THE TRUTH SEEKER

Exploring the Mysteries of the

Metaphysical and the Multidimensional

Identity of Humankind

Joan L Boler

Published by:
Siobhan Pty Ltd
23/818 Pittwater Road
Dee Why NSW 2099
Australia
www.thetruthseeker.com.au

Copyright © 2015 Joan L Boler

All rights reserved. No part of this document or related files may be reproduced, stored in a retrieval system, or transmitted in any form by any means (electronic, mechanical, photocopying, recording, or otherwise), for commercial purposes, without the prior written permission of the publisher.

First Edition 2015
This Edition 2016

Siobhan Pty Limited

The Truth Seeker
Exploring the Mysteries of the Metaphysical and the Multidimensional Identity of Humankind
by Joan L Boler

ISBN-13:978-0-9944116-3-1

Cover Picture: "©iStock.com/agsandrew" with additions and alterations by Joan L Boler

Dedication

This book is dedicated to those seekers of truth who, through their efforts, knowledge and research have enabled me to provide proof or supporting evidence for the validity of many of the assertions in this book.

Acknowledgements

First of all, I feel both fortunate and grateful to have secured the editing skills of Kim Farnell, an amazing lady who has contributed to the quality of my book on a number of levels. Her editing skills have given polish to my writing without interfering with my individual style. Her conscientious and intelligent approach along with her extensive knowledge on the subjects about which I have written, has ensured a degree of accuracy and excellence I could not have achieved without her input.

My thanks to my family, friends and acquaintances who have supported and aided me in this challenging project.

To my extraordinary siblings: Sonia, my multi-talented sister who with the patience of a saint spent countless hours teaching me how to structure my writing and who insisted I must support my knowledge and experience with evidence. Without her help, this book would have floundered, and likely failed, in its infancy. I owe to her my many thanks for converting my book file to the PDF requirements for publishing, assembling the book cover and providing guidance regarding publishing and promotion procedures. My appreciation also goes to my other special sister Yvonne, who contributed her experiences and who critically examined a number of the book's chapters. To my unique brother John, who introduced adventure into my life when we were children, and who spent many hours working with me to achieve detail and accuracy in recording his life experiences which he has kindly allowed me to present in my book.

To John's son Robert goes my appreciation for his time and effort in setting up my website and familiarising me with cyberspace.

My thanks to others who read and critiqued chapters, offered ideas, experiences and encouragement. Among these were my daughter Sharon and my friends Susie, Sally, Penny, Joy, Cheryl, Sieglinde, Margaret, Gunta, Maureen, and Paul. Thanks also to Zac and his family who shared their delightful and interesting stories. And to Robert who provided the story of his young son Shaun's past life memories.

My friends and astrologers Patricia, Norman and Frank contributed their time unstintingly researching information for me and answering my queries. To them also goes my gratitude and thanks.

Last, but not least, thanks to my good friend Treve, who with her provocative and challenging comments inspired me to expand my approach.

Contents

Introduction vii

Chapter 1 - Ancient Wisdoms—Modern Physics 1

The Search for Truth 1
The Spiritual Quest 2
The Paranormal Experience 4
Soul Sciences 10
Reincarnation 11
The Scientific Search 13
Truth 16

Chapter 2 - Astrology—the Science of the Soul 19

The Study of Human Energy 19
Astrology – An Ancient Science 20
The Human Blueprint 24
Sensing Energies 28
Physical Appearance of the Astrological Signs 30
Combining the Skills 33
Astrological Charts and the Influences they Reveal 34
Universal Order 41

Chapter 3 - Reincarnation—the Journey of the Soul 45

Reincarnation – Belief or Truth? 45
The Past and Reincarnation 46
The West in Recent Times 49
Evidence of Past Lives Revealed During Psychic Readings 52
Indication of a Past Life 54
The Recovery of Past Life Memories through Meditation 55
Past Life Recall through Hypnosis 56
Personal Evidence of Other Lifetimes 59
Countless Lifetimes 61
Birth Marks and Birth Defects 62
Research and Living Memories 65
Possible Supporting Evidence 70
Continuation of Life Skills and Awareness 71

Chapter 4 - Transformation 73

- Cause and Effect 73
- A Wild Child 75
- Water and Sailing 76
- Trouble, Trouble, Trouble 77
- A Colourful Character 80
- The Legal Challenges 82
- Life, After Life, After Life 84
- South Node in Taurus 91
- North Node in Scorpio 92
- Teacher and Student 93
- Trust the Weaver 94

Chapter 5 - Our Extraordinary Senses 97

- Psychic Ability 97
- Scientific Evidence 98
- Awareness of Psychic Ability in Today's World 100
- Prediction 101
- Clairvoyance 104
- Clairsentience 106
- Cleansing 107
- Clairaudience 108
- Telepathy 110
- Deliberately Influencing Others 112
- Psychometry 113
- Intuition 115
- Revelation in the Palms 117
- Remote or Distant Viewing 119
- 'I Know' 120
- Avoiding Pitfalls and Developing Skills 124
- Potential 126

Chapter 6 - Mind Powers, Magic and Miracles 127

- Manipulation of the Physical World 127
- Scientific Breakthroughs 128
- Cause 131

The Creative Abilities of Each and Every Human Being 131
Fuel of the Soul 136
Powerful Energy Sources 140
Healing 142
Belief and the Manifestation of the Miraculous 145
Sword of the Soul 147
Ego 151
Motivation 152
Oops 153
Consciousness 154

Chapter 7 - Our Multidimensional Identity 157

Supernature 157
Non-Physical Bodies 158
Auric Fields 160
Vulnerable Psychic and Spiritual Bodies 162
Chakras 163
Awareness of Energy Centers 168
Connections and Disconnections 171
Coinciding Events 174
Kundalini 180
More than Physical 182
Healing the Damaged Chakras and Auras 183
Spiritual Within 187

Chapter 8 - Love—the Universal Law 189

Love and its Aspects 189
Spiritual Evolution 191
The Middle Road 194
The Hook 196
Unconditional Love 196
Romantic Love 197
The Judge Within 199
Religious Laws 203
Freedom's Song 207
Personal Responsibility 208

Chapter 9 - Revealing the Unconscious 211

The Search for Happiness 211
Healing the Psyche 212
The Trance State 215
Hypnotherapy 217
Respecting the Unconscious Mind 219
Dream Analysis 220
Divination 222
Tarot 224
Changing the Future 228
The Psychic Reader 230
Psychics and Sensitivity 232
Interference in Readings 235
The Search for Self 236

Chapter 10 - Extra Dimensional Travellers 239

Our Multi-Dimensional Universe 239
The Research 240
The Etheric Body 243
Consciousness outside the Physical Body 244
Pronounced Dead 245
A Super Hero 247
The Dream State and Multidimensional Travel 251
Expanded States of Consciousness 254

Chapter 11 - Encountering the Afterlife 257

Death 257
The Near-Death Experience 258
Consciousness, the Brain and the Near-Death Experience 261
Near-Death Experience Research 263
The Clairvoyant View 266
After Death Contact 267
An Anomaly 269
Ascension 270
Lost Souls 273
Judgement 276
The Afterlife Kingdoms and their Occupants 279
Ancient Beliefs in the Afterlife 280
The Near-Death Experience and Religious Belief 284

Chapter 12 - Human Interaction with Non-Physical Beings........285

Inter-dimensional Interaction 285
Humankind in the Heavens 287
Validity of Spirit Contact 288
Intervention 291
Communication with Passed-Over Human Beings 293
Angelic Assistance 295
Spiritual Help for the Sick 297
Archangels 299
Expanding the Consciousness 300

Chapter 13 - The Invisible Creatures of Earth 303

Our World and its Creatures 303
Researching Information on Elementals 304
Memories of another Lifetime 307
Jane's Faerie Queen 308
The Faerie Narrative 310
An Extraordinary Child 313
Zac's Helpful Spirit Relatives 315
Frightening and Unpleasant Aspects of the 'Sight' 316
Angels and Angel Cards 319
Dwarves, Faeries and Elves 319
The Travelling Elf 321
Real or Not 324

Chapter 14 - Religion, Belief, Spirituality and Truth..................327

Religion 327
Truth in Religion 328
The Gods of the Ancient World 330
Myths and Legends of Old 333
The New Testament Scriptures 336
Who Was Jesus? 341
Following in the Footsteps of Jesus 348
Authority 350
The Reign of the Church 354
A Religion Built on Fear 357
Perfection and Idealism in the Church 359
Karmic Consequences 364

Spiritual Victory 367
Belief 369
Religion – The Future 371

Chapter 15 - Mysticism - Mystical Heritage..........375

Secrets of the Cosmos 376
Kabbalah and Creation 379
Defining the Mystical Experience 381
All That Is 386

Chapter 16 - Our Intelligent and Spiritual Universe..........389

Our Intelligent Universe 389
Astrological Ages 390
The Open Mind 392
Quantum Mechanics and Consciousness 395
Creation 396
Creation and Evolution 399
The Truth Within 401

Introduction

Take the attitude of a student, never be too big to ask questions, never know too much to learn something new.

Og Mangino[1]

The landscape of my life has been coloured by many varied paranormal experiences that have been breath-taking, exciting, wonderful and enchanting. These experiences have enhanced a driving force within me; a force that has driven me to seek the truth and to uncover the mysteries surrounding phenomena such as intuition, telepathy, clairvoyance, the application of the power of the mind in producing magic, and the accessing of the non-physical dimensions that transcend the physical.

Back in the 1960s when I first began experiencing the paranormal, the risk of being considered mentally unbalanced kept me from sharing my new awareness with others. Each time a new experience presented itself, I questioned why and how. The conflict between society's teachings and what my experiences revealed to me evoked denial. My logical mind kept saying, *This is impossible!* However, nothing could erase my deep conviction that my experiences were real and not simply created by my unconscious mind.

Why was I having these experiences? Was it something I was doing? If so, what? How could I achieve these experiences at will when they seemed to occur without provocation or warning?

In order to understand the underlying causes of how the metaphysical worked, and to come to terms with who and what I truly was, I began my lifelong search for answers. I delved into the mysteries of life through science, religion and personal experience. My experiences had revealed irrefutable truths that I used as a guide when studying. I devoured books that provided insight into the paranormal, the spiritual and the scientific. As I read what had been written, I found for the most part I was able to discriminate between the truth and what was born from superstition or misinterpretation.

---

[1] Augustine 'Og' Mandino (1923-1996), American author.

My search for answers as to the true nature of humanity in the light of the paranormal was intensified by my need to search for solutions to the emotional pain experienced in personal relationships. I dabbled in psychology, attended classes on dream analysis, and studied palmistry, tarot and astrology. Each of these sources of knowledge explored human nature from different vantage points.

In 1991, after many years of developing my psychic skills through regularly attending classes, I decided to spend some time each week reading psychically for people. It wasn't long until I began to seize a growing number of opportunities to give lectures and teach people who were eager to understand more about metaphysics. This helped me to express a creative aspect of my nature that was to be the precursor to teaching through writing.

In my writing, I have attempted to relate as accurately as possible some of the many experiences that have enhanced my life, and at the same time show how they reveal a part of the greater picture of the non-physical aspects of the world and its non-physical residents. That picture is so incredible and awesome that nothing in our experience of the physical world can possibly compare.

I can provide you with evidence of my experiences that have given me *my* proof. I can show you the evidence contained in the experiences of others, and I can provide details of scientific research, but I can't give you *your* proof. While science offers some evidence and even absolute proof of the some of the paranormal, for the most part authentication comes from personal experience.

Each person prepared to put in the effort can develop the necessary psychic skills and discover their own proof. There can be no journey more exciting or interesting than to travel the road that leads to the truth of who and what we are and to the personal experience of the paranormal powers we can each possess.

THE TRUTH SEEKER

Chapter 1

Ancient Wisdoms—Modern Physics

Of all the liars in the world, sometimes the worst are your own fears.

Rudyard Kipling[2]

The Search for Truth

Are you a truth seeker?

A truth seeker is an individual who is prepared to shed garments of security and walk into the unknown where an open mind provides a doorway to the truth.

An open mind forms a foundation for genius that can lead into worlds of fascinating realities and possibilities. In the absence of free thinking, those hints of what is real are distorted by the caged as the gaps between the bars of fear and ignorance allow only glimpses of the truth.

As human beings, we embrace structure—especially if that structure is absolute. We keep building structures within science, religion and in our perception of whom and what we are, and we don't easily adapt when the unforgiving sea of truth sweeps away an apparently solid foundation.

Fuelled by curiosity, and using both scientific and spiritual approaches, the educated people of antiquity sought to explain the many mysteries of our world including those relating to the source and purpose of human life. Their conclusions, that formed the basis for the religions of today, included a belief that the celestial bodies were gods who played a role in the destiny of each human being. Whilst over time some of their explanations have dissolved in the face of science, as we sift through the many sources of accumulated knowledge with an open mind, is it possible to discover truths that have remained unchanged since earliest recorded times? Studies by sages over millennia included not only geometry and mathematics,

---

[2] Rudyard Kipling (1865-1936) English novelist, short story writer and poet.

architecture, medicine, science and astronomy, but also the information found in astrology, numerology and palmistry. Is it possible today, for those who are scientifically minded, discerning and insightful, to access verifiable knowledge from these fields of learning regarding the nature and purpose of life?

The revelations of today's scientific accomplishments show that knowledge and understanding is constantly advancing. Air and space travel, computerisation and complex technology which almost eliminates the need for manual labour in many industries, were, for the most part, make-believe before the twentieth century.

Science has held beliefs that today are negated with the emergence of the new science of quantum mechanics that developed after the splitting of the atom and provided evidence of a multidimensional universe. Scientists are now unveiling an amazing array of truths about the cosmos, our world and humanity that parallel the claims of mystics and psychics. As we consider the implications of a universe with non-physical dimensions, possible credibility is given to the existence of beings like gods, angels and elementals and the continuation of the human soul through reincarnation. As we wade through the bodies of knowledge and evidence, both current and ancient, some of that which was believed to be scientifically true is now known not to be. And many claims of the paranormal rejected as invalid by science in the last few hundred years, can in fact now be supported by evidence. Perhaps it's time to critically reassess our understanding of whom and what we are and look to science and the evidence provided by research in order to discover the truth.

The Spiritual Quest

For millennia, human beings have sought answers to what lies beyond the physical. Religions reveal humanity's experience and understanding of the spiritual. Throughout history, religions have risen to great heights only to eventually disintegrate, leaving no more than remnants of their passing. Today, we examine the records of their existence found in folklore, ancient writings, structures built thousands of years ago, and artefacts excavated by archaeologists in various parts of the world. The god or gods worshiped by the faithful reveal the ancients' perception of the supernatural and, as they evolved through the ages, so did that perception. In both East and West, major religions that have survived for thousands of years reveal an evolving awareness and understanding of our true nature.

THE TRUTH SEEKER

Throughout history, in all cultures, there have always been individuals who have clairvoyantly seen spirit beings or entities not of the physical world. There has been evidence of the arcane, the supernatural and the paranormal. Enlightened individuals have passed on their knowledge and the truth as they see it—individuals from all parts of the world who understood the laws of nature and experienced the spiritual within. Since ancient times, humanity has revered and listened to these people and attempted to record their knowledge. As a result, the following writings have had enormous lasting impact on humanity:

The Vedas, which come from India and are written in Sanskrit. The *Rig Veda*, the oldest of the four Vedas, is the oldest book in any Indo-European language and was written around 1500 BCE (before common/current/Christian era).[3]

The *Avesta* (ancient scriptures of Zoroastrianism, which was founded by the Prophet Zoroaster (Zarathustra) in ancient Persia (Iran) 1500-1000 BCE.[4]

The *Egyptian Book of the Dead* which is dated around 1500 BCE.[5]

The *Bible* which has influenced three of the world's great religions—Judaism, Christianity and Islam. The first five books are thought to have been written between the sixteenth and twelfth century BCE by Moses, but Jean-Louis Ska provides arguments in favour of the sixth century BCE.[6] Deuteronomy is thought to have been written between the eighth and sixth century BCE.[7]

The *Zohah* which is the foundation text of Kabbalism was written in the second and third century CE (common/current/Christian era), and after being hidden for nine hundred years emerged around the twelfth or thirteen century CE.

The *Qur'an*—the sacred book of Islam, is based on revelations from the Archangel Gabriel to Muhammad, who was born around 570 CE[8].

---

[3] 'The Vedas', *Internet sacred text archive*. www.sacred-texts.com/hin(accessed 8 May 2014)
[4] 'Zoroaster', *BBC Religions*.
www.bbc.co.uk/religion/religions/zoroastrian/history/zoroaster_1.shtml (accessed 8 May 2014)
[5] Taylor, John H. (Editor), *Ancient Egyptian Book of the Dead: Journey through the Afterlife*. British Museum Press, London, 2010.
[6] Ska, Jean-Louis, *Introduction to reading the Pentateuch*, Eisenbrauns, 2006, USA, p.217.
[7] Miller, Patrick D, *Deuteronomy*, John Knox Press, 1990, pp.2–3.
[8] Goldman, Elizabeth, *Believers: Spiritual Leaders of the World*, Oxford University Press, Oxford, 1995.

So much wisdom and so many truths from the Masters of the past. Revelations of the spiritual are recorded for those eager for knowledge and enlightenment. Comparisons of the various teachings of the Masters reveal common knowledge and understanding, such as the way to live spiritually and reach spiritual goals. However many of the wisdoms recorded are mixed with, and coloured by, racial and cultural beliefs.

There are two approaches to the search for truth—the external and scientific where physical evidence is sought and examined, and the experiential inner search that can take the seeker on a journey into the very essence of who and what humankind are, and can reveal the nature of the cosmos that surrounds us. Both approaches are valid as they are two sides of the same coin. In evaluating the great variety of conclusions reached worldwide about what spiritual truths are, one is left in confusion unless the spiritual approach to life (as taught by the Masters) has been followed and the journey within has begun.

The Paranormal Experience

Paranormal experience breaks the rules laid down by those whose feet are firmly planted on the ground and who deal only in the physical. When a person is cocooned in a safe world where all knowledge seems solid and reliable, the shock of a first-time paranormal experience can be overwhelming. Yet the truth of the supernatural, which is so often elusive, has found that person. First-hand experience can't be underestimated, as it offers individual proof and insight into the mysteries of life. To underestimate or ignore personal experience and the knowledge that can be gained from it, is to guarantee misunderstanding and confusion when dealing with both metaphysical and scientific matters.

There are many possible paranormal experiences, each of which offers an aspect of the truth. Out-of-body travel confirms the truth that we don't require the physical body in order for consciousness to survive. Seeing a departed loved one confirms the truth of their continuing life force and identity. Recall of a lifetime lived in another place and another era confirms the reality of reincarnation. A visitation from an angelic being confirms the truth of their existence.

The paranormal can provide an explanation for timely warnings that prevent disaster, leaving one questioning whether there has been intervention from a spiritual source or if the individual's intuition has been the saviour.

THE TRUTH SEEKER

For example, one night as I was driving from Sydney to the Central Coast in heavy rain, I approached a familiar pedestrian crossing not far from where I lived. Ahead on my left, in front of a church that bordered the footpath, dense bushes grew. No streetlights lit this dark area. On the opposite side, a street light sent its beams on to the road illuminating the crossing.

Suddenly I sensed I should slow down and I immediately braked. Two seconds later when I was within thirty feet (ten metres) of the crossing, a person ran out from behind the bushes on to the crossing. The coat over their head blocked their side vision and ability to see my car. There was no time to sound the horn. In the split second before possible impact, horror and fear took over. Although my foot had already floored the brake in an attempt to avert disaster, I put all my strength into depressing my foot harder into the floor. At the moment my car came to a halt at the edge of the crossing, the pedestrian ran directly in front of my vehicle.

Only two seconds separated a close call and what could have been a serious accident.

How did I know to brake? One explanation is that on an unconscious level I psychically sensed the person's presence, and possibly their intention to run into the road. Or perhaps there was a spirit present, impressing on me the need to slow down.

Personal psychic experiences can provide valid insights and knowledge. However, hallucinations and mental illness can cause delusions and such experiences can be confused with genuine psychic experiences. Because of this, when evaluating personal experience, it is advisable to seek supporting evidence. The nature of evidence can vary depending on the type of experience and the capability of the psychic. For example, when in communication with a person who has passed over into the non-physical dimensions, it is possible to gain confirmation through information only the recipient of the message would know.

Some years ago my friend Carol (name changed) requested that I contact her father who had died a number of years before. Her father had been a minister of the Uniting Church, and since I had met him, his energy was familiar to me and I was able to contact him with little effort. He appeared to me as a young man, and in the vision I could see the ethereally beautiful place where he now resided. I was enchanted as I looked upon a scene that included beautiful flowers, hillsides and an expanse of water.

As Carol's father stood in front of me, he placed a halo on his head and then removed it. He repeated this activity a number of times. I found this amusing, especially considering his earthly vocation. Laughing, I described his behaviour to Carol who immediately recognised his actions. She told me he often used to entertain his wife and daughters by placing her mother's hats on his head and then removing them. Such confirmation does not provide scientific proof of life after death, but it provided Carol with evidence her father's spirit was indeed there, especially as she was aware I had no prior knowledge about his amusing behaviour.

So why do such experiences happen? How can they be explained? What laws govern them? What is and what isn't paranormal? Could there be a metaphysical reason for experiences of a coincidental or synchronistic nature? All over the world, people experience happenings that defy the law of probability.

In 1970 I left New Zealand to live on Norfolk Island where I met Carol who had recently arrived from Australia. She and I quickly became good friends. I returned to New Zealand fifteen months later on my birthday and at my youngest sister's suggestion, celebrated by accompanying her to a party. Apart from my sister, I knew no one at the party so I joined a group of people in the kitchen who were chatting. In response to questions, I said I'd just returned from living on Norfolk Island. One young man said to me, 'Do you know Carol H......s?' When I answered in the affirmative, he said, 'When she spent three months in New Zealand last year, she stayed at my place with my family.'

Three months after my return to New Zealand, I moved to the Central Coast of Australia some forty-three miles (seventy or so kilometres) north of Sydney. A few weeks before my arrival, Carol's boyfriend, who had originally come from Sydney and who worked for the Commonwealth Bank, returned to Sydney accompanied by Carol. Within a week of my arrival, I travelled to Sydney to register with an employment agency with a view to obtaining work in the area.

After my interview in the city, I walked along George Street. Upon noticing a sign that read *Immigrants' Information Centre*, it occurred to me I might be able to obtain some useful information. I proceeded down the steps, and as I reached floor level, I realised I was in the Commonwealth Bank. *Well*, I thought, *Since I'm here, I might as well ask about transferring my Commonwealth Bank account from Norfolk Island.*

I stood in the queue and waited for my turn to be shown into one of the three offices where bank employees were dealing with customers' needs. Before long I was sitting in front of a young man and advising him I wished to transfer my bank account from Norfolk Island. A surprised expression

THE TRUTH SEEKER

preceded the announcement, 'You must be Joan!' Astounded, I stared at him. He explained he had spent the previous weekend visiting Carol and her boyfriend and they had informed him I was flying into Sydney that weekend.

In order for such unlikely connections to occur, people, time and place need to coincide. Are these random coincidences, or are there are laws involved that ensure such occurrences?

Is it possible the human mind is the key that unlocks the doors to the paranormal, especially to those experiences related to mind powers? José Silva began investigating parapsychology in 1944. After twenty-eight years of experimentation and research, he founded *Silva Mind Control*, which teaches how to unlock and use the mind more effectively. He had discovered it was possible to use the mind to affect and increase not only the intelligence of individuals, but also to create changes in the physical body and possibly cure disease! Also, he showed that strong mental focus could attract a desired result or outcome![9] Among those who had ventured into using the power of the mind in the past were the Eastern yogis, Brahman priests, Australian aboriginals, the tribes of South Africa and practitioners of magic.

Can we really cause something to happen in the way we want? Knowledge revealed by those who practiced mind skills motivated me to attempt such feats, and I have accomplished a desired result on many occasions.

Some years ago, during the first month after moving from apartment to another, my costs shrank my available funds. The move had been expensive, but as I had recently commenced a new job, I'd anticipated the expected income would cover any deficit. It didn't. As I stood in my lounge, my frustration and anger rose as I faced the impossible task of finding the required money. As my anger peaked, I expelled it in a spontaneous mental demand that I receive $500 by the first day of the following month when the rent was due. Immediately I'd made the demand, I forgot about the situation. All thought of rent and my concern about how I was to pay it disappeared.

As I'm an independent person, it hadn't occurred to me to ask for help from family or friends or mention my situation to anyone. Just prior to the end of the month, I received a notice in the mail that there was a registered item at

---

[9] Silva, José, *The Silva Mind Control Method*, Harper Collins, London, 1977.

the post office awaiting collection. I walked up to the end of the street and across the road to the post office where I signed for an envelope:

Inside was a money order for $500. So effectively had my need for $500 for rent been purged from my mind that it skipped through possible explanations. *There must be some mistake. This can't be for me. Perhaps it's for the bush walking group!* I checked the name. Yes, it was made out to 'Joan Boler'. *Who would send me $500?* There was no sender's name anywhere. I couldn't even see from where the envelope had been posted. The memory of my demand for $500 resurfaced and I realised my command had been effective!

Around eight weeks later, I was again short of money for the rent, but this time I needed $800. *Well,* I thought, *it worked before, so I'll try it again!* On the Sunday before the rent was due, I went out with the bush-walking group. I returned home, opened my door, and there on the floor was an envelope addressed to me:

It contained $800 in $100 bills.

The writing on this envelope was different to the one that had contained the $500 money order. Did two different people come to my aid? No one has come forward to claim responsibility for either amount.

This wasn't a coincidence. Twice, the exact amounts I had requested mysteriously manifested within the time stipulated. Nor had someone responded to a verbal announcement of my financial shortfall, as I'd said nothing. How the knowledge got out there, was received and responded to, can't be explained by conventional means.

Another aspect of the paranormal that seems to defy accepted understanding of the impossible is divination. Tools like the tarot reveal not only what's happening in a person's life, but also offer helpful information regarding a problem.

I once did a reading for a young man, and as I tuned into his energy, I could feel a lot of pain in his back, especially around the neck area. He told me he'd been in an accident and was still suffering a lot of back pain. I selected a single card from the cards that were face down on the table with the intention it would provide me with information helpful to the young man. The card I selected was *The Hanged Man.*

There was no need for me to question what this meant. For years, I had suffered from a back problem. In my search for solutions, I had purchased a

THE TRUTH SEEKER

Gravity Guidance System back machine upon which I could hang upside down and then exercise. I had gained a great deal of relief from using this machine, and so advised the young man an inversion machine could help him.

Out of the seventy-eight cards in the tarot deck, I had selected the one card that would indicate the way in which he could relieve his back pain. Was it coincidence he came to me for a psychic reading? How many readers would have known about the back machine? Is it possible the young man's desire for release from his constant pain caused his unconscious mind to prompt him into arranging a reading with me?

All over the world, intelligent, respectable people claim to have had a wide range of paranormal experiences that deserve serious consideration.

For the individual, the proof of such experiences is usually inherent in the experience. Without the benefit of personal experience, consistent reports of the paranormal that are multiplied hundreds, thousands and millions of times (as are many of the experiences related in this book), provide weighty supportive evidence. Albert Einstein said, *A theory may be verified by experience, but there is no road leading from experience to the creation of a theory.*[10] Perhaps scientists need to extend their thinking and study the evidence provided by the massive number of reported paranormal experiences. Although testing many of those experiences is outside the scope of current scientific tools, study of metaphysical experiences can provide consistent information. Searching for explanations has the potential to contribute towards scientific understanding.

In the West, paranormal experience has been suppressed in the past due to superstition and fear of reprisals from the Christian church. However, today many more people welcome experiences that can provide the individual with proof. Many people, in every age, have demonstrated supernatural gifts and knowledge, and there is no reason to believe only the Masters of ancient times were qualified to speak of their spiritual and paranormal experiences and their resultant understanding. In fact, it's difficult to accurately interpret many of the spiritual wisdoms in ancient writings without the understanding that comes from first-hand experience.

---

[10] Einstein, Albert, 'Autobiographical Notes', *Einstein, Philosopher Scientist,* Tudor Publishing Company, New York, 1951.

JOAN L BOLER

Soul Sciences

The search for truth demands we understand our own nature.

In modern times, the unconscious mind has been exposed. Psychology evolved in recognition of the fact many of our negative emotional responses are born from unresolved past experiences, the memories and effects of which are buried in the unconscious. To deal with this, counselling in a variety of forms has become widespread to address the deeper causes of emotional and mental problems. For example, hypnosis and dream analysis are two tools through which fears and phobias can be revealed and healed.

Carl Jung (1875-1961) has had a profound effect on our understanding of dreams, archetypes and symbolism. His research into and understanding of the unconscious mind, reveals a depth of insight that has contributed greatly towards the overall mental and emotional health and well-being of many in developed countries today. He introduced the concept of the 'collective unconscious', which explains the mind's unconscious knowledge of, and access to, archetypes and symbols that come from our deep past and cannot be accounted for by personal experience. What is this universal unconscious and is there more to it than Carl Jung discerned?

Behavioural and emotional problems and the need to understand what makes the individual a productive member of society have not just been the territory of the intuitive thinkers of recent times. The scientific approach today to understanding the human soul—the essence of the individual identity—finds its parallel in studies that reach back into ancient times.

Astronomy and astrology evolved over thousands of years. The ancients studied the movements of the planets and they also studied the impact of those movements on human life (in the past most astronomers were also astrologers). Numerology and palmistry also take the influence of the planets into account. In spite of scientific rejection in modern times, these wisdoms have had a long and respected history. Each of these studies into the workings of the human soul provide the student with information that enables possible identification of the mental, emotional, and physical aspects of each and every human being on the planet.

Studying the social sciences of astrology, numerology and palmistry provides evidence that supports the idea the cosmos is intelligently designed with a purpose to ensure spiritual growth in all life forms. Consideration of this leads to the question as to how one lifetime could provide a human being with the necessary experience to achieve the desired goal of spiritual perfection. Therefore, the scenario we live many lifetimes is a possibility that needs to be investigated.

Reincarnation

Does the idea of reincarnation inspire wonder and curiosity in you, and is this subject worthy of thorough investigation? Since the pathway to truth is paved with time and effort, I invested both in researching this subject. I read countless books, encountered a surprising amount of research, and found it is not uncommon for people of all cultures and religions to claim memory of, and reveal details of, other existences in previous times. In a trance state, I relived experiences from lives both in recent times and in the distant past.

The concept of reincarnation—the migration of the soul (individual essence along with conscious awareness) from one life to another—has been part of Eastern philosophy for thousands of years. Many years ago I was fascinated when I read about the spiritual leader of the Tibetan Buddhists (the Dalai Lama) who is believed to be a Master, a soul who has evolved spiritually beyond the need to incarnate into a human body, and who chooses to be reborn. When the Dalai Lama dies, the High Lamas begin a search for his next incarnation. The fourteenth and present Dalai Lama, Tenzin Gyasto, was found in 1935 and proved his identity when from among a range of objects he recognised those that had belonged to the previous Dalai Lama.

While early Christianity had followers who accepted reincarnation, the Church of Rome promoted a one life belief. However, many in Western society today have been exposed to the concept of multiple lifetimes. Reincarnation could explain phenomena like the massive variations in the innate physical, mental and emotional capabilities of each human being, including childhood genius. Individual advantages and disadvantages could be seen as a rightful inheritance. The reason for a strong attraction to some people and repulsion to others on first acquaintance suggests prior connection of the individuals involved. The sense of being *at home* when visiting a different place or country or the feeling of being comfortable around foreign paraphernalia, makes sense when the unconscious memories of a past life are taken into consideration. Questions as to the why of the internal longing for types of experience others lack interest in are also answered by looking to a previous existence. While our genetic makeup and social environment contribute to the individual each of us is, reincarnation offers reason to many of the variations in the human experience.

JOAN L BOLER

In the search for reasons for my current life attitudes and circumstances, I looked to my other lives. When I was around the age of seven, I experienced a strong desire to become a teacher. That desire persisted until I had reached the age when I needed to make a decision. *Should I enrol in a secondary school that focused on an academic education that would prepare me for a future career in teaching, or should I consider a commercial education?* It should have been a simple decision, but it wasn't.

My mother, who had been a teacher like her older sister, convinced me to put my efforts into another career. Some years later, my youngest sister became a teacher. By the time I reached my early twenties, I regretted not following my instincts as the desire to seek and share knowledge was strong within me. My gift for teaching was expressed over the years when training employees in my commercially-orientated work, in passing on knowledge about the various subjects that fascinated me, and in teaching classes on psychic and spiritual development.

Where did the ability and desire to teach come from? Did I from ancient times possess teaching skills and enjoy imparting knowledge? Among the past lives I have recalled while in a trance state is the following.

In around 600-500 BCE, I lived as a male in a male-dominated, but civilised society—probably more civilised than many communities on the planet today. I felt the location to be in the Canaan/Palestine area. The people of this community usually wore light coloured, ground-length robes and the women covered their heads. The buildings of the walled city were organised as sections of adjoining rooms (mainly square) constructed out of a solid material that had a flat, even finish and was light in colour. Usage was varied, with some being living quarters while others were used by those skilled in the arts and crafts that contributed to the community as a whole. Still others were for community use. This was an independent, thriving community.

When I was about fourteen, I left that community and travelled by camel in the company of an adult male to a great city that was the then hub of greater learning. I was impressed by its large buildings and sophisticated infrastructure. I remained in that city for many years and learned from the best teachers society had to offer. Some of my learning time was spent in a high-walled, domed, round room that was like a small auditorium with seating for approximately twenty male students. The students were from different cultures and included Egyptians. My studies included mathematics and the sciences, one of which was astronomy. In this environment, I led a much freer lifestyle than was typical for a young man from my home city.

THE TRUTH SEEKER

After I returned to my own city when I was around twenty-eight, I was provided with the facilities to work with my knowledge. My inventive and scientific skills were in demand in the community. When time permitted, I experimented in order to discover how available resources could be used more effectively. From amongst the most talented and enthusiastic students (all male), I selected those to whom I would teach advanced knowledge. In one memory, I experienced a stimulating discussion with my students debating information contained in a scroll.

I was a greatly respected member of that society and my presence out of doors was an invitation for those of all ages to gather around me. In this impromptu classroom, I used the environment to demonstrate the information I imparted. I recall one occasion when stones close by became planets as I discussed the heavenly regions. In my later years, I left civilisation and went into the wilderness to spend my final years in seclusion.

Could my aptitude for and interest in teaching be attributed solely to my genetic inheritance? Or is it possible that genetics, my character, personality and accumulated abilities combine in a like-meets-like attraction to produce the person I am in my current life?

Investigation into reincarnation brings the understanding that all souls experience a circular process of descending to the physical world and then ascending back to the spiritual or non-physical realms. This process enables the soul to gain layer upon layer of learning through experience. The density of the physical world (for the most part) severs the soul from the realms of the non-physical and its awareness of its spiritual identity. What emerges at birth is the accumulated soul identity that has been fashioned through the experiences of many lifetimes under the influence of astrological forces. Gradually, as each soul evolves, it begins to link to its psychic and then spiritual potential until it can unite its spiritual self with the soul in the physical body.

The Scientific Search

Our planet has been home to many people with brilliant inquiring minds, and many of these people find their way into the sciences. As early as 3000 BCE, the Egyptians had developed knowledge in physiology, geometry and mathematics. At the same time, astronomy and astrology had developed side by side. In China, chemistry, astronomy, astrology mathematics and medical knowledge were developing independently.

Science of the past walked hand in hand with the spiritual beliefs that dominated at the time. Ptolemy, an astronomer, mathematician and geographer, lived in Alexandria, Egypt around 150 CE. His geocentric model was the same as that of most of his predecessors and supported his conviction that the earth was the centre of the universe. Christianity, the dominant world religion for the greater part of the last two thousand years, endorsed this view. It was not until 1543 that Nicolaus Copernicus published findings based on both observation *and* experimentation and invalidated Ptolemy's theories.[11] There were other scientific findings at that time that were based on experimentation and hands on investigation. Andreas Vesalius (1514–1564), was an anatomist, physician, and author of *Concerning the Fabric of the Human Body* who, rather than following the teachings of Claudius Galen (129-200/ 216 CE), which were based upon the dissection of animals, dissected the bodies of dead criminals and revealed many errors made by Galen.[12] With long held beliefs being refuted, science began to move in a different direction from religion, and observation combined with experimentation soon became the accepted method of the scientists. Observation alone was no longer considered scientific.

The seventeenth century saw further significant changes take place. Physicist, mathematician, and astronomer Isaac Newton (1642-1727), using Galileo's theories as a basis, proved through its effects, the three laws of gravity. Both he and Gottfried Wilhelm von Leibniz (1646-1716), independently developed calculus (a branch of mathematics), which considerably advanced the ability to test and understand the laws that governed the world and the universe.[13] [14] Over the next couple of generations, this change of approach began to have an impact on the sciences. Science came to be about the physical alone rather than incorporating the spiritual, and a belief emerged that everything that existed and was real could be measured with scientific tools. The new scientific approach began to create changes in scientists' concepts, and gradually the scientific view moved from humans being connected spiritual creatures to being physical beings separate from their environment. It was at this point that humanity's accumulated understanding of the world as a spiritual creation was scientifically voided, and God and the spiritual were excluded from the world of science.

---

[11] 'Nicolaus Copernicus.' *Stanford Encyclopedia of Philosophy*, plato.stanford.edu/entries/copernicus/ (accessed 8 May 2014)
[12] *The World Book Encyclopedia*, Field Enterprises Educational Corporation, Chicago, 1974, 'V' p.273.
[13] 'Isaac Newton's Life.' *Isaac Newton Institute for Mathematical Science*, www.newton.ac.uk/newtlife.html (accessed 8 May 2014)
[14] Smith, David Eugene, *A Source Book in Mathematics*, McGraw-Hill Book Company, New York and London, 1929.

THE TRUTH SEEKER

The following generations of scientists and academics dealt only with the physical, to the point where eventually, for many scientists, the belief emerged that anything that was not of the physical could not exist. When metaphysical experiences were brought to their attention, since the non-physical did not come within the boundaries of their scientific *belief,* they attributed all such experiences to the imagination, the creative mind of the individual, hallucinations, or more recently to the collective unconscious. This disbelief has extended even to those instances where scientific testing has validated claims.

An interesting study was done involving the acceptance of research on extrasensory perception (ESP).[15] It was found that scientific tests for a new medical drug with a success rate of only a few per cent were accepted as valid. However, research by the Koestler Parapsychology Unit at the University of Edinburgh, Scotland on ESP, that followed all the scientific guidelines and revealed impressive results, failed to gain acceptance by most scientists. Mainstream scientific response to research on the paranormal has been to ignore it, assume the tests could not be repeated, or conclude the tests were inefficiently carried out or there was some other cause that could be explained in terms of the physical.

Physics from the seventeenth to the early part of the twentieth century encompassed only the physical and measurable. Then near the end of World War 1, New Zealand born British physicist Ernest Rutherford (1871-1937), who is considered to be the 'Father of Nuclear Physics', split the atom. Physics was now in trouble as its laws were unable to explain the behaviour of subatomic particles. A new approach was needed. Quantum mechanics emerged and, as with gravity, its theories could only be proven by effects. The effects revealed that subatomic particles are the potential of all their possibilities until they are observed or used. Additionally, these particles are interconnected with all other particles. This contradicts the previously accepted laws of physics and the conclusions reached that everything, including human beings, were separate. This new understanding provides a framework through which the paranormal can be explained and understood.

Unfortunately, many scientific theories are treated as fact both by the scientists themselves and the public at large. Until we have a 'theory of everything' that can be proven, we may not be able to scientifically prove such possibilities as life after death and beings existing in other than the physical realm.

---

[15]Matthews, Robert. 'Extrasensory perception—ESP, evidence, criticism, Parapsychology.' *New Scientist,* London:13 March 2004, vol. 181, Iss. 2438; pp. 39-42.

JOAN L BOLER

Albert Einstein, who contributed greatly to our knowledge of physics, was full of curiosity and was still seeking answers when he died. He was especially interested in finding a 'unified theory of everything'. Unfortunately, he died before he found the answers he was seeking. His curiosity extended to religion and it was his belief that there should be no conflict between science and religion. In his opinion, 'Religion without science is lame and science without religion is blind.'[16]

Truth

Humanity is adrift in a world where the need to know ensures that answers to the mysteries of the scientific and spiritual laws are sought. As each individual travels through time and space on planet Earth, time and again new knowledge challenges previously held understanding.

Recognition that truth is earned through diligence and effort leads to all sources of information being tested. Conversely, truth itself demands we recognise the limits of our knowledge, as the very parameters we use in the testing may be faulty. By acknowledging we don't know all the answers, we ensure we are open to new information. Believing, either scientifically (as in scientism where only those things that can be proven via the scientific method are worthy of recognition[17]) or spiritually (where fundamentalism demands strict obedience to doctrines validated solely by scripture) binds the would-be seeker.

Religions today reflect the impact of past beliefs, and through these religions many seek spiritual truths. The spiritual knowledge to be found in the scriptures that form the basis for the largest world religions was written by those who lived in earlier times, and over time rewritten or interpreted by those who lived in a different era and sometimes had a different culture and language to the original authors. Personal understanding influences each individual's interpretation of these earlier writings. For this reason, there are many different beliefs within the many religions of the world, and sometimes the original truth has become obscured. Paranormal experiences along with scientific research and knowledge (such as that gained through archaeology), can contribute towards discovering the truth when discerning the validity and accuracy of the original texts and their meaning.

---

[16] Einstein, Albert. 'Science and Religion II'. *Science, Philosophy and Religion, A Symposium*, 1941. www.sacred-texts.com/aor/einstein/einsci.htm (accessed 9 May 2014)
[17] Sorell, Thomas 'Tom, *Scientism: Philosophy and the Infatuation with Science*, Routledge, 1994, p. 1ff.

THE TRUTH SEEKER

A healthy respect for the truth raises questions. Are we, as many esoteric sources claim, multidimensional beings living in a multidimensional universe? Is it possible the information on the paranormal that has been discarded by many provides knowledge of and evidence for our true nature and that of the universe?

We live in an age where much of what was in the past beyond the reach of science is now being examined using scientific strictures. Solid evidence that psychic ability and reincarnation are not whimsy is available to the seeker. And who can dismiss the reports by the large numbers of apparently sane people who throughout time have claimed contact with those living around our planet who do not reside in a physical body? Can more scientists let go of the fear of ridicule and the bias of inflexible disbelief long enough to seriously study and test paranormal experience?

Does modern physics now suggest a possible scientific framework for the supernatural, and could science when it finally proves a *theory of everything*, confirm the truth of our spiritual nature? Is it possible the truth will bring science and religion back together with greater insight and understanding? And will science of the future once again encompass the wisdoms of astrology and numerology?

Belief infiltrates both science and religion, claiming truth where only shadows exist and confusing the seeker. The enemy of truth is fear, the author of rigid thinking, superstition and obedient belief. However, no belief supersedes truth and all that is false is destined to disintegrate along with the fear that gave it birth.

JOAN L BOLER

Chapter 2

Astrology—the Science of the Soul

A physician without knowledge of astrology has no right to call himself a physician.

Hippocrates

The Study of Human Energy

When my son was thirteen his pet guinea pig died. Holding back tears, he pleaded, 'Mum... Would you bury him for me, please?' I gently picked up his pet and experienced a sudden shock of realisation. The little body had no life force. The energy, which I had hardly realised I felt whenever I made contact with another living creature, was gone.

Every life form in the universe is made up of, and expresses energy. Furthermore, the energy of each individual creature varies to some degree from others of its species. This is especially true in the case of humans. What are the common denominators and why are there differences? Quantum mechanics maintains that everything and everyone is connected. Can these connections explain a possible link between the planets, our other astral neighbours and the earth and its inhabitants?

Through the ages, humanity has been searching for answers to these questions. Generations of wise men and women have accumulated a huge body of information and understanding that can be found in writings on astrology, palmistry and numerology. Palmistry and numerology are based on astrology. In palmistry, the planets' energies are mapped out on various parts of the hands, while in numerology the planets' energies are linked to numbers. According to the Greek philosopher and mathematician Pythagoras (582-500 BCE?), *The world is built in numbers manifest in form.* Astrology, palmistry and numerology describe the way in which each of us is individually endowed with intelligence, creativity, emotion, sensitivity, practicality and artistic ability.

According to astrology, the planets in our solar system, along with the signs of the zodiac (which are made up of constellations along the ecliptic, the path of the Sun through the heavens), reveal the nature of each human being. The way in which they do so is described in the astrological archetypes. The notion that the planets have an impact on humans is evident in the etymology of the word 'lunacy', which is derived from the word 'lunar' and describes the emotionally unbalanced behaviour some people display at the time of a full Moon.

Is it possible, as astrology maintains, that body shape, bone structure, skin and hair type, along with the facial features of every individual, are the physical manifestation of a variety of identifiable archetypal energies found in varying degrees in each of us? This concept seems, at least in part, to find validation in Albert Einstein's formula $E=mc^2$. Einstein maintained that energy and mass are the same and that they are interchangeable.

Astrology, which also claims a potential for prediction regarding the lives of individuals and world events, was a respected science for millennia. More recently however, this has changed, and the academic community has labelled astrology a pseudo-science. *Astrology is generally considered to be a pseudo (erroneous) science, and should not be confused with astronomy.*[18] Science is based on research and evidence. Has the academic and scientific community investigated thoroughly and disproven the wide range of knowledge that astrology covers? Or has isolated knowledge been examined with a lack of understanding of the dynamics involved, and with the intent to invalidate what they assume *must* be deluded ranting? Have astrologers throughout the ages developed a belief system that has no basis in fact? Or has astrological knowledge developed through the research and efforts of scholars over time, gradually building up a vast resource of knowledge that is incredibly revealing and accurate? The evidence I have encountered confirms the latter statement.

Astrology – An Ancient Science

Early records reveal the gradual evolution of astronomy and astrology which were, until recent times, the same field of study. Early astrologers painstakingly studied the planets, and mapped the celestial bodies traversing the heavens. While astrology started out as a study of the elements that influenced the daily lives of the ancients (for the planting and harvesting of

---

[18] 'Astrology', *The World Book Encyclopedia*, Field Enterprises Educational Corporation, Chicago, 1974, A Vol 1 p. 784a.

crops), it gradually evolved into much more. Its influence, in varying degrees, is seen not only in the religions of the past that saw the celestial bodies as gods or angels, but also its wisdoms form the basis for the religious beliefs of today.

The history of astrology reaches back to Mesopotamia (Iraq) and the Sumerian civilisation some four thousand years ago. The Sumerians were astronomers and mathematicians. Since the nineteenth century, thousands of clay tablets with cuneiform writings on astronomy and astrology have been found, the oldest dating to 1875 BCE.[19] Over millennia, astrology found its way into India where Vedic astrology evolved. Although Chinese astrology evolved in a different way, the knowledge gained also provides accurate information.

The Greek community within Mesopotamia adopted astrology and adapted it to reflect Greek mythology. In addition to being versed in the ways of palmistry, Hippocrates, the 'Father of Medicine' (130-200CE), was also an astrologer and in his work *On Airs, Waters, and Places* he discusses the diagnosis and treatment of illness taking the astrological influences into consideration.[20]

The Jews were also familiar with the concepts of Hellenistic (ancient Greek) astrology. The *Treatise of Shem* (Shem was the son of Noah), thought by scholars to have been written towards the end of the first century BCE, reveals knowledge of its workings. Further confirmation as to Jewish acceptance of astrology is revealed in the 'Dead Sea Scrolls' found at Qumran which included a variety of writings on astrology.[21]

In a climate of acceptance of astrology, the New Testament records the birth of Jesus. The scriptures mention the wise men from the East (the magi).

Matthew 2: 1-2 NIV (New International Version) *[1]After Jesus was born in Bethlehem in Judea, during the time of King Herod, Magi from the east came to Jerusalem [2]and asked, 'Where is the one who has been born king of the Jews? We saw his star in the east and have come to worship him.*[22]

---

[19] 'Bibliography of Mesopotamian Astronomy and Astrology.' *Institute for history and foundations of mathematics and the physical sciences* www.staff.science.uu.nl/~gent0113/babylon/babybibl.htm (accessed 19 Jun 2014)
[20] 'Astrology—History'. New Advent. www.newadvent.org; (accessed 11 Sept 2011)
[21] Ness, Lester J, Astrology and Judaism in late antiquity, Miami University Oxford, Ohio, 1990 www.smoe.org/arcarna/diss1.html (accessed 3 Oct 2011)
[22] *Biblestudytools.com*. www.biblestudytools.com (accessed 10 Aug 2010)

These learned wise men were probably astrologers. However, it is not surprising that over time, mixed attitudes towards astrology are found in both Christian and Jewish communities, when the Bible includes statements such as the following:

Deuteronomy 18:9-12 (NIV) *⁹ When you enter the land the LORD your God is giving you, do not learn to imitate the detestable ways of the nations there. ¹⁰ Let no one be found among you who sacrifices his son or daughter in the fire, who practices divination or sorcery, interprets omens, engages in witchcraft, ¹¹ or casts spells, or who is a medium or spiritist or who consults the dead. ¹² Anyone who does these things is detestable to the LORD, and because of these detestable practices the LORD your God will drive out those nations before you.*[23]

Kocku von Stuckrad, Professor of Religious Studies and Dean of the Faculty of Theology and Religious Studies at the University of Groningen in the Netherlands, notes that as early as the second century BCE, Jewish and Christian documents reveal the use of an astrology adapted to align with religious belief. Although Jewish and Christian attitudes conflicted with the astrology of other cultures due to the deification of the planets and deterministic belief, they did not deny that astrological knowledge provided the means by which heavenly signs could be interpreted, and they sought, and made use of, astrological information. Von Struckrad cites the Qumran writings, the records of the Jewish historian Josephus, gnostic documents—especially the Nag Hammadi texts, and the early Christian Origen's non-fatalistic astrology.[24] [25]

By the first century CE, two forms of astrology had emerged: the first (judicial astrology) drew on knowledge that revealed the past, present and future[26] while the second (natural astrology) covered the weather or medical astrology or meteorology. The hierarchy of Christianity determined that judicial astrology involved divination was therefore was heresy, and in 321 CE Constantine issued an edict that threatened the Chaldeans (astrologers)

---

[23] *Biblestudytools.com.* ibid. (accessed 11 Nov 2011)
[24] Von Stuckrad, Prof. Kocku, *Jewish and Christian astrology in late antiquity—A new approach*, Koninklijke Brill NV, Leiden, 2000.
[25] Rasmussen, Adam. 'Origen on Astrology.' *Acadamia.edu* www.academia.edu/3623649/Origen_on_Astrology (accessed 20 Aug 2014).
[26] Campion, Nicholas, *A History of Western Astrology*, Vol. 1, The Ancient World (first published as The Dawn of Astrology: a Cultural History of Western Astrology. London: Continuum, 2008, pp. 173-174.

and followers of the Magi (priests of the Persian Zoroastrian religion) with death. This ensured that fatalistic astrology lost its appeal for many.[27]

During the time of the Byzantine Empire (Eastern Roman Empire) which lasted to the fifteenth century CE, natural astrology remained acceptable, but in spite of the danger judicial astrology was not eradicated. The fifteenth century CE saw a rise in the popularity of astrology. Popes Sixtus IV (1414-1484), Julius II (1443-1503), and Paul III (1468-1534), had their own astrologers, while Leo X (1475-1521) and Clement VII (1478-1534) were served by the court astrologer Lucas Gauricus.[28] These astrologers were called upon to aid in decisions such as to whom, and when, an audience should be given, and who would best be suited to becoming a cardinal. Kings and emperors also had court astrologers. Nostradamus (1503-1566), a French astrologer, physician, and gifted clairvoyant, was appointed court physician to King Charles IX of France.[29] By the end of the seventeenth century, astrology began to lose favour with the Church, which today views it as false science.[30]

Judaism garnered its share of followers of astrology over the centuries, especially with those who studied the Kabbalah. The Zohar (Splendour), the foundation text of the Kabbalah, was hidden for around nine hundred years from the second century CE and is believed to have been written by **Rabbi Shimon Bar Yochai (second and third centuries CE)**. The Zohar assumes astrological influence. *All the stars and constellations in the heavens were appointed to be rulers and commandants over the world ... there is not a single blade of grass in the entire world over which a star or a planet does not preside, and over that star one [angel] is appointed who serves in the presence of the Holy One Blessed Be He, each according to his merit.*[31] Until the sixteenth century CE, only spiritually advanced males over the age of forty were permitted to study the Kabbalah. However the Holy Ari, Rabbi Isaac Luria (1534-1572), studied, understood and explained the basics of the Kabbalah's wisdoms to his followers. His teachings were recorded and their clarity resulted in his Kabbalistic knowledge becoming sought after by those

---

[27] Astrology—Astrology under Christianity.' *New Advent*, www.newadvent.org (accessed 24 Nov 2011)
[28] 'Astrology—History.' *New Advent*, www.newadvent.org (accessed 11 Sept 2011)
[29] 'Nostradamus.' *The World Book Encyclopedia*, Field Enterprises Educational Corporation, Chicago, 1974, N-O Vol. 14 p. 428.
[30] 'Astrology.' *New Advent* www.newadvent.org/cathen/02018e.htm (accessed 14 June 2014)
[31] 2:171d; see Mishnat ha-Zohar, Tishbi-Lachower trans. vol. 1, 1957, p486.

from other races and creeds seeking spiritual knowledge and understanding.[32]

While Kabbalists accepted astrology from the eleventh century onwards, there were those Jews who rejected astrology. In spite of this, many greatly respected rabbis, preachers, and teachers looked favourably on astrology. Rabbi Abraham Ben Meir Ibn Ezra (1089-1167 CE), was of the opinion that the powers of the seven planets and their various alignments with each other and within the various zodiac signs controlled the welfare of each human being until freedom resulted through spiritual perfection. Some Jews, over the next few centuries, became court astrologers.[33][34]

After checking and rechecking, astrologers over time have ascertained that as well as influencing world events, the Sun, the Moon and the planets' energies reveal human emotional, mental and physical strengths and weaknesses. They also determined that the planets influence the attraction of positive and negative situations into our lives, and that they have an impact upon the events in the world around us.

It would be a mistake to assume the astrologers of any age were ignorant and naïve. A few thousand years is but a moment in time as far as the evolution of humanity is concerned, and the learned individuals of past times were every bit as intelligent as the scholars and scientists of today. These people were not misguided fools. Although they sometimes lacked in the scientific knowledge now available, they based their opinions on research, not belief. In so doing, they laid down the foundations for a science that today is used and respected by many learned people and can be supported by evidence as to its validity.

The Human Blueprint

Deoxyribonucleic acid (DNA) reveals biological family connections. Like DNA, astrology reveals energies passed from one generation to another. The astrological connections between family members reveal links that cannot be considered mere chance.

---

[32] 'Astrology'. *Jewish Virtual Library*. www.jewishvirtuallibrary.org/jsource/judaica/ejud_0002_0002_0_01531.html (accessed 15 Jun 2014)
[33] Altmann, Alexander. 'Astrology.' *Jewish Virtual Library*. (accessed 15 Jun 2014)
[34] *Bnel Baruch Kabbalah and education and research institute.* www.kabbalah.info/engkab/mystzohar.htm#.U50Lf_mSySo

THE TRUTH SEEKER

When the time and place of birth is known, it is possible to plot an astrological chart that will reveal which energies the individual is endowed with and the impact of those energies. Layer upon layer of aspects (positions of the planets and their significance in the individual chart in relation to other celestial bodies at the time) identify each of us as an individual. Of particular interest are the positions of the Sun, the Moon and the ascending sign (the sign that rises in the east at the time and location of birth), each of which identifies a dominant energetic aspect of the complex and unique individuals that we are.

As the Sun moves across the sky and passes through each of the zodiac signs, the sign it is traversing at the moment of an individual's birth is described as that person's Sun sign. Most people know this sign as their 'star' sign. Those who check the detailed astrological description of their Sun sign will recognise a dominant energy in their makeup.

Without the time and place of birth, the 'ascendant' or 'rising' sign cannot be determined accurately without considerable research. The energy identified by the ascending sign reveals the individual's persona. In fact, on first acquaintance initial impressions of a person will most likely reflect the nature of the ascending sign.

The Moon and the sign that it falls in reveals the individual's moods, emotions, intuition and how resolved each person is in remaining constant in their decisions.

The astrological charts of family members reveal a whole range of similarities, including the same significant signs running through the charts of each family member. The family diagram shows links in my own family. Unfortunately, my generation and the previous generation do not know their times of birth and therefore their ascending signs. Years of experience in discerning signs in people allows me to recognise, through physical appearance and personality, the likely missing astrological signs, and I have taken the liberty of entering those signs on the chart in italics. In the case of my siblings, the signs I consider to be their likely ascending signs appeared as Sun signs in one of their children, further supporting my choices.

As shown in the chart 'Astrological Family Links', (Figure 1, page 27) strong family connections can be seen in the following signs:

- Aquarius: The Sun sign of both my sister and me is Aquarius. Our younger sister has her Moon in Aquarius while both my children have Aquarian ascendants. My son's daughter also has her Sun in

Aquarius. If I am correct that my father's ascending sign was Aquarius, then that link came down to us physically through him.

- Taurus: The Sun sign of my father, my youngest sister and my son is Taurus. My son was actually born on my sister's birthday. My mother's Moon is in Taurus, as is my daughter's. My second sister, my son, his father and I all have three planets in Taurus.

- Aries: My mother, my daughter and her father all have Aries as their Sun sign. In fact, my daughter was born on her father's birthday.

- Leo: My son has his Moon in Leo, as does his maternal uncle.

When I began to study astrology many years after I married, I could not miss noticing the astrological similarities between my mother and my husband. If I am correct that my mother's ascending sign is Gemini, then she and the man I married both had Gemini ascendants. Also, and perhaps more significantly, both were born under the sign Aries, which expresses the 'I AM' ego energy. They both had controlling natures that did not easily allow for individual expression in others. This observation gave me insight into the reasons for my attraction to the man that I had married. Once I learned the lesson that dominating Aries energy had to teach me about claiming my own power, I left the marriage.

An in-depth study of a family's astrological birth charts would show many more connections, including generational lessons being learned. The chart of an older family member could show the first stages of learning in a specific area of his or her life. The chart would show unavoidable and inevitable conflict between the individual and their environment, leaving the person with no alternative other than to confront and live in the hostile environment. In the chart of a member or members of the next generation, the same lesson could have progressed to its next stage. The second generation, which has had the opportunity to learn from the actions of the previous generation, must in turn resolve the next stage of the issues such experience causes. Once again, avoidance is out of the question and action, or reaction, is inevitable. Should the lesson reach the third generation's chart/s, it will reveal yet another stage of the same lesson. The number of generations a lesson can encompass is variable.

THE TRUTH SEEKER

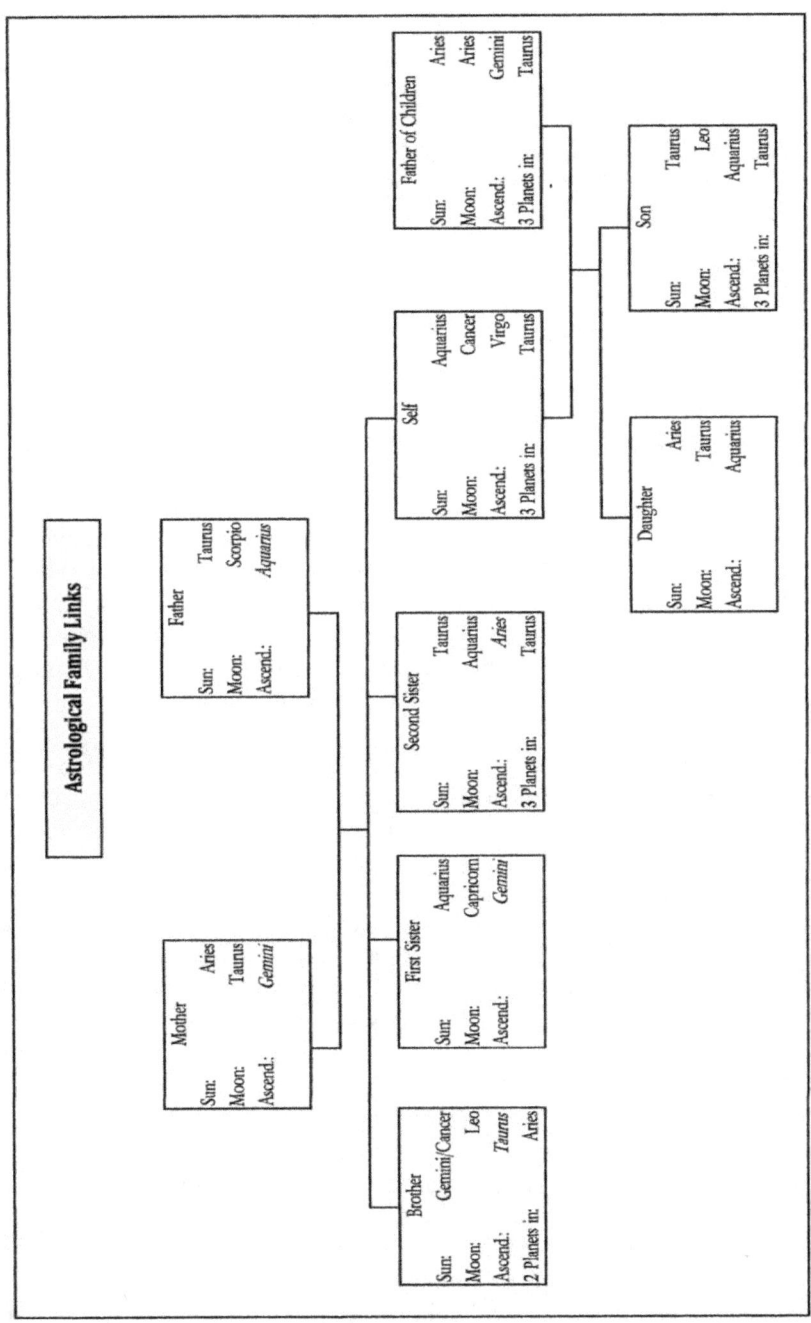

Figure 1 – Astrological Family Links

JOAN L BOLER

All life is energy. DNA is a code that determines our energetic physical, mental, and emotional makeup. Astrology describes the nature of that makeup. An individual who seriously wishes to discover the validity of astrology would find the study of the astrological genealogy of their family a convincing place to start.

Sensing Energies

I was born under the sign of Aquarius and therefore, I am not only humanitarian in nature, I possess a focused, scientific and enquiring mind that takes in the large picture. Intensifying the Aquarian impact is the presence of Mercury (the planet that relates to intellect and communication) and Venus (the planet of love and harmony) in Aquarius. Complimenting my Aquarian mind is my Virgo ascendant, which is expressed in an analytical mind and an eye for detail. It was perhaps inevitable that someone like me would be fascinated by people and what makes them tick. I was easily drawn into the study of the diversity of energies to be found in people and linking the knowledge gained, to the astrological archetypes.

There are many different types of energy, the structure of which science can describe. But science cannot describe what that energy feels like. With the exception of personal emotions, psychically sensing energies is the domain of the clairsentient psychic who can feel, and identify, a wide range of human and other energies. These sensing abilities are, in the main, to be found in those endowed with the astrological water or emotional signs, and my Moon in the water sign Cancer doubtless contributes towards my ability to extend my studies through tuning into and feeling the energies related to the character, attitudes, and emotions of other people.

Individuals are complex, and the study of their energetic makeup through astrology can provide in-depth knowledge and understanding. When we prepare a meal, we draw on a variety of foods and seasonings to produce an interesting and tasty culinary experience. Each of the ingredients has a unique taste and texture. While some people are able to do so, not everyone can identify every ingredient in a prepared meal. For the most part though, the majority of us are able to recognise the main ingredients. During our lifetime we consume an incredible variety of foods, and we learn to recognise the tastes that we experience. In a similar way, each of the energies that make up the nature of a human being can be felt, recognised and defined by those people who sense these energies.

THE TRUTH SEEKER

For a long time I sensed energies around people without consciously knowing what those energies were. Like many people, I could sense when I met a person whether or not I was going to like them. The instant negative reaction to some individuals originally caused me to feel I was being unfair, so I decided I should ignore my intuitive warnings. Closer interaction with these individuals revealed that there was indeed a good reason to avoid them.

On one occasion, during the time I was married with young children, I responded to a knock at the door. When I opened the door, I was confronted with the energy emanating from the two men standing before me. The sun was in my eyes blinding me, so I was unable to discern their faces or expressions. However, my ability to sense their energetic nature enabled me to realise that these were very dangerous men. They had clever, calculating minds and were ambitious. I sensed both had a total disregard for human life and would kill in an instant if they deemed it necessary. What surprised me was that in spite of their treacherous natures, I could not sense in either a tendency to be vicious or vindictive. Instead, I sensed a total lack of emotional caring that indicated that at some prior time the ability to feel for another person had been purged from their makeup, precluding, for the most part, emotionally charged responses.

'Is your husband home?' one of them asked.

'No. He's at work,' I replied. While I knew that these men should not be provoked in any way, I also intuitively knew I wasn't in any danger from them.

'Where is he working?' was their next question. Once again my intuition told me their intentions were not threatening, so I provided them with the address.

That night when my husband arrived home, I asked him if the two men had found him.

To his 'Yes,' I responded, 'I would not have anything to do with them if I were you!'

He was insulted by my advice and retorted, 'I'm not stupid—they belong to the Mafia!'

Some years later, I decided that whenever I felt an energy I did not recognise, I would ponder its nature. Over a period of time I discovered I was beginning to recognise energies and relate them to the signs of the zodiac. I found that when looking at photographs I was able to tune into the energy of the person in the photo and recognise and identify their dominant astrological energy. The person who had given me the photo invariably confirmed the individual in the photo was born under that sign.

The sensing of energies makes it possible to avoid, for the most part, those in society who are likely to cause problems. Intuiting and recognising astrological energies provides a key to in-depth knowledge of the behavioural patterns of those whose nature incorporates those energies. In order to be competent at sensing the energies of others, it is necessary to have the ability to understand other people from their point of view. The person who is able to intuit the motives and feelings of others is not only armed to deal with any situation involving people, they have also developed one of the main abilities required in order to become a good astrologer.

Physical Appearance of the Astrological Signs

My study of astrology provided me with the information that there were consistent subtle physical likenesses to be found in people born under the same sign of the zodiac. Initially, when I began to discern the physical characteristics common to a specific sign, it happened not because of any deliberate study on my part, but because of an incident that caused me to see the possibilities.

I was at my place of work, which at that time involved office administration and bookkeeping. In a social moment I was expounding on the accuracy of astrology and how the personalities of people could reveal the sign of the zodiac they were born under. I was receiving some flak, especially from one young man who worked with me. A gentleman who was engaged in a consulting capacity for the company happened to be in the office at the time and challenged me with, 'What sign was I born under?'

After a few moments I answered, 'Pisces!'

'Yes,' he confirmed, as though it were the most natural thing in the world for me to have been able to provide the correct answer, even though I had no apparent way of doing so. Pisces people tend to be accepting of the unexplained, as most people born under this sign experience some degree of intuition or psychic ability.

Since I could have chosen any one of the twelve signs, even my loudest critic was silenced!

THE TRUTH SEEKER

So how did I get it right? I had not known the gentleman very long and had only spoken to him a few times, so I had not, as yet, discerned his nature through exposure to his attitudes and behaviour. Since I had read that zodiac signs had an impact on the physical appearance of a person, as I looked at him, desperately trying to find answers, I noticed that the overall structure of his face reminded me of a Pisces man that I knew...

After that incident, whenever a person's looks reminded me of another's, I made a point of asking them which zodiac sign they were born under and I frequently found that they were born under the same sign. Gradually my perception increased and I was able to recognise, in much more detail, the dominant features and body structure of each of the signs of the zodiac.

My ongoing observations revealed it was not by chance, or as a result of a long-ago myth or legend, that most of the signs were represented by a specific creature. Frequently, I noted a likeness to the creature that represented the sign in the appearance of those born under a particular sign. It would appear that in earlier times, astrologers had also recognised the physical similarities to specific animals and included that knowledge in the naming of the signs or the creature associated with them. Also, the gods that represent some of the signs, when illustrated, have usually been given a physical appearance resembling that of those born under the sign. Such is the case with the Gemini person, who I have noted has the look of the winged messenger god Mercury (Gemini is ruled by the planet Mercury) with the physical appearance of a long face and body. An interesting aspect of the earth sign Capricorn, which is symbolised by the goat, is that it can produce a look of the horned god Pan. Those born under this sign often have the appearance of the 'trickster' and usually have a particularly mischievous aspect to their nature.

Those born under the sign of Pisces, a water sign with two fish as its symbol, sometimes have a subtle fishlike appearance with a glassy look to the eyes, and sometimes they even have long noses and pursed lips. Others of that sign remind me of penguins with large eyes and rounded bodies. One Piscean person I know, although he is quite attractive, has a wide mouth allowing one to interpret a likeness to a frog or a wide-mouthed fish.

My observations revealed that those born under the sign of Cancer, which is represented by the crab, often have eyes that can give the impression of *standing out*, and they are usually barrel-chested. The bull represents the sign of Taurus, and those born under this sign often have thick necks, strong noses, large square teeth and broad, powerful shoulders. I have frequently recognised those born under the sign of Scorpio as they remind me of an eagle in appearance, with their eyes very strongly focused and a winged brow.

Leo people tend to have a cat look about them, and just as there are many different kinds of cat in the animal kingdom, those with a Leo Sun sign take on the look of different types of cats. Most noticeable about them is the mouth—their lips, teeth and mouth shape. Their smile is usually charming, and of all the signs of the zodiac, they are the most likely to be charismatic and creative.

In a bored moment during a break at a dance one night, I began to read a gentleman's palm. As I looked at his heart line I noted that it was almost identical to a Leo friend's heart line.

Always looking to gain insight and confirmation, I asked, 'What sign were you born under?'

'You tell me,' was his reply.

The man had a huge ego that in itself indicated Leo as a possibility and the features of his face reminded me of the animated Pink Panther.

'Leo!' I stated.

'Funny you should say that,' he responded. 'I was born on the cusp of Leo.'

Over the years, I have noted that people often have the appearance of creatures and other life forms that are not named in astrology. Some Aries people have the look of a ram (the symbol for the Aries sign), especially around the eyebrows and nose, while others of this sign possess a rooster-like appearance, and have sharper features. Each zodiac sign lasts a month and during that month, as the degrees change, it seems possible that the essence of the dominant energy also changes. I am of the opinion that each of the signs relate to a range of similar energies that are to be found in a number of nature's life forms rather than to one or none.

The question arises as to why a person can not only display behaviour attributed to a particular creature, but also possess a subtle physical similarity to that creature. The answer is found in the knowledge that energy has shape. When an aspect of the nature of a human being is similar to the dominant energy of an animal, then the shape their appearance takes on will reflect that similarity. It is not coincidence that such similarity is confirmed in their astrological chart.

THE TRUTH SEEKER

Over time, I began to recognise more than one dominant look in the appearance of an individual, and as my sensing abilities increased, this recognition of form was confirmed by my psychic sensing of its energetic counterpart. On numerous occasions I was able to select two or three signs dominating the individual's appearance and energy. Those who had had their astrological chart drawn up were often able to confirm that I had picked their Sun, Moon, and ascendant signs. Since signs run in families, with those who did not know their Moon or ascendant signs, I asked for the star signs their parents and siblings were born under. Almost always the signs I mentioned were found in their immediate family's star signs.

In most people, a mixture of the Sun, Moon and ascendant signs can be found in their appearance while in some people, the Sun sign dominates, and in others it is the ascending sign or even the Moon sign. Why this is I don't know, but it would make an interesting study. This three-way mixture of energies, each of which has an impact on and modifies the others, plus the many other influences revealed in the astrological chart, explains why people born under a particular sign can vary considerably in both personality and appearance.

We look the way we do because of our energetic natures. We are born with definable characteristics and potential, and our appearance reflects all that our soul brings into this life. Over time, how we live this life is also reflected in our appearance as an overlay on the original architecture. For those versed in the physical appearance of energy, the reading of character is possible.

Combining the Skills

When I eventually began to work as a psychic reader, I was able to combine the ability to not only feel and identify a person's energy, but also to recognise the physical manifestation of those energies in a person's appearance. Additionally, by that time I had developed the ability to see clairvoyantly and to use tarot cards intuitively. Each of these abilities contributed towards a greater degree of accuracy in the information I obtained.

A young lady, who worked in the same shop as I did, came to me for a psychic reading.

'I don't want to know when I'll meet the person with whom I will settle down. I just want to know if there is a relationship coming in for me soon.'

Unlike most young ladies who wish to know when they will meet the 'love of their life', she was only interested in information relating to the possibility of a less permanent relationship.

First, I used the tarot cards, which revealed that a relationship would come into her life in approximately three months' time. I then focussed upon receiving a clairvoyant vision of him. The image I clairvoyantly saw revealed a man with light-coloured skin and hair, a lean body structure and a long, oval face. His appearance reflected the physical attributes of a person with Gemini energies. At the same time, I felt a very strong Gemini energy and advised her of this.

Three months later she met a young man who physically matched the description I had given and he was born under the sign of Gemini.

Over the ensuing three years or so that they were a couple, I came to know the young man fairly well. His interest in astrology guaranteed a number of mutually enjoyable conversations. He informed me he had five planets in Gemini which meant, because mental stress and instability can be a confronting factor for those born under this sign, he was likely to have mental problems. In fact, he was schizophrenic.

Time and again in readings confirmation came as I advised people of their astrological makeup, their attitudes and their interests. And then, just as accurately, I described the makeup of those close to them even though they were not present. Often, the person I was reading for became a little freaked out and said something like, 'I feel as though you just got inside my head.' Personal experience has been my proof with regard to the validity of astrology and its ability to identify the nature of people, but does astrology also reveal influences that have an impact on the events in our lives and the world around us?

Astrological Charts and the Influences they Reveal

Astrologers over time have worked to uncover the secrets of life. Layer upon layer of understanding has translated into calculations and formulas based on observations of the heavenly bodies in our galaxy and their verifiable influence on individuals and the world at large. What astrologers have discovered, and are still discovering, is that we appear to be part of a gigantic programme that encompasses forces that have an impact on billions of life forms, including human beings. In addition, each person is programmed through life experiences in a unique way, so the type and intensity of the impact of the astrological forces is directly related to the individual's programmes. Today, the impact of and reaction to all that an individual encounters can, for the most part, be correctly ascertained by astrologers.

Prediction of a probable outcome from the information available is commonplace in our lives. The difference between one form of prediction and another is the degree of accurate information to which the forecaster has access. In our daily lives we are constantly guessing at probable outcomes. We see a driver on the road taking dangerous risks and predict that they are an accident waiting to happen. An encounter with an arrogant self-absorbed person leads us to the conclusion the individual will meet with problems in relationships. As we come across those whose behaviour is dictated by drug or alcohol addiction, we can predict failure rather than success in most areas of their lives. While we look at others and predict, we do so with relatively limited information. This is not the case with astrology, as all the basic data contained in the individual's programme is revealed astrologically at the time of birth.

Today, research is still going on. Astrologers like Norman Pallas, a friend who spent many years painstakingly recording the time and place of events, running charts, making comparisons and finding common denominators, have recorded their findings. Norman's special interest is degrees. His research follows on from that done by Maurice Wemyss (1892-1980).[35] The study reveals that the degree indicated in an aspect, reveals a particular influence depending on the sign involved. It was found that each degree impacted in the same way, on not only the individual sign, but also its opposite sign. For example, the ankle degree has an orb that includes 18, 19 or 20° Pisces *and* Virgo.

Astrology has now evolved to the point where it can not only provide strong pointers as to what is likely to confront or surprise a person and have an impact on their life, it can also give precise information about possible events on any given day. In evidence of this, since I had recorded in my diary the date and time that I broke my ankle, the relevant astrological charts can be examined and compared with the actual incident, which took place on a hot sunny day as I prepared to leave for work.

My attire that day reflected the warm weather and included 2½ inch (6.4cm) high-heel leather sandals, the straps of which had, over time, stretched a

---

[35] Wemyss, Maurice. *The Wheel of Life or Scientific Astrology*, Modern Astrology Office, London, 1927.

little. In spite of this, I chose to wear the cool sandals rather than closed-in footwear. On my way out, I negotiated the staircase from the upper level of the house and was part-way down the stairs when abruptly, my right foot slid slightly within the sandal and as a result I turned my right ankle. (Later my eight year old niece, who was at the base of the stairs mentioned that she had heard a 'crack', but she said nothing to me at that time. It would seem that her hearing was more acute than mine. Had I heard the sound myself, I would have stopped immediately.) Rather than stop and check my ankle thoroughly, I put my weight on my foot and as it felt fine I continued on down the stairs and proceeded to the front door and the outside stairs.

There were sixteen stairs and I had no problems moving down them—until I reached the last step. Suddenly my right leg collapsed and I was unable to prevent a headlong crash on to the concrete. My sister-in-law, after phoning for an ambulance, came down to where I was sprawled on the driveway. She noted I was sweating from the heat from an already warm day, and as I was not going to be moving before the ambulance arrived, she gave my niece the task of holding an umbrella over me to protect me from the sun.

My unwise decision to wear the sandals resulted in my tibia and fibula being shattered at my ankle, which was also dislocated. In order to effectively repair such a bad break, screws were embedded in the bone on one side of my ankle while on the other a plate was screwed into the bone. The one positive aspect was the presence in the hospital on that day of the top bone surgeon in New South Wales, and it was he who performed the operation. A long and painful recovery ensued.

Although I have studied astrology, and am adept at recognising and understanding astrological energies, I am an amateur when it comes to reading charts, and I have no knowledge whatsoever of degrees. In order to bring together the relevant astrological information, I needed the help of my three astrologer friends, each of whom has previously helped me with answers to astrological questions. Frank Soria spent time and effort researching my charts to produce the initial information, and from time to time he contributed additional knowledge. My good friend Patricia Chardon did further research, and assembled it along with the relevant charts. Norman Pallas, who taught Frank and Patricia, was available as advisor when needed. In the late 1980s, Norman had, through research, ascertained the time of my birth so charts could be calculated.

The following information, gleaned from the charts, reveals the astrological influences that had an impact upon my life at the time I broke my ankle. With Patricia's help, I have translated the astrological terms and attempted to give a plausible explanation as to the significance of each astrological aspect and the data that it reveals. For those who do not wish to labour through all the information provided, reading the summaries (in italics) will provide the probable meaning of each astrological aspect. The relevant astrological charts are at the end of this book so that those who wish to, can study these reports in depth (Figure 9—Geocentric Natal Chart, Page 406; Figure 10—Geocentric Event Chart, page 407; Figure 11—Heliocentric Natal Chart, page 408; Figure 12—Geocentric Progress Chart, page 409).

Natal and Event Geocentric and Heliocentric Charts

An examination of the 'geocentric' (perspective from Earth) and 'heliocentric' (perspective from the Sun) of the natal and event charts, reveals aspects that need to be interpreted in order to gain insight into the way in which the influences will have an impact. The 'natal' chart is the birth chart. The event charts reveal transits (relationships between the planets in the birth chart and their positions at the time the event) for the day, time and location that I broke my ankle (21 December 2000, 8:45 am, Sydney, Australia). The main trigger should be, and is, revealed by the transiting Moon for that month.

- The transiting Moon (deals with the unconscious and the unseen and is a trigger or source) at 8:45am was at 4°36' (touch/slippery) Scorpio (provokes intense emotional response) and was in (90°) square (stress/obstacles) aspect to transiting Neptune (vague/nebulous/impractical thinking and ruler of Pisces which relates to the feet) at 4°57' Aquarius (physically, Aquarius rules the ankles). *An impractical decision to wear loose sandals, allowed my feet to slip resulting in an excruciatingly painful broken ankle that caused an enormous amount of physical and emotional distress.*

- Neptune (vague/nebulous) was in opposition (disruption and conflict), to the Moon (unconscious) square (stressful) the Natal geocentric and heliocentric Pluto (provokes sudden change and is associated with the eighth house and can trigger accidents) at 4°33' geocentric Leo (vitality and self-expression) and 4°39' heliocentric Leo. *Due to lack of depth of thought, circumstances suddenly changed with an accident that resulted in restriction and limitation.*

- On the event chart, transiting heliocentric Chiron (wellness, wounds and healing) was at 20°31' (change to luck) Sagittarius (can be reckless) and was conjunct (acts together with) transiting heliocentric Mercury (mind/communication), which was at 20°44' Sagittarius (recklessness/unplanned). *Reckless thinking and lack of communication from niece resulted in negative change that involved wounds.*

- In my natal chart, both these planets were on the cusp of the 4th house (home). Both Chiron (wounds) and Mercury (confused/blocked communication) were in square (stressful) aspect to the ankle degree, which has an orb (range) that includes 18, 19 or 20 degrees Pisces (vague thinking/feet) and Virgo (affects analytical/detailed thinking). *While at home that morning, I unknowingly wounded my ankle while walking down the stairs. My niece's lack of communication and my lack of in-depth consideration by me, of possible injury, resulted in further damage.* The transiting Moon (unconscious) at 4°36' Scorpio (intense feelings) was semi-square (tension) Chiron (wounds) and Mercury (confused/blocked communication), which were semi-square (tension) transiting Neptune (feet) at 4°57' Aquarius (ankles). *Lack of communication contributed to further wounding to my ankle through the feet, and the wounding resulting in excruciating pain.*

- On the Event chart, the transiting Moon (unconscious) was squaring (stress/obstacles) the transiting ascendant (represents the physical body) at 7°42' (skin) Aquarius (ankles). *Points to physical body stress on skin and ankles.*

- The transiting Sun (self) was at 29°20' (brittleness) Sagittarius (spontaneous/reckless) in the fourth house (represents the home), and was afflicting my Natal Neptune (vague/nebulous/impractical) at 29°40' (fragmentation) Virgo (perfection/critical/discrimination) in the 1st house (relates to self). *My reckless and impractical decision at home that morning lacked good judgement and resulted in the shattering of my ankle bones.*

- Natal Uranus at 26°22' Taurus is in permanent square affliction to natal Mercury at 26°22' Aquarius in the 6th house. This affliction will only be triggered when a transiting or progressed planet arrives to trigger one of these two degrees either, 26°22' Taurus or Aquarius. On the day, transiting Saturn (associated with bones) was at 25°10' (fractures/dislocation) Taurus (physical senses), and was conjunct (acts together with) my natal Uranus (sudden and unexpected events) at 26°22' (breakages/fractures/dislocation) and conjunct (acts together with) my natal heliocentric Saturn (bones) at 27° (destiny/the inevitable/fate/karma) 43' Taurus (senses). In addition, Saturn (bones) and Uranus (sudden and unexpected events) were conjunct (acts together with) 25–27° (degree of fractures) of Taurus and Scorpio. *Suddenly and unexpectedly fate stepped in and I experienced pain and shock from badly broken bones and a dislocation.*

- Heliocentric Mars (the fiery planet) on the event chart was at 27° (one of the heat degrees 27°05') Virgo.

THE TRUTH SEEKER

It was a hot day.

The Progressed chart

In order to obtain a progressed chart and reveal the influences for a specific time after birth, the natal chart is adjusted to allow for relocation from New Zealand to Australia, and progressed to the year 2000 by advancing the chart twenty-four hours for each year. For a part of a year, each month equals two hours. The progressed Moon is extremely important in triggering an event.

- The progressed Moon (deals with the unconscious, the unseen and is a trigger) was, in December 2000, at 26°39' (communication degree) Leo (vitality and self-expression) and in opposition (disruption and conflict) to natal Mercury (mind/confused/blocked communication) at 26°22' (breakages/fractures/dislocation) Aquarius (ankles) in the 6th house (health) on the natal chart. *A secondary trigger, which had an impact on the severity of injury, was contributed towards by my niece's failure to communicate that she had heard a 'crack'. Dislocation and shattered bones in the ankle followed.* It was also afflicted by a square (stress/obstacles) aspect to my natal Uranus (the unexpected) at 26°22' (breakages/fractures/dislocation) Taurus (physical senses). *Unexpected stress caused breakages and dislocation, resulting in extreme physical pain.*

- Progressed Mars (relates to action/is ruler of the 6th house of health) was in the eighth house (accidents). Mars (action) was also the traditional ruler of the chart, on that day and at that time. Mars (action) was at 13°03' (accident/mobility) Gemini (affects mental state) and afflicted the progressed North Node at 13°18' Virgo. This affliction can cause mishaps. Progressed Mars at 13°03' (accident/mobility) Gemini (affects mental state) was also square (stress/obstacles) the natal North Node at 13°54' (changeability) Virgo and this North Node on my natal chart is conjunct (acts together with) my natal ascendant (physical body) at 12°36' Virgo. *Action impacting upon health of physical body. Activity involves accident, change in mobility and mental stress.*

- Progressed Mercury (mind/communication) was at 18°03' (ankle degree) of Pisces (feet/impractical thinking) and was afflicting by square (stress/obstacles) natal heliocentric Mars (the planet associated with accidents which is also the ruling planet of the natal 8th house, a house which is associated with accidents or sudden events) at 18°39' (affects positive outlook) of Gemini (affects mental state). *Sudden accident contributed to by the lack of thought given both towards wearing practical footwear and checking the ankle after turning it, plus lack of communication from niece.*

- The progressed Sun (self) at 7°56' (surgical operations) Aries (affects self-expression) was afflicting, by square (stress/obstacles) aspect, 8–10° (bone degree) Cancer and Capricorn, (a degree which is also related to falls), and the Sun (self) was also afflicted by a semi-square (problems), 25–27° (fracture degree) Taurus and Scorpio. *After the fall, I was no longer free to follow my usual responsibilities and interests. Instead, it was necessary to have an operation to repair the fractured bones caused by my fall.*

- Transiting Venus (harmony) was at 22° (surgeon) Aquarius (ankle) and was trine (powerful and positive) the Part of Fortune (brings good fortune) in the 8th house (operations). *The best bone surgeon in the state of New South Wales was present at the hospital, and was available to perform the operation.*

All relevant information on the events of that day is revealed in the charts, and most of the probabilities are repeatedly confirmed, from different viewpoints, by a variety of aspects. The presence of the bone specialist in the hospital at the time (the only real positive on that day) is an argument buster, refuting the possibility of coincidental alignment of all the influences.

Although my chart was accessed after the event which made interpretation of the aspects easier, the exact same charts could have been run before the event and would have predicted accurately that I would break, wound and dislocate my ankle on that day. The evidence provided by the charts confirms it is possible to predict likely happenings for any given time. The cosmos follows patterns and laws that command and control the output of all types of energetic influences. I imagine that these influences have an impact much like the weather. If a storm is predicted, most people stay indoors, but there are always those who don't have a choice and must endure the inclement weather.

Astrology indicates that certain events, if not all events, are fated to happen. Is it possible that there is a computer-like consciousness of the universe that contains all knowledge of every aspect of every living creature and its world and that accurately reveals how, at any given time, the cosmic influences will have an impact on each and every individual on the planet? If this is the case, is it possible to reduce antagonistic influences or enhance the impact of positive aspects? History records that people have been using astrological knowledge to their advantage over a long period of time, but was that advantage predicted in their charts?

THE TRUTH SEEKER

While fate may be predetermined, free will is intrinsic to the human state. Free will is not about our ability to control all that is in our environment, for such a belief is an illusion. Free will is the ability to be in charge of our innermost thoughts and feelings: to employ wisdom in our choices and to respect the right of others to do the same. Each of us chooses our attitudes and what we care about. Whether we harbour the negative or nurture the positive, that which is within us will be revealed in what we attract and in how we react to life's challenges. All individual choices may well be foreseeable as they are the outcome of prior experience and the moment-to-moment decision-making each person is engaged in throughout their lives.

It is awe-inspiring that the powerful tool of astrology can accurately access such an amazing range of detailed knowledge and can assist us in understanding and making the most of our lives.

Universal Order

The study of human nature through astrology, palmistry and numerology has evolved over thousands of years, and scholars throughout the ages have respected such studies. For those who study astrology in depth, it proves its ability to provide accurate data relating to the personal details of an individual's makeup and possible life experiences.

In modern times, many gifted and intelligent people have studied and appreciated the information that can be gleaned from astrology. One such person was Carl Jung (1875–1961), the Swiss psychologist who, with his theory of the collective unconscious, developed analytical psychology. In his writings, Jung recounts how he used astrology to help him to understand the psychological makeup of his patients.[36] As astrology deals with archetypes, such understanding and knowledge influenced and contributed towards his work.

There have been many in recent times who have sought to discredit astrology after a superficial examination of some aspects of astrological knowledge. It is not possible to properly assess astrology without a thorough investigation into all of its knowledge. Just as life is complex, astrology is also complex, and because the understanding of it requires not only a scientific mind, but also an intuitive one, not everyone can be an astrologer

---

[36] Jung, Carl — *Letter written to Hindu astrologer B V Raman*, 6 September 1947

or is competent to judge the accuracy of astrology. In the words of Carl Jung:

> *While studying astrology I have applied it to concrete cases many times.... The experiment is most suggestive to a versatile mind, unreliable in the hands of the unimaginative, and dangerous in the hands of a fool, as those intuitive methods always are. If intelligently used the experiment is useful in cases where it is a matter of an opaque structure. It often provides surprising insights. The most definite limit of the experiment is lack of intelligence and literal-mindedness of the observer.* [37]

As we look to the celestial bodies in our solar system, it is easy to accept without question the idea that our world and its neighbouring constellations are separate and have little to do with human beings on a personal level. But astrology shows this is not the case. In fact, what happens out in space affects each of us in significant ways.

Energy is found in all life, and although it may change the way in which it manifests, it never ceases to exist; nor does new energy come into being. In physics, this is known as the 'law of conservation of energy'. From the moment a human birth takes place, the positions of the celestial bodies in our galaxy can be used to accurately discover the energetic nature of the new life. This knowledge raises a number of questions.

Is it possible that we as souls plunge into the physical realm, gathering to ourselves the dominant energies surrounding earth at a given moment? Or alternatively is our own soul energy compelled down into the denser realms of the physical by those cosmic energy fields that interact with our own? Evidence indicates that we live in a 'like attracts like' universe perhaps because it is a 'like connected to like' universe. Since both psychically and on a subatomic level there is no distance between one physical object and another, credence is given to the possibility that we are in some way, through the various energies in our makeup, connected to similar energies in the cosmos. Is it possible that an archetypal energy in the great bodies of the planets resonates with a like energy in our human makeup? As far-fetched as this might sound, it provides an explanation for the verifiable links between the astrological bodies and the human state.

As we study the remarkable complexities of humanity, the wonders of nature all around us and galaxies near and far, can we truly believe that all

---

[37] Jung, C G,: *Letters*, Volume 2, 1951-1961, Princeton Press, 1976, pp. 463-464, letter to Robert L. Kroon, 15 November 1958.

aspects of the cosmos are random and without purpose and design? Is it not possible that the universe is filled with an order and purpose that guarantees a perfect outcome for all life?

JOAN L BOLER

Chapter 3

Reincarnation—the Journey of the Soul

As long as you are not aware of the continual law of Die and Be Again, you are merely a vague guest on a dark Earth.

Johann Wolfgang von Goethe[38]

Reincarnation – Belief or Truth?

Is the idea of having lived before part of a belief system adopted by the naïve or is it based on real experience and evidence that has been seriously researched?

The concept of reincarnation has a long history, the details of which have been recorded throughout time by those who remember their previous sojourns into the physical dimension. So much has been written about the idea that we have lived many lifetimes, both over the ages, and during recent times, that there is no lack of information for the interested seeker.

Reports come from all over the world of children who recall a lifetime preceding their current life, and who can give verifiable, in-depth information about the person they claim to have been. How is this possible? And has science verified that birthmarks and birth defects can provide extremely convincing evidence for a person having lived previously, in another body, and in another place and time?

As we look to the varying skills, abilities and innate wisdoms we are born with, can they be explained by prior existence? And can valid evidence be gained through the dream state, meditation, hypnosis and psychic readings?

For those who research this subject, all these possibilities render answers and more questions. The significance of reincarnation as a fact of life cannot

---

[38] Johann Wolfgang von Goethe (1749–1832) (German writer, pictorial artist, biologist, theoretical physicist.) Selige Sehnsucht in his *Buch des Sängers of the West-östlicher Divan*, 1819

be underestimated, for it underpins our attitude towards both life and death. In the largely Christian West, that has for the most part excluded a belief in past lives, proof of reincarnation could have a profound effect on the consciousness of billions of people.

The Past and Reincarnation

For millennia, a number of the world religions have taught the concept of one soul living many lifetimes. Each soul is said to progress through repeated lifetimes of learning from life's difficulties and challenges. Although the religions that accept reincarnation disagree in their understanding of what represents the soul and whether the human soul migration includes animals, they accept that life is a continuing process and rebirth is a part of life. Even those peoples who have for countless generations been isolated from the beliefs and knowledge accumulated by other cultures, like the Australian aboriginal tribes, support the belief that the spirit will be reborn.[39]

Among the major world religions that have held with the concept of reincarnation are Hinduism and Buddhism (from the Sanskrit word 'buddh' meaning 'to awaken'). The Bhagavad Gita (Song of God 250 BCE–250 CE) is a sacred Hindu text written in Sanskrit. Chapter 2:27 refers to death and rebirth—*For certain is death for the born. And certain is birth for the dead. Therefore over the inevitable, Thou should not grieve.*

Records reveal that the Greeks were no strangers to the concept of reincarnation. The Greek mathematician, scientist, astronomer and philosopher Pythagoras (580-500? BCE) taught numerology along with the wisdom that the human soul was immortal and moved on to another body after death. Plato (427?-347? BCE), a Greek philosopher, believed in the immortality of the soul and that after death the soul finds itself in the *realm of the pure forms*.[40] He also maintained that after spending some time in this other realm, the soul reincarnates into another body and returns to the physical world.[41]

While today mainstream Islam rejects the idea of reincarnation, there are those who claim the Qur'an speaks of reincarnation. Sura 2:20:11 states: *Ye*

---

[39] *World Book Encyclopedia*, op. cit. 'A-L' p.14.
[40] *World Book Encyclopedia* op. cit.
[41] *World Book Encyclopedia* op. cit. 'P' vol. 15 pp. 504a and 813.

THE TRUTH SEEKER

were dead and He gave you life; Next He will cause you to die; next He will restore you to life: Next shall ye return to Him.[42]

It is difficult to gain information as to early Jewish attitudes towards reincarnation, and to date there is no conclusive proof that Judaism held a belief in reincarnation during the period 516 BCE to 70 CE.[43] In spite of this, there are Biblical verses that suggest the idea was not excluded and could have been accepted by at least some: Job 14:14 (NIV) *[14] If a man dies, will he live again? All the days of my hard service I will wait for my renewal to come.* Malachi 4:5 (NIV) *See, I will send you the prophet Elijah before that great and dreadful day of the LORD comes.*[44]

The writings of the Jewish historian Titus Flavius Josephus (born Jerusalem 37 CE) provide some information as to the attitudes towards *gilgul* (reincarnation) of two of the Jewish religious factions of the time: the Pharisees, who are seen as a source for Judaism today, and the Sadducees.[45] According to Josephus in Jewish Wars 2:8, *[14] '...the Pharisees... They say that all souls are incorruptible, but that the souls of good men only are removed into other bodies, - but that the souls of bad men are subject to eternal punishment. But the Sadducees... take away the belief of the immortal duration of the soul, and the punishments and rewards in Hades.*[46] In the twelfth century, Kabbalistic knowledge was expressed in the *Sefer ha-Bahir*. At this time it revealed a limited acceptance of the transmigration of souls. Early in the fourteenth century, a broader understanding of reincarnation was included that accepted reincarnation in all forms of life.[47]

From a background of Judaism, Christianity emerged with the life of the Jewish rabbi, Jesus. The attitudes of the Pharisees towards gilgul, seems to be known to the disciples. In the Gospel of Matthew it is suggested that the soul of Elias (the Greek equivalent of Elijah who was a prophet of Israel in the ninth century BCE[48]) had returned as John the Baptist. Matthew 17:10-13 (NIV) *[10] The disciples asked him, 'Why then do the teachers of the law say that Elijah must come first?' [11] Jesus replied, 'To be sure, Elijah comes*

---

[42] Rodwell, J M (tr.), *The Koran,* Dover Publications, London, 2005.
[43] Scholem, Gershom. 'Gilgul'. *Encyclopaedia Judaica,* Jewish Virtual Library, www.jewishvirtuallibrary.org (accessed 10 Oct 2011)
[44] *Biblestudytools.com* www.biblestudytools.com/ (accessed 10 Oct 2011)
[45] 'Pharisees, Sadducees & Essenes.' *Jewish Virtual Library.* Source: Mitchell G. Bard, The Complete Idiot's Guide to Middle East Conflicts, NY: MacMillan, 1999. www.jewishvirtuallibrary.org/jsource/History/sadducees_pharisees_essenes.html#top (accessed 15 May 2014)
[46] Titus Flavius Josephus.*The Wars Of The Jews.* www.ccel.org/j/josephus/works/war-2.htm (accessed 15 May 2014)
[47] Scholem, Gershom, 'Gilgul'. *Encyclopaedia Jucaica,* Jewish Virtual Library, www.jewishvirtuallibrary.org (accessed 10 Oct 2011)
[48] 'Elijah.' *Wikipedia.* en.wikipedia.org/wiki/Elijah (accessed 10 May 2009)

and will restore all things. ¹² *But I tell you, Elijah has already come, and they did not recognize him, but have done to him everything they wished. In the same way the Son of Man is going to suffer at their hands.'* ¹³ *Then the disciples understood that he was talking to them about John the Baptist.*⁴⁹

Another example of an acceptance of reincarnation is found in the Gospel of Mark that indicates the past life beliefs of the people of the town. Jesus did not revoke that idea. Mark 8: 27-28 (NIV) *⁷ Jesus and his disciples went on to the villages around Caesarea Philippi. On the way he asked them, 'Who do people say I am?' ²⁸ They replied, 'Some say John the Baptist; others say Elijah; and still others, one of the prophets.'* Yet another verse that could imply a belief that a blind man was being punished for his actions during a previous lifetime is found in the New Testament: John 9:2 (NIV) *His disciples asked him, 'Rabbi, who sinned, this man or his parents, that he was born blind?'* ⁵⁰

According to available records, early Christianity's approach to reincarnation was split between those who accepted reincarnation and those who did not, just as was the case with Judaism. While most of the writings on reincarnation were later banned by the Church, the works by Basilides (130-160 CE) and Valentinus (100-175 CE), both of whom were influenced by Plato's teachings, survived.⁵¹

When Constantine became Emperor in 312 CE, he declared that Christianity was to be the religion of the Roman Empire. Over the years that followed, all beliefs that did not adhere to the new Christian dogma were defined as pagan and did not survive Rome becoming the custodian of Christianity. The concept of multiple lives that allowed for spiritual growth through experience and learning, along with the need for atonement through reparation for the wrong deeds committed in previous lives, did not sit well with the Church's claim that spiritual salvation was dependent on believing in Church dogma in order to gain the approval of Jesus and therefore entry into heaven. The Gnostic Gospels, some of which have, amazingly, survived to this day and contain teachings by Jesus, were rejected by the Roman Catholic Church. The following reveals a statement by Jesus regarding reincarnation. *Souls are poured from one into another of different kinds of*

---

[49] *Biblestudytools.com.* www.biblestudytools.com (accessed 11 Oct 2011)
[50] Ibid.
[51] Jenson, Elizabeth. 'The argument over reincarnation in early Christianity'. *Historia: the Alpha Rho Papers.* University of Utah E Publications. epubs.utah.edu/index. (accessed 22 May 2013)

THE TRUTH SEEKER

bodies of the world..[52] By 553 CE the concept of reincarnation had disappeared completely and the Church's one life policy was established.

Whether or not reincarnation is an actuality is best determined by looking at the facts, and not by a *belief* dictated by those who have claimed authority. If our soul is reborn into a physical body again and again, it is part of the Creator's grand design and as such, the evidence needs to be investigated without prejudice by all religions interested in spiritual truth.

The West in Recent Times

As Christianity has dominated the Western world for many centuries, minimal exposure to the concept of reincarnation has led to an almost total acceptance of the one life belief. But in spite of the majority following the indoctrination that prevailed for over sixteen hundred years, many famous people maintained multiple lives were a reality. Among them were the following:

> *It is not more surprising to be born twice than once; everything in nature is resurrection.* — 'Voltaire' François-Marie Arouet (1694-1778), enlightenment writer, historian and philosopher.[53]

> *Our birth is but a sleep and a forgetting; The Soul that rises with us, our life's Star, Hath had elsewhere its setting. And cometh from afar.*—William Wordsworth. (1770-1850) English romantic poet.[54]

> *The soul comes from without into the human body, as into a temporary abode, and it goes out of it anew it passes into other habitations, for the soul is immortal. It is the secret of the world that all things subsist and do not die, but only retire a little from sight and afterwards return again. Nothing is dead; men feign themselves dead, and endure mock funerals... and there they stand looking out of the*

---

[52] Mead, G R S (tr.) 'Pistis Sophi'. *The Gnostic Society Library*. gnosis.org/library/psoph.htm (accessed 25 Aug 2014)
[53] Quoted in French in Lady Caithness (Marie Sinclair), *Old Truths in a New Light*, London, 1876) p. 394.
[54] Wordsworth, William. 536. 'Ode Intimations of Immortality from Recollections of Early Childhood' in Quiller-Couch, Arthur, *The Oxford Book of English Verse*: 1250–1900, ed. 1919.

window, sound and well, in some strange new disguise. — Ralph Waldo Emerson (1803-1882), American essayist, lecturer, and poet.[55]

Why should we be startled by death? Life is a constant putting off of the mortal coil - coat, cuticle, flesh and bones, all old clothes. — Henry David Thoreau (1817-1862), American author, poet, philosopher.[56]

I know I am deathless. No doubt I have died myself ten thousand times before. I laugh at what you call dissolution, and I know the amplitude of time. — Walt Whitman (1819-1892), American poet, essayist and journalist.[57]

I have been born more times than anybody except Krishna. — Mark Twain (1835-1910), American author and humourist.[58]

When the physical organism breaks up, the soul survives. It then takes on another body. — Paul Gauguin (1848-1903), French Post-Impressionist artist.[59]

He saw all these forms and faces in a thousand relationships become newly born. Each one was mortal, a passionate, painful example of all that is transitory. Yet none of them died, they only changed, were always reborn, continually had a new face: only time stood between one face and another. — 'Siddhartha', Herman Hesse, (1877-1962), German Novelist.[60]

Over the last two or three hundred years, the influx into the West of those from the East, along with more frequent travel and modern media, has exposed those in the West to the spiritual understandings of the East. Theosophy (a Westernisation of Eastern religious teachings with Christian ideas and ideals integrated), played a significant role in increasing awareness. As a result, open investigation of the religious outlooks that include reincarnation has become fairly widespread today.

---

[55] Emerson, Ralph Waldo, and Brooks Atkinson. *The Essential Writings of Ralph Waldo Emerson,* Modern Library, New York, 2000.
[56] Thoreau, Henry D, *The Writings of Henry D Thoreau,* Journal, vol. 2 1842-1848 Princetown University Press, 1984, p. 211.
[57] Whitman, Walt, 'Song of Myself' *Leaves of Grass,* 1860
[58] Autobiography of Mark Twain
[59] Lester Pleadwell, Frank (tr.), *Modern Thought and Catholicism,* privately printed, 1927. www.harekrishna.com/col/books/KR/cb/chapter1.html (accessed 4 Nov 2014)
[60] 1922.

THE TRUTH SEEKER

Extraordinary people have contributed towards the general population's awareness of the possibility of multiple lives. Edgar Cayce (1877-1945), was a Christian who became known as 'The Sleeping Prophet'. Cayce was a family man who was also a photographer, a Sunday school teacher and a keen gardener. While in a trance state, Cayce was provided with the name and address of the person requiring his help regarding health problems. He then accurately diagnosed and prescribed for the medical conditions of these people. That these diagnoses were confirmed, and the prescribed cures successful, brought Cayce recognition. During his lifetime he performed over thirty thousand readings.

Gradually, while Cayce was in a trance state, other information emerged and/or was sought. Among the abundance of knowledge revealed were answers confirming the validity of astrology and reincarnation.[61] Cayce could relate one or many of the past lives an individual had experienced. He explained the reason one person was spending his life in a wheelchair was because this person needed to learn to appreciate life as he had committed suicide in a previous lifetime. This theme of the consequences of actions incorporating learning was repeated in many stories involving difficulties faced by individuals during their current lifetime.[62] When Cayce died in 1945 he left behind a foundation dedicated to researching the data provided by his readings.

The screen legend Shirley MacLaine has also contributed towards increasing awareness of the existence of previous lives in the modern Western world. In a number of books, MacLaine revealed details of many years of her life and her spiritual journey. Remembrance of other lifetimes was an integral part of her experiences. Had MacLaine not been so highly respected, very little attention would have been given to her claims. Although there were sceptics, MacLaine's willingness to be open about her knowledge and experiences meant many in the West opened up to the concept of multiple lifetimes.

Today some Christian religions such as the Gnostics, the Christian Spiritualist Movement, the Liberal Catholic Church and the Rosicrucian's teach reincarnation, while others leave opinions on multiple lives to individual choice.

As the idea of reincarnation receives the attention of the West, it is like a breath of fresh air as it infiltrates the Christian consciousness that has been

---

[61]Sugrue, Thomas, *There is a River*, Holt, Rinehart and Winston. New York – Chicago – San Francisco, 1942
[62]Langley, Noel, *Edgar Cayce on Reincarnation*, Warner Books, New York, 1967.

programmed to believe, rather than to search for evidence in order to discover the truth.

Evidence of Past Lives Revealed During Psychic Readings

At the psychic development classes I attended in the 1980s, I learned how to psychically tune into and retrieve details of previous lives lived by another person. Initially, when I related the information accessed regarding a previous existence to the person I was reading for, I didn't anticipate confirmation other than the person admitting an interest in the relevant country or culture. To my surprise, confirmation was often much more specific.

On one occasion, a woman requested past life information. As I tuned in, I found myself viewing a life that dated back hundreds of years. She had lived and worked in a castle. Her heart was linked to that of a man who was often away fighting—I could see him riding away in his armour with the other fighting men. She was very happy when they were together. I described details of the castle and the man in her life. As I watched her working in the castle, I had difficulty determining exactly what her position was. I advised her of this and from the activities I saw her involved in, I came up with a possible answer.

Upon the completion of the reading, she advised me she remembered that lifetime and confirmed all I had told her—with the exception of my conclusions as to her work position. The work I described her doing was accurate, but I was wrong about her appointed position.

Repeatedly during past life readings, it emerged that the skills and interests of those earlier times had found their way into the current life of the person. Such was the case with a woman I read for. Images came to me of her living as a man some twelve hundred years ago in a forested area I felt was in England. He lived with a group of people in a timber fort, the walls of which were about ten foot (three metres) in height. As I observed him, I realised he had been an expert marksman with a bow and arrow. I could see him shoot from a heavy bow that enabled him to shoot straight and fast. Upon the completion of my providing details of that previous lifetime, the woman commented that archery was a sport she had been involved in for many years.

A young man requested I reveal something of his past lives. I immediately saw a very large Japanese man who was a sumo wrestler wearing his long

THE TRUTH SEEKER

black hair tied up in a ponytail (not the knot frequently seen today). Then I saw him in another lifetime, once again as a Japanese man, but this time, although he was strong he was not a large man. He was involved in a great deal of fighting as a Samurai warrior. He carried a sword and was skilled in martial arts. Upon my providing further details on this life, the young man confirmed the information and advised me he had dreamed of the lifetime in which he had been a Samurai warrior. Although not Asian in this incarnation, he had a deep interest in martial arts and was already a skilled teacher.

Sometimes, even though one does not recall a past life, it is evident that the memory is there and often this comes through during early childhood. I began telling a young woman she was going to travel to England. She confirmed she had already booked her trip. I advised her she had had a recent past life in Ireland and had married a young man with the surname Kelly. She looked surprised and advised me that as a young child, for a couple of years, she had insisted on being called Kelly.

A young man I read for would stand out anywhere! He walked through the door wearing a long dark overcoat that rather than making him look ridiculous, on his frame made him look impressive. He advised me he was currently dating two ladies, one blonde and one brunette. He was having difficulty choosing between them and asked I reveal his past life connection to the two. I was drawn to the Middle Ages. As I viewed the great hall inside a castle, I noted that on the wall were a shield and some swords. The shield had a fleur-de-lis engraved on it. I intuitively knew the young man had been given responsibility for this castle and had married a woman with blonde hair. As I continued to receive information, I saw him on a horse on the land nearby, meeting with a dark haired lady.

He advised me another psychic had described the same past life, and I had confirmed the details for him. I told him I thought it likely he would settle with the blonde woman.

A week later, as I was reading for a young dark haired woman, I clairvoyantly saw images from a past life during the Middle Ages where she was talking to a young man on a horse. It seemed to be the same couple I had seen clairvoyantly the previous week when I read for the young man. She confirmed this was so.

After many readings where I received confirmation, surprise ceased to be a part of my reaction and my confidence in the information I was receiving increased. Evidence of this type is convincing for the person who experiences it. For those who don't, more evidence is needed before conclusions can be drawn.

Indication of a Past Life

Sometimes there are reports about those who have detailed knowledge of places they have never visited or possessed any prior information about. Perhaps such situations indicate the possibility of a previous life. I have known Paul for over thirty-five years and he tells of a rather unusual experience. Paul was born in Yorkshire in England, and it was not until he was in his mid-years that he came to live in Australia. This is his story:

> At around eighteen or nineteen years of age I was accepted into the RAF regiment band stationed at Catterick in North Yorkshire, England. The new bandmaster decided that we would take commissions as far away from the camp as we could, and that would mean that we would have to fly everywhere. The band members, including myself, thought that would be marvellous. We began to play concerts all over England. On one occasion we were flown to the south west of England. From there we were to be trucked into either Somerset or Devon.
>
> On the way to that evening's concert we stopped in a small town and the driver advised, 'Boys you've got fifteen minutes.' (To have something to eat).
>
> So we went and found a little café and grabbed a meal. One of the boys said, 'I've got to find the post office. I've got this letter and I've got to mail it.'
>
> I answered, 'Ah yes. When you leave here, if you do a quick left, go to the end of the street, do a left again and about fifty yards on the left, there's a post office.'
>
> 'I'll be able to do it then.' The young man left to mail his letter.
>
> Later on during the meal one of the men said, 'Paul, when were you last here then?'
>
> 'Pardon?'
>
> 'When were you last here in this town?'

THE TRUTH SEEKER

'I've never been here. As a matter of fact I've never been in the county.'

'Well how did you know exactly where the post office is then?'

'Well, I don't know.' Since I had been correct about the location of the post office the boys of course thought I was lying. But I thought, *'I've not been here.... Or have I? Past life. That's the only way I could have been here.'*

Paul's automatic response to the young man's query about where to post a letter revealed knowledge he didn't know he had. A similar story was told to me many years ago by an extended family member, Bill, a New Zealander who had been in the armed forces during the Second World War. When he was on leave in Paris and needed to find a shop that sold cigarettes, he looked around and inexplicably recognised the area and went straight to a shop around the corner that sold cigarettes.

In both cases, the knowledge hadn't come from an experience gained in this lifetime. While the information could have been accessed intuitively, it is also possible the knowledge came from past life memories stored in the unconscious mind.

The Recovery of Past Life Memories through Meditation

Trance states provide a way to access a wide range of knowledge and experiences. A guided meditation (through listening to a tape or a facilitator) has become a common way to recall past lives.

In my experience, the memories recovered during meditation tend to be re-experienced in flashes. Just as lightning lights up the sky and can strike an object on the surface of the planet, so too can a thought or desire direct the illumination of a past life experience. In spite of the speed with which the experience takes place, the knowledge received usually encompasses a great deal of information that would normally take a lot longer to absorb. Such flashes can include visual and emotional recall, but can also simultaneously be revealed from an observer point of view. While the mind is in a trance state, it is responsive and reacts to suggestion rather than initiating thought. A deliberate self-directive to retrieve sought after knowledge during a meditation can be an effective way to gain information.

JOAN L BOLER

Some years ago, I was at a past life workshop and my friend Sally (the facilitator) was about to commence a guided past-life meditation. There were eight people in the group attending this workshop. Immediately before we commenced, I gave myself the instruction, 'I am going to go back to a lifetime in which I knew Paul.'

The group was guided first of all into a relaxed state and then into recalling a past life. From high on a hillside, I could see the sea to my left and a majestic sailing ship not too far from shore. To my right were houses on a hill that sloped up from the sea. Then I was looking down to the wharf where Paul, wearing captain's clothes and with long black wavy hair, was striding along. I heard the word 'Cornwall'. Then my position moved and I was the young woman inside one of the buildings on the side of the hill. With me was our young son who had hair as dark as his father's. I intuited that in that lifetime Paul and I had been married.

Although I had heard of Cornwall and knew it was in England, I had never been there. Nor did I know where in England it was as I had never studied the geography of England. Paul had given me a beautiful book on England some years earlier. As soon as I arrived home, I scanned through it until I found information on Cornwall. It *was* on the coast, and a photograph of the Cornwall area revealed a scene that, though not identical to the one I had witnessed, had very similar homes to those I had viewed from my vantage point high on the hillside.

The limitation of meditation as a way by which to recall past lives, is the lightness of the trance state that tends to limit the depth of knowledge gained, if any is gained at all. While directives have the potential to enable the access of specific knowledge, after the first flashes of memory in response to the original instruction, the unconscious mind is unlikely to produce further information.

Past Life Recall through Hypnosis

The trance state provides a doorway to the unconscious mind. Perhaps the most effective method of working with the trance state in seeking information on previous lives is through a person trained in the process of enabling access to the unconscious memories of other lives through hypnosis. Both meditation and hypnosis induce trance states. Hypnosis can take the individual into a deeper trance state and enable access to many more details of a previous life. As the practitioner prompts the individual to describe what they are experiencing, ongoing questioning can result in a much more detailed description of the life being accessed. Those who drop into a deep trance sometimes recall the name of the person they were in that previous time, and the location of where they had lived.

Re-experiencing means just that. Therefore, emotional and physical pain can be part of the process, so only an experienced hypnotist who understands the potential dangers should work with the deep trance state.

The information gained through trance states is only as reliable as the people working with it. The unconscious mind can be manipulated, so where possible, it's important to obtain substantiating evidence as to the accuracy of the information obtained. Sceptics have used hypnosis to show it is possible to manufacture a past life memory. The unconscious mind is extremely versatile and will follow the instructions given or implied by the practitioner. The unconscious mind is creative and has the ability to fabricate when required or desired. Such ability does not disprove or negate the past life evidence found in many genuine research cases; it simply reveals the versatility of the unconscious.

The traumatic experiences from previous lives lie below the surface of our conscious awareness. There has been a number of qualified practitioners who have, when using hypnosis to guide a patient back to the original cause of their phobia or problem, found they are dealing with the person describing another lifetime. A common result of this experience is the removal of a phobia or emotionally destructive behaviour.

Among those in the academic world who have discovered evidence of past lives is Dr Brian Weiss, a respected graduate of Columbia University and Yale Medical School. Dr Weiss is a psychiatrist who made the difficult transition from sceptic to believer based on the evidence he received during hypnotherapy sessions. Weiss's first book on the subject, *Many Lives Many Masters*,[63] covered his ground-breaking discovery of the other lives of one of his patients, along with evidence relating to his own spiritual identity. As a result of his clinical experience in dealing with regression, his first book was followed by a number of others that reveal how through past life regression he was able to effectively enable healing in the mind, body and soul, of many of his patients. He also encountered those who, when in the trance state, spoke fluently in a language they had no prior knowledge of in this lifetime.[64]

---

[63] Weiss, Brian. MD, *Many Lives, Many Masters*, Simon & Schuster, Sydney, Australia, 1998.
[64] Ibid. p. 218.

Another practitioner who uncovered the other lives of his patients was Dr Bruce Goldberg. Goldberg has a dental surgery doctorate, a BA in biology and chemistry, and a master's degree in counselling psychology. Goldberg witnessed the healing effects of past life recall time and again. His second book, *The Search for Grace*[65], traced forty-six of the past lives of a woman and the man who murdered her in twenty of them. The woman recalled a previous life in Buffalo in the 1920s as Grace Doze. Research substantiated her previous identity and confirmed twenty-four of the facts she provided. This was filmed and presented as *CBS Movie of the Week*.[66]

One of the early pioneers in past life research was Dr Helen Wambach who worked as a senior psychologist and clinical psychiatrist. She taught college psychology and introduced progressive ways for working with disturbed adolescent girls, many of whom were a product of the drug culture. In addition, she lectured on parapsychology and researched, through hypnosis, the memories of past lives and life between one life and the next.[67]

Wambach studied 1,088 subjects under hypnosis over a ten-year period, regressing them to various periods during the last four thousand years. During each regression, she allowed her subjects to recall a life lived in one of a number of periods and in any part of the world. Historic data was obtained and checked, and included such verifiable information as the detailed description of coins, market places, food, architecture, clothing, footwear, language, landscape, climate, and religious ceremonies.[68]

The impressive results revealed that of the 1,088 subjects, only 11 (1%) did not provide information that was consistent with historic records.[69] When considering the garments worn, Wambach concedes her subjects could have seen illustrations in books or examples in museums, but she found that her subjects made no errors. In each case they described accurately the type of clothing that matched their position in life.[70]

One of the interesting discoveries that came out of Wambach's research was that time between lives varied from four months to two hundred years and short periods seemed more likely after a violent death.[71]

---

[65] Goldberg, Dr Bruce, *The Search for Grace*, Llewellyn Publications, St. Paul, MN, 1994.
[66] Goldberg, Dr Bruce, *The Search for Grace* (www. drbrucegoldberg. com/SearchForGrace. htm) (accessed 11 Oct 2011)
[67] Wambach, Helen, Ph. D. *Reliving Past Lives*. (1978) New York, Harper & Row
[68] Ibid. Ch. 7.
[69] Ibid. p .112.
[70] Ibid. p. 127.
[71] Ibid. p. 122.

THE TRUTH SEEKER

The evidence in these and many other such past life regressions cannot be discounted. Time and again, detail after detail of factual evidence has been found. The healing aspect alone makes past life regression worthwhile. Perhaps in the future this method of healing will become more mainstream as Western society becomes more informed and aware.

Personal Evidence of Other Lifetimes

It is impossible to convey to another person the utter conviction of reality that accompanies the genuine experience of a past life. The sense of 'this is real' is irrefutable. Personal experience gives proof to the experiencer.

Hypnotic regression has not taken me into the deep trance state that enables the recovery of names of people and places and actual dates. Past life recall for me is about flashes of memory where I relive the moment in time I find myself in. As the experience takes place, I am aware of myself as the observer and at the same time, I am the person I am observing. What makes it different from recalling a childhood memory is the re-experiencing of the emotions and the physical impact of whatever activity is taking place.

In the present moment, we see all that is going on around us, and feel all that is making an impact on us physically, mentally, and emotionally. All information from past experience, along with all learned knowledge, is contained in the memory, and although such knowledge is revealed in reactions, it is not part of the present moment's conscious thoughts. As a result, during a regression where the experience is of the moment, learned knowledge and memories are not necessarily consciously accessed. Because of this, my re-experiencing of a past life situation does not give me the learning, language, and all the memories of that lifetime.

Over the years, I have returned to the experiences of a number of my previous lives. Each time I have done so, the alignment with and recognition of the self is absolute. Although the life lived may reveal the influences of a different economic, racial and social environment to those of the current life, there is recognition on a deeper soul level. Consideration of behaviour, attitudes, emotional capacity, capabilities and experiences of the earlier self, illuminate not only the constancy of identity, but also the growth of the soul through experience.

While in other lifetimes my appearance may vary due to race, gender and lifestyle, I find there are similarities in the way I look. On one occasion, I recalled a past life I had lived as an American Indian man around six to eight hundred years ago. What amazed me about this recollection was that when I looked into a mirror a few hours later, I could see remnants of my American Indian face integrated into the structure of my face in this lifetime. The fact that this time around I am of English and Irish descent did not prevent the shadow of that past life impinging upon my present day physical appearance.

Although in some lifetimes I have lived a sophisticated life style and in others a simpler one, my essence remains the same. In the same way that I can identify with my own essence, I sometimes find it possible to identify those people in that past existence who are also around me in this lifetime.

My very first past life recall was spontaneous and occurred when I was in my late twenties. I had not sought this experience and at that time would have had no idea of how to do so. My access to the much earlier lifetime seemed to be have been triggered by my emotional reaction to a particularly difficult time in my life. Suddenly I plunged into a past existence that mirrored my pain-filled state. One moment I was in the present, in the next my consciousness was transported back three thousand or so years. I was a man standing in front of a South American style pyramid. In that time, I had not known how to change my circumstances and my resultant depression and the feeling of helplessness and isolation, was overpowering. As my mind returned to my current life and its difficulties, the memories of that previous lifetime motivated me to act. Unlike in that previous time, I now knew it was within my power to take control of my circumstances and move forward.

A word of warning to those who seek to discover the details of their other lifetimes: most of us have lived through dangerous and painful times that may have involved war, religious persecution, poverty and lawlessness. In order to survive, we have done what we felt we needed to do. Some of it is not pretty. Non-judgement and forgiveness of self and others is essential on such a journey into the secrets of the soul.

One night I guided the psychic development class I was taking into a meditation to recover past life memories. A woman, who I had previously intuited was compelled to always do the right thing and as a result was very hard on herself and perhaps also on others, began crying. In a previous life as a young girl, she had become an unmarried mother and was ostracised. Post-natal depression was no doubt exacerbated by her loneliness and she drowned her baby. This was a traumatic and shocking experience for a woman who prided herself on always following the morally correct path.

THE TRUTH SEEKER

Personal experience of previous lifetimes proves to the individual they have lived before. Since relatively few people experience spontaneous past life recall or dream of other lifetimes, those who are looking for personal proof could possibly find it through hypnosis.

Countless Lifetimes

How many lives do we live?

On a number of occasions during this lifetime I have spontaneously entered into an expanded state of consciousness where greater awareness allows knowledge not normally accessible to become available. The information gained is always totally accurate and true.

On one occasion, I had decided it was time to bring a little more exercise into my life. As I have never been interested in exercise for its own sake, my preference was to become involved in activities that had added benefits such as emotional involvement or mental stimulation. First, I enrolled in dancing classes, and then I joined a newly-formed bush-walking group. On our first weekend away there were five of us—four ladies and one man. The man disturbed me. For some reason I couldn't explain, as soon as he started talking he felt familiar and well-known to me. This, my logical mind maintained, was ridiculous—I had never met the man before. But it was impossible to dismiss the feeling I *knew* him.

At the conclusion of the third weekend, I was in the kitchen helping to tidy up the dishes. Suddenly and spontaneously my conscious awareness expanded. Knowledge I had not been previously aware of, became available to me. *Oh! It's you!* I realised as my gaze rested on the man. I was aware I knew his soul as well as I knew my own. This man's soul had been part of my life throughout eons of time and during countless lifetimes. I felt the ages as I followed our connection back through time for a million, if not millions of years. The discovery I had lived so many lives shocked me. Many of the people I associated with had thought we lived anything from five, to five hundred, lives. I now knew I had lived many more. My new knowledge was confirmed by Shirley MacLaine, who claimed in one of her books she had lived thousands of lives.

Why so many lifetimes? From my own knowledge of my past lives, I realise we learn by experience and just one aspect of learning can take many lifetimes.

JOAN L BOLER

Birth Marks and Birth Defects

The first time I heard that physical trauma resulting in death could cause birthmarks and birth defects on the physical body that was to host the soul during its next lifetime was in 1971 when I was living on Norfolk Island. I had joined a small group of people studying comparative religion through a correspondence course from the University of Sydney. These people were extraordinary. Each of them was searching for answers and had followed many avenues of learning. Discussions dealt with the major religions from viewpoints that were far removed from views held by the major Christian religions at that time. It seemed reasonable to me that the shock of a fatal wound could be carried by the soul and have an impact on the physical body in its next life. I was born with a small hole (a pocket in the skin) in my back between my shoulder blades and over my backbone, the opening of which was just over half an inch (1. 5cm) in width. When I was thirteen, the depth of this pocket was measured by a surgeon, who found it went straight up under the skin for approximately one inch (2.5cm). The surgeon advised my mother that as it might predispose me to cancer at some time in the future, it should be cut out. Since swimming usually invited comments such as, 'How did you get that hole in your back?' I welcomed this solution.

Over the years I wondered. *What, in my last life, could have caused such an injury? A bullet? A knife? But if either of these, why straight up my back?* A possible answer came one night during the psychic development classes I was running. We were each reading another member of the class. The young man who was reading me said, 'Joan, you were a pilot in the Second World War!' Of course—flak from an anti-aircraft gun would go straight up. It fitted. I envisaged a small projectile penetrating the plane and entering my back at the entry point of the hole in my back. *Was this how it happened?*

My friend Sally, a hypnotherapist, agreed to work with me. On a number of occasions, she guided me into a trance state and back to the life immediately preceding this one. On the first occasion she did this, Sally asked what I was wearing. My immediate visual of myself was as a young man of around eighteen to twenty, of slender build and wearing a blue Royal Air Force (RAF) uniform. Then I kept flipping backwards and forwards between the pristine blue air force uniform and brown trousers and jacket. I was confused by these inconsistent images until I checked on the internet that night and found both were RAF uniforms worn during the Second World War. The more casual brown uniform was worn on active duty.

I was born in England around 1913. The houses in my street were built close together and the modest house I lived in with my family was comfortable, with high ceilings and heavy dark varnished wood furniture. My family

THE TRUTH SEEKER

consisted of my parents and a sister who was around ten years younger than me. My mother was a fairly short, fuller-figured woman with blue eyes who wore her hair in a bun. My father, who was of slim build, was an academic and smoked a pipe when relaxing. He was a placid, reserved man with a dry sense of humour. My sister, whose hair was fair and almost straight, was a constant source of delight as her effervescent personality lit up the room whenever she walked into it. From her early years, her antics brought laughter to those around her.

As my father saw my education as important, I was sent to an all-male public school where I received an above average education. The impressive school buildings were built of stone and were the location for learning, playing cricket, and boyhood mischief.

At around eighteen years of age, I joined the air force and spent the next few years learning and developing my skills as a pilot. My closest friend was a fun loving extrovert who ensured that my more conservative nature didn't result in my missing out on the social activities available to us. We enjoyed both our time on the base and our free time. This was a strong friendship where there was deep unquestioning trust.

In September 1939, when I was around twenty-six, England declared war on Germany and life changed dramatically. The first months of the war, I flew a single engine fighter aircraft. As squadron leader I relayed information through the radio transmitter to the rest of the squadron. Time and again, I flew towards the coast intercepting, and firing upon, enemy aircraft coming from across the Channel. At other times, I crossed the Channel and took part in air battles that involved high speeds and aerial acrobatics.

The highest loss of life of the British forces during the war was experienced in the air force, and this could have resulted in low morale. But it didn't! There was an incredible contrast between the gravity of confronting the possibility of imminent death along with coping with the loss of those who had been companions for years, and how everyone on the base lived their lives on a daily basis. A cheerful, positive attitude permeated the base. Discipline, instead of being imposed by superiors, seemed to be inherent in each individual. Senior officers were respected and in turn treated everyone with respect and comradeship. All air force personnel were linked in an optimistic brotherly solidarity. The potent energy generated expressed itself in friendly teasing, joking and enthusiastic cooperation along with an overall determination to contribute to an efficient, well-run base. Every individual on the base was attempting to achieve the impossible together.

JOAN L BOLER

Sometime after the war commenced, I met a young lady in the mess hall. She was in the Women's Auxiliary Air Force (WAAF) and her administrative duties included coordination and communication. This very attractive young lady had blonde shoulder length hair and a peaches and cream complexion. As our relationship grew, we argued over my refusal to marry before the war ended.

I transferred from the single engine fighter planes to bombers sometime during 1940. Over the next months, reconnaissance and bombing raids on targets perceived to be a threat followed discussions between crews and air force personnel. One night I was piloting a bomber across the Channel. We continued to fly over water until we were parallel to the target area and then we turned inland. The target that appeared before us seemed to be a factory. As I flew over it, the bombardier released the bombs and I immediately swung the plane up and off to the left away from the explosions that followed. Then we made our way back to base.

It was daytime during 1940 or 1941. I was in the air over Europe sitting in the pilot's seat on the left hand side of the two-seater cockpit. The navigator/bombardier's seat was vacant. From my position inside the plane, I could see the aircraft was painted in brown camouflage. The sky was filled with planes of different shapes and sizes. Action was intense and plumes of black smoke belched from a number of the planes. At that moment, forward and to my left, a single-engine aircraft burst into flames. Then, through the joystick, I felt the aircraft shudder. At this point, I viewed the scene from above and outside the bomber. Black smoke was coming from the tail section.

The plane went into a spinning dive. All I could see was the colour brown. Suddenly, there was an explosion where my seat and seat back joined. Small projectiles penetrated my body. My upper legs and stomach received blasts that were at once painful and shocking. I registered pain in my lower back, while at the same time another projectile penetrated my upper back and probably continued up through my neck and into my brain—but consciousness had left my body by then.

In the moments immediately following my death, as I looked upon the destruction taking place below me, I felt a deep connection to and caring for humanity as a whole, and great sadness that good men on both sides were killing each other. This in no way invalidated the strong belief I held that Hitler needed to be stopped. I realised such wrongness was brought about by the lack of awareness and understanding of the power of love and its ability to bring happiness and fulfilment and to heal all that is evil in the world. In that moment, a strong desire emerged from within me to communicate this knowledge to all those who would listen.

With the memories of this past life came the recognition of the identity of my sister in that lifetime as my younger sister Yvonne. In both lives, during her childhood her bubbly nature captured all those around her while her blonde straight hair, similar face and body left little doubt as to her identity. My good friend in the air force was another person who has connected with me again in this lifetime at a time when I was going through major changes in my life. Susie and I met on Norfolk Island and quickly became friends. She supported me during the first breakdown of my marriage that resulted in a separation that lasted a year. Once again, this vivacious soul played a part in pulling me into the fun and enjoyment to be found in the social activities on the island. Not only did she display a similar nature, there were considerable physical likenesses in her appearance in this lifetime to that of her previous life. Her male features were reflected in a female version in this life, and if placed side by side the impression of brother and sister would be gained. The full friendly smiles were identical as were skin and hair colouring. Her fair hair was once again, in contrast to mine which was dark.

It is not only birthmarks that reveal the traumatic death experience of a previous life. Damage experienced at the point of death can be revealed in physical weaknesses in the subsequent life. Since childhood, tension in my stomach has resulted in discomfort and pain and blood sugar problems. For many years I experienced on-going back pain at the point where the shrapnel penetrated my lower back.

Only in the light of past life memories is it possible to see the continuity of an individual life force, and to bring understanding to the whys of the undesirable such as birth marks, health issues and fears. While my past life memories do not offer proof to others, there is a great deal of research that does provide convincing evidence for those seeking answers.

Research and Living Memories

Not all past life evidence is dependent upon recall through hypnosis. During the twentieth century, the academic community was confronted with stories of children claiming to have been another person prior to being born into their current family. This resulted in the many cases being investigated. The evidence found in relation to verifiable memories and the supporting biological evidence is nothing short of astonishing.

JOAN L BOLER

In the following a father tells of when as a young man of twenty-two he was shocked when confronted by his son's past life memories.

'Dad, when my other family put me in the hole in the ground—I can't remember them. When you put me in the hole in the ground, can I take something with me so I can remember you?'

And that's exactly the way it came out. It was just after Shaun's second birthday. His grandparents had given him a red pedal car and he and I had been playing around with it. We'd had a great day and he was tired. He went to bed reading a picture book. Then he had called out to me and I went in and he looked up at me and blew me away with his question. The hairs on the back of my neck stood up and I felt a cold shiver.

I went out to my wife and explained to her what had happened and she said, 'Well, just don't leave it like that. Go back in and talk to him!'

I went back in and spoke to him and said, 'Hey mate, why did you ask me that?'

He said that his other family, his sister and his mum and dad, put him in a hole in the ground and he can't remember what they look like any more, and he wished he could. He then asked, 'When you put me in the ground, can I take my red car with me?' And he wanted a picture as well.

I just said to him that we would not need to do that as that was not going to happen. But he was very insistent that this was going to happen because it had happened before. So I said to him, 'Tell me a little bit about your other family.' He described what seemed to be a very sparse older style two-roomed wooden house with a big open fireplace that was used for cooking. He told me that there was a big fire. He said that the car sat out the front. It didn't seem that he saw his dad so much because he spoke more about his mother and sister. Then he was tired and wanted to sleep.

Kim and I spoke about it and then the next night when he was settling down into bed, I asked him about it again he talked about living near water. I was not sure if he was talking about his previous family or us as we lived near water. But when he was around four or five he grabbed a rope to make a knot. I asked him, 'What are you doing there?'

THE TRUTH SEEKER

He said, 'I'm tying a blood knot.'

'There's no such knot,' I said. He was very insistent that that's what this knot was called. He tied the little trailer on to his little red peddle car using what he insisted was a blood knot. I dismissed it with, 'You don't know what you're talking about,' until I did a course on ropes under tension and knots and learned that a blood knot is used in fishing and boats.

When Shaun was about five we did a lot of camping and after the first time we had a camp fire, he screamed all night saying, 'Don't let the fire get me. We've got to get out. We've got to get out.' Every time we went camping and we had a fire, he reacted the same way. The only thing we could relate it back to was what he had told me when he was two—that there was a big fire. We thought the fire got away in the house he had lived in with his other family and he was burnt to death.

When he was about four we went on a holiday and we happened to go past a vintage car show and as we drove past the old cars, Shaun said, 'Look, that's a 56 Chev,' and went on to point out and name other old cars.

Kim and I looked at each other and I said, 'How do you know that?'

And he said, 'I just do.' We did not have books on the old cars and nor did we watch movies with the old cars—he knew them!

Sometimes he described things about his previous family, like, 'My dad when he used to drive, he put me in the boot.'

I said to him, 'Who put you in the boot? I would never put you in the boot.'

He said, 'No, my other dad.' And what we figured out was that it was a Model T Ford with the dickie seat. They used to open the back (boot) *and put the kids in the dickie seat* (fold out seat) *when they were going to town. He had never seen one of those cars and he hadn't seen one in a picture and yet he described it to a 'T'.*

He is twenty now and still has a fascination for the old cars.

When I talk to him now about his early memories he says, 'Oh Dad, what are you talking about!'

Shaun, like most children who, during their early years recall memories of their previous life, has not retained those memories.

In some cases, children interviewed by the academic community have total recall of the person they claimed to have previously been, along with all the emotional attachments to that previous life. Having the whole of the previous life as a current memory is quite different to recovering flashes of memory through hypnosis. The children researched were able to recall incredibly detailed information leaving absolutely no doubt as to the authenticity of their knowledge. The results gained from studying these children were so startling that further research followed.

Dr Ian Stevenson (1918-2007), was a Canadian psychiatrist. Before he retired in 2002, he was Director of the Division of Perpetual Studies at the University of Virginia. Earlier, he had been the head of the Department of Psychiatry at the University of Virginia. Over a forty-year period, his research covered over three thousand cases of the past life memories of children born all over the world. Dr Stevenson personally checked the stories of many of these children, interviewing them, their families and those who had had a close association with the person who the child reporting the past life claimed to have been. The evidence was overwhelming. The information provided by the children regarding their previous existence, time and again proved accurate and contained information that only the person they claimed to have been could have known.

Some of these children also reported their memories of the time between lives. One such case involved a Japanese soldier in Rangoon in 1945. He and his three companions retreated as far as Rangoon Zoo, and rather than be captured by the British, all four committed suicide. He had died as a result of slitting his own throat. He remained at the zoo as a disincarnate soul until one day in 1972 when he followed a man two hundred and fifty miles (four hundred kilometres) to his home. Not long after, when the man's pregnant wife gave birth, the Japanese soldier's soul, which had merged with the body of the baby, was reborn. The child was born with a horizontal scar-like birthmark across his neck. His father confirmed the visit to the Rangoon Zoo. [72] [73]

---

[72] Stevenson, Ian, *Where Reincarnation and Biology Intersect,* Praeger Publishers, Westport CT USA, 1997, p. 31.
[73] Stevenson, Ian, *The pioneer of reincarnation research*, near-death.com/experiences/reincarnation01. html (accessed 15 Sep 2008)

THE TRUTH SEEKER

Confirmed past life memories alone build a strong case for reincarnation, but when that study took Dr Stevenson into the realm of the physical evidence, it brought proof that at least the people investigated had lived before.

Dr Stevenson's many case histories into birthmarks and birth defects reveal a relationship between the causes of death in a previous life and the presence of a birth defect or birthmark in the current lifetime. Where possible, his research included death certificates and post-mortem reports (of the previous life), and excluded those cases where birthmarks might be genetically inherited or caused by other possible reasons such as the mother suffering viral infections or exposure to chemicals during pregnancy. Of the many birthmark cases he studied, there was a considerable number that involved more than one birthmark. A number of cases were investigated where the entry and exit points of gunshot wounds recorded in the autopsy report were uncannily reproduced in small and large birthmarks on the body in the current lifetime.[74][75]

Shocking evidence was found in those cases that carried forward extreme damage to the body, as in the case of the young girl who was born in 1967 with a congenital absence of the lower leg. In her previous life in 1966, she had been run over by a train that first severed her leg and then ran over her body.[76]

The evidence gained from past life research is convincing. Sceptics and those from the academic community agree that genuine knowledge is being obtained. Alternative explanations to reincarnation have been suggested, one being that genetic memory could be involved. This is not unreasonable, as there have been many cases where individuals have reincarnated back into the family with which they previously lived. On the surface genetic memory might seem a plausible answer, but since there is frequently a change of race and/or country from one incarnation to the next, this explanation falls short.

In attempting to explain how the individual has connected to the memories of that other person from a previous time, some suggest the source is the collective unconscious, which is thought to hold a record of all that has ever been. This theory suggests that the child accesses the recorded memories of the dead person. However, some of the children have been shown to have received not only the memories but also the physical imprint of the previous

---

[74] Stevenson, Ian, *Where reincarnation and biology intersect,* Praeger Publishers, Westport CT USA, 1997.
[75] Stevenson, Ian, *The pioneer of reincarnation research,* www.near-death.com/experiences/reincarnation01.html (accessed 15 Sep 2008)
[76] Stevenson (1997) pp. 122-123.

death trauma in the form of birthmarks or birth defects. This indicates the emotional content of the dead person's life was also integrated into the makeup of the new life at the time of birth. The recall by some of the children of the time between the lives, adds weight to the idea that consciousness is continuous and the individual identity does not end at death.

Possible Supporting Evidence

Consider again the scientific fact that energy always *is*. It can change, but it cannot disappear. Nor can new energy come into being. So what happens to our soul energy (which is on a higher frequency than our physical energy) when we die if energy cannot disappear? Does it disintegrate or does it continue its conscious existence?

In an interview in 1988 with parapsychologist Dr Jeffrey Mishlove, Dr Nick Herbert, physicist and author of *Quantum Reality*, explained that once particles have interacted, they remain connected.[77] What does this mean when applied to a person's soul? Some very strange information seems to give credence to the ongoing connectedness of the soul.

In an experiment, white cells were taken from the mouth of a subject and placed where they could be monitored with electroencephalogram (EEG) instruments. The subject was then exposed to a variety of stimuli and their reactions recorded. The reaction of the white cells corresponded with the subject's responses.[78] It appears that the soul of the individual did not recognise the physical separation of the white cells. This indicates the soul operates on a level that does not recognise space or distance. While we are connected to the physical body, at least while it or any part of it is still alive, the soul remains connected. This adds weight to the idea that while the physical body disintegrates at death, the soul, which operates beyond the physical and incorporates the consciousness and individual identity of each person, remains connected outside space and probably also outside time.

---

[77]Herbert, Nick, 'Consciousness and quantum reality: Interview with Dr Jeffrey Mishlove' *Thinking Aloud: Conversations on the Leading Edge of Knowledge and Discovery*, 1998, http://www.intuition.org/txt/herbert.htm (accessed 22 November 2014).
[78]Backster, Cleve and Stephen G White. 'Biocommunications Capability: Human Donors and In Vitro Leukocytes.' *The International Journal of Biosocial Research*, 1985, vol. 7 (2): 132:146.

THE TRUTH SEEKER

Continuation of Life Skills and Awareness

What impact does the recognition and acceptance of reincarnation have on the way we view life? As we consider natural talent, inborn desire of and attraction to certain people, along with the many anomalies that exist between the advantaged and disadvantaged, what sort of answers emerge?

My observations and research have provided me with much evidence that rebirth of the soul can result in a physical match that compliments the character, attitudes, personality and the various energies we developed in our other lives. The individual awareness and concept of right and wrong that emerges can differ from that of others and is dependent on the range and type of previous experiences. For this reason, when being reborn most gravitate towards people, ideals and beliefs that reflect our inner self and therefore past experience.

When we connect to and form bonds with people in one lifetime, our connection brings us together time and again—sometimes in order to learn through conflict, and sometimes for support. Not only do we experience lives as both male and female, we also may play different roles in each other's lives in different lifetimes. Husband, wife, brother, sister, cousin, aunt, uncle, lover, friend, and business associate—*all* are interchangeable. These relationships are called soul mates. We often recognise soul mates when we first meet them. There is an inner sense of knowing them, or there can be a strong physical attraction and a love of lifetimes can be revealed causing a person to fall in love on a first encounter.

Natural talent in any area, when seen as a prior skill developed during previous lifetimes, removes the idea of random selection and bias and replaces it with skill and ability being the result of effort. Child genius is an example of continuing talent the child has worked for and deserves. Wisdom, perceived to be a gift that comes with age, when seen in the light of past lifetimes explains why sometimes the young confound us with their perception, and why many people do not display wisdom even in their later years.

Then there is the question of our unconscious emotional reactions and responses to the world around us. The response from within that reveals an interest in, or fear of, particular countries or places can reveal a forgotten past. How we choose to decorate a home, what hairstyles and clothing styles appeal to us, and what represents our life interests and passions can also indicate influences from a past we do not consciously recall.

Validation of reincarnation immediately changes one's perspective of the world and of the self. It removes injustice and bias, and places responsibility for each person's experience squarely on the shoulders of the individual rather than on an accident of birth. It opens the door to so many possibilities, and the view from that door holds the promise of time—time to experience everything under the sun; time to develop and grow; time to share with loved ones; time to live. Of course, it also opens Pandora's Box, as consideration is given to the time between one lifetime and the next that confirms continuation of consciousness outside the physical.

Chapter 4

Transformation

Have you learned lessons only of those who admired you, and were tender with you, and stood aside for you? Have you not learned great lessons from those who braced themselves against you, and disputed the passage with you?

Walt Whitman[79]

Cause and Effect

The story of our lives is woven through time like an incredibly beautiful and intricate tapestry. Only through time do we see the greater work of the Weaver. From a view that sees back into a past beyond conscious memory, the interaction between souls over lifetimes and the interests and passions of the individual identity is revealed. Astrological lessons and karma give reason to life's circumstances and difficulties as the needle of life penetrates the weave of the soul, bestowing pain as it adds colour and beauty. And examination of the complex and sometimes obscure circumstances in which the soul finds itself reveals a teacher of daunting capability who is never fooled or eluded.

There are many life forms in this universe of great diversity and complexity, and many of these life forms evolve their consciousness and potential through the process of rebirth in the physical. All progress along different pathways through their different life forms. Souls that require a human body in order to express and evolve are born into a physical body that manifests the current life energy associated with that soul. For humans, physical life serves the metaphysical by providing a vehicle whereby consciousness can experience and grow, and death provides a way to discard what has been outgrown. Throughout countless lifetimes, each human being encounters and responds mentally and emotionally to the physical world and its inhabitants.

---

[79] Whitman, Walt, 'Debris', *Leaves of Grass*, 1860.

JOAN L BOLER

Astrology explains the concept of evolution of the soul and gives reason to the on-going variety of experiences the soul encounters. The universal energies create a classroom-like structure around our world that enables each soul to progress from one life to the next following a pattern of lessons that compel growth. Each soul learns through experience. Just as children first attend kindergarten, followed by primary school, and then move on to intermediate and higher education, learning happens sequentially and in layers. Through behaviour that might invite judgement, great gifts can emerge, and the difficult and challenging situations in life can bring us face to face with the strength or lack of it, that lies within.

Much is spoken today of karma. The Sanskrit word 'karma', means action or work. The word 'phalam' means the result of actions. To many in the West, karma has come to mean a system of reward and punishment according to past deeds. However, reward and punishment is not an accurate assessment of what attracts the various experiences into our lives. Each soul is a continuing life force that is reborn again and again. Imbalance within the soul attracts energies that confront in order to bring balance. Love is the law that balances, and recognition, understanding and application of the laws of love removes painful physical, mental and emotional consequences. Lack of awareness of what the laws of love are, is not *wrong* or *evil*, but ignorance can and will be confronted—usually painfully. Therefore, a disaster in this life can, but does not necessarily, indicate a judgement of wrong doing in a past life. Such challenges to the soul, whatever the cause, allow for spiritual growth.

An integral part of our growth comes from our interaction with others. As each individual soul progresses through a wide variety of lifetimes, and forms many relationships with other souls, the emotional connections established in one lifetime can ensure reconnection in other lifetimes. While some souls come into our lives to support, others come to confront. Amid confusion, imperfection, challenge and achievement, all humanity is walking together in unconscious accord towards a common spiritual goal.

While you have your agenda with life, it has its agenda with you. My brother's current life, along with his preceding lives, reveals a fearless soul that thrives on adventure and loves the sea, both through sailing ships and exploring its depths. His soul, that has a loyal heart, lacks boundaries in dealings involving the property of strangers. From childhood, my brother John's lack of fear invited death as he carelessly used up more than his proverbial nine lives. Through his experiences, it is possible to see the lessons woven through time that are brought about by the Weaver through the workings of astrological forces.

THE TRUTH SEEKER

A Wild Child

I sometimes wonder if our parents ever questioned how between them they produced a boy who had the stamp of an adventurer, and who, even during his early years had absolutely no concept of following the rules. In spite of his wild ways, which seemed to be driven by a deep-seated curiosity and a zest for any exciting activity, this generous warm-hearted lad had a strong sense of loyalty and his own brand of morality. From his earliest years, he seemed to have a natural attraction to trouble that, at least in part, was due to his total lack of physical fear or consideration for the consequences. He was my brother and he brought excitement and adventure to my childhood years.

We grew up in New Zealand's North Island in the Bay of Plenty where a small country town provided a playground for John's adventurous and fertile imagination. In the days before television and computer games, children played outside. Outside could mean at home or anywhere within walking distance. Impulsive in his search for excitement, John turned his world and that of those around him, and that often included our sister Yvonne and me, into a constant source of thrills and excitement. John was generous about sharing his explorations and adventures, and on many occasions led us into all sorts of wonderful and interesting escapades. As the oldest, he became teacher and when necessary, the rescuer.

John introduced us to an outdoor adventure that involved the local railway tracks. I recall hurtling north along the railway lines on the 'borrowed' railway jigger. While John and I operated the jigger, Yvonne clung desperately to its side. This was an exciting experience and not dangerous—as long as we didn't encounter a train. In response to my query as to when the next train was due, John revealed he had no idea! As I turned and looked ahead to the bend not too far distant, excitement warred with dread as I was taunted with imaginings of a train bearing down upon us.

Sometimes the experiences that evoked thrills challenged my more responsible nature. Such was the case one cold miserable day when John decided to build a fire under the family home. The warmth the fire threw out was inviting until the flames licked the timber floorboards. My comments on the danger were refuted by John, who no doubt would have immediately applied water had the floorboards actually caught alight. But I was unconvinced and although reluctant, called our mother—an action that put me out of favour with John for some days.

JOAN L BOLER

Inclement weather found us playing in the family shed from time to time. It was in this location that on one occasion John's fallibility was brought sharply into focus. As youngsters, climbing anything and everything was a common activity. On one occasion, when John was between six and seven, he was playing in the shed with our two year old sister Yvonne and me. John and I climbed up on to and crawled around on the shed rafters. Yvonne was too young to climb to such height. In order to ensure she didn't attempt to do so, we told her we had invisible wings and couldn't fall, but *her* wings hadn't grown yet. We got away with that story for some time, but on this occasion after we had all played contentedly for a while, a sudden noise drew Yvonne's and my attention and we stared appalled as John crashed down from the rafters. Yvonne's fury at being deceived was expelled in a sequence of loud, indignant, disparaging statements.

We graduated from the rafters in the shed to the rafters in the house. When Mum and Dad were out, John took us up through the trapdoor at the top of the wardrobe in our parents' bedroom. He then gave Yvonne and me a guided tour, advising us to place our weight *only* on the rafters and to watch out for the electrical wiring.

That I was a tomboy became clear under John's tutelage. I listened and followed John's instructions eagerly as he taught me how to catch eels in the creek not far from home. With John's guidance, my sister Yvonne and I enjoyed thrills and excitement as we flew down the side of the hill on the sleds Dad had made for us, ensuring that as we neared the bottom of the hill we either fell or jumped off before reaching the banks of the creek. Although adventurous by nature, I probably would never have thought up ideas like underground tunnels that led into the next door neighbour's place; climbing neighbour's fruit trees and eating the fruit with (according to John) the owner's permission and predictably, getting caught; climbing a Norfolk pine tree to dizzying heights and scaring the living daylights out of myself! But of course John was there to rescue me! Boredom was unlikely when my brother was around.

Water and Sailing

John's life-long love affair with boats and water emerged during his early years. In his determination to go boating on the local river, John found a sheet of corrugated iron and envisaged a canoe. By folding one end of the corrugated iron over a piece of wood and nailing both sides to the wood, then repeating the exercise at the other end, he had the shell of the canoe. He then used yet another piece of wood to spread the centre and provide a seat.

THE TRUTH SEEKER

All that was left was to fill the holes at each end where the corrugated iron joined the wood. He decided the readily available clay would work.

The canoe was ready to launch! John experienced the heady feeling of being in his canoe, on the water—for all of five minutes. Then, as the clay popped out and the canoe sank, a disappointed, bedraggled John struggled back to the river's edge.

John's desire to master the river with his own craft lay dormant for a time. Then he saw potential in an old bathtub. With great effort, and using trolley wheels, he dragged the bath the considerable distance to the river. He plugged up the drain hole and proceeded to paddle it out into the middle of the river. Our sister Yvonne and I stood on the riverbank—I eagerly anticipated our promised turn while Yvonne faced the prospect with trepidation. As we watched, John and bathtub slipped ignominiously beneath the water's surface!

Dog-paddling in the local river was fun, but for John the swimming pool offered thrills the river didn't. At age nine, John, instead of spending his time in the shallow end of the pool, as he had been instructed, joined the older children high-diving. Hours of this activity saw John's energy drain to almost zero. After he had completed yet another dive, whilst still in the depths of the pool, he experienced a feeling of such serenity and contentment that instead of pushing himself to resurface, he happily remained in his peaceful environment. His next conscious memory was of being resuscitated at the side of the pool.

John's thirst for boats and water activities was not dimmed in the slightest by the consequences of his early encounters.

Trouble, Trouble, Trouble

While John's nature, that did not understand the meaning of caution, was attracted to dangerous situations, they also seemed to be attracted to him.

Our dad nurtured John's interest in trains and gave him a Hornby steam train that ran on methylated spirits. The family experienced many hours of enjoyment as Dad, with his off-sider John, got the train to chug around the tracks. Due to the flammable liquid, Dad's presence was a requirement when John played with his train. In the post Second World War period, scarcity and limited funds resulted in most families reusing items to a degree that would delight the most conscientious of twenty-first century recyclers.

JOAN L BOLER

Dad used a passion-fruit soft drink bottle as a container for the methylated spirits and placed it in one of the kitchen cupboards that contained cleaners and the like and was *not* used for food or drink.

When John came home from school one hot day, parched and desperate for a drink, he found the bottle. In his haste to quench his thirst, he swallowed around six ounces (150ml) straight down before he gagged on the taste. Sick to the stomach and light-headed from the effects of the alcohol, he sent me to the neighbour's for help. John's stomach was pumped out, but he never fully recovered from the damage to his throat.

The knowledge he definitely should not engage in an activity never held John back from an adventure. One day after school, he joined a friend on his farm. This friend had watched his father work with explosives on a number of occasions and claimed he knew all there was to know about them. With mischief in mind, and explosives and fuses in their possession, the lads headed off out into the countryside. A likely target was sighted. The boys dug a hole under a tree stump and placed the explosives into the hole. They set the fuse, packed the explosives down, lit the fuse, and ran behind the next tree stump. The explosion blasted the tree stump and dirt into the air. The crouching boys huddled down as a mass of dirt and bits and pieces of tree stump rained down upon them! Two very subdued boys returned to their respective homes.

Even a game of cowboys and Indians spelt trouble for John. One day he was playing with a group of boys in the sports grounds. The changing sheds were used as forts. As John crept up to the fort that had been taken over by the Indians, he noted a small hole where a knot in the wood had popped out. Seizing the opportunity to spy on the Indians, John peered through the hole. An overly enthusiastic Indian with bow and arrow in hand let fly with the arrow aimed directly at the hole. John experienced shock and pain as the arrow penetrated his eye. At the sight of the arrow protruding from John's eye, the braves reverted to scared little boys and ran away. John and arrow found their way unaided to the doctor's residence. After three weeks of blurred vision out of the damaged eye, John's sight began to return to normal.

Cowboys and Indians was for the most part tame compared to the excitement John experienced when he, on a regular basis, after sneaking out of the house in the early hours of the morning, joined his friend and his friend's father, who doubtless had been told by John he had permission, and for the next three hours (till around six in the morning) rode bareback on one of their horses using only a bridle.

THE TRUTH SEEKER

Like all young boys at that time, John knew how to fight with his fists and arguments were often solved that way, or if not solved brought to an end by the winner of the fight. One day John and the minister's son had an argument in the church that developed into a fistfight. (This was the same church in which the boys often played cowboys and Indians). Both boys were extremely angry and John stormed out and went home.

A couple of days later, John went down to the shops with our grandmother who was visiting at the time. At each side of our gate were ten-foot (three metre) tall dense Cupressus Macrocarpa trees. Upon their return home, as John walked through our gate a solid object slammed down on his head driving him to his knees. Stunned, he shook his head and looked up to see the minister's son, hammer in hand, hanging out from the tree. Blood welled up from the head injury and ran down John's face. When he saw the bloody wound, his friend jumped out of the tree and stood there in shock. John passed out and woke at the doctor's place. He lost consciousness again and was taken to hospital where they found the hammer had punched a hole in his skull and the bone was floating. The doctor pulled the bit of bone back into position and over the next few weeks, John healed.

John's close calls were not over and at age thirteen he was electrocuted and pronounced dead—Chapter Ten, 'Extra Dimensional Travellers', covers this incredible life and death experience.

The family relocated to Auckland during John's teen years, where, apart from an incident when he decided some interesting looking poisonous berries would provide him with a tasty bite, his adventurous spirit was more constructively occupied—at least some of the time. Dad built a twelve-foot (3.33m) yacht with John's help. John then competed in the yacht races on Auckland Harbour. Adversity brought out the best in John and stormy weather and heavy seas became an advantage as he used all his innate skills to sail an extraordinary race and win the eleven to twelve foot (three and a half metre) class yacht race, in which only five out of twenty yachts finished.

From his very early years, John revealed behaviour patterns experience may have modified, but did not change. His curiosity and love of adventure ensured a constant sequence of interesting experiences. No amount of discipline from parents, teachers and other adults in authority, put a stop to his undisciplined and often dangerous activities. While he didn't like punishment, and did his best to prevent his mischievous activities being found out, he never really feared the penalties incurred and as a result they were never a deterrent.

JOAN L BOLER

John's character was of the adventurer who displayed the courage of someone used to facing down dangerous situations. He was a lover of boats from an early age and had a wildness in him that indicated a lack of respect for discipline—unless he himself saw the wisdom in it. His lack of fear in dangerous situations usually allowed his natural resourcefulness to find solutions to difficulties when they arose. Such a strong and definite character was bound to have past life experiences that had made him that way. Who was he before his current sojourn into the world?

It would be many years before answers were sought and found.

A Colourful Character

John survived to adulthood, and as the years flowed by his life continued to reveal his constant need for challenge and adventure. Work over the next few years reflected his restless nature. His occupations included roadwork, truck driving, farm work, car mechanics, washing machine repairs, factory work, freezing works, and not surprisingly some dangerous work in land development that saw him trapped under a five or six ton bulldozer that back in the 1960s had no safety cage.

John's dance with death continued. He rode bulls in rodeos. Cuts, bruising and broken limbs resulted, but never held him back. Other hobbies included hunting deer and wild boar. John's love of the underwater world saw him not only snorkelling, but also scuba-diving. On one occasion, he was snorkel diving for paua shellfish and crayfish when one of the men he was with got caught in a rip. John went back to help the terrified man and although he attempted to calm him, in the next moment he was being held under the water to provide buoyancy for the man who was totally mindless with fright. In those moments, John's life flashed before his eyes and he experienced a vision of himself lying in a grave with the family all around, crying. Somehow, John gained his freedom from the man's deadly grip. Another man who had seen what was happening came to help and all three made it back to shore. Years later a broken sternum and a punctured lung—the consequences of being a passenger in a car involved in a serious accident—forced John to give up diving and underwater activity.

John grabbed at opportunities to sail. In June 1975, he was sailing from Fiji back to New Zealand in a forty-foot (12.2m) ketch with the captain/owner of the boat and one other man. Two days out, the other man became seasick and stayed in his cabin day and night surfacing only for meals prepared by the other two men. This meant John and the captain were on four-hour

THE TRUTH SEEKER

shifts. Approximately sixty miles (ninety-six kilometres) north of New Zealand's Whangaparaoa Peninsula, they ran into the first storm. Then some twelve hours later, another storm hit—side on to the first. As a result the waves built up to sixty and seventy feet high (eighteen to twenty-one metres). Running on adrenaline, John steered the boat as it went up and up each wave. From the middle of a wave, John was able to see a wall of water in front of him and a large trough behind. The weather was so bad it was necessary for John to tie a short lead from himself to the boat to avoid getting flipped or washed out of the cockpit.

As the boat reached the top of a wave it came up to pivot point and then banged down. Twenty-four hours of this punishing treatment split a plank in the hull. John was on shift that night. At around eleven o'clock, in need of a coffee, he tied the steering wheel and stepped down into the cabin—and found himself knee deep in water. Tired from his share of the responsibilities, the boat's owner was asleep in one bunk while the other crewman was asleep in another. The bunks cleared the water by only a few inches. They were sinking!

John woke the captain who attempted to radio for help. Then John switched on all the bilge pumps and started pumping with a hand pump. The next two hours saw both men bailing. They had begun to make some headway when the bilge pumps began to block up. The tinned food (mainly baked beans and spaghetti) had been stored below and now all the labels that had come off the tins were blocking the pumps. The water-logged boat was sluggish and in danger of flipping over, so it was vital they reduced the volume of water in the boat. Non-stop bailing and pumping to get the water down to floor level was necessary.

Once the water levels were under control, John and the captain cleared the bunks away so John could get to the hull to check it. But the ketch had concrete ballast and access to the leak was impossible. Unfortunately, the option of putting a sail around the hull in an attempt to seal the damage was out of the question. Because the winds were so strong, in such rough and dangerous weather it was essential all the sails be used in order to keep headway. During the journey, five of the six sails blew out and had to be repaired. In order to aid in keeping the boat's nose into the wind when the wind was blowing them back, a sea anchor that floated under the water creating drag was used as well. Unable to fix the hull, John returned topside.

Over the next twenty-four hours, the two men had almost no sleep. The captain attempted to mayday any ships in the area, but because of the troughs and high waves, he received no response. Finally, one of the American oilrigs off Mount Egmont, picked up their call, and with their high-powered radio contacted Radio New Zealand. A search was implemented, and the three ships in the area began a triangular search pattern. Using radar, they attempted to hone in on the ketch's radio signal, but because of the high seas, their efforts failed. When advised the next day one of the ships were nearby, they fired flares from the ketch. The 'Union Wellington', that had been delayed on its way from Australia to New Zealand by a day due to the high seas, found them.

The Union Wellington was a container ship and could only stop for twenty minutes. As it turned sideways, the men pulled the ketch alongside. Immediately, the seasick crewman went straight up the approximately three stories high rope ladder. The crew then hauled up their clothes, radios and whatever gear they wanted to get off the ketch. They were on the windward side, and every time the ketch touched the side of the container ship, the force of the water pushed the decks up into a curve and the pressure created started to crack the deck. As they climbed on board the container ship, the Royal New Zealand Air Force Orion aircraft, which had been helping in the search, flew overhead. Twenty minutes after they boarded the ship, the Orion's pilot advised the ketch was gone.

After the three men disembarked the Union Wellington in Auckland, a reporter asked how they felt about their experience. John revealed his sense of adventure and cavalier attitude to danger in his reply, 'It was a terrific experience even right until we had to abandon ship.' In an era when the use of illicit drugs was becoming commonplace, adrenaline was John's drug of choice. John found his thrills and enjoyment of life through dangerous and challenging experiences.

The Legal Challenges

John came to live in Australia in 1979 and over the next few years, his life became more focused on the domestic scene. Within two years of his arrival in Australia, John met a special lady, and over the next few years they built a life together. John's interests now focused upon bringing more security around himself, his wife and his children. He built up a reputation renovating older, beautiful homes, and that business did well. John and his wife bought an older building on the Northern Beaches of Sydney, on a prime block of land with sweeping sea views. Then John built a two-bedroom unit at the rear of the property, where they lived while he pulled down the old house, planning to build a beautiful new home. After years of effort, the new home was built and it seemed his hard work had provided him with financial security such as he had never experienced before. In his leisure hours, he could sail his twenty-one foot (6.4m) yacht.

John had met and been close friends with Brian[80] for around ten years before he went into business with him. John, his wife, Brian and his wife spent considerable time enjoying each other's company. Such was their friendship, John and his wife trusted the other couple completely. When Brian became interested in going into a business, but didn't have the necessary finance, as he only had a small interest in his own home, he asked John and his wife to join him in this venture.

As the business proposition sounded promising to John, he and his wife allowed their home, the sum total of some fifteen years of effort and sacrifice to be put up as part collateral against the loan to purchase the business. When Brian advised John he didn't need to hire his own lawyer as Brian's lawyer could attend to all the legals, John and his wife agreed. There was another party (two men) who would also put up properties in order to secure the loan. The three-way partnership with John and his wife holding one third, Brian and his wife holding one third and the other two partners holding the remaining one third, was legally locked in.

A short time after they had purchased the business, Brian convinced John that the other partners, who were actually working in the business, were stealing goods. When they were accused, an altercation took place that ensured an on-going enmity between John and those other partners. Court action some time later by the other shareholders resulted in an agreement that those partners' shares were to be purchased by John and Brian for $180,000.

At the time of the court case, the partnership business, which was being managed by Brian and his wife, had been running for a couple of years. Eventually, after many requests, the first year's figures were received. They revealed a loss and no supporting documentation could be produced. The business had been profitable when purchased. John and his wife managed to wrest control of the business from Brian. Investigation into the business records revealed that at the time the business was purchased Brian had transferred the alcohol licence into a company he owned. An amount of $90,000 of the bank finance for the business had been placed into a bank account belonging to a business Brian owned. A number of other lesser anomalies were found.

---

[80]Name changed.

As Brian could not raise his half of the $180,000 to purchase the other partner's shares, this situation became a tug of war as Brian sought ways to gain control of the shares and at the same time, prevent John from buying them. Brian was a wily person who knew his way around the legal system and he was effectively able to give John hassles in ways that were daunting. Time after time over the next two years, John and his wife were involved in court battles that cost in excess of $400,000 of their own money. As a result, their financial resources were stretched to breaking point and that, along with long working hours, in order to make more money, added to the unrelenting stress that had taken over their lives. Finally, the partnership business was sold at auction. But this did not bring an end to the nightmare.

The other party now sued for the $180,000 plus huge damages for the shares it had been impossible to buy due to Brian's devious activities that included threatening the bank and ensuring no properties could be released.

These years, that moved John's focus from physical to legal challenges, were horrendous and resulted in the breakdown of John's marriage to the loving and supportive lady with whom he had spent the previous twenty years.

Life, After Life, After Life

John left Sydney and moved over five hundred miles (845km) away to Queensland's Gold Coast. The situation continued to deteriorate. On one of my visits to the Gold Coast, I suggested to John perhaps it could be helpful to look to his past lives in order to gain insight into what was going on, and as far as possible resolve any harmful emotions that connected John to Brian in his other lifetimes.

Since he had first discovered Brian's betrayal, John's every waking moment had been focused on Brian and the consequences of his association with the man. The on-going pain of being imprisoned in circumstances he had no control over ate into his soul. A permanent knot in his stomach made him feel sick when he ate. Upon waking up each morning, John obsessed over Brian and how to get even with him, and how to get access to Brian's and his wife's assets. John was an angry man and in his frustration, he upset his family and friends. I guided John into a meditative state and proceeded to question him about his past relationship with his ex-friend. There were three previous shared lifetimes. The following revealed John's love of the sea.

THE TRUTH SEEKER

John found himself in the late 1700s on a ship. He was wearing clothes from the Nelson era—double brass buttons, a blue vest, buckles on his shoes and white pants made out of sailcloth-like material. John was a lieutenant who was experienced at reading charts, and was very familiar with the area in which they were currently sailing. Brian was the captain of the ship who wanted to take a short cut through what John knew to be, a dangerous passageway. John said, 'No! You can't go through there. It's too dangerous because of the rocks. A smaller ship might get through but this one won't.'

'I'm the captain and I'll say where we go!' Brian stated.

'With all due respect,' said John, 'I know the area, and you can't go through there. There are too many rocks.'

Brian was deaf to his arguments and angry at having his authority questioned, especially in front of three other seamen. Directing his attention to those seamen, Brian ordered them to throw John in the brig for insubordination and at the same time, gave the order to turn the ship into the passageway.

The four-by-four foot (1.4m x 1.4m) brig in which John found himself was below the water line. To his left were iron bars, and to his right was a plank timber wall. In the area around the brig were provision barrels. To the rear left, was a stepladder to a hatch. Suddenly, some fifteen minutes after he had been confined, John was thrown backwards as the ship jolted and shuddered from the impact of hitting solid rock. The tearing, scraping sound of wood against rock followed as the ship's momentum forced further damage. The side of the ship caved in and water poured into the front of the brig. John leaned back against the iron bars of the door.

At this point, John wasn't unduly concerned. He listened to the uproar as men shouted and screamed on deck, indicating they were making efforts to fix the hole in the side of the ship. Then he began to realise that at the rate the water was coming in, there must have been more than one source. When, after five or six minutes, the water was rapidly moving up around his ankles and no one had come to let him out, he started shouting. And shouting...

A short time later, John heard the captain's orders to abandon ship. Sounds of activity followed as the longboats were lowered into the water. Quiet stole over the ship and John watched the water inch higher. As it reached his waist, John was aware only a short time was left before the brig became submerged. Then he heard a sound. In the next moment, a key turned in the brig door as a shipmate unlocked it. John felt he recognised a brother-in-law, Rob,[81] from his current life. The descent of the ship gathered momentum, and as Rob dragged John out of the brig, the water reached his chest. Both men struggled against the force of the water to reach the steps to the hatch. Suddenly a rush of water pushed them both straight up and through the open hatch to the surface.

The fight for life was not yet over. John, in his heavy clothing, was immediately dragged back under the water. Rob followed him and determinedly grabbed him and helped him to swim back to the surface. Then Rob dragged John along as they swam until they reached the rocky beach. An exhausted Rob collapsed at the water's edge and John dragged him up on to the beach and then fell to the ground exhausted.

Around fifteen minutes later, they heard the sound of raised voices. John sat up and looked to his left to see the captain, who was about three to four hundred yards along the beach, pointing in their direction. Following their captain's orders, two seamen with muskets headed towards them. Rob, assessing the situation, said, 'Don't worry about me. I'll look after myself.'

Since it was apparent there was little likelihood of survival if he remained, John took off along the beach and around the point, where he began looking for somewhere to hide. As he ran, he spotted a low, shallow cave. He lay down and managed to wedge himself into it. John stilled as the two seamen chasing him ran straight past. Time passed... The sounds of searching continued. Some hours later, darkness fell and it seemed that the search was over. John vacated his cave and walked approximately another two miles (3.22 km) along the beach until he came to an inn.

John took stock. The coins he had were sufficient to provide for food and lodging for a short time, but to find some way to earn money was vital. A change of clothes seemed wise, so John accepted the offer from the innkeeper's wife of some ragged old clothes in return for his uniform.

---

[81] Name changed.

THE TRUTH SEEKER

A few days later, John was talking to some local men at the inn and advised them he was looking for work. 'We can get you a job on another ship,' they offered. These were rough and ready men and it was not surprising that the ship turned out to be a pirate ship. John's life was about to take a significant turn as he accepted this dubious opportunity. It didn't take long for the captain to appreciate John's abilities and place him in the position of first mate.

Life at sea was what John knew and enjoyed. One day, they captured a Spanish ship and were transferring people off it when one of the lookouts spotted an English ship bearing down on them. Fevered activity erupted as the crew prepared to immediately cast off. There was no chance of outrunning the British ship as it was the same size as theirs and it already had its speed up while they had been stationary. As the crew turned their ship towards the approaching British ship, John studied it through the telescope and saw that the captain was his nemesis, Brian. John knew how Brian's mind worked, and he sought to use that knowledge to advantage. Apprehension and excitement warred within John as he prepared to meet the challenge to bring about Brian's demise.

In the face of imminent danger, they loaded all guns on the port side and built up what speed they could. The English ship came past and fired. The return fire from the pirate ship hit not only the English ship's centre mast collapsing it, but also the hull of the ship at the waterline. The pirate ship did a left hand tack right behind the English ship, and then chased them.

The English ship had lost sail, was taking water through the hull, and was slowing down. The pirate ship caught up and used its forward cannons to increase the damage to the other ship. The English ship was now at a significant disadvantage, as, with no guns at the rear of their ship, they couldn't return fire. John and his shipmates came alongside and using grappling hooks, they boarded. After a fifteen to twenty minute fight, they had taken control of the British ship.

John's history with Brian was already known to the captain of the pirate ship who said to John, 'Do you want to handle this?' John answered in the affirmative and when a couple of the sailors brought Brian towards them, the captain stood aside.

John faced a beaten Brian. 'We meet again! You,' contempt dominated John's voice, 'left me in the brig of a sinking ship. I think I should give you the same privilege!'

Gone was the arrogant self-opinionated captain. Visibly scared for his life, Brian turned into a gutless shaking mess as he begged and pleaded with John to spare his life. John, more than a little disgusted, didn't answer. At a signal from John, his shipmates moved forward to take Brian away. Brian didn't see the wink and nod John gave his shipmates as they dragged a still begging Brian to what he believed was his eminent death. Instead, he was taken to the brig in the hold of the pirate ship. The rest of Brian's crew, which did not include Rob, were already down there, along with some of the Spanish ship's crew. The pirate ship set sail and within a day came to an island. It was here that all the prisoners from the brig, including Brian, were deposited.

As the pirate ship sailed away from the island, a livid Brian shook his fist at John.

John knew that if he was rescued, Brian would never be given another ship after losing two. That knowledge, along with the realisation Brian had been beaten, brought a broad happy smile to John's face.

While that was then end of their contact in that life, it was not the end of the story, as the feelings provoked by their encounters ensured there would be further confrontation. The next lifetime in which the two connected was on an American battle ship.

John found himself on board an American, steam-driven battle ship as part of the crew. The crew's quarters included an area with double rows of hammocks and benches. Brian was also a member of the crew and a recognised tough guy who didn't play by the rules. There had been a number of questionable situations on board indicating Brian wasn't to be trusted. On one occasion, when members of the crew were sitting playing cards in a circle on the floor, one of the sailors accused Brian of cheating. Without hesitation Brian pulled a knife with the apparent intention of taking down the sailor who had dared to accuse him.

John, in an effort to prevent the situation from escalating into bloodshed, stepped in to try to pacify the two men. In the scuffle, Brian stabbed John in the stomach. John experienced excruciating pain. It felt as though his stomach was being ripped out. He collapsed to the floor. The others tried to stop the bleeding, but there was too much damage and blood kept pouring out. John could feel his life fading. Everything went grey and he couldn't see anymore...

THE TRUTH SEEKER

Brian's stabbing John in that life did not bring an end to their connection through the release of negative energies on the part of either party, ensuring another encounter.

It was the First World War and on this occasion, Brian was a lieutenant while John was a corporal in what was probably the Italian army. John was wearing a brown uniform with a cap that had a flap from the sides to the back that could be raised or dropped. They were in the thick of the fighting. Brian, who should have been leading his men into battle, was ordering the men into unnecessarily dangerous situations, resulting in the death of many. He had no care as to how to achieve the best result without the wholesale slaughter of his men. Repeatedly, they came back with fewer and fewer men. John became angrier and angrier regarding Brian's lack of leadership abilities and his cowardice. The men were continually coming to John saying, 'This is crazy. We don't want to die for nothing.'

Initially, John tried to get Brian to talk to the sergeant who had a lot of battle experience. Brian's answer was to warn John against insubordination. Then John requested, on a number of occasions, that Brian come with them into the situation so he could see the problem. Brian refused. After continued efforts to get him to see reason, John accused Brian of being a coward. Finally, when Brian ordered them to walk straight into gunfire, rather than going around and attacking the left flank, John refused to take his men into another situation that would result in a wasteful loss of life. Brian said, 'I'll shoot you for cowardice.' John ignored him and turned to walk away. As Brian shot John in the shoulder he said, 'I can kill you at any time.' The bullet smashed John's shoulder blade and he fell to the ground unconscious. After a while, the medics came and took him away.

So there we had it. The source of the energy that was the basis for the conflict between John and Brian in this lifetime! As long as these two were connected on an energetic level, any contact would bring conflict and invite threatening or dangerous situations. John needed to let go his connection to his old enemy who would only bring him more pain and grief!

Anger, fear and judgement are among energetic attractions that determine who is drawn into our lives to teach us lessons through painful experiences. John had drawn Brian's soul into his life on at least four different occasions, and unless the negative energy was cleared, such connections would continue. I advised John to release any emotional attachment and judgement, and to thank Brian for the lessons and experiences they had shared in each of their lives, including the current one. Fortunately, John recognised the need to have positive feelings towards Brian, to wish him well, and to lose all feelings of attachment to the situation.

After the work to clear the negative energy between himself and Brian, Jane,[82] a spiritual healer, also worked with John. He followed her recommendations and attended a course that focused on letting go of negative feelings and realigning his way of perceiving situations. As a result, the anger and frustration that had been an obsessive force for years disappeared completely. The pain that had been gnawing at his gut since he first discovered Brian's betrayal, dissolved. John felt light and liberated. He no longer wanted to beat Brian to pulp, and although he would like to see him get his just dues, John had no emotional attachment to that eventuality. Even now, some years after the work John did to clear the situation, his feelings remain neutral regarding Brian's role in the years of battles and his devastating losses.

A few weeks after the past life work, Brian's lawyer advised he didn't know Brian's whereabouts and had no way of contacting him. John had let go emotionally and now Brian had disappeared out of his life, ending the on-going, expensive, legal tangle he had been creating for John. The cost to deal with the case in full would have been exorbitant and not worth the effort as Brian and his wife did not have the finances or assets to recompense them. Since they did not appear to defend their case, a judgement of $200,000 was awarded against Brian and his wife.

Of course, collection of the $200,000 wasn't possible as Brian and his wife were nowhere to be found. Although this finalised the situation with Brian, the other partnership was yet to be dealt with. These two men sued John and his wife for the $180,000 plus massive damages they believed they were entitled to as a result of the failure of the earlier agreement for their shares to be purchased—an agreement that couldn't be fulfilled due to Brian's manipulations. Many years, and a number of very costly court battles later, this finally resulted in the loss of John and his now ex-wife's remaining assets as the court ordered payment of the $180,000 plus costs. Although the court rejected the damages claim by the other party, the court costs were crippling.

In the aftermath, virtually everything was lost. The soul-destroying devastation had laid waste to a lifestyle that had appeared to have so much

---

[82] Name changed.

THE TRUTH SEEKER

potential. In the greater picture, how could good come out of such a crippling experience? We looked to astrology to provide answers.

South Node in Taurus

No one on the planet escapes the relentless energies that rule it. Not only are we learning to develop our energies to their full potential, but also, according to those astrologers who have researched the karmic influences in a chart, the position of the Moon's Nodes (the point where the Moon crosses the ecliptic) can define the direction the greater life lesson will take. Of the books that I have read by astrologers that deal with karma, I have found that the writings by Martin Schulman[83] and also those by Jan Spiller and Karen McCoy[84] reveal great depth of insight, and I have drawn on their knowledge when presenting explanations.

The South Node (the Dragon's Tail), indicates the habits and behaviour (karma) of past lives that need to be brought into balance. The North Node (the Dragon's Head) is in the opposite sign and reveals the sign that can bring balance. As the focus of learning comes under the dominion of particular signs, attraction to situations that confront the designated area of learning also activates. The fact that John was born with his South Node in Taurus reveals that at some time in the past this energy had gone out of balance and needed to be stabilised.

Taurus' lesson is about learning to have a balanced outlook on prosperity. Imbalance can result from a belief that spirituality must be compromised in order to have abundance. To have, or not to have, financial abundance does not have an impact on spirituality—to see abundance as immoral, or to gain it through immoral means is what compromises the soul. John, in his life as a pirate, and possibly in other lives, had gained property through dishonest means, ensuring that eventually recompense would require the loss of what he had earned through hard work and effort.

The *need* of Taurus is inner strength that includes self-respect. John found his inner strength in courage and daring. He had managed to superficially compensate for his loss of self-worth through his bravery that gained him the respect of others. The nature of Taurus, is the indulgence of the senses

---

[83] Schulman, Martin, *Karmic Astrology*, Samuel Weiser, 1975, pp. 50-51.
[84] Spiller, Jan and McCoy, Karen, *Spiritual Astrology*, Simon & Schuster, New York, 1988, pp. 187-194.

that for John were fed by the adrenaline rush he experienced when confronting danger. John did not feel the need to change. He fearlessly faced down all opposition, physically, mentally and emotionally. These patterns of behaviour were his strength, his base and his fulfilment.

In this lifetime, it was determined that John, who had become too comfortable with his established patterns of behaviour, would bring balance and clarity to his Taurus energy. It was time to destroy the conflict in his unconscious and bring about a true liking and acceptance of self.

North Node in Scorpio

Scorpio is the opposite sign to Taurus and as such, provides an opposite and balancing energy. While Taurus seeks inner strength through self-respect, Scorpio causes transformation through destruction. This is not likely to be an easy experience for the soul. With knife-like precision, Scorpio's forces cut deep, removing external supports and exposing internal motives, strengths and weaknesses.

The destruction of John's world saw him suffer years of stress and loss of his peace of mind. The on-going court battles over eight years brought about a scarcity of money and the loss of his assets. He saw his wife's health deteriorate under the pressure and their previously loving relationship destroyed, leaving a gaping hole in his heart. He saw his children suffer from the loss of stability and security he had sought to provide for them.

After such a devastating experience, it takes time to recover, just as it does from a long and painful illness. The shattered soul has to come to terms with the pain and loss and the changed circumstances. More importantly, it needs to grow into new and different approaches to life. Scorpio transformation provokes change in the Taurean energy in the following ways:

- From reacting to inner feelings of inferiority to understanding those feelings, and introducing the disciplines that ensure self-respect
- From dependence upon the opinion of others to belief in self, and independence of thought
- From hanging on to old behaviour patterns to forging new pathways
- From holding on to old hurts and judgements to freeing the heart of burdens

THE TRUTH SEEKER

Through skill, honest hard work and self-discipline, John built a beautiful home and developed a successful home renovation business of which he was justifiably proud. During those years, his self-esteem grew as he began to recognise and acknowledge his own worth. Then Scorpio's knife cut John to the core. Betrayal and the resultant court battles robbed John of all he had worked hard for. The props that had revealed him as a success to the world, and to himself, were removed—and yet his self-respect remained.

Brian had betrayed John and as a result, John lived through many relentless, harrowing years. John's judgement of and anger towards Brian crippled him emotionally. Yet when the opportunity arose to let go of those potentially destructive energies, John didn't hesitate to put in the necessary effort and as a result he reclaimed his power over his own emotions. Scorpio, through consequences, also taught the necessity for more in-depth study of situations and the underlying motives of others.

Such growth to the soul reveals the causes of, and reason for, the pain and suffering encountered in our lives—not as a judgement of wrongdoing, but as a gift of infinite value.

Teacher and Student

While general knowledge such as reading, mathematics and science can be learned from others, it is through experience and often pain that we grow in emotional depth and learn life's wisdoms. Life is the lesson giver that utilises each of us in the dual roles of involuntary teacher and the often-reluctant student.

Very little difference can be seen between the character of John in his three previous incarnations and in his current life. He continued to display the same lack of fear, lack of respect for rules, love of adventure, and a sense of loyalty and fairness. His passion for the sea and his natural sailing ability, were clearly revealed during his childhood and have continued to be important in his life to this day.

It takes little imagination to see that Brian also revealed the same characteristics throughout each of the lives recalled by John. In two of the three lives, Brian was in positions of trust and responsibility, revealing his ability to convince the right people of his worth. John's and Brian's attitudes, behaviour and feelings during each lifetime expose a continuation of the same life force in each of the men.

JOAN L BOLER

We may not like them, and we may seek retribution from them, but we need the Brians of this world, as it is through them we learn some of our lessons. Brian's absolutely convincing performance as a good friend to John shows the mark of a truly gifted con artist—because he deludes himself into believing at least some of his own spiel. As such, he is used by the life forces as a teacher. Without a doubt, Brian was also learning through his connection to John and the other people he used and treated badly.

Those who seek to rescue their loved ones from the consequences of their actions, take from that person the opportunity for greater learning. They may effectively delay pain and suffering, but they leave the rescued person feeling inferior and powerless. That person is then likely to attempt to regain their power through negative methods such as subjugating and deriding others. Alternatively, drugs and alcohol can provide escape mechanisms—at least for a time. It's better for a person to learn through the consequences of their actions and become empowered through the lessons learned.

Where the gaining of wisdom through experience is an integral part of the picture, judgement that condemns those who think differently, in turn, invites the judgement of those with a different outlook. Judgement that discriminates and wisely avoids, or handles, the antisocial behaviour of others ensures freedom from undesirable consequences. Growth emerges through both positive and negative behaviour and experiences, and the wrong-doing of a person during a lifetime can provide not only invaluable lessons, but also result in the development of character and skills. Each individual is a work in progress, so even those whose antisocial behaviour causes pain are in the process of developing qualities that are laying the foundation for the spiritual.

Trust the Weaver

As we attempt to control and direct our own life and the lives of those we care for, we can find ourselves frustrated and powerless.

Eventually, we come to understand that life is the Weaver, and we who would weave our own patterns must first of all open to the vision of the Weaver—the true artist. And as we join with the Weaver to view the tapestry, we can share the joy in the beauty so far revealed, both in ourselves and in those with whom we share our journey. Then we can relax as the Weaver rests for a time. And inspired by the magnificence yet to be created, we can once again join the Weaver as the needle of life is threaded with another colour.

THE TRUTH SEEKER

Trust the Weaver of the tapestry that is your life.

JOAN L BOLER

THE TRUTH SEEKER

Chapter 5

Our Extraordinary Senses

People who say it cannot be done should not interrupt those who are doing it.

Anonymous[85]

Psychic Ability

What is psychic ability? How does psychic ability work? Who are the people that possess the abilities that break the accepted rules? Telepathy, prophecy and visions have been an integral part of the past in all cultures. For thousands of years the writings of old have recorded the words of the seers of their time. In spite of the scientific evidence that proves psychic ability is possible, denial by many in the scientific world of the existence of *any* paranormal abilities has resulted in the psychic being considered either a charlatan or a delusional person by large numbers of people. Denial of such abilities by science, along with past religious attitudes that included a superstitious fear of witchcraft, has inhibited the development of these amazing senses.

Each of us is born with varying degrees of potential regarding a wide range of skills, including those related to our psychic senses, which in the most of the population lie dormant. This is not surprising as until recently, very few psychics in the West dared to discuss their paranormal abilities and experiences, and the idea of developing them was dangerous. Those who were talented psychics were left bereft of information that could provide understanding as to how and why paranormal experiences occur. Like many others of my generation, I couldn't share with loved ones part of who I was and what I was experiencing. My reticence in advising close family and friends of my spontaneous paranormal experiences was because I would be considered to be mentally unbalanced by most people, and evil by some. I

---

[85]George Bernard Shaw often credited but unverified and disputed.

was in my late thirties when during a discussion on psychic phenomena with my friend Joy, whom I had known since my teen years, it emerged we were both psychic and had for many years been dealing with the metaphysical.

Paranormal abilities and experiences are often viewed as the domain of just a few select souls. But that is simply not the case. Almost anyone can have a paranormal experience of a prophetic, telepathic or intuitive nature. The state of consciousness conducive to bringing about such experiences can be entered into accidentally or deliberately. Dreaming, daydreaming and during the times prior to sleeping and immediately after awakening, are occasions when the mind is in the same state as is experienced in meditation. Times of intense emotion such as following the death of a loved one can also predispose the individual to experience the paranormal.

When activated, psychic talents can bridge space and time. While visions come easily to some, others hear voices. Intuition and gut feelings can give timely warnings while a sense of knowing can offer truth. None of these abilities can be explained in physical terms, as they breach the boundaries of the physical. That does not make them impossible or unreal, as is shown by scientific research.

Psychic ability is the potential of every human. Realising that potential is the destiny of humanity.

Scientific Evidence

What does science have to say about this subject?

Although the scientific community has, for over three hundred years, been consistent in its rejection of the paranormal, there is now an abundance of evidence creating change in the scientific world. Dr Dean Radin has held appointments at Princeton University, the University of Edinburgh, the University of Nevada, SRA International and the Interval Research Corporation. In 2000 he co-founded the Boundary Institute. Since 2001, he has been the senior scientist at the Institute of Neotic Sciences. He also holds an adjunct appointment at Sonoma State University, and is on the Distinguished Consulting Faculty for Saybrook Graduate School.

According to Radin, who has spent over twenty years engaged in the scientific investigation of psychic phenomena, scientists tend to avoid researching potentially career damaging psychic phenomena, and for the most part have assumed those who report such occurrences are delusional.

THE TRUTH SEEKER

But that is simply not so! Radin and other scientists have for the last hundred years been accumulating evidence in the form of repeatable experiments that prove that psychic abilities such as clairvoyance, telepathy, distant viewing, precognition, and influencing others through the power of the mind are possible for some talented people.[86]

Psychic ability was used during the Cold War. Russell Targ, an American physicist who was a pioneer in the development of the laser, co-founded the Standford Research Institute. Targ is the author of 'Limitless Mind' and is also co-author to a number of books on the mind and psychic abilities. At the Institute, investigations undertaken into the capabilities of the human mind revealed a range of capabilities including remote viewing. Specially trained people were given the latitude and longitude of a location (that could be anywhere in the world) and were expected to remotely view the location and obtain useful and detailed information. Government intelligence agencies, including the Central Intelligence Agency (CIA), were so impressed with the abilities of some subjects that from 1972 until around 1989 they used and supported the Institute's resources for top-secret projects—such as obtaining specific information relating to the Soviet Union during the Cold War.[87]

In 1984, Targ, under the supervision of the USSR Academy of Sciences, organised for Djuna Davitashvili, a Russian healer, to describe where his colleague would be hiding in two hours' time. From 10,000 miles away Davitashvili accurately provided details of the colleague's future whereabouts in San Francisco.[88]

Telepathy in humans and animals has been researched extensively by Rupert Sheldrake, writer of over eighty scientific papers and ten books. Sheldrake studied natural sciences at Cambridge University, achieved a double first class honours degree and was awarded the University Botany Prize. After studying philosophy and science history at Harvard University, he returned to Cambridge where he completed a doctorate in biochemistry.

Sheldrake's research with humans used telephone calls, SMS (short message service) and emails. With telephone calls, recipients (who had previously selected the four possible callers) announced the identity of the caller prior to answering the phone. All sessions were videotaped. In a total of five

---

[86] Radin, D. Ph.D., 'On science and psychic phenonema'. *New York Times*, Vol XIII, No. 5, October, 1997.
[87] Targ and Katra (2001).
[88] Targ, Russell and Katra, Jane. 'Alternative Therapies in Health and Medicine' *Aliso Viego*: May/Jun 2001. Vol 7, Iss. 3; pp. 143-150.

hundred and seventy trials, the average hit rate was forty percent which is above the chance level of twenty-five percent. Similar findings were reported at the universities of Amsterdam, Holland[89] and Freiburg, Germany.[90] Email and SMS trials revealed like results. Fifty participants took part in five hundred and fifty-two trials with an average hit rate of forty-three percent. Sheldrake concluded that while tests for precognition failed to show results, the psi effects indicate telepathy that in all likelihood would be more pronounced in an environment free of the artificial demands of the experiments.[91]

Sheldrake's research into telepathy in animals included the ability of animals to intuit their owner's intentions, especially dogs that anticipate their owner's return. The tests confirmed they can in fact do so.[92]

As we look at the world of scientific research into the paranormal, we may not see one hundred per cent accuracy, but what we do see are results that consistently exceed the expected average, sometimes with startling results. What we are looking at is proven potential. Psychic ability has been suppressed and ignored. Given the potential benefits, can we continue to allow ignorance to place limitations on skills that can enhance the lives of billions?

Awareness of Psychic Ability in Today's World

The number of people who recognise the reality of psychic ability today is increasing as exposure to knowledge on the subject becomes increasingly available. In this age of media coverage of anything that might attract an audience, psychic ability has received considerable attention. Many movie and television productions base their public appeal on the sensational and imaginative, though usually highly improbable, paranormal abilities of the characters. Not all productions deal in make-believe. In live shows, psychics

---

[89] Lobach, E. and Bierman, D.J. Who's calling at this hour? Local sidereal times and telephone telepathy. *Proceedings of Parapsychology Association Annual Convention, Vienna, 2004:* 91-97, 2004.
[90] Schmidt, S., Erath, D., Ivanova, V. and Walachm H.: Do you know who is calling? Experiments on anomalous cognition in phone call receivers. *The Open Psychology Journal* 2: 12-18, 2009.
[91] Sheldrake, Rupert. Telepathy in Connection with Telephone Calls, Text Messages and Emails. *Journal of International Society of Life Information Science* Vol.32, No.1, March 2014
[92] Sheldrake, Rupert. 'A dog that seems to know when his owner is coming home.' *Journal of Scientific Exploration.* 14, pp. 233-255 (2000) sheldrake. org/homepage. html (accessed 23 Oct 2011)

have exposed themselves and their psychic abilities to the scrutiny of public at large, usually under conditions not conducive to successful outcomes.

The television programme 'Sensing Murder' (a joint Australian and New Zealand production) features the amazing psychic abilities of Sue Nicholson (a New Zealander originally from England), Kelvin Cruickshank (New Zealander) and Deb Webber (from Australia). These psychics set out to gain information about cold cases through communicating with the dead victim. Two psychics are separately asked to investigate each case and each psychic is accompanied at all times during the investigation, to ensure no outside resources are used to access information.

The information gained is incredible. Much of it is confirmed by the investigators of the case. The psychics provide a detailed description of the victim along with at least their first name and their age at the time of their death. In addition, they often give the year, month and sometimes even the day when the victim was killed. They reveal how and why the person was murdered and usually pinpoint the location of the murder (sometimes on a map, sometimes they direct the driver to the area). On arrival at the scene, they point out the spot where the murder took place. They often name the killer or killers, although the viewers aren't privy to this information.

Since psychics can't prove the killer's guilt, and the cases are cold, even though the information gained is passed on to the police the killer is unlikely to be charged with the murder. But the knowledge obtained helps the families to find closure.

Other programmes that reveal psychics' talents are 'Psychic Detectives' (USA) and 'Psychic Investigators' (a Canadian/United Kingdom co-production).

Many in our society can provide evidence of the paranormal, sometimes at a cost, as lack of information still causes many people to ridicule, demean, or fear those who attempt to reveal their psychic abilities. It is important to recognise that paranormal ability is a part of life and the potential of every human.

Prediction

Many novels include incidents of foretelling by gypsies where the predictions turn out to be true. Real life does not necessarily follow fiction. My own experience with psychics regarding prediction is that although most offer helpful information, prediction is for the most part a hit or miss affair with some predictions accurate and some not—unless the psychic is especially gifted.

Early in 1972, I returned from Norfolk Island to Auckland, New Zealand. Shortly after my return, I visited a psychic for a reading. This lady, who was the most accurate psychic I have encountered, turned out to be a gypsy.

Firstly, she advised me I had not long returned from living overseas. She then said that within a short time I would once again be living overseas. However, I was not returning to the place where I had recently lived. She advised me I would receive two letters from overseas in the next few days, and one would be significant with regard to my once again moving overseas. I had had no plans to move to Australia, but a few weeks later, I did just that!

A letter arrived from Australia from my husband, from whom I had been separated for almost a year. He offered to pay for our children to fly over to join him for the school holidays in May. As my son had been fretting for his father, I wrote back suggesting that if he could arrange temporary accommodation for the three of us, I would also come over with the intention of remaining there. The other letter was from my Norfolk Island friend Carol advising that she and her boyfriend had just moved from Norfolk Island to Sydney, Australia, so I realised that if I moved to Australia, my good friend would be close by.

The gipsy went on to advise that before I travelled overseas, I would go on a trip within New Zealand. My parents lived in Wellington while I was in Auckland. Once plans were made for travel to Australia in May, I travelled, with my children, to visit my mum and dad.

The gipsy advised that not long after I arrived in Australia, I would find myself in a relationship. I had absolutely no intention of returning to my marriage, and at that time, the possibility did not even occur to me. But after a few weeks in Australia, I caved in to pressure and agreed to give the marriage another try thinking it was the best for all concerned—except me. This didn't work out and once again I ended the marriage.

The gipsy also said, 'In five years' time, you will be invited to a party and you will receive a head injury which could kill you…' Pause… 'No. No, it won't kill you.' She went on to suggest I avoid the party.

Almost exactly five years after the gypsy's reading, at the end of March 1977, I was invited, with my two children (then in their early teens) to a

THE TRUTH SEEKER

barbecue that was being attended by a number of friends and their children. By this time, I had forgotten the prediction. I had for some time been experiencing conflict with a man who had threatened me on a number of occasions. This man was at the party when I arrived, so I only stayed for a short time. I left with two ladies to attend a concert at the local country club ten minutes away. Since the concert would not be over for some time, I left early and promised the ladies I would return to collect them later after I had picked up my children. When I arrived back at the barbecue, I was confronted by the very angry, very drunk male I was trying to avoid. The uppercut that connected with my chin lifted me off the ground and sent me flying through the air. Shocked friends subdued him.

After dropping the children home, I returned to the country club to collect the two ladies. He intercepted me as I exited the club with them. He was a well built, strong man and almost twice my eight stone (51 kg) in weight—physically, there was little I could do to defend myself against him. He grabbed me by my upper arm and turning, flung me up through the air. The momentum lifted me off my feet and then, as he let me go, I crashed to the pavement. He repeated this action three more times. The fourth time he threw me, he had turned and I went backwards, full force towards the brick wall of the club—the side of my head connected with the brick windowsill ledge. He picked me up again and half dragged me to his panel van. Then he threw me face-first into the door of the van.

He took me back to my place where he beat me over the head with the phone book before he finally left. The injuries I sustained included a slight dent in my skull, a broken nose, the misalignment of around seven vertebrae, concussion, and scrapes and bruising over almost every part of my body. The next day, because of his drunken state, he remembered nothing of what he had done. Even had I (prior to this traumatic experience) recalled the gypsy's prediction, I doubt I could have avoided the attack. After a threat from him a few weeks earlier, I'd sought help from the police but they advised me they could do nothing. They assured me that on most occasions, it never happened. I took him to court where the lawyers conferred before our case was called. Then his lawyer warned him that if the court case went ahead, he could find himself in prison that day. The threat of prison doubtless contributed towards his agreeing to his lawyer's advice that he agree to stay away from me. His lawyer also warned him he could expect immediate imprisonment if he failed to do so. On his signed agreement he would keep his distance, I dropped the charges.

Even though I had had psychic experiences, I had never thought of myself as psychic, especially as I had never foreseen anything. But the gypsy lady had said to me, 'You are the most psychic person I have ever met. I could teach you to do what I can do.' I had no idea how she came to that conclusion!

She had talked about her relatives in spirit who were talking to her and giving her information. In spite of having read information on communication with those souls who had died, my knowledge was sketchy, and whilst I had no problem with her doing so, the thought of speaking to those in spirit, at that time, sounded somewhat daunting, so I didn't accept her offer. Fifteen years elapsed before I felt I was ready. It was then I began to attend classes where I learned to develop a number of psychic skills.

That reading was the first I had received from a psychic, and the predictions she made were one hundred per cent accurate. She had confirmed, for me, accurate psychic prediction was possible.

Clairvoyance

Clairvoyance, or experiencing visions, is the ability to see what is beyond the normal physical visual spectrum and is the most commonly known of our extra-sensory abilities. Those who use this ability were called seers in the past and clairvoyants in more recent times.

The visual area we use when we picture images in our mind is appropriately described in the East as 'the third eye' and is located in the centre of the forehead. This viewing area can be compared to a television. Just as it is possible to view different programmes by switching channels, it is also possible to receive images in the mind from a variety of sources, providing the desired information is tuned into. When a specific target is focused on, the pictorial information can be played out in the mind of the seeker. The need to know of past events can result in intimate information being revealed. In the following incident, all the information received played out visually like a movie, even though the original event had long passed.

In the 1980s, I was attending a psychic development class. A young man who was writing a book presented the class with the photos of three people—two men and a woman. He mentioned the murder of one of the subjects and requested that we discover what we could about each of these people. As I didn't wish to view bloody and ghastly sights (it's possible to place boundaries on what type of information will, or will not be received), I immediately declared to myself I would not see anything gory.

THE TRUTH SEEKER

The photo of the young woman became my first target. A scene appeared in my mind. From my visual vantage point above the eucalyptus trees, I saw the young woman being hunted. Her terror invaded my psyche as she ran through the trees. Then she reached an escarpment. Suddenly the scene shifted. I was now with her inside a house. The chaos I viewed in the kitchen and dining area revealed she had been fighting for her life. I felt a heavy blow to her head and I psychically knew the blow had killed her.

Next, my attention was drawn to the photo of one of the men. A vision of this man pursuing the terrified girl through the treed area passed before me. At the same time, I felt the man's loathsome, ugly, violent, spine-chilling energy. With each moment I was connected to the man's vicious energy, I was aware of the power and pleasure he experienced from the pain and terror he instilled in others. There was no doubt in my mind this man was a killer. Then the scene shifted to a house with a white vehicle outside.

With what little time was left I tuned into the energy of the other man and became aware of a feeling of total disconnection. This shell of a man was devoid of personality and emotion. At this point, I had run out of time.

After the psychic exercise, members described what they had seen; some giving details of the dismembering of the body. The man who had brought in the photos provided us with the available facts relating to the murder. He advised us the two men were brothers, and then he confirmed the following.

- The man I had psychically known was the murderer was in jail, convicted of the murder of the girl.
- At the time of his arrest, he owned a white vehicle.
- The woman died from a blow to the head.
- The body was dumped off the escarpment after being dismembered.

There was little doubt my mind had travelled to the time leading up to and including the woman's murder.

Clairvoyance is an amazing ability that can transport the psychic's consciousness to the past or to the future where it is possible to clairvoyantly view the events sought. While visions of the past can be confirmed when the accounts are accurate, that is not the case when dealing with the future, as only time can confirm whether life pans out as predicted. Although clairvoyant ability makes it possible to *see* images of the future for a person, a country or the world, it should not be assumed predictions of the future reveal fate. It is possible they foretell a likely future that can be altered through changes in patterns of thinking and the behaviour of the people involved.

JOAN L BOLER

Clairsentience

The empathic person is clairsentient and able to sense the energies of others. Such sensing can include not only the emotional, but also the mental and physical state of another person.

My experience of the murder situation not only provided clairvoyant images related to the murder, but also bombarded me with the attitudes and emotional energies of the victim and the murderer. The fact the murder had happened ten years prior to my tuning into it made no difference to the intensity of the experience.

By the conclusion of the psychic investigation into the murder, I felt violently ill! The experience and the energy I had encountered were so vile that my stomach churned. I voiced my feelings to the other members of the class and they spoke of similar reactions. Such an experience is horrendous! The ghastly energies that had permeated my being left me feeling tainted, and as a result with a need to cleanse myself. The horror of the experience stayed with me for days. I can only admire those psychics who subject themselves to such gruesome experiences in order to help law enforcement solve violent crimes. Perhaps they are able to practice such psychic investigations without becoming exposed to the emotions of those involved. I can't seem to do so, and so I choose not to use my abilities in this way.

Nowhere near as intense as emotional sensing can be is the sensing of the mind of another. Such an activity can reveal clear, concise minds, that process rapidly; slower detailed minds that need time to sift through all the information at their disposal; minds that flit, never seeming to access the depths, and minds that cannot rise above the fixed knowledge that absorbs them. Motivation (the emotional intent behind any mental activity) adds another dimension to the energetic signature. The devious individual's mind, as it analyses self-serving possibilities, is different to the mind that employs a scientific approach in its analysis of available facts. Those dominated by emotion may have little use for their minds and translate each situation into cause for emotional reaction on their part!

I recall an occasion when I was tuning into a young man's mind. It felt all but dead, and capable only of mechanical thought. The entertainment of creative and stimulating ideas was impossible for him. In response to my query, he revealed he was on medication for a mental condition. Each mind is complex and different—but those differences can be felt and interpreted, and can enable the psychic to relate to people on their own terms.

THE TRUTH SEEKER

Physical energies can provide valuable information. It is not unusual for me to feel the pain or physical discomfort a person is experiencing. Some people aren't aware when their physical body is in distress, perhaps because the symptoms have developed so gradually that the mind has suppressed or ignored them. One day, I tuned into a young lady whose lungs felt badly impregnated with toxins, and I knew the damage was not due to the usual lung trauma caused by smoking. My queries as to a possible cause revealed she worked with leadlight glass. I advised this young lady to consider the damage she was doing to her body and suggested she took steps to protect her lungs from the serious dangers associated with her chosen career.

On another occasion when I tuned into the health of a lady, I felt that an area of her chest had been badly burnt. The life force normally present throughout the bodies of all physical beings was absent in the area she informed me had been treated with radiation in order to destroy the cancer there.

When sensing the physical energies of a person, I invariably feel the energies through my own body. One night, a few minutes after a psychic development class had ended and I was still in highly receptive state, someone handed me a pen and requested I give them information about its owner. Intense pain shot through my hand. I dropped the pen! The owner had been in a car accident some weeks before and had received extensive and painful injury to her hands. While I am only deeply sensitive when my mind is in a trance state, and when I deliberately tune in, some psychics continuously absorb the feelings of those in their environment. Since I am a person who is normally strongly focused on what is happening around me, constantly considering and analysing all information, I naturally exclude my psychic talents most of the time.

Clear sensing is a resource that is neither recognised nor used to any great degree. Since it can be applied to ascertaining the mental, emotional and physical health of an individual, it has a wide variety of possible uses and would greatly enhance a medical provider's ability to diagnose illness. Just as I learned to do this, so can others.

Cleansing

What action does one take after absorbing energies that are unpleasant or horrific? Energy manifests. Energy entering the physical body has an impact on the cells of our body, our moods and our energy levels. The implications of this give reason to the undesirability of retaining negative energies in the psyche. Expelling them is necessary in order to avoid personal contamination physically, mentally and/or emotionally. While absorbing the negative energies of others may at times be unavoidable in order to psychically diagnose and assist, such energies are destructive. For those who are practicing psychics, or who are ultra-sensitive to the energies of those around them, cleansing is essential in order to ensure continued health and well-being.

Prayer and spiritual cleansing can prevent and negate contamination. After any activity that involves the use of my body as a conduit for the energies of others, I consciously clear my body of residual energy. While there are doubtless many ways of clearing, I prefer to ask the aid of those in the spiritual kingdoms, as I visualise a pure spiritual white light from above, raining down, over, and through me. As the light penetrates my being, I visualise and mentally affirm the light removing all negative energy and transforming it into positive energy.

Clairaudience

Clairaudience is the word used to describe the receipt of audible information, usually from those in other dimensions but sometimes from those living. While clairaudience is the ability to 'hear' voices inside the head, such communications operate on a different frequency to that of a person communicating physically with someone in the same room. For this reason, knowledge from those dimensions not of the physical often combines limited verbal information, conceptual knowledge and symbolic visuals.

Although on occasions I 'hear' in my mind an actual voice talking to me, it is not the usual way I receive psychic communication. The crystal-clear voice that answered my question during the following incident was an exception rather than the rule.

At the end of 2002, I was on holiday at my brother John's place on the Gold Coast in Queensland, visiting family and generally enjoying a break from work. On the Saturday, I drove to Brisbane to visit friends and then went on to join relatives for a barbecue. I ignored the unsettled feeling in my stomach and joined in. That apparently had not been such a good idea, as I began to feel worse and as the evening wore on, I guessed I had contracted a stomach bug.

THE TRUTH SEEKER

I stayed overnight. It was not a good night. The next morning I decided to return to the Gold Coast where I rested all day, drinking only water. Common sense departs with illness. It was not until the following morning when the pain moved from the centre of my stomach to the right hand side, that the thought occurred to me I could have appendicitis. John took me to his doctor who advised me to go to hospital immediately.

Upon my arrival at the hospital, they lost no time in taking my temperature and giving me a blood test. My temperature was up and I had a bacterial infection. Because of my allergies, they decided not to have me ingest anything before x-raying me. The doctor explained it would be necessary to operate and although I wasn't quite with it, I gained the impression the situation was probably very serious. An operation, which lasted almost three hours, proved the problem to be a ruptured appendix. The surgeon did keyhole surgery and followed up by prescribing a number of different antibiotics, none of which were on my allergy list.

The following afternoon I was lying in bed feeling annoyed. I complained to those beings in spirit who were there to aid me when I did psychic readings for people. *Why did this have to happen while I'm on holiday?'*

A clear voice replied, 'Otherwise you'd be dead now.'

I wondered if I had needed to be in a hospital that did not have a build-up of patients awaiting attention from an overworked staff, as was normally the case in Sydney hospitals at that time—and more so during the Christmas break.

While clearly spoken words are obviously possible, the way in which I usually receive information is through conceptual ideas that drop into my mind. This process seems to allow access to a complete knowledge I have only to consider in order to unravel and understand all the information contained therein. Frequently, information is relayed through pictures. I might be shown a person involved in a particular physical activity, displaying an emotion of sadness or happiness, or perhaps the blindness of a person refusing to look. Images are frequently used that employ the symbolism I have learned over the years through my study of dream analysis and tarot cards.

When messages are received for others, because much of the information imparted by those in spirit requires interpretation, it is not always easy to accurately assess the meaning of that information without a degree of feedback from the person the message is for. This feedback confirms the reader is on the right track. Unfortunately, this activity can provide fodder for the sceptic. While it's possible to receive words telepathically, the different frequencies involved in communication between non-physical and physical beings leads to the likelihood that information will be received via concepts that are often accompanied by visual symbols.

Telepathy

Telepathy, the mind-to-mind communication between people, can happen in a variety of ways.

On occasion, a thought deliberately sent to another person may be received by that person. However, the most common form of telepathy is of a linking of minds between closely connected people. This mental connection is often found in twins or those who have shared their lives for long periods. The frequency with which mind-to-mind communication occurs is difficult to determine as it is only when a comment is made it is revealed the other person has the same thoughts.

I recall having a telepathic rapport with Allan. I worked with Allan over a number of years and as we were both born under air (mind) signs, we thought alike and our minds operated on similar frequencies. My work responsibilities included office administration and the handling of accounts. Frequently, I would suggest to him an idea that had not been under discussion, or remind him of something that needed to be done only to have him tell me he was already thinking about it or actually doing it.

Over the years, I have tested my various psychic abilities in a number of ways. 'Mastermind' is a game where one person selects from eight differently coloured pegs, four pegs of differing or the same colour. Then the chosen pegs are placed in shielded peg holes.

The other player attempts to guess the colour and position of the pegs hidden by the first player, by placing four coloured pegs into peg holes at the opposite end of the board. The first player then marks the result that reveals the number of correct colour choices in the correct position and the number of correct colour choices in the wrong position. Which colour is right or wrong, isn't revealed. The possibility of guessing the four-peg colour combination from eight differently coloured pegs is one thousand, two hundred and ninety six to one.

When my sister Sonia visited from New Zealand, we went on a bus trip to the Blue Mountains. I had a pocket size Mastermind with me and we

THE TRUTH SEEKER

decided to play a game. My sister took the first turn and placed her pegs. I said to myself, *I will pick out the same colour pegs, in the same order she has.* I then selected the four correct pegs and placed them in the correct holes. Stunned, she cried, 'How did you do that? Yvonne, (our sister) said to watch out for you!' I explained what I had done. I wasn't able to successfully repeat the exercise.

Another person I found myself to be on the same wavelength with was Susie—one of the friends I met on Norfolk Island. Over the years, we have had many experiences of a telepathic nature. Susie remained on Norfolk Island when I returned to New Zealand for three months before I moved to Australia. Over the next three years, we communicated regularly by mail. In all that time, we never really replied to each other's letter. Each of our letters crossed in the post. In one letter, she mentioned the day and time she was writing to me, and when I calculated the time difference between Norfolk Island and Australia, I realised we had been writing to each other on the same day and at the same hour.

Susie returned to Australia and communication continued with visits and telephone connections. Often, as I thought, *I must phone Susie*, the phone rang and Susie was on the line. At other times when I phoned Susie her first comment to me was, 'I was just thinking about you.' Many such experiences are not seen for the telepathic connections they actually are, and are labelled coincidences.

When Susie and I decided to play Mastermind, I realised almost immediately she was reading my mind. On her very first turn, she picked the correct colours, but didn't place them in the right order! This error was corrected with her next effort. I took three attempts to guess the colour and order of her pegs. Then it was her turn to again guess my colours. *Okay*, I thought, *I'll focus my mind on different colours to the ones I have placed on the board.* Susie immediately chose the colours I had focused on. My spontaneous and delighted laughter demanded explanation, and I advised her what I had done. I then had some regrets, as subsequently it didn't matter which colours I concentrated on she always selected the correct colours, but sometimes took one or two turns to get them in the correct position. Likewise, I always managed to place the correct colours in their correct position in one to three turns.

With both my sister and Susie, I experienced spontaneous and deliberate mind connection. I deliberately misled Susie using mental focus. But once she knew I was focusing my mind on the wrong colours, she was able to bypass any mental suggestion and successfully access the information she required from my mind. On the other hand, when playing with my sister, after I was able to accurately access the knowledge relating the colours and positions of each peg and advise her of this, I was no longer able to do so. It is possible to deliberately block our mind to others, and in this case my sister had effectively done so. Since Susie and I did not bother to block our intended actions from each other, we continued to access the information we needed.

Deliberately Influencing Others

As the following story indicates, it is possible to influence others whether they are in your presence or not. While most telepathic connections are usually not deliberate, the deliberate sending of messages in order to influence the behaviour of a person (even though the recipient may have no conscious knowledge of having received the message) is possible.

Early one Saturday morning I climbed out of bed, still tired from a week of working nine to five. Motivation kept me moving as I prepared to join the bush-walking group for a weekend down the south coast. After the usual ablutions, breakfast et cetera, I packed the car with food, clothing and sleeping gear and was on my way. I successfully negotiated the harbour bridge and enjoyed the feeling of freedom I always experience when I leave the city for a country destination.

Suddenly my subconscious, finding my mind no longer busy, interrupted. It replayed the last minute functions of turning off this and that electrical appliance. Then it stopped at the curling wand. Frustration surged as in my mind's eye I could see the light on the curling wand. *I am NOT going back!* I determined.

My problem solving abilities kicked into overdrive as I considered my options. My daughter, who lived nearby, would be calling around to my place during the afternoon to feed our cat. So Sharon was volunteered as the solution—not that she had any say in the matter. This was during the 1980s so there were no cell phones. My problem was—how could I ensure she would turn off the curling wand when the possibility of talking to her on the telephone was limited to the time she would actually be at my place feeding the cat and who knew when that would be? The alternative was sending her instructions mentally. *Could I do it?*

With great determination, I visualised the curling wand on the dressing table, with its light on and then I spoke to my daughter forcefully in my mind, **Sharon!** *Look at the light on the curling wand!* **Sharon!** *Turn off the* *curling wand!*' After repeating the exercise two or three times, I relaxed and enjoyed the drive to my destination. I had a pleasurable weekend and returned home to find the curling wand switched off.

On Monday, the phone rang and after I answered, the voice of my daughter accused, 'Mum! You left the curling wand on! I *never* go around to that side of the bed,' she stated emphatically. She continued to reiterate how she couldn't understand why she had gone around to the side of the bed where the dressing table was, as there was no reason for her to do so. Nor could she understand why she had sat down on the bed. It was of course from this vantage point she could see the light on the curling wand. Sharon had no conscious awareness she had heard my message. In order for her to respond to my instruction, she found herself moving without conscious thought or intent, to the best place from which to see the curling wand, so she could execute the task I had set her.

How often do other people influence our behaviour as I did with Sharon? My emotional and psychic connection to my daughter no doubt played a significant role in the successful outcome. While it is important to realise such influence is possible, it is unlikely such a connection could influence another to do anything that goes against their own ideals and wishes.

Psychometry

Just as we record on CDs and DVDs, life itself records events on all manner of objects. Psychometry involves the sensitive person focusing on an object and using clairvoyant, clairaudient and/or clairsentient abilities in order to gain the information the object has recorded. Traumatic events that impose a strong energetic impression on the environment are the most likely recordings to be felt or seen by the sensitive person. Sound, pictures, and all the emotions of the original event can be accessed by the psychic. On many occasions where a ghost is observed, what is in fact seen is a recording of the past—the soul of the individual has long gone.

Many materials record information. When practicing psychometry, psychics usually find that tuning into metal jewellery is much easier than using other personal belongings as metal easily records and retains the events that happen around it. Psychics have tuned into historic happenings through the energetic recordings in buildings, stone and even in the countryside, where, for example, battles have been fought. Validation of information accessed provides confirmation the data gained is not a product of the imagination.

JOAN L BOLER

In the earlier years when I was developing my psychic abilities through classes, I was often surprised when feedback supported my findings, as frequently I was unable to tune into anything at all. I recall one night in a class of around sixteen people. A lady had brought in an item wrapped in a cloth for us to read psychically. We were asked to discover as much as we could about the object, including from what part of the world it had come.

I was the second to last person to read. As I tuned into the item, the vision that invaded my consciousness included a castle surrounded by grass, trees and forest. I did not see other buildings. Since geography is not my strong point, as I viewed the image in my mind of the map of the world, I was drawn to the British Isles. Had I been as familiar with the British Isles as I am with New Zealand and Australia, I might have been able to be more specific regarding location. I then intuited what I was viewing dated back to the Middle Ages. From my vantage point above the castle, I could see the guards on the parapets. Their helmets were made of metal and had a sharp spike moulded into the centre at the top/back of the helmet.

Of the fourteen class members preceding me with their descriptions of what they had sensed, none had mentioned anything about a castle. Since I didn't have a lot of confidence in my clairvoyant capabilities, I was more than ready to dismiss what I had seen. However, my teacher was always saying, 'Whatever you see, say it, no matter how way out it might seem.' And so I spoke up.

The lady who had brought the item into class revealed what looked like an ordinary piece of stone. She explained, 'It is a small piece of stone from the family castle in Ireland.' The castle had apparently been built around the 1300s, and when her daughter had travelled to Ireland and visited the castle, she had decided to bring a small piece of it back with her.

The helmets worn by the castle guards fascinated me—the spike especially intrigued me. I could not recall ever having seen the like in any movie, book or documentary. A check at the library revealed the helmets were in use in Ireland from around the end of the fourteenth century to the sixteenth century.

Psychometry offers another way to gain insight into times passed. To compare known data to that obtained by the psychic at such places as archaeological digs will perhaps be something we will see in the future. Such information can only enhance our knowledge and understanding of our past.

THE TRUTH SEEKER

Intuition

An intuitive or gut feeling of trepidation or joy can be accompanied by a flash of illuminating knowledge. A valuable resource is often wasted in a world where many don't acknowledge the paranormal and even those who do can become too caught up in a busy lifestyle and ignore the feelings that can come and go in a moment.

One of the areas Dean Radin researched involved experiments where a subject sat in front of a blank computer screen. Electrodes were attached to two fingers on the left hand of the subject in order to measure changes in skin resistance. An electrode was placed on their third finger to monitor blood flow. Forty photos were randomly flashed on and off the screen while the computer measured the subject's reactions *before* each photo appeared. Reactions hardly changed at all before peaceful photos were shown. It was before the emotional photos appeared that the blood flow dramatically changed. Radin found his results difficult to accept as true. A disbelieving professor at the University of Amsterdam, Dr Dick Bierman, ran the same experiment and obtained the same results. Others have since performed the same tests with similar outcomes.[93]

We absorb massive amounts of data from our surroundings on an unconscious level. This data is obtained through our visual, tactile, audio and psychic senses. In a computer-like manner, and without conscious thought or awareness, information received is assessed against previous knowledge and can result in timely warnings or a confirmation of 'rightness' or 'wrongness'. Often I experience vague feelings of unease that come and go in a split second. A busy mind can block or ignore such messages, and in today's hectic world we often move too fast to listen to these timely warnings, as I did in the following situation.

The rain was pouring down as I made my way into a café in Glebe. Water dripped everywhere as I stopped inside the entrance. I noted a container holding a number of very wet umbrellas. As I folded my new black umbrella and placed it with the others, a feeling of disquiet accompanied the thought, *Someone might take my umbrella by mistake.* In that moment, I was distracted from the split second thought as my focus shifted to finding a table. When I went to collect my umbrella, it was gone but there was an old navy umbrella of a similar size remaining that did not belong to anyone in the café. It's reasonable to assume the presence of an umbrella similar to my

---

[93] Radin, Dean. 'Is there a sixth sense?' *Psychology Today*, New York: Jul/Aug 2000. Vol33, Iss. 4; pp. 44-51.

own triggered my unconscious mind to send a warning even though I had no conscious memory of having noticed the other umbrella. However, such visual observations cannot account for all such feelings.

Some years ago, I was looking for accommodation for my daughter, myself and our cat Sam and I was yet to find suitable housing. The real estate agent had given me the key so I could view a place. As I checked the street numbers, I realised the next building on the right was the correct house. My gaze moved to the building itself, and for no apparent reason, a euphoric feeling invaded my psyche. The house was ordinary and the grounds very basic—certainly not a place to evoke such an intense feeling. So what had caused such a potent reaction in me?

I viewed the interior of the small three-bedroom home and decided the place would suit our needs. Upon my return to the agent, I signed the lease. We moved in. To my dismay, I discovered there were two large dogs living next door on one side, and one little one on the other side. Images of Sam cowering and hiding from the beasts came to mind and I rebuked myself for not checking more thoroughly before signing the lease.

The cat moved in and in no time at all was king of his castle. Many was the time I would note him in one of his favourite places—next to the hedge where the large dogs lived—an activity that tormented them to distraction. From being a cat that shot out the door and ran for cover, he became secure and happy in his kingdom. Passers-by laughed at Sam spread-eagled on his back on the front lawn in the sun in a deep and contented sleep.

Sam was not the only one content in the household. My daughter and I both found it perfect for our needs and we were happy during the time we lived there. Had I not experienced the remarkable feeling, I would no doubt have checked further into the suitability of the environment for the cat. The discovery of the presence of the dogs would have sent me looking elsewhere. The feeling told me beyond a shadow of a doubt this was a place where I would be happy, and for now at least this was where I was meant to be.

There are many reported instances of people avoiding dire consequences because they listened to their intuition. In eliminating scepticism, the use of intuition could become widespread, so this natural and valuable tool could play a part in avoiding and/or preventing, undesirable circumstances. When we respond to our inner voice, our lives become easier and trouble can often be avoided or minimised.

THE TRUTH SEEKER

Revelation in the Palms

Palmistry involves both the intuitive and the scientific. Every aspect of our physical form reflects our individual essence. Over time, palms have been used by many as a visual and intuitive way to analyse the nature of the soul through its expression in the palms. Through studying palms, the perceptive person is able ascertain the nature of the individual and determine the directions the soul is likely to take during its lifetime.

The use of the palm by the psychic as a conduit to the soul of the individual, so the reader can clairvoyantly access past events and likely future, is not the more scientific palmistry that has been studied over millennia. Rather, like psychometry, it uses the physical connection to the person (rather than an object) to obtain direct access the soul. Detailed predictions like, 'You will meet a tall, dark stranger' are not gained from palmistry. Such predictions are the domain of the clairvoyant and prophecy.

Palmistry is thought to have originated in the East, as references to palmistry are found in the ancient Vedic text 'Vasishtha'. It was practiced in India two thousand years before the birth of Jesus, and was a widespread and respected art.

There are Chinese texts on palmistry dating back to before the fourth century BCE. Plato (c. 427-347 BCE), Hippocrates (130-200 CE) and Galen (129-199 CE) were some of the people of great standing who respected and practiced the art. Aristotle (384-322 CE) mentions palmistry and the meanings of the length of the lines in the palm in his 'De Historia Animalium'. The accumulated information over this great period of time includes valid understanding and knowledge, and information based on superstition and the attitudes of times long gone.

The palms of the hands reveal our total identity. Just as the brain has two hemispheres that operate in harmony with each other, each performing a part in the day-to-day activities we are involved in, so too do the hands display the way in which our brains are 'wired'. Because of this, it's possible to discover the personality and potential of the individual through reading their palm.

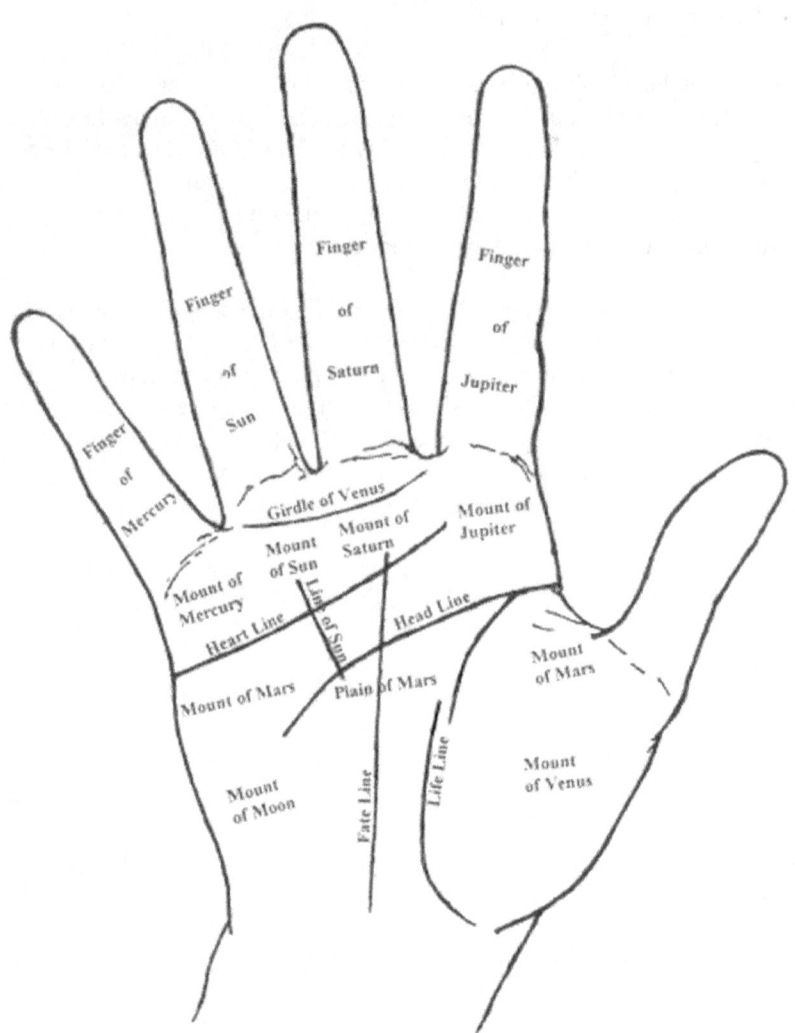

Figure 2 - Palm with broken life line

THE TRUTH SEEKER

Prediction of likely situations in a person's life, along with the challenges and difficulties they might face and why, is possible. However, it should be noted that through changes in attitudes and behaviour, new pathways can be created in the brain which will result in changes in the palms, and as a consequence changes to the person's future. Since people do not readily change their behaviour, in most cases the type of experiences a person will encounter can be accurately assessed years in advance.

Over the years, I have tested ideas put forward in the many books I have read on palmistry, and discovered that while some sources of information provide extremely valuable insight, others are inaccurate and poorly researched, especially the predictive information. Often, authors simply repeat what they have read without testing for accuracy.

From time to time, I have encountered people who have been advised by palmists they were going to die at a specific age—in some cases whilst they were still relatively young. Naturally, this information caused them considerable distress. The predictions were wrong! They were based on the belief that when the lifeline on the palm is broken and not joined by another line, the break indicates death (Figure 2 – page 118). My observations over the years have provided me with evidence that the broken line usually means the person will experience a complete change in their life at the time of the break. For many, a break in the line signifies a change of state or country. This change will cause them to leave behind all that is familiar. In fact, you could say the *old life* is dead to the person—not that the person is dead.

To those who have unravelled its secrets, palmistry provides a quick way of obtaining a wide range of information about a person, including their personality, intelligence, creative ability, emotional status, potential health and likely life path. While intuition plays a part in ascertaining the way in which the makeup of the individual is expressed, and how the life path is played out, essentially, like astrology, palmistry is a scientific study.

Remote or Distant Viewing

Remote or distant viewing is seeing clairvoyantly what is happening in another place and/or in another time. As unbelievable as it might seem, it is possible for the conscious mind to access distant places and times. The experience can include the 'hearing' and 'sensing' of what is being said by people at the chosen location.

There is little difference between an exercise where one tunes into a past crime via an object as in psychometry and distant or remote viewing. 'Distant viewing' is an exercise where one directs their mind to access a specific place and possibly a specific time. In order for an individual to achieve this, mental focus on their objective and belief their mind is capable of accessing places *any* physical distance from the body is necessary. As mentioned earlier in this chapter, the practice was used by America during the Cold War as a spying technique. In 1974, Russell Targ, along with his colleague Hal Puthoff, demonstrated to the CIA that retired police commissioner Pat Price could obtain details of a Soviet weapons laboratory in Siberia, with only its latitude and longitude as a guide. So successful was this effort, it resulted in a congressional investigation.[94]

Those who are able to view the future of individuals and predict the cataclysmic events of our world are called prophets or seers. But what is it they are really doing? Are they tuning into the likely future of the person or a location, or are they accessing a future time? Perhaps both of these possibilities can occur. We can only theorise on the complexities of time as viewed from differing perspectives.

Scientists who are investigating psychic phenomena are attempting to get their heads around the fact the mind is able to access knowledge from distant locations and from the past or the future. They are asking deep questions that go beyond the realm of science as we know it. No doubt in time the answers will be discovered.

'I Know'

An aspect of most genuine psychic experiences is the absolute 'knowing' that accompanies them.

I have spoken to women who have *felt* the exact time when conception has taken place. This may be due to the fact they are tuned into their physical body, or they have gained the information intuitively. Both are possible. Some women I know have simply known they were pregnant and some, like my friend Susie, knew not only that conception had taken place, but also what sex the child would be.

---

[94]Targ, Russell and Katra, Jane. 'Alternative Therapies in Health and Medicine' *Aliso Viego*: May/Jun 2001. Vol 7, Iss. 3; pp. 143-150.

THE TRUTH SEEKER

My friend Susie's psychic abilities extend beyond the telepathic experiences revealed as a result of our friendship. Sometimes Susie 'knows', although she can't explain how she knows.

Susie and her husband decided it was time to start a family. With excitement and anticipation, not to mention conscientious enthusiasm, they focused their efforts upon the task at hand. Unfortunately, ill health dogged Susie during this time and saw her in hospital on a number of occasions, so in spite of all their determined efforts over the next two years, each month revealed the same disappointing outcome.

Then one evening Susie and her husband went out to dinner with friends. The following morning Susie awoke, opened her eyes, and experienced a crystal-clear, unqualified knowing.

'I'm pregnant!' Susie announced to her husband. Then she added they were having a boy.

After breakfast Susie phoned her mother in Sydney and informed her she was pregnant and it was a baby boy. 'Oh dear God,' her mother replied, 'That's wonderful. What did the doctor say?'

'Well, I haven't been to the doctor yet. It only happened last night,' Susie explained. 'You said you wanted to be the first to know, so I'm telling you.'

Predictably, her mother reacted with, 'Oh good God, girl. Don't be ridiculous!'

Nine months later Susie gave birth to their son.

Their little boy was only nine months old when on the morning after Boxing Day 1978, Susie opened her eyes and said to her husband, 'I'm pregnant.'

He responded with, 'Oh-oh! Are you sure?'

'I'm positive and it's a little girl.' Susie confirmed. Then one or two mornings later Susie opened her eyes and said to him, 'It's *twin* girls!'

A week or so later, Susie took her nine-month old son to see her Irish doctor. 'Guess what Michael? I'm having twin girls!'

'Glory be to God, girl. You're not pregnant again?'

Susie confirmed she was pregnant with twin girls.

'Jesus, Mary and Joseph, and what would be makin' you think that?' he asked.

'I don't know, but I know it as clear as a bell and I need a referral back to the gynaecologist.'

The doctor shook his head. He had twin boys himself, and up until a short time before their birth he and his wife had had no idea they were having twins. And now here was Susie telling him, within days of conception, she knew she was having twin girls! He laughed.

At fourteen weeks, Susie had a show of blood and her doctor said they had better get a scan done. 'Oh good,' she said, 'I'll be able to see my twins.' He laughed. But this was an opportunity for Susie to ensure not only that her two little girls were fine, but also that the doctors were aware of both babies so they would receive the medical care they needed.

In 1979, there were very few ultrasound machines in Sydney. Although they did not have the sophistication of more recent models, they were capable of providing the information needed to confirm the presence of twins. It was with considerable anticipation and excitement that Susie went along for her ultrasound. As requested, she drank three pints (a litre and a half) of water before climbing on to the table. Once there, her stomach was covered with gel and the ultrasound probe was moved backwards and forwards over her stomach. After a little while she was told, 'It's all right. The baby's head is over the mouth of the cervix, and that's what has caused the pressure you have been experiencing that resulted in the show of blood. Everything is perfectly normal. The heartbeat is fine!'

Susie said, 'Well, that's good, but where's the other twin?'

'I beg your pardon?'

'Well, there's twin girls.'

The doctor pulled out the letter from Susie's doctor and commented, 'It doesn't say anything about twins here.'

Then the radiographer asked, 'What makes you think you're having twins?'

Susie explained that she *knew* she was having twin girls, and since she knew the examination would end at this point, she pleaded with them to take another look. They relented and checked further. By this time, Susie's

THE TRUTH SEEKER

bladder situation was becoming urgent, especially as they kept pushing down with the probe.

Once again the conclusion was reached—there was only one baby.

Susie hadn't anticipated finding both babies would be so difficult! She was determined she wouldn't leave the table until they had found the other twin. It was time to use extreme measures. From past experience, Susie knew no medical person could resist the chance to view her two completely separate, functioning reproductive systems. It was possible, she advised them, that the other baby might be in the second uterus.

That got their attention!

Three more medical people came into the room as they began the search for the second uterus. Amazement and excitement took over when the other uterus was revealed on the ultrasound screen. They viewed with fascination one uterus with a baby in it and the other uterus that was about the same size, alongside it. No additional baby was found.

The doctor told Susie, who was still insisting there was another baby, to calm down. He patted her on the shoulder and said he would write a report for the gynaecologist, and then he turned away and walked towards the door.

As the doctor reached the door, the nurse, who still had the probe resting on Susie, turned around to speak to him. As she did so, the probe zipped right up over Susie's navel and went *blip-blip.* The doctor stopped. The nurse turned back to Susie and guided the probe backwards and forwards just below her navel. Again it went *blip-blip, blip-blip* and then the nurse said, 'There's another baby! Doctor, look at this.'

The doctor was already at her side. Pandemonium broke loose. Excitement spilled over to the patients in the waiting room who were waiting for their turn with the ultrasound.

It occurred to them perhaps the baby had somersaulted, and so they put a cross where that baby was and then moved the probe down and confirmed the presence of the first baby. Enthusiasm and excitement completely replaced the earlier scepticism. This was the first set of twins to be detected with the ultrasound machine in this clinic!

A teary-eyed nurse asked Susie, '*How* did you know?'

The old machines didn't print out like the newer models, so someone rushed out and found a Polaroid camera to photograph the ultrasound screen showing the twins.

Desperation to get to the bathroom overruled all else as Susie begged temporary leave of them. The fuss continued. One of the nurses offered to make her a cup of tea. The radiologist offered the use of his office so she could phone her husband to tell him the good news. A vindicated Susie couldn't resist. 'Oh, I told him the news ages ago!'

Susie gave birth to two beautiful healthy daughters.

At no time did Susie question the truth of either the fact she was pregnant with twins, or the gender of the babies. Even when faced with the conviction of the doctors that there was only one baby and the lack of evidence from the ultrasound, Suzie didn't waiver—so deep was her conviction that what she knew was true.

The knowing comes from experiencing an expanded state of consciousness. This state of consciousness transcends our normal awareness and incorporates more of our total identity. It seems that at this stage of our evolution, expansion of consciousness only operates during trance states, such as is experienced during the first moments we emerge from sleep—as is evidenced by Susie's insights upon awakening.

Avoiding Pitfalls and Developing Skills

Each of the psychic abilities can provide us with a larger view of life. Over many years of involvement in the world of psychic ability, I have found not all psychic experiences are reliable. The individual who experiences the paranormal can be certain of its validity if the extraordinary knowing that accompanies powerful experiences is present. As not all experiences are accompanied by this knowing, feedback becomes important in validating the experience itself and the interpretation placed on the experience.

One night I was teaching a class. On this particular night, the psychic exercise was psychometry. Each of us had placed a personal belonging made of metal into a covered box. Then we each withdrew someone else's object from the box and proceeded to tune into it and search for specific information relating to the owner and their home environment.

THE TRUTH SEEKER

I began to psychically read the object I held in my hand, describing the home and surroundings of its owner. After each comment I made, a gentleman who was doing this exercise for the first time commented, 'I got that.' After he repeated this comment four or five times, I was curious as to why he was seeing the same images as me as he was supposed to be tuning into the object he held.

The gentleman was holding the object that belonged to me and when he focused upon it, he tuned directly into the information I was receiving. Whilst he showed ability, he needed to learn to tune in specifically to the information required. Feedback resulted in him being aware of his mistake and future exercises were error free. The most effective way to eliminate such inaccuracies is to, before beginning, define in the mind the subject and the purpose of the exercise.

There is a number of ways in which information obtained can be misunderstood and placed in the wrong context. Some naturally talented clairvoyants receiving images and knowledge don't know how to discern the specific person or environment to which the images belong. Sometimes they will attribute occurrences that relate to other family members or close friends to the person they are reading for. Once again, prior specification or identification as to who the information received is to be about can eliminate such confusion.

It is also possible for a psychic to tune into a person's wishes and desires that might, or might not, come to fruition. Many years ago, I received a reading that contained specific forecasts that confirmed my dearest wishes and desires for my future. But not one of the promised forecasts happened. The psychic had tuned into valid information—but that information was my dreams for the future, and not my actual future.

There are psychics who attribute their own emotions to the person for whom they are reading and twist the information accordingly. Strong belief, fear and lack of clear focus, can influence experiences and produce inaccurate and/or misunderstood results. For example, if a psychic believes the future they *see* psychically can't be changed, a doom and gloom attitude can dominate a reading.

Everyone can learn to draw, but not everyone can become an artist. In the same way, the different psychic skills can be developed, in varying degrees, by those who wish to put in the effort. Groups are the best way to work, as group energy enhances one's abilities. Over time, the energy of the group is no longer necessary as the psychic energy of the individual is boosted through the ongoing practice of deep relaxation and the resultant centring and healing of the soul. A group also provides an environment where information received can be tested. As knowledge and experience increases, high levels of accuracy can be achieved.

Potential

It is important to recognise that paranormal ability is a part of life and the potential of every human. It is time to let go of disbelief in what is already proven and to squash the superstition that is the aftermath of religious fanaticism. Psychic ability has a lot to offer humanity as a whole and its practice can enhance the life of each individual prepared to work to develop themselves and their latent skills.

Scepticism is a healthy approach to knowledge that is not personal experience. The sceptics in our society who reject the paranormal need to avail themselves of the knowledge gained through stringent research over many years. Die-hard fundamentalist sceptics who reject in the face of proof are not capable of unbiased judgement.

Evolution towards spirituality manifests in the opening of a person's supernatural connections to the psychic and spiritual worlds. The more a person expresses spirituality, the greater their access to the higher dimensions and the knowledge and understanding found therein. As each person grows into their potential, they reap the rewards of the inner self revealed along with an amazing array of paranormal skills and abilities.

Chapter 6

Mind Powers, Magic and Miracles

Every Cause has its Effect; every Effect has its Cause; everything happens according to Law; Chance is but a name for Law not recognized; there are many planes of causation, but nothing escapes the Law.

Le Kybalion[95]

Manipulation of the Physical World

Mind powers, magic and miracles are words used to describe manipulation of the physical world. In essence, although techniques and tools may vary, all who work with the natural laws that govern who and what we are, and every aspect of the cosmos we are part of, can create what they will and achieve magic. In fact, each of us is already a creator, and as children at play, we innocently create what comes into our lives each day. Awareness and understanding of our own involvement in what manifests in our lives is important if we are to become empowered and achieve our dreams.

The understanding of how we ourselves, as part of creation, operate is intrinsic to unlocking the mysteries of magic. Long accepted scientific rules have been proven to be false. New science that has not only taken scientists out of their comfort zone, but left them floundering has also enabled greater insight into the workings of magic.

Most religions have a history of belief in paranormal powers. Religion is not a pre-requisite in the manifestation of miracles, nor does belonging to a particular religion bestow an exclusive right to create miracles. Such ideas deny not only the basic spirituality of all human beings, but also that paranormal ability is the rightful inheritance of all.

---

[95] Anonymous (the 'Three Initiates'), *Le Kybalion* (Hermetic Philosophy), Yogi Publication Society, 1908.

In spite of differences in race and ideologies, the Masters of the past have bequeathed us with knowledge of how to become a miracle worker. The teachings of the Masters insist on our ability to perform miracles through command and belief. Buddhist monks spend years perfecting their mental and miraculous skills using discipline and trance states. Most followers of witchcraft and the natural religions of today know of and understand not only the power of the mind, but also the power contained in physical, terrestrial, cosmic and celestial energies.

Magic and miracles are within our capabilities. In order to achieve success, it is necessary to be aware of and to work with the laws involved.

Scientific Breakthroughs

Scientists from the seventeen hundreds until recently have denied the possibility of their physical laws being breached and demeaned or explained away happenings outside the realm of their science. As a result, a large percentage of the world's population make decisions and run their lives based upon a range of beliefs, thought to be backed by the science they were taught, that are simply not valid.

Not everyone has accepted scientists' teachings. Those versed in magic, have been defying the beliefs of the scientific community and achieving magic. One such person was French occult author and magician Eliphas Levi (1810-1875). He stated, *Magic is the traditional science of the secrets of Nature which has been transmitted to us from the Magi. By means of this science the adept becomes invested with a species of relative omnipotence and can operate super-humanly—that is, after a manner which transcends the normal possibility of man.*[96]

New science now explains at least some of what the miracle workers and magicians of the world have been achieving throughout the ages.

Quantum mechanics has amazed those in the scientific community who have not only had to reassess their opinion as to what is and isn't possible, but have also been placed in a position where they need to explain the inconceivable. Physicists, though they are as yet unable to explain this, have proved that consciousness affects the behaviour of photons (the smallest particles that do not break down into even smaller parts). In his famous 1909

---

[96] Levi, Eliphas, *Dogme et Rituel de la Haute Magie (Transcendental Magic: Its Doctrine and Ritual)*, 1854 and 1856.

double-slit experiment with light, English physicist Geoffrey Taylor revealed that matter and energy can display the character of both waves and particles.[97] In 1998, members of the Condensed Matter Physics Department at the Weizmann Institute of Science conducted further testing using more sensitive technology and confirmed the earlier results. It was also discovered that observation affects reality and the more focused the observer, the greater the effect.[98]

The implications of these experiments take us into the realms of possibility previously ascribed to science fiction by most people. By simply observing our environment, we can direct and change it. Or through our thoughts and constant beliefs, each of which has its own frequency, we have an impact on our environment.

In view of the mind's impact upon photons, it is not surprising research is now revealing the plasticity of the brain. Until recently, it was believed the brain became fixed after childhood and brain cells began to die, never to be replaced. Evidence now reveals this is simply not so. No matter the age of the person, if brain damage occurs, it is possible for the brain to create new neural pathways in another part of the brain.[99] While scientific understanding of the power of the mind is yet to be fully grasped, neuroplasticity nevertheless confirms the mind is more capable and versatile than previously thought.

In spite of there being no conclusive proof, scientific understanding has generally held that the brain is the source of the mind. American born neurosurgeon, Wilder Penfield Graves (1891-1976) worked with patients who suffered severe epilepsy for many years. Along with his colleague Herbert Jasper, he invented the 'Montreal Procedure' that involved the destruction of the nerve cells in the region of the brain in which seizures originate. In order to isolate the area of the brain involved while the patient was awake, he stimulated various areas of the patient's brain with electric probes.[100] The fact that patients maintained they were *not* responsible for the body movements that stimulation of the cortex evoked, and also that since the centrencephalic system (neurons in the central core of the brainstem, that

---

[97] Taylor, G I, *Interference fringes with feeble light.* Proc. Camb. phil. Soc. 15, pp.114-115 (SP IV, 1).
[98] Buks, E. , R. Schuster, M. Heiblum, D. Mahalu and V. Umansky. 'Dephasing in electron interference by a 'which path' dectector. ' *Nature*, 1998: 871:874
[99] 'Definition of Neuroplasticity.' *Medical Dictionary,* www. medterms. com (accessed 28 Oct. 2011)
[100] Jasper, H and Penfield, W *Epilepsy and the Functional Anatomy of the Human Brain,* Little, Brown and Co, 1954.

connect the two hemispheres) were fully active during cortical stimulation, the brain could not be shown to be responsible for consciousness.[101]

According to Dutch cardiologist and scientist Pim Van Lommel, in spite of there being no scientific proof, the conviction that brain function produces our mind has been taught as though there is no question as to its validity. The evidence he puts forward negating such a belief includes reports of patients who had been declared brain-dead by their physicians. When they subsequently regained consciousness, they maintained that during the time they were in a coma they experienced full conscious awareness while out of, and above, their body. During this time, they were able to *see* the people who came around them.[102]

Today, some in the academic community is questioning the validity of the belief the brain is responsible for consciousness, as evidence suggesting the mind is independent of the brain increases. Evidence for reincarnation, near-death experiences and out-of-body experiences certainly suggest strongly this is the case.

As a result of quantum physics, there is another aspect of scientific discovery that brings further understanding to the why of magic. Back in 1670, German philosopher, mathematician and physicist Gottfried Wilhelm Leibniz stated, 'Reality cannot be found except in One single source, because of the interconnection of all things with one another.'[103] Such ideas were seen by mainstream physicists to be unscientific until the twentieth century when quantum physics revealed Leibniz had been correct.

David Joseph Bohm (1917–1992), was born in Pennsylvania in the United States of America. A quantum physicist who worked for a time with Albert Einstein, Bohm contributed significantly to physics in the area of quantum mechanics and relativity theory. According to Bohm, in the current view of quantum physicists the idea of independent elementary parts as a fundamental reality has been replaced with the quantum interconnectedness of everything in existence.[104]

---

[101] 'Penfield, Wilder Graves.' *Complete Dictionary of Scientific Biography*. 2008 Encyclopedia. com. www. encyclopedia. com/doc/1G2-2830905999. html (accessed 11 Feb 2014)
[102] Van Lommel, Pim. 'Near death experience, consciousness, and the brain a new concept about the continuity of our consciousness based on recent scientific research on Near-death experience in survivors of cardiac arrest.' *The Journal of General Evolution*, Jan 2006, vol. 62, pp. 134-151.
[103] Philosophical Writings, 1670.
[104] Bohm, D.J., Hiley, B.J. *On the intuitive understanding of nonlocality as of physics,* Mar 1975, Vol. 5, issue 1, Implied by Quantum Theory, Foundations of Physics.

THE TRUTH SEEKER

Science is changing our view of the world and of humankind. Science says we are all connected on a quantum level, not only to each other, but also to all that is. Objects and entities in the physical, that we can see and touch and which appear to be separate, have an inner core that connects them to all else that exists. Connectedness, in part, clarifies much that has lacked explanation both scientifically and spiritually. This knowledge becomes important in the understanding of magic and miracles, as it seems to explain (at least in part) how it is possible to access and influence people, objects and situations, no matter the physical distance.

Cause

Order is omnipresent in the cosmos. No happening is without cause, and although many situations are thought to be random, causes are found within causes. The Universal Law is the first cause. All the Laws come under one law: the Law of Spiritual Love. Everything that exists is subject to this law. Through its governing astrological forces, it rules all life forms, all the planets, all the universes, and all that is.

The Law of Love causes the mirroring and attraction of like energies. For example, suppressed anger attracts violence, while guilt attracts punitive consequences. It is a shocking fact that the fearful victim consciousness is attracted into the environment of the aggressor or the predator. This results in the fear being confronted with the fearful. This understanding has eluded those who have a one-life belief, as they cannot see how the 'innocent' victim can have contributed towards the violence and abuse dealt out to them. It is through the law of Like attracts Like that we learn to change that within ourselves which does not reflect the Law of Love.

On a very basic level, we attract our environment. Astrological influences trigger a specific aspect of what lies within, which in turn attracts what comes into our life at that time. Through understanding the Law of Like attracts Like, we are not only looking at the answers to the why of the events in our lives, we are also looking at one of the underlying factors involved in the creation of magic and miracles.

The Creative Abilities of Each and Every Human Being

We are creators! Along with the scientific evidence proving we have an impact on and change the photons in our environment, there is little question we create what comes into our lives. When we also recognise how we are responsible not only for our current state of being, mentally, physically and emotionally, but also our environment, we can begin to reclaim our power. We all work with the basics of magic, whether we do so consciously or unconsciously. The natural abilities that enable us to do so are neither good nor evil—they exist because our greater spiritual nature has ensured this is so. The individual who is the conscious creator knows every thought, word and deed, past and present, not only has an impact on themselves, but also on their environment.

Our soul carries the sum of who, and what, we are. Each and every one of our previous life experiences has had an impact on our soul, and the resultant fears, beliefs, and emotions are stored in our unconscious. In addition, even though we may have no memory of decisions that have been made prior to our current life experience, previous determination to achieve desired goals also plays out in our lives. Whether those resolves are born of spiritual intent or not, the consequences are revealed in our life experiences. We are creators, albeit for the most part unconscious ones. We are author of both the happiness and the chaos that comes into our lives.

If our desires are strong and we wish to achieve our goals, we will attract the opportunities to fulfil those goals. That may mean skills need to be developed and knowledge gained. That some become bogged down in learning their lessons does not mean the law has failed. It means the goal is only reachable through experiential and sometimes painful learning that may take any length of time—from days to lifetimes.

Since our minds affect our environment at all times, the impact of our thoughts, both conscious and unconscious, is daunting. It is not possible for it to be otherwise. But how far does the power of the mind extend? What are we doing with this amazing power and exactly what are we creating? Like all those who have discovered the power of the mind and emotions, I have studied, observed and experimented, and although not always finding answers, I have come to many conclusions supported by evidence gained through experience.

A simple example of the effect of the focused mind, even when dealing with the most benign of thoughts, can be found in an incident that occurred a few years ago. I was on my regular morning walk when I noticed bushes with blue and mauve flowers gracing the gardens of the homes I passed. Images of my mother's garden remembered from my childhood years came to mind. In spite of my efforts to recall, the name of the flowers eluded me. Over the next two or three days, each time I walked past the bushes, I prodded my memory. Then suddenly, the name was there. Hydrangeas! I determined I

THE TRUTH SEEKER

would not forget their name again, and so, over the next couple of weeks as I passed these bushes each day, I repeated, *Hydrangeas, hydrangeas, hydrangeas.* Christmas arrived and I received a gift from my friend Carol. I opened the box and inside I found a cup, bowl, plate and tablemat, each of which was imprinted with hydrangeas. Was this random coincidence? I think not!

The multiplicity of ways in which our souls attract is endless. As we look deeper into the events in our lives, we begin to obtain answers as consistency confirms causes. Programmes like my *When I **need** money it comes to me,* ensure financial surprises in times of financial need. Over the years, I have successfully challenged my unconscious to solve the problems that have appeared in my life. When I command or demand with strong mental focus and deep emotion, my unconscious works upon a recipe for solutions. However, it is not necessary for me to make a deliberate demand. In the following experiences, as I viewed them in retrospect, I was able to see the probable underlying causes and forces that seem to have contributed towards creating the events that solved my transportation problems and aided my finances.

My little Mitsubishi Colt had required a replacement engine in January. The reconditioned motor had a three-month warranty and, wouldn't you just know it, around three weeks after the three months were up, the car began to expel suspicious looking smoke. Annoyance and agitation hovered over me during the next few weeks of driving.

June arrived. My plans to travel to Hawaii with two friends kept me focused on all I had to achieve before my departure. A few days before I was due to leave, Sydney was deluged with unusually heavy rains. As I was driving home in the continuous downpour, I noticed the windscreen was leaking. The new windscreen I had had installed a few months back had not been sealed properly. *Just what I needed!* I arrived home, parked my car at the roadside, opened up my umbrella and ran around to the back of the car to retrieve belongings from the boot. The boot was leaking.

I DON'T WANT THIS CAR ANYMORE, I silently screamed in my frustration.

At that time, I was living with my brother and sister-in-law. On the day of my departure, I handed the car keys to my sister-in-law and advised her that if she wanted to, she could use the car while I was away.

I returned from my holiday to a car that was written off. My sister-in-law had been driving around a corner in our street when a car driven by a

JOAN L BOLER

European lady coming from the opposite direction on the wrong side of the road appeared in front of her. The head-on collision, though not at speed, not only did extensive damage to the front of the car, it also left my sister-in-law with whiplash. I was not unhappy the car was written off, especially as the insurance value was about to drop by a thousand dollars with the renewal due in three weeks' time. I received $4,000 for my Mitsubishi Colt—around $2,500 more than I would have received had I attempted to sell it—if I could have sold it in the condition it was in!

Was my unconscious responsible for the demise of my Mitsubishi Colt? Did it carry out my strong emotional wish regarding my not wanting the car anymore?

I was dismayed as the possibility occurred to me that my frustrated outburst on that wet rainy day, prior to my departure, was probably responsible for not only my vehicle's demise, but also for the whiplash my sister-in-law received. I needed to be much more careful about how I expressed my feelings when I was emotional, as I knew it was possible the energy I expelled in my comment could have provided the energetic power needed to execute the wish contained in my outburst. The next time I wished for anything, I determined I would use words that ensured no one, including myself, was hurt.

I replaced my Colt with a Ford Laser. Five years later, around April, my then ten-year-old Ford Laser wasn't running well and, since I had spent $2,800 on it before Christmas, I decided to dispose of it before it cost me even more money. I was fed up with spending money on second-hand cars, so this time I determined I would buy a new car, even though it would place my finances under considerable pressure and mean extreme tightening of my belt. I felt my peace of mind warranted such a step.

It didn't take me long to decide which car to buy—a beautiful, blue Hyundai GETZ. Initially, all I was offered as trade-in on the Laser was $1,000. I was shocked and made it clear the amount was unacceptable. They upped it to $3,000. I wasn't happy, but after checking on the internet as to values and considering the unpredictable condition of the car, I did the deal.

The day before I was due to pick up my brand new car, I drove the seventy-five kilometres to Gosford on the Central Coast. On the return trip, whilst travelling along the motorway listening to music and allowing my mind to wonder, my unconscious produced an unsolicited idea. *It would be good if this car was written off.* My previous programming produced an immediate response. *Not in an accident!* Consideration of what I had said followed. *How stupid. How can you possibly write off a car without being in an*

THE TRUTH SEEKER

accident? End of story and end of self's discussion with self. My mind immediately switched back to everyday thoughts.

I had almost arrived home when the car stalled. *Oh no! Don't say I have to take this car to the repairers before I can trade it in.* After two or three tries, it started again, and relieved I drove around the corner and into my driveway. As I swung across the grass before turning into the carport, the car stalled again. In search of answers, I scanned the dials on the dash and noted the petrol light was on. 'That's ridiculous,' I said, recalling reading the petrol gauge some half an hour earlier. 'I have half a tank of petrol!'

Suddenly there was a *whoosh* and flames shot up all around the bonnet. Images of the car exploding propelled me into action. My frantic move to get to safety was stopped by the still fastened seat belt. I snapped the fastener open and jumped from the car, forgetting my handbag still on the passenger's seat. I raced around the rear of the car where the grass was on fire. My neighbour called me into her flat as she phoned the fire brigade.

Every part of me was shaking. My kindly neighbour plied me with tea and biscuits while a short distance away my car burned furiously. Ten long minutes later, the fire brigade arrived and doused the fire. The car was gutted. The front and side windows were blown out, the dash was warped and the seats were blackened holes.

'It's only in the movies that cars blow up—in real life, they rarely do,' the firemen advised—too late to be of benefit.

An hour later, I spoke to my insurance company. I listened dazed as I was advised the pay-out was $11,400. 'But you will have to pay the excess of $450.' The $3,000 trade-in I'd agreed to had been replaced with a pay-out of $10,950. The motor vehicle insurance company took care of everything. The car had been leaking petrol. Had the minor repairs done on the car two or three weeks before contributed to that? There was no way of establishing that possibility as fact.

The next morning, the car dealers phoned to confirm my new car would be ready for pickup that afternoon and I arranged to take $3,000 instead of the trade in vehicle. When I arrived to collect my new car, they advised me Hyundai had reviewed their prices with the result I would be paying $1,500 less than originally agreed. I think it probable the change in price had more to do with the fact they didn't have to absorb the cost of the trade-in. Since I had recently paid the registration on the Laser, I received $120 back. In addition, because the damage happened on the property where I lived, my householders' insurance covered the $430 replacement cost of the personal items destroyed inside the car. I was better off by a total of $9,450.

Was my unconscious mind the designer and executioner of the events that led to both my Mitsubishi Colt and my Ford Laser being written off? My strong emotional wish in both cases was to rid myself of problem vehicles. On each occasion, vehicle costs were putting my finances under considerable pressure that doubtless challenged my unconscious to comply with the programme *when I need money, it comes to me* and rectify the situation. The circumstances were exacerbated when, after two unreliable vehicles, I determined to buy a new vehicle, making it possible my extended credit was placing me in an untenable financial situation. My unconscious not only found a solution, it acted upon it, taking into account the car was *not in an accident*! What we have programmed into our unconscious is powerful and awareness of this enables us to take care as what programmes we allow to take up residence in our unconscious.

Each individual has multiple programmes within. Programmes that are the result of experience—programmes that may be the result of vows made in a previous lifetime; programmes that emerge as fears as a result of past abuse or accident; programmes that are born of relationship experiences or any of a wide range of experiences that may be of a positive or negative nature. Each of these programmes is exposed at some time or another. The timing of such exposure can be revealed in the study of the astrological climate for the individual at any given time.

We bumble through life trying to control it while believing the creator of our problems is a deity or some other person or circumstance in our lives. In fact, we are the deaf, dumb and blind creators of our circumstances when we could be the conscious creators of exciting, interesting and enjoyable events in our lives. Power is in the hands of those who understand this basic truth.

Fuel of the Soul

Energy is the fuel of the soul. It is what drives our body and enables us to function in the world. Insight into the workings of magical happenings can be gained through considering the characteristics of various energies in our environment and their impact on the human body. Like all else in nature, patterns or programmes within dictate the identity and behaviour of every cell in our body. The study of the interaction between each cell and other energy, whether our own or introduced, reveals interesting information.

THE TRUTH SEEKER

Our mental and emotional attitudes have an impact on our physical body. An example of this is the hypothalamus, which produces a chemical for every emotion. Happy and positive chemicals are released with positive emotions, whilst negative chemicals are released with negative emotions. Good mental, emotional and physical health is dependent upon a positive outlook. Emotions such as fear, guilt, suppressed anger and stress are the cause of much of the disease our bodies experience.

Attributed to Buddha but not his saying is: 'Every human being is the author of his own health or disease.' This statement continues, 'Disease is the result of disobedience to the immutable laws of health that govern life.'[105] This is correct up to a point. But it would be a mistake to pass judgement on the health or otherwise of an individual. While much can be attributed to personal mental and emotional energies, they are not the only cause of disease. The external world should also be taken into account. As revealed in quantum physics, the thoughts of others can have an impact on the composition of the smallest particles within us, and those particles in turn can impact on the physical. Since all we come into contact with has the power to have an impact on our physical, mental, and emotional state, awareness of the quality of our environment along with all we ingest is important. It is as well to also consider that in order to achieve certain goals, to become more powerful in the face of the destructive, or to learn from suffering, we as souls may have chosen to manifest in a world that has become dangerously polluted. The consequences of those choices that can result in distress in the physical body can reveal we saw more to gain spiritually in what such a life had to offer.

Those who have researched the impact of energy on the human body have provided us with fascinating insights that should cause us to consider reviewing our approach to healing.

Homeopathy was developed by the German physician Samuel Hahnemann (1755-1843) and is based on the energetic Law of Similars. Homeopathy is a safe, effective treatment that has research to back it up. Whilst many clinical trials have produced evidence as to the effectiveness of homeopathy, some haven't. The results of clinical trials by Linde (1997),[106] Cucherat (2000),[107] and Shang (2005)[108] that found homeopathy to be ineffective

---

[105] Swami Sivananda (1887-1963), founder of The Divine Life Society and author of over 200 books. From *Bliss Divine* p. 202.
[106] Linde K, Clausius N, Ramirez G, Melchart D, Eitel F, Hedges LV, Jonas WB: Are the clinical effects of homeopathy placebo effects? A meta-analysis of placebo-controlled trials. *Lancet* 1997; 350:834–843.
[107] Cucherat M. Haugh MV, Gooch M Boissel J-P: Evidence for clinical efficacy of homeopathy. A meta-analysis of clinical trials. Eur J Chin *Pharmacol* 2000;56:27-33.

were examined by Robert G Hahn, a Swedish anaesthesiologist who had spent thirty years in research and had neither studied nor practiced homeopathy. Hahn, who was not supported financially for this work, refuted their findings bringing attention to the serious weaknesses and distortions.[109] In his review article 'Scientific framework of homeopathy: Evidence-based Homeopathy.' Belgian doctor Michel Van Wassenhoven presents data showing there is sufficient indisputable scientific evidence validating the effectiveness of homeopathic medicines in the treatment of both humans and animals. He is of the opinion that in consideration of the rights of patients, they should be informed of *all* available treatments. Therefore, homeopathic medicines should be included in general medical practice and in hospitals.[110]

Homeopathy is a treatment prepared by introducing an ingredient into a water and/or alcohol base and then vigorously shaking. A small portion of that now *pattern impressed* base is taken and added to another water/alcohol mixture and the process is repeated a number of times. This ensures none of the original ingredient remains. In spite of this, the potency of the pattern or vibration of the original substance has been retained in the formula. However, in those cases where the ingredient in its original form was poisonous, it has become non-toxic.

That homeopathy works I have proven to my satisfaction through personal experience. At twenty-eight, I contracted a virulent bacterial infection. Numerous doses of antibiotics failed to rid me of the symptoms. After four years of intermittent prescriptions, my body began to react to the antibiotics that invaded my system. In the search for the cause of my severe chest pains, I was tested for a heart condition. After two more such attacks, I realised I had been taking antibiotics on each occasion. The doctor decreed he could do no more for me. Over the next few years, I continued to suffer from frequent bouts of tonsillitis and ear infections, and on one occasion, I became very ill with pleurisy. Around ten years after I first contracted the infection, a brilliant homeopath was able to clear my bacterial infections. I have since successfully employed homeopathic treatments for a number of health issues including a viral infection.

The concepts of homeopathy were extended by Dr Edward Bach (1886–1936) to include the healing of emotions. Dr Bach was a medical

---

[108] Shang A. Huwiler-Münterer K. Nartey L, Jüni P: Dörig S, Sterne JA, Egger M: Are the clinical effects of homeopathy placebo effects? Comparative study of pacebo-controlled trials of homeopathy and allopathy. Lancet 2005;366:726-732

[109] Hahn, R G 2013. *Homeopathy: Meta-Analyses of Pooled Clinical Data*. Forshende Komplementarmedizin; 20(5): 376-381

[110] Michel Van Wassenhoven (MD). 'Scientific framework of homeopathy: Evidence-based Homeopathy.' *Int J High Dilution Res 2008; 7(23): 72-92,* June 2008.

THE TRUTH SEEKER

practitioner who became frustrated with the limitations of orthodox medicines and treatments. He worked with homeopathy and through personal experimentation, developed a range of flower essences to aid in the alleviation of emotional suffering.

The idea that since our bodies are made up of around sixty per cent water, water itself can have considerable impact on our health and well-being was researched by two Japanese men. In his books, 'The Healing Power of Water'[111] and 'The True Power of Water'[112] Masaru Emoto reveals his incredible research into water. Emoto graduated from Yokohama Municipal University. While his degree was not in science, he gained the help and support of Kazuya Ishibashi who had obtained his scientific background at Kumamoto University. After much trial and error, they were able to produce crystals formed from water.

The apparent power of the written word was revealed with an experiment that involved taking two containers of the same water and placing a positive word on one container, and a negative word on the other. When the water was crystallised, it was discovered that negative words produced crystals that ranged from unformed to unpleasant. Positive words produced a variety of beautiful crystals.

Does this mean that each word in every language absorbs the energy that accompanies its usage? Or does it indicate the energy directed by the current user alone is transmitted to the water? Perhaps both contribute. Personally, I am of the opinion every word carries the emotional energy related to its usage over time. Consider words like, *error*, *mistake* and *sin*. Each word has a similar meaning, but as each word is used, the feelings that accompany it are different—especially the word 'sin', which has strong emotional judgement of wrong-doing associated with it. Each time we use a word, we invite the energy of that word into our lives.

Emoto documents his successful treatments of physical disease through healing water designed to cancel the negative emotions of fear, guilt, depression and distrust. All healing is dependent on positive energy. That which mimics a specific positive energy or negates a negative energy has the potential to heal. Unfortunately, scant attention seems to have been given by those involved in orthodox medical research to the composition of energy and the way in which its vibrational output has an impact on health.

---

[111] Emoto, Masaru. *The Healing Power of Water*. Hay House, Sydney, 2008.
[112] Emoto, Masaru, *The True Power of Water*, Beyond Words Publishing Inc. Oregon US, 2005.

Arguments against actual healings, through the abovementioned means, include the placebo effect. The placebo effect itself provides evidence that the patient's belief in the positive outcome of treatment generates positive energy that can result in healing. While some cures may be attributed to the individual's belief in a cure, the placebo effect is unlikely to be the cause of all healings, such as in the case of the healing of young children who have no belief whatsoever. Of course, it's possible the healing practitioner, or family members, could have sufficient belief in the healing to bring about a healing in the sufferer, since all directed energy, whether mental, emotional, or physical, has an impact on a situation.

Whether the positive healing energy comes from the belief in a cure, or from a physical potion that mimics the energetic imprint of a healthy state or eliminates the unhealthy condition, transformation from sick to healthy is the outcome. In essence, cures are brought about by a vibrational energy that replaces or cancels out the negative pattern of the energy that has caused the illness. Spiritual healing uses this knowledge.

Energy is powerful, and its ability to affect physical change, is one of the underlying ingredients in successful magic!

Powerful Energy Sources

When bridging the worlds of the physical and the psychic, all types of energy, including our own, can be used to bring about change and produce magic. There are great variations in the nature of energy. Celestial and spiritual energies not only exist, they can contribute greatly towards the efforts of the miracle worker and the magician.

As a specific astrological energy bombards our planet, the like energies within each soul are aroused and attract or repel situations that confront or support depending upon the state of the soul regarding that aspect of their life. Those who understand these influences realise that if they use, and work in harmony with, the prevailing celestial energies, positive and even miraculous results are possible. Most practitioners of witchcraft consider astrological timing important in ensuring desired results.

Miracles are about harnessing and/or commanding power. The celestial energies include not only the cosmic energies from our solar system, but also the finer energies of the higher dimensions. Spiritual energies and entities like white light, deities, angels or spirits are some of the power sources effective in the creation of miracles. When these energies are called on, it's either to invoke (to direct energies into self) or evoke (to direct energies outside self). The energy is used to assist in manifestation of the desired result.

Miracles have been reported through different religions for thousands of years. Whether or not the reports are true can't be ascertained today. What science can prove is that the human mind has power over the photons found in everything that exists. What science has not yet established is that the power of energy has the ability, when directed, to cause change in miraculous ways.

Claiming responsibility and power opens doors that enable the fulfilment of desires and the defeat of undesirable circumstances. Just as there are many types of celestial energies, there are also many techniques for accessing and using them. My own experience has caused me to make regular use of spiritual white light and to beg the aid of those in spirit when the situation warrants.

The first time I attempted to work with white light outside the class environment where I learned of it, the results were convincing enough to ensure I used it time and again.

In the late 1980s, I went with the then man in my life to a spectacular fireworks display on Sydney Harbour. As the location of the display was a pontoon on the harbour close to Lady MacQuarie's Chair, we arrived early and found a prime spot on the grass, close to the water's edge. After we sat down on our blanket, an almost continuous flow of people began to troop past us.

In spite of the grassed area between the next person's blanket and ours, someone tripped over my left foot. A few minutes later, another careless, inattentive individual did the same. Since the blanket had covered my foot, I uncovered it. In spite of this, within a very short time, two or three more people tripped over that same foot *and* it was still daylight! By now, my battered foot was receiving my undivided attention. *How could I solve a problem that shouldn't have been a problem?* There was very little viable free space left, so moving wasn't an option.

Desperation no doubt contributed to my recalling my psychic development teacher's instructions regarding using white light to protect. Admittedly, he had not described its use in this context, but under the circumstances, anything was worth a try. I focused my mind and visualised a white light surrounding my left foot with the intent my foot would be protected by the light. Dusk was now predicting imminent darkness. As dark descended, the fireworks commenced and throughout the next two hours, people continued walking past, just as they had before. The difference was that now the pedestrians were aware of my foot and completely avoided it.

That successful outcome lead to other experiences where white light influenced the situation—many of which related to calming the energy of those who were angry, upset, or stressed. One such situation occurred during the period I worked as a bookkeeper for Allan.

One day, a rather loud discussion was taking place about an outstanding account between Allan and a lady who was organising advertising for him. I have a very strong focus when I am working and it took a while for me to move my attention to the voices and what to do about, what was to me, a disruptive noise. I thought, *I'll just put a white light around myself*, and proceeded to do so. Then as an afterthought, *Oh, I'll put a white light around them as well.* Immediately, the loud voices lowered to a murmur and left me free to continue my work in peace. The woman left around ten minutes later. I asked Allan if he had sorted the problem out.

He replied, 'Most of it. There is still a little more we'll have to discuss further.' I then advised him of the white light, to which he responded, 'I felt the change in energy.'

There is perhaps no limit to the ways in which energy can be used to have an impact on situations in our world. The power of energy is revealed in virtually every aspect of life—in the home, in the office, in industry, in transportation. The difference in the use of the energy used in miracles is that the energy accessed is from different sources and is directed by the individual mind, rather than by a diversity of manmade devices.

Healing

Accounts of psychic and spiritual healing have been recorded since Biblical times. Certainly, Jesus was credited with healing powers. While methods used by healers may vary, records of their successes can be found in the both the writings of old and in those of recent times.

Remote healing has received attention from the academic community with interesting (though not always conclusive) results. Psychiatrist Daniel J Benor investigated over one hundred and fifty controlled studies on remote healing. These studies used differing methods of healing—mental, psychic and spiritual. While some of these experiments involved humans, others were performed on animals and plants, while still others involved cell cultures, bacteria, enzymes and yeasts. The results showed that over half of these studies revealed substantial healing.[113]

Fred Sicher, MA; Elizabeth Targ, MD; Dan Moore II, PhD; and Helen H Smith PhD, did a six-month study at the California Pacific Medical Centre that involved forty AIDS sufferers. In this double-blind study, the men, who were advised they had a fifty per cent chance of being in the group to be treated, were paired as close as possible, taking into consideration likeness in age, CD4 (T-cells) count and the number of AIDS-type diseases. The healers were from a variety of backgrounds including Christian, Buddhist and Native American, and all had had over five years' experience. At the end of the six months, the results showed that the treatment group experienced a significantly better quality of life than the control group with fewer visits to doctors, fewer days hospitalised, fewer new illnesses and less emotional distress.[114]

When I broke my ankle in December 2000, the damage done was extensive. My leg swelled and became very painful. A psychic I knew offered to send me healing at a pre-arranged time. A few minutes before the allotted time, I was lying on my bed when I felt energy engulf my leg from the calf down. This energy was quite strong, lasted around twenty minutes, and could not be mistaken for anything other than the promised healing. I did not experience pain relief, nor was I aware of any physical change that took place—but that does not mean there wasn't any! Perhaps daily treatments would have been necessary for significant change.

For a number of years, I visited a spiritual healer. Each time I visited Jane[115] I became aware of very strong energy activity in the area of my body she worked with. When I commented on the powerful energy directed at me, she commented that most people didn't feel it. After each healing I experienced a wonderful feeling of lightness combined with an almost euphoric emotional state.

I don't consider myself a psychic or spiritual healer and don't have experience in healing work such as that practiced by Jane. However, from my early thirties, after reading an article in the Reader's Digest regarding a man whose boat sank many miles from shore and his swim back to land that was made possible by the energy sent to him by those who loved him, I too

---

[113]Benor, Daniel J, MD. *Healing research*, vol. 1, Munich, Germany: Helix Verlag 1992.
[114] Sicher, F , Targ E, Moore D, Smith, H. 'A randomized double-blind study of the effect of distant healing in a population with advanced AIDS.' *Western Medical Journal December 1998,* vol. 169, no. 6.
[115] Name changed.

began to send energy. It occurred to me it would be helpful to send loving and supportive energy to those experiencing emotional trauma or serious and painful health issues. I seem to have access to an endless supply of spiritual, loving energy I can draw on when needed, and for these types of situations, that energy source seems to be appropriate. Over a period of days or weeks, depending on the need, whenever I think of the person I send energy. One such case was the following.

A young woman had been sent to my classes by a psychic who didn't know me, but who during the reading she was giving the young lady, received my name from her guides in spirit. This young woman had begun to experience the presence of the spirits of dead people that seemed to invade her space, causing her to become extremely fearful, so the psychic advised I could help. After a phone call to me, the young woman arrived for my class. In an attempt to remove her fear, that night I spoke personally with her and also discussed in detail during the class, the dynamics involved in dealing with those who are no longer in the physical. Since I felt support during the following week would be beneficial, I frequently sent loving energy to the young lady. The following week, when she arrived for my class, she stated, 'You sent me energy during the week!'

There are many types of energy used by the healer. The use of a healer's own psychic energy can be draining to the healer and the energy sourced possibly less effective than the spiritual alternatives. On the few occasions healing of the physical has seemed appropriate for me, I have requested help from beings in the spiritual realms. There are those in spirit who can assist and direct the appropriate energy to the healer who then becomes the conductor of that energy to the person in need of healing. In the following situation, I called upon those in spirit to aid me.

A man who had attended my classes phoned me one evening in a very distressed state to tell me his wife had given birth to premature twins (a boy and a girl) who were suffering complications. 'My little girl is having a very difficult time, and the doctors are very concerned and don't hold a lot of hope for her. Please pray for my little girl.'

As this man was familiar with the concepts of spiritual healing, I assured him I would attempt to send some healing as soon as I could. That could not be until the following evening as I was packing to travel to Canberra the next day. Although I was tired when I arrived at my hotel the following night, I took the time to look to the healing of the tiny girl. I lay down on my bed and focused my attention on feeling into and sensing the condition of the child.

As I opened psychically to the baby, I began to feel her energy as though her body was directly in front of me. Every part of the tiny mite's body seemed to be wracked with pain and her energies were very weak. Concern filled me as I prayed for spiritual healing energy to be directed through me by my spirit helpers. Such spiritual energy is only directed through me if it is 'right' and doesn't interfere with what an individual soul has chosen to experience in this lifetime in order to achieve spiritual goals. If a healing isn't meant to happen, or happen in that way, no healing energy is made available to me. The energy made available works in a way right for the individual at that time.

On this occasion, as soon as I prayed a powerful energy flowed through me and I directed that energy into the child. Gradually I began to feel the baby's energy grow stronger and as it did so, the pain receded. Finally, after around twenty minutes, the healing energy slowed and stopped.

I was very busy working over the next few days, but on the following Monday evening, I received a phone call from the baby's father. He was very excited. 'It's a miracle. Her health suddenly improved so much. The doctors can't believe it.' He then stated the time the remarkable change had taken place and confirmed for me what I already knew. It had occurred on the same night and during the very same hour I had been directing healing energy to the child.

Each of us can call upon power, by whatever means seems appropriate, in a given circumstance. When appealing for, or commanding, a miracle for another, consideration should always be given to the 'rightness' of interfering in another's life. All miracles work in accordance with physical and spiritual laws, and when all is in accord, nothing can prevent the manifestation of the desired result.

Belief and the Manifestation of the Miraculous

Theodore Roosevelt said, *Believe you can and you're halfway there.*[116] An understanding of the power of belief is important when looking to become a conscious creator. Belief, especially reinforced belief, is an integral part of our unconscious mind and has enormous power. The conscious mind also has power, but conflict between the beliefs of the unconscious and the

---

[116] Roosevelt, Theodore, Works: Presidential addresses and state papers, Dec. 3, 1901, June 1910, and European addresses, vol. 8, p. 1433, The Review of Reviews Publishing Company, 1910.

thoughts and attitudes of the conscious mind leads to disappointment and failure.

Belief can enhance or limit our lives, depending on what we believe. Whether belief is the consequence of reaction to experience or programmes received from elders, its impact on our lives is no small matter. Conflicting messages such as *I need money* and *I don't believe I deserve to have money* or *Money is the route of all evil* ensure financial rewards are likely to be spasmodic at best. Patterns of thinking and belief play out in each person's life. In changing self-defeating and erroneous programmes, we change our lives for the better.

For almost two millennia, Christians have been taught to believe they are worthless sinners. This is a destructive programme that not only results in a self-image of inferiority, it also causes the attraction of the negative into the life of the *underserving* individual. It is not surprising that *all* apparent miracles are attributed to God or to a spiritual being rather than being recognised as the result of the individual's own power to create a miracle. Jesus taught: Matthew 17:20 ((NIV) *He replied, 'Because you have so little faith. Truly I tell you, if you have faith as small as a mustard seed, you can say to this mountain, 'Move from here to there,' and it will move. Nothing will be impossible for you.*"[117]

The contradiction between the teachings of Jesus and Christian religious belief has ensured that the devout individual has been stripped of belief in their own power. The unexplained is seen as a miracle and is attributed to God, Jesus, or one of the saints. While this could be the case, as the individual's mind has the power to draw in whatever or whomever it needs in order to produce the desired result, and this can include beings in spirit, it is not necessarily so. In spite of the fact the believer does *not* command in their own right, if there is a strong belief the request will be granted, then it can be that belief that ensures the result. It is in fact likely, that at least some of the miracles attributed to a divine source have been created as a result of the unconscious mind of the believer.

Stigmata are wounds likened to those received by Jesus when he was nailed to the cross. Such wounds have manifested on the bodies of some members of the Roman Catholic Church, and although some claimed cases of stigmata have proven to be false, there are others that simply can't be explained. These cases are seen by members of the church as being bestowed upon the worthy by a divine source. That it is the power of the

---

[117] *Biblestudytools.com.* www.biblestudytools.com (accessed 28 Oct 2011)

individual's own emotional feelings, mental focus and beliefs producing the stigmata is revealed in the actual wounds.

Most crucifixes show the nails piercing the centre of the hands. The only way the body of Jesus could have been supported on the cross was by placing the nails in his wrists. Therefore, the stigmata in the hands of devout Catholics could have only been produced by the unconscious mind of the individual. The crucifix, on which the person fixed their attention, became the model for the expression of a profound love for Jesus, combined with an intense empathetic focus upon his sufferings. These people are powerful psychics who, through lack of guidance, are misusing their power.

Spiritual beings, not of the physical world, can be authors of the miraculous. But so can we. If we truly believe we can, we can.

Sword of the Soul

The mind is the sword of the soul. The power of the energy of the focussed mind is daunting. Those who have achieved greatness have done so through focusing clearly on their goals. While the power of the conscious mind is amazing, by aligning it with the unconscious mind and accessing other dimensions, the magician can achieve incredible results.

My original forays into the use of mind powers involved charging my unconscious to provide me with required information. It was my practice to focus on, and mentally voice, a query with the expectation of an answer. Within a short period of time, usually within three days, the answer dropped into my mind or appeared in my environment—perhaps I'd pick up a book somewhere that just happened to provide the answers I was searching for, or someone would happen to mention the desired knowledge. Although the ways in which the information arrived were many and varied, it always arrived.

My attendance at psychic development classes provided me with the opportunity to learn other methods of using the power of the mind—like visualisation and writing down a desired outcome. Visualisation requires that the mind drop into a meditative state where the unconscious can be accessed. Once there, the mind focuses on visually creating a template of the desired objective, bringing into play the law of Like Attracts Like. Providing that image isn't weakened by fear or denial, the unconscious mind works to manifest creation in the physical world. The energetic imprint of the visualised desire (like the karmic content each soul carries) attracts or creates it's like in the physical world. But if this image comes into conflict with strong opposing beliefs in the unconscious, and is not strong enough to negate those inner programmes, failure will be the outcome.

I have personally found that expression of the desire through the written word can be very effective. This method helps to bring the mind's focus to the details of a situation. Once written down, absolute faith at all times thereafter is necessary. Another important aspect of the practice that ensures success is to treat the outcome as though it's a fixed part of the future.

The unit I had been living in for about four years was to be refurbished, and the residents were advised they had eight weeks to vacate. I decided to be specific about what I wanted in my next unit, and as clarity of thought was important in the achievement of this, I wrote down a list of my requirements. The following is what I asked for:

- A two bedroom unit
- Facing north
- Sea views
- Location—North Shore
- Above ground level
- Balcony
- Undercover parking
- Space in kitchen for dishwasher
- Rent over $195 and under $250 per week

In all situations where mind powers are used, it is important the requirements are realistic. The rental price range I stipulated reflected current prices in the area. The subconscious knows what's realistic, so asking for rent at $150 per week would have brought conflict between the conscious and unconscious and immediately negated my efforts.

I was into my fifth week of searching and had been tempted by a lovely unit for $245 on the second level, but facing south. My mind refused to let go of my ideal of a northerly aspect. Then I found it! It was perfect and fitted all my criteria exactly *and* it was only $210 per week. For around four years, I delighted in this perfect unit that had glorious panoramic views of the harbour.

Affirmations can also be a very effective way of working. Affirmations that are repeated over and over can result in reprogramming of the brain—the negating of old programmes replacing them with new. Sometimes, when immediate results are required, a strong on the spot affirmation is appropriate. Many are the times when I quickly decide I will achieve the

THE TRUTH SEEKER

result I want. That might be a parking space or the mental blocking of phone calls from people at an inconvenient time. Or it might be the wish to have an arranged meeting or event cancelled by the other party when the timing does not work for me. There are many ways in which this method can be used, as in the following circumstances when time was short.

It was Friday night. No more work for three weeks as the next morning I was flying out to New Zealand. My youngest sister was celebrating her fiftieth birthday and as I had not yet purchased a present for her, I quickly made my way to the shopping centre. Time was not on my side. I still had to go home, eat, and pack. I raced into the department store and as I stepped on to the escalator, I looked at my watch and thought, *I need to get a present within ten minutes.* I then determined that when I stepped off the escalator, I would go directly towards the area where I would find an item my sister *really* wanted, and would happy with. This affirmation was spliced with a high dose of non-negotiable determination.

As I left the escalator, I moved to the right. This took me toward handbags. I headed past the bags and stopped at the display of wallets. My eyes were drawn to a beautiful, boxed, black leather wallet with a matching key holder. I checked out the wallet. I had my present.

'How did you know?' my sister demanded as she beamed approval of her present. She retrieved her old wallet that was literally falling to pieces with stitching coming undone and edges torn. It had definitely passed its use-by date. 'I have been intending to replace this for ages,' she said, 'But I just hadn't got around to it.' We each have our own ideas of what represents to us, a workable wallet. Her complete approval was guaranteed, as the old wallet and the new one were all but identical, even to the logo on the front.

I often use 'command' or 'demand', especially when I have become impatient with the current situation and decide to take immediate steps to obtain results. When my requirements are straightforward, I focus my mind on what I desire and frame the wording of that desire with as much clarity as possible.

Some months after I moved into the previously mentioned unit, I decided I needed a cleaner, as I had been so busy that cleaning had been neglected. For three weeks, I watched for the local weekly paper and its classifieds, but for some reason it wasn't delivered during that time. Sunday morning arrived and my place was a mess. Once again, there was no time for me to clean up—I was not about to miss out on the planned bushwalking outing. It was urgent I *did* something! I focused my mind and commanded, *I need a cleaner who is capable, honest and reliable; someone who has similar thinking to me, and I who will get along with!*

When we stopped for lunch on the walk, my house-cleaning problem popped into my mind and I mentioned it to the three or four people in the group I was sitting with. One woman said, 'I know a lady in your area who does cleaning.' That night I phoned her. When I explained my need, the woman spoke up, 'I am sorry, but I don't have time to take on anyone else, but I can give you the name of someone who may be able to help you.' At the end of my next phone call, I had my cleaner. Over the next few years, we enjoyed a friendship and many a discussion on subjects that interested us both, and whilst we now live in different parts of the country, we remain in touch.

Some time after I gained my new cleaner, new neighbours, a couple, moved into the unit below me. It wasn't long before it became obvious they were noisy and he was verbally abusive and used foul language. Her distressed crying was audible on a regular basis.

Over the next few months, the situation interfered with my peace of mind and enjoyment of my environment. I loved where I was living and had no desire to move. As I focused on the situation, I determined I was entitled to a harmonious environment, and so I decided *they* would move. I commanded in my mind they move to a place more suited to them at a time convenient for them. Six weeks later, they were gone.

While there are subtle differences in the mental techniques used, each approach requires clear definition and strong mental focus. Mental focus is, like every other ability, something we are born with and further develop during our current life. If we can learn to remain in control mentally in the face of dangerous and traumatic situations, and apply mental focus to finding answers and solutions, we can develop it. Astrology can reveal to the individual, the degree to which the power of the mind has developed at birth. The sign Aquarius, unless negatively aspected, reveals cleverness of mind along with an ability to apply intense mental focus. My astrology chart at the time of my birth shows that the Sun (expression of self), Mercury (intellect and communication) and Venus (love and harmony) are all in Aquarius bringing that sign's influence into each of these areas of my makeup. When mental focus has enough strength, the mind can cut through apparent obstacles as easily as a sword slicing through water.

THE TRUTH SEEKER

Ego

A balanced ego is an important ingredient in the creation of magic and miracles.

Confusion abounds around the perception of ego. Some see ego as a negative and a barrier to spirituality and set out to destroy it. The ego is our sense of self. The healthy ego, that values and loves the self and also loves and appreciates others, provides a daunting source of power. While appreciation and love of self and others empowers, inferiority and lack of self-love disempowers. While many seek power through controlling their environment and those in it, such people lack the real power that comes from within. Fear, the hidden destroyer, is behind the ***need*** to control. In order to claim our power, we need to let go of fear.

Self-esteem that deserves to receive, along with humility in one's attitude and behaviour, reflects an ego that is mature and balanced. Humility is not about abasing oneself. It is about seeing the world and all in it through eyes that are appreciative and caring. It is about the lack of need to demean or judge the self or others. Essentially, it sees neither the superior nor the inferior and sees the value in all. One of the reasons a healthy ego is important is that if a person doesn't feel worthy of receiving their desire, their emotional commitment is sabotaged by a lack of self-love and appreciation.

We are in the early stages of recognising and understanding the natural laws of the cosmos. In the greater scheme of things, we are individuals, and yet we are also part of all that is. We are spiritually connected to all beings, even though we are not consciously aware of being so. Everything we experience incorporates what has been created or provided by others. Whether those others are of the physical world or not, it behoves us to appreciate that when we receive, we are beholden to many sources within our universe. While an ego is a valuable ingredient in the successful manipulation of our world, gratitude to all the silent contributors to our success is the healthy response of a balanced ego. Gratitude is an emotion that releases positive and powerful energy. It acknowledges our spiritual connection to all in the universe and is accompanied by joy in the fulfilment of wishes, along with peace and contentment in the knowledge it can always be so. Since like attracts like, gratitude attracts what we will be grateful for.

It is an unwise person who believes that creating magic makes them superior and their ability gives them licence to ignore the rights of others. Such lack of wisdom brings its own consequences. Just as in our everyday activities, in the practice of any form of magic or in the use of mind powers and when invoking miracles, care should always be taken not to invade another's world and limit or take away their freedom of choice, except in circumstances where their actions are a threat to others.

When we combine a healthy ego with humility, we create balance in our life. A healthy ego recognises its unique place in the universe, experiences a loving connection to all that is, and trusts in the spiritual laws. The arch-enemy 'fear' is then defeated so nothing can stand in the way of achieving what we will.

Motivation

With all power of mind and miraculous manifestations, strong motivation plays an important role in ensuring that interference blocks in the unconscious mind, such as those caused by fear and disbelief, play no part in obstructing the execution of the intent. Perhaps the most potent motivation is the capacity to care deeply. If I am going to have problems in achieving a successful outcome, it will be because I am not motivated. If I am not earnest in the belief I should attempt to create change, or my heart isn't in it, it doesn't happen. I can't manufacture motivation—it's either there or it isn't. Its source is in the accumulated attitudes and beliefs lodged in my soul.

In magic, as in any aspect of life, boundaries are important. Through trial and error, we discover where our boundaries should lie. Some years ago, using the powers of my mind, I sought to help a friend to solve a personal problem. I was successful in aiding her, but my help entangled me in her life in a way that limited my own life for some time. I now react to such situations with caution.

My understanding of, and belief in, my own paranormal ability, has motivated me to attempt time and again what most people would deem impossible. That the possible includes the amazing is revealed in the following occurrence that took place in the 1990s.

It was Saturday morning and it was pouring with rain. In between racing for the taxi that picked me up, and my arrival in the city, I recalled that the Mardi Gras was being held that evening. Since there was little likelihood the rain would cease, I decided I would take action to ensure the event all those people had spent months preparing for did not turn into a disaster. My determination was inspired by a story that had been told to me recently by a lady who had travelled to Dharamsala in India where the Dalai Lama resided. On the day she was due to fly back to Australia, inclement weather caused her concern. One of the monks advised her he would take care of it, and it wasn't long before the weather cleared and she departed in beautiful sunshine. *Well*, I thought. *If he could do it, so can I!*

Upon my arrival at the place I was to work for the day, I sat down and began to meditate. I then focused my mind to extend it out into the skies above Sydney. As my mind expanded, so did my awareness of the power within— an all-encompassing power. As I merged my consciousness with the wind and the rain, I became aware of the earth below me. In my empowered state, I extended my consciousness to the storm's boundaries that in the south reached as far as Canberra, (around a hundred and eighty-six miles or three hundred kilometres away by road). I could feel the massive area I was, for the moment, part of. As the prevailing wind herded the clouds in a north-easterly direction, I reached back to its source, joined with it and focused on willing the winds to turn east. With unlimited power at my disposal, the execution of my wishes was easily accomplished. I returned to my normal state of consciousness and to the room where I was to spend the rest of the day. The weather cleared and the Mardi Gras was a success.

Had I really changed the weather, or did my imagination create the scenario? Over the years, I have found valid experience has a reality to it that imagination and wishful thinking lack. Actually feeling the energy and power of the storm was an integral part of the experience. I could feel the force of the wind and its direction in relation to the land. With the immediate conscious awareness of my own power, I never doubted my ability to change its direction. The fact my mind could expand over such a large area and how it felt to do so was mind-blowing.

Being highly motivated, knowing and believing the apparent impossible can occur when the conscious mind takes charge and decides what will and will not be, are essential ingredients in achieving success. Providing the expanded or altered state of consciousness is entered into, taking the practitioner into the dimension used by all magicians and miracle workers, what is desired can be created.

Oops

Most magicians have experienced mistakes in one form or another. When working with powers capable of causing miraculous change, it is as well to ensure the laws are understood. Precision is extremely important as the computer-like unconsciousness not only lacks judgement or conscience, it may also interpret literally.

It's easy to spontaneously react to a situation, especially one causing frustration. For some time I had been working hard and under a great deal of pressure. I knew I shouldn't allow such stress and pressure to continue. But what could I do about it?

Impulsively I commanded, *I need time out. I need a break.*

Three days later, as I was helping someone lift a table up some stairs, it dropped on my foot breaking some small bones. Not the kind of break I had in mind! Had the automated part of my mind taken my words literally and implemented the breaking of bones as a result of my command? I don't know. But I did get my time out! My biggest mistake was that I had not included a command no harm would come to me or anyone else. Added to the pain of broken bones in my foot and being temporarily incapacitated was the disappointment of missing out on a fun weekend away down on the South Coast.

As we learn without fear or prejudice to draw upon our own power and paranormal abilities, our worldly experience is enhanced. By incorporating responsibility and awareness when invoking the powers within, it is possible to avoid undesirable consequences.

Consciousness

Consciousness. What is it? How come it possesses such extraordinary power? If consciousness can operate on a non-physical level and through connection to all that is access places outside the physical body and be aware of and influence other environments, is it reasonable to consider the mind is dependent on the physical? Our past perceptions of the brain being like a machine and the mind a product of that machine has caused us to stagnate. Humanity in the Western world has become the victim of a false belief. As a result, our natural powers have been suppressed rather than developed.

Miracles that have been defined as happenings that defy the laws of nature do not in fact do so. The new scientific knowledge reveals we can and do have an impact on and create change on the atomic level of existence.

Belief and trust are powerful forces that contribute towards the power of the magician. Such power needs to be respected and used in the right context.

THE TRUTH SEEKER

Blind belief, as in blind religious or scientific belief, creates boundaries in the mind that have the ability to block personal power and leave the individual a victim for one or many lifetimes. For those who wish to claim their power, following the teachings of the Masters, who are recognised by their profound understanding of and adherence to the Law of Love, and whose transcendental experiences have revealed spiritual truths, can lead to the Master within.

If we can take responsibility for our own circumstances and change in the unconscious that which is causing limitation, and if we can recognise and gain dominion over the powers within, our world changes and we can no longer claim to be powerless victims, dependent on the apparent whimsy of the natural or the supernatural.

JOAN L BOLER

THE TRUTH SEEKER

Chapter 7

Our Multidimensional Identity

What lies behind us, and what lies before us are tiny matters, compared to what lies within us.

Unknown[118]

Supernature

Mysterious forces dwell within every human being. Such is the awareness gained by those who travel the internal road into the secret world of the spirit within where enlightenment is experienced as wondrous truths are revealed.

Ancient writings regarding the make-up of our spiritual nature can be found in the Vedas (knowledge) from India. These texts were written in Sanskrit and discuss humankind existing on five levels and identify each person as a multi-dimensional being. Today most writings by psychics discuss the presence of seven bodies, each of which extends further and further out from the physical body and are seen as auras. However, the number of inter-dimensional layers to the soul of each individual can't at this point in time be considered definitive.

Supportive of the idea that we are multidimensional beings are the theories of a multi-dimensional universe put forward by theoretical physicists who, in their efforts to provide a theory of everything, came up with 'string theory'. String theory suggests that electrons and quarks within the atom are dimensional oscillating strings. Over time, string theory became five string theories. Then a more fundamental unifying theory, 'M-theory', that incorporates the basics of each of the string theories and includes eleven

---

[118] Earliest appearance found: "Meditations in Wall Street", author unknown. (1940) William Morrow & Company. http://quoteinvestigator.com/2011/01/11/what-lies-within/ (accessed 14 Nov 2014)

space-time dimensions, was introduced by American theoretical physicist, Edward Whitton.[119]

Each of the dimensional bodies possess energy centres called 'chakras' (wheels) which are today also known as energy channels, doorways or gateways. Carl Jung called chakras *the gateways of consciousness*[120] with good reason. These powerful centres have the ability to link the individual with the various dimensions. Through the chakras it is possible for the conscious mind to access the various levels that make up the greater part of who and what we are, and to gain knowledge not normally available to the conscious mind. Psychic abilities and the paranormal also operate through these doorways.

Barbara Ann Brennan, author of 'Hands of Light', provides many insights into the workings of both chakras and the various non-physical bodies.[121] Brennan, a physicist who originally worked as a research scientist for NASA, has spent the past thirty years researching the human energy field. Brennan's own well-developed psychic abilities have enabled her to study the impact of psychological issues on the chakras and auras. She has developed spiritual healing techniques that are now taught to people all over the world.

As supernatural, inter-dimensional beings, we are capable of expressing ourselves in the physical world in ways that challenge our accepted understanding of our human existence. Deeper investigation of our chakra centres reveals they play a part in our evolution as souls and are fundamental to psychic and coincidental happenings.

Non-Physical Bodies

While we generally think in terms of *the* body, in reality we're made up not only of the physical body, but also a number of non-physical bodies that can function independently of our physical bodies (Figure 3, page 159). Extra dimensional bodies reflect the sensual, passionate, emotional, creative, mental and spiritual energies that spring from within and reveal the various

---

[119] Dowell, William. 'Juan Maldacena: Finding physics' missing link [*TIME International Special*].' 2000: (idisk.mac.com/wdowell-Public/ WilliamDowellF/Maldacena/htm
[120] Shamdasani, Sonu (ed.), The Psychology of Kundalini Yoga, *Notes of the Seminar given in 1932*, Princeton University Press, 1932.
[121] Brennan, Barbara Ann, *Hands of Light – A Guide to Healing through the Human Energy Field*, Bantam Books, New York, 1987.

aspects of our soul. Each of these extra-dimensional bodies operates on different frequencies and is made up of energies that vary in nature and density. As discussed in Chapter Six 'Mind Powers, Magic and Miracles', scientific evidence indicates the possibility that consciousness is not a product of the brain. In order to appreciate the true state of our being, it is necessary to allow for the possibility that consciousness (the energetic essence of other dimensions) rules the physical and is not dependent upon it.

Dimensional Bodies

7. ***Ketheric or Spiritual Body:*** Gold/silver light. Divine awareness. One
   with Creator. Past life connections.

6. ***Celestial Body:*** Pale pearl-like colours with beams of light that reveal
   spiritual love.

5. ***Etheric Template Body:*** Spiritual will. Cobalt blue template for
   physical manifestion.

4. ***Astral Bo****dy*: Humanitarian love revealed in clouds of colour.

3. ***Mental Body:*** Thought forms – usually yellow.

2. ***Emotional Body:*** Emotional feelings—usually revealed in clouds of
   colour.

1. ***Etheric Body:*** The bluish energy that binds the physical body.

Levels 1-3: Physical world
Level 4:   Astral plane
Levels 5-7: Spiritual plane

Figure 3 - Dimensional Bodies

The validity of the presence of separate dimensional bodies is consistent with:

- Instant mind access to distant places

- The ability to be outside time and to access knowledge from previous times

- The impact of the human mind upon protons

- Twentieth century scientific discoveries that have challenged boundaries previously laid down by physicists, and resulted in theories that endorse a universe of extra dimensions

Auric Fields

Each of our bodies extends beyond the physical body, and can be seen as an aura. The aura is, in part, an electromagnetic energy field that radiates from all forms of life and can be measured by a number of instruments including the electroencephalograph and the electrocardiograph. Science is making inroads into discovering the microcosmic. Today it is possible to capture the light emitted by a single photon from a human body using a specially adapted sensitive charge-coupled-device camera.[122] Doubtless, before too long, greater understanding of our makeup as humans will be achieved.

Colours in the aura are identified by their vibrational speed, and the colours themselves indicate different types of energy. The way in which humans express and use energies is reflected in the layers of colourful energy fields around the physical body. Each layer of the aura varies in density and is made up of materials of the dimension it belongs to. The energies that radiate from life forms expose the nature of that life form. From the simple to the complex, auras provide details of the nature within.

The aura layer that reflects current moods and attitudes of an individual, the emotional body, can be seen with the naked eye. Many years ago, I attended a lecture given by a male witch. The timing of his lecture coincided with my having recently learned to put my eyes out of focus in order to see a

---

[122] Kobayashi M, Kikuchi D & Okamura H. (2009) 'Imagining of Ultraweak Spontaneous Photon Emission from Human Body displaying Diurnal Rhythm.' *PLoS ONE* 4(7): e6256, dio:10/1371/journal.pone0006256

THE TRUTH SEEKER

person's aura. The result was much more pronounced when the person was receiving the attention of a group of people. As I focused on the witch, I was able to see a beautiful, bright, emerald green aura extending around three inches (7.6cm) from his body. Since green reveals feelings of harmony and love, this was what the man was feeling at that moment in time.

A few weeks later, I attended a lecture given by a lady who belonged to a group that practiced raja yoga. As she talked, I viewed a beautiful purple aura around her. Purple indicated she was in a pure, or holy, state of mind. She explained her beliefs and methods used in meditation, and then guided the group into a meditation. At this point, her aura from the shoulders up changed to gold revealing the expression of higher spiritual energies.

In both these instances, I was viewing energies related to the moment. In the case of the witch, the harmony and balance, and even the loving energy he was displaying, was his response to the attention and respect he was receiving from his audience. However, challenge to or conflict with his ego would produce entirely different colours. The lady's colours indicated her spiritual attitude and intent throughout her lecture, especially during the meditation.

While basic aura levels can be seen with the naked eye, for me at least, clairvoyance is necessary in order to see the higher levels. As other levels of aura are seen, clouds of colour reflect the nature of the total person. These auras reveal the other bodies of each person that progressively become finer and finer and express a multitude of colours that at higher levels can be pearl-like. The energy of the total self extends beyond the body in an egg shape, the outer edge of which is protected by an energetic field that prevents the penetration of negative energies.

While the first layer of the aura extends to around one inch (2.5 cm) from the body, each additional layer extends a little further. The average distance from the body is around a yard (metre), but this varies depending whether the individual is focused inward or outward. As psychic and spiritual abilities develop, the distance becomes greater.

In the late 1970s I was living on the Central Coast. On this particular day, I was listening to 2GO, the local radio station. In the wake of Uri Geller, a guest who claimed mind power abilities was encouraging listeners to attempt to bend spoons using the power of the mind. At the conclusion of the exercise, the announcer advised that the guest was about to prove his abilities under test conditions. The announcer ended his spiel. Suddenly there was dead silence. The radio station was off the air! Music from the relay station ended the silence one minute later. Five minutes elapsed before the station came back on air with a very flustered announcer attempting to get his head around the fact the radio station had been shut down—apparently by the guest.

A few days later, I went shopping in the Imperial Shopping Centre in Gosford. A gentleman was standing on a platform surrounded by a group of people for whom he was giving psychic readings. As I stood some twenty feet (6.2 metres) away, I could feel his aura extend through and past me. The huge auric energy I encountered was powerful and loving. I had little doubt this was the man who had shut down the radio station.

The aura can be a beautiful and powerful field of energy that reflects both the current and the more complex total state of being. While some psychics see colours in the aura, others sense the nature of the energy. A highly skilled psychic will be aware of both. Accurate interpretation of auric energies depends on the ability of the seer to access the various aura levels. Superficial sight will only reveal the current mood and not the actual character and personality.

Vulnerable Psychic and Spiritual Bodies

As we progress through life and encounter its challenges, the field of energy that surrounds and protects all layers of the whole person can be breached, resulting in soul damage. Healing is then required to reinstate the natural protective barriers and rebuild auric health.

There are consequences when the boundaries of the auric protective shield are eroded. Exposure to negative energies can result in unaccountable mood swings as the happy or unhappy moods of those who are close by, are absorbed. It is also possible to become the victim of a psychic attack or to attract a 'lost soul' (a soul that's died and is still attached to the physical world) into the energy field. For the large numbers of people who are open to, and absorb into themselves, the energies of those around them, reasons vary:

- Empathetic, emotional, sensitive people who care about others are at risk until they learn to ensure their protective boundaries are strong.

- Sufferers of long-term mental, physical or emotional distress or abuse can become vulnerable due to the ongoing negative energies in their life.

THE TRUTH SEEKER

- Drug or alcohol abuse destroys the protective energy field. The auras of drug users seem to me to be not only torn, but also the substance of the aura seems lifeless and in the process of disintegrating.

Due to the lack of knowledge of this subject in the West until relatively recently, most people are ignorant of the damaging consequences of mental, emotional and physical abuse. Nor do they have access to the possible ways of healing such damage as established medical knowledge denies the presence of the spiritual. It is through gaining insight into the multidimensional workings of the total person that true healing methods can be recognised and used.

Chakras

Our multiple bodies have gateways called chakras. These gateways connect us to people in the physical world about whom we feel strongly. They also offer the possibility of accessing other dimensions and are the doorways through which the paranormal operates.

Chakras are energy centres found throughout the body. In order to keep it simple, I will deal with the seven dominant ones (Figure 4, page 164). With the exception of the crown and base chakras, each of the chakras on the front of the body has a connecting chakra at the back. These energy centres in the human body are located in areas where there are nerve networks and glandular centres and are thought to be the control behind these systems (Figure 5, page 165). They are also the centres through which psychic abilities operate.

Each chakra provides access to a dimension that controls or influences an aspect of the physical body. Each time/space dimension is less dense than the previous one until the highest of all dimensions—of pure spirit—is reached. As consciousness expands through the various levels of awareness, knowledge not usually available to the physical senses becomes accessible. At the higher levels, contact with beings in spirit, including beings of light, is possible.

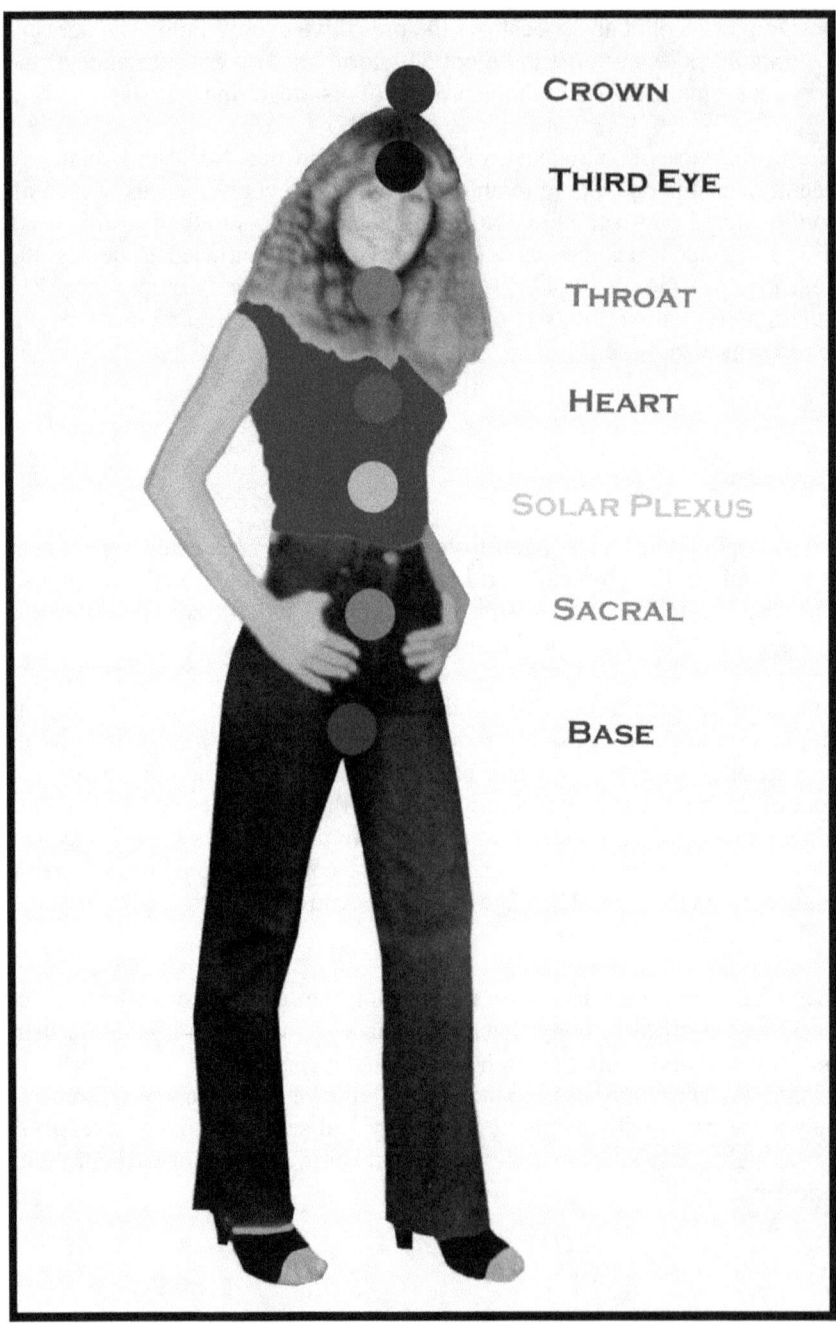

Figure 4 - Main Chakra Energy Centres

THE TRUTH SEEKER

Chakras

7. **_Crown—violet, white and gold._** This chakra when open indicates spiritual awareness. When closed there is no concept of the spiritual.
Controls: Pineal gland

6. **_Third-Eye—indigo._** Front: Love reflecting higher mental concepts. Comprehension. Practical mental and creative ideas.
Back: The ability to implement ideas.
Controls: Pituitary gland

5. **_Throat—sapphire blue._** Front: Ability to communicate needs. Understanding others. Listening to internal voice.
Rear: Self-realisation.
Controls: Thyroid

4. **_Heart—emerald green._** Front: When balanced will love and care about
all life on the planet. Rear: self-love which enables the attraction of opportunities.
Controls: Thymus

3. **_Solar Plexus_** *—yellow.* Front: Thoughts and beliefs. Self-esteem and ability to trust the environment. Reflects outlook on life and contains the fears that block. Rear: Caring for health.
Controls: Adrenals

2. **_Sacral (Hara)_** *—orange.* Front: Emotional and sexual feelings. Creativity. Happy, friendly people show balance in this chakra.
Rear: Sexual power.
Controls: Pancreas

1. **_Base—bright red._** Relates to the will to live, sense of touch and interpretation of physical pleasure and pain.
Controls: Gonads

Figure 5 - Chakras

Most people's energy centres open and close automatically as they go about their daily lives. When a person suffers trauma, pain, rejection, failure or abuse, the chakra related to that aspect of their lives can close down or become deformed. When chakras close down, they can't access the life giving energies necessary for a healthy and balanced life. Such a state, if prolonged, can result in physical illness.

Comparatively few in the West have knowledge or understanding of the chanting of mantras common to Buddhist monks. The first and most important of the mantras is **OM**. When one chants this and the other mantras correctly, it sets up positive vibrations throughout the body. When a group of people comes together, the combined vibrations created increase in intensity and the effect on the body of each individual is more pronounced.

Chakra	Chant	Pronounced
Crown	Silent	
Third Eye	OM	Aum
Throat	HAM	Hahm
Heart	YAM	Yahm
Solar Plexus	RAM	Rahm
Sacral	VAM	Vahm
Base	LAM	Lahm

Figure 6 - Mantras

These mantras create vibrations that harmonise with the chakra centres which in turn interact with the hormonal system of the body and create a build-up of psychic energy. This psychic energy can be used in the manifestation of magic. The real benefit of chanting is the effect on the psyche. As our emotions, thoughts and all aspects of our character are made up of energy, vibrations from the chanting have an impact on these energies. They clear and balance—clearing the negative and replacing it with the positive. As a consequence, those who practice chanting experience joy, calm and emotional balance, which can lead to a loving and positive attitude towards the self and others. Those who practice unconditional love for themselves and others are likely to have clear energy centres. As harmony within ensures a balanced and positive expression of the life forces, the outside world reflects that harmony back to the individual.

THE TRUTH SEEKER

Each of the chakras provides a doorway through which one or more psychic skills can operate. These skills can activate automatically, especially in times of great emotion or need. Whether or not they're aware of doing so, most people react to the psychic activities of the chakras. There are many who have felt compelled to turn their head to face someone because of an uncomfortable feeling of being stared at. Our energy centres can act as receivers and enable us to become intuitively aware of attention. The psychic receptors that operate through the chakras are also responsible for our intuitive feelings about circumstances in our environment. More advanced psychic activity is likely when a person's energy centres become free of problems or blocks and the person is centred.

While it might seem reasonable to allot specific psychic abilities to each of the chakras, frequently more than one chakra is employed in the execution of a paranormal activity, so I cannot always assign responsibility to one chakra.

Crown chakra:

The crown chakra is the doorway to the spiritual dimensions. Journeys of enlightenment that can involve communication with high spiritual beings like the angels, archangels and the Masters, can occur when all chakras are aligned. The crown chakra is also the main chakra involved when a spiritual presence channels spiritual love and healing energies.

Third Eye chakra:

Front — The domain of clairvoyance that can include the viewing of distant places and times and can be called into play in for the purpose of creative visualisation.

Rear — Mind-to-mind connection as in telepathy, and the mental will of the focused mind that can be used in mind powers.

Throat chakra:

Front — Clairaudience (hearing voices and sounds from the astral and spiritual dimensions).

Rear — Sensing directed interest as in someone staring.

Heart chakra:

Front — Expresses love for others which plays an important role in healing.

Rear — Implementation of will due to caring. This can be a very powerful force in mind powers and magic and also in healing. There are many ways to heal, and each method can call upon one or more of the chakras including the two additional chakras in the palms which can be used to expel healing energy.

Solar plexus chakra:

Front — Scans the world around us and brings messages through intuition.

Rear — Relates to the healing of self.

Sacral chakra:

Front — Clairsentience and partially responsible for the magnetic charisma that captivates others and encourages their goodwill and cooperation. (Perhaps the heart chakra is also involved in this.)

Rear — Psychic power in the physical world—energy used in mind powers.

Base chakra:

Kundalini

There are doubtless many more abilities that can be expressed through the chakras, and time will bring more clarity to the powers that become available as humanity lifts its soul and consciousness to meet the divine within. Whilst we all wish to access our potential powers, spirit has ensured that while limited access may be gained by those who are still caught in their ego, full access to paranormal abilities accompanies the spiritual evolution of the soul.

Awareness of Energy Centers

My Christian upbringing did not provide me with knowledge about my chakras. I was unprepared for the experiences that revealed their presence and ill equipped to handle those experiences. I certainly didn't know that these centres could become connected to another person's chakras. My

THE TRUTH SEEKER

discovery that these powerful energy centres existed sent me on a journey of searching that enabled me to use the knowledge I subsequently gained.

After my marriage broke up, I became attracted to a man with whom I did not wish to form a close relationship. In the fallout from my unhappy marriage, in which I had been the recipient of daily rejection in one form or another, I knew any attraction would reflect the state of my slowly healing ego that still battled with feelings of inferiority.

The attraction expressed itself as an intense energy located just below my stomach (sacral chakra). This man was also attracted to me and approached me on a number of occasions with the intention of taking the attraction further. In spite of my determination not to allow the attraction to develop, sometimes when I was out I would turn around and look straight into a car that was passing without consciously knowing why. It would be the car he was driving. At other times, although I had no prior knowledge of his presence, I would turn and look directly at him on the other side of the street. I found it weird that this sort of incident happened so frequently.

The strong magnetic pull towards this man continued for over a year and showed no sign of abating. I had no idea how to stop it. Then one afternoon I was on the bus when suddenly the strong energetic pull on my sacral chakra ceased. One moment it was there, the next it was gone! A week later I saw him. The attractive lady he was with had his undivided attention. It would appear that he had been locking my energy to his because of the intensity of his attraction to me. When he met someone new who attracted his interest, he let me go.

We may connect to another person's energy centres for many reasons. Which of our energy centres connect will depend on the type of energy involved in the connection. However, I've found in most strong energy connections between other people and me, the sacral chakra is involved. In the above case, the chakra connection that had locked me into his energies had resulted not only in the distracting attraction, but also the unconscious awareness of his proximity whenever he came near.

Around two years later, although I still had little understanding of the workings of the chakras, I was aware of the power of the focused mind (third eye) and of intuitive awareness (solar plexus) along with the sensing that came from the heart (heart). At this time, I met Paul. I felt an immediate attraction to him that exposed a deep emotional response in me. Disappointingly, when I next saw him he didn't seem to remember me. As I passed him on the street, I said, 'Hello,' and then dropped into an expanded state of awareness that involved my heart chakra and allowed me to feel loving energy radiating from him. It was like thousands of tiny beads of beautiful, exhilarating energy flying at and through me. This beautiful experience reveals how one person's energy can penetrate and have an impact on another's.

The experience confirmed Paul was a person I wanted to get to know. Ladies didn't directly approach men when I was in my teens, and twenty years later at the beginning of the eighties I hadn't caught up with the more equal interactions between men and women. So I needed to come up with a subtle way to attract his attention. Paul was a member of the band at the club I attended on Saturday nights when I went dancing. There was always a variable lapse of time after the conclusion of a dance bracket before he came out to the bar area. Occasionally, he would stand in the queue of around five to ten people to obtain a drink from the free coffee machine.

What I needed to do was arrive at the machine at the same time as Paul. It would be too obvious if I sat in the bar area and jumped up to join the queue when I saw him, so I looked for an alternative. I needed to walk through the dance hall doors, into the bar area and straight to the queue without having previously had the opportunity to see him.

Each week at the conclusion of one of the dance brackets, I headed into the bathroom in the dance hall with the intent this would be the break during which I would connect with Paul. I then focused my mind (third eye) and said to myself, 'I will go out into the bar area in time to be next to Paul in the queue.' And then I waited until the time felt right (solar plexus) to leave the bathroom. I exited the bathroom and walked through the dance room doors to the bar area towards the drink machine.

There were no misses—near or otherwise. Each time I joined the queue, I was either immediately ahead of or immediately behind Paul. After five or six nights, he looked at me and said, 'We have to stop meeting like this!' The ice was broken.

Whether consciously or unconsciously, we all react to the subtle activities of the energy centres that are part of who and what we are. As we become aware of the inner workings of the chakras, we can begin to use the forces that are as much part of us as our eyes and ears. Chakra activation can be a subtle feeling as in my determined actions regarding my meeting with Paul, or they can seem like a strong ongoing pulling energy as in the case of the attraction that followed my marriage breakup. Alternatively, they can produce a powerful vortex of energy as happened after our cat was hit by a car.

THE TRUTH SEEKER

Our two cats (mother and son) brought us much enjoyment and pleasure. Lady, the mother cat, was great company and followed me around talking constantly. Her communication was so full of expression, it was clear she was voicing very definite opinions. One evening I answered a knock on the door. A lad of around twelve stood in the doorway. 'A cat ran in front of our car and was hit,' he said. He then noted the cat (Lady's son Sam) sitting on top of the fridge and continued, 'It looks like that one.'

Blood dribbled from Lady's mouth as she lay still but conscious. The vet advised she should be left with him overnight and we should call the next morning to check on her condition. Torn and distressed, I returned home to spend the night restlessly tossing and turning, never losing awareness of the shadow that hung over our heads.

When I woke, my first thought was for Lady. It occurred to me I might be able to help her by sending her love energy (heart chakra). As I did so, I immediately connected psychically to her dead body through a powerful vortex of energy extending from below my waist (sacral chakra). Through that energy, I could feel the cat's body as though it were right in front of me. There was no life energy in what was now a very solid dead form. When I phoned the vet, I was advised that Lady had died during the night.

Considering the importance of the existence of our non-physical bodies and their gateway chakras, it's surprising Christianity seems to lack knowledge of them. There have no doubt been Christians over the centuries who have experienced chakra activation and the resultant psychic and spiritual experiences. Some must have reported details that came into the hands of the Church hierarchy. Perhaps they were ignored because their reports conflicted with the Church's beliefs, or perhaps superstition led them to believe such experiences were an aberration and the work of the devil. Ignorance of our spiritual nature needs to be removed, and the real truth of who and what we are needs to be recognised and understood so we can discard whatever is holding us back from fulfilling our spiritual destiny.

Connections and Disconnections

At the highest levels of existence we are all connected. As we move through the progressively denser levels of all we are, separation comes into effect. The connections that then take place are individual and relevant to the chakra level associated with the energy involved. We are connected to those people we care about in the physical world through bands of energy at all times, and these connections can be helpful in times of trouble. However, when the connections are destructive, action needs to be taken to sever the energetic links.

There are all sorts of shared energies between people and one or more chakra connections are usually in place with people who are close. I have found in all chakra psychic connections between people, the sacral chakra activates. Common intellectual interests will create connections between the third eye chakras and can result in telepathic interaction. Emotional connections involve the heart chakra and empathy.

In the following case, actual knowledge of the thought processes of the person were revealed to me through the automatic activation of my chakras. I had met a man at the psychic development classes I attended and was attracted to his sensitive nature and clever mind. Although we were in the early stages of getting to know each other, we had already formed chakra connections.

It was Saturday morning, and I was changing the sheets on my bed. Suddenly I became aware of a vortex of energy in the region of my sacral chakra connecting me to this man. I 'heard' his thoughts (throat chakra). He was focused on making a decision involving me and was considering the impact knowing me would have on how he dealt with a situation in his life. He ran the different aspects of the situation through his mind, and I was aware as he made the decision and what that decision was. A week or so later I informed him of my knowledge and was confronted by his shock followed by his confirmation as to the accuracy of all the details. I had not deliberately tuned into this man, but when he focused his attention upon me, the psychic connection took place because of the linking of our chakras.

Sometimes the connections between people aren't healthy and are therefore better severed. Through phone calls over a number of weeks, I was informed of an escalating conflict between my friend and her partner and one of their neighbours. Time and again, the neighbour's dog kept my friends awake during the night. Requests that something be done were met with a hostile response. In fact, the neighbour had taken to regularly yelling abuse at the couple as she passed their place.

My distraught and angry friend asked me what she could do to make the problem go away. Since she was familiar with the concept of chakras, I explained to her that when there are strong feelings between people, a cord of energy is established from one or more of the person's chakras to those of the other person. Which chakras connected depended on the type of energy involved. My friend was horrified at the thought she was connected in any

THE TRUTH SEEKER

way to the lady concerned. Even more so, when I advised the other woman's energy could pass through this connection and into her.

A revolted, 'Yuck!' followed. 'What can I do to stop it?'

The most effective way to dissolve this energetic link, I explained, was through love energy. My friend felt incapable of feeling love for the lady. Since she was determined to do something to end the nasty situation, I suggested white light as an alternative.

'First of all, relax into a meditative state and clear your own energy by letting go of any negative feelings towards the woman. Then visualise the other woman and see the energy links between you in the colours you feel represent the thoughts and feelings involved. Then visualise a white light from the spiritual realms coming through your crown chakra and moving down and out through your chakras and along the cords of energy connecting you to the other woman's chakras. Then visualise the white light dissolving all the negative energy until there is no connection left between you.' I then went on to advise her she should repeat this exercise for each of the chakras she felt were compromised through their association.

If done wholeheartedly, the exercise would sever *all* connections between them—even in the physical world. For this reason, I advised my friend she needed to be aware that a separation in their physical proximity to the other woman was a likely consequence of this exercise, and either the woman or my friend and her partner would find it necessary to move.

My friend decided to go ahead with the exercise.

Two or three weeks later, I asked my friend about the woman. She replied she hadn't seen her. Shortly after, she and her partner received notice from their landlord that they needed to vacate the premises as he wished to refurbish the building.

We each have choices as to how we feel towards others. What most people don't realise is the impact our feelings can have on another person, and how we can be affected by how others feel about us. Letting go of hostility towards others ensures opposition on their part disintegrates or they're removed from our environment.

Our energetic connections to each other can offer positive support or a negative drain. The workings of such connections can be seen in incidents of serendipity and coincidence. Whether those incidents are positive or negative depends on the nature of the link.

JOAN L BOLER

Coinciding Events

Being in the right place at the right time, and attracting the right people and situations when needed, can be described as 'coincidence' or 'serendipity'. Most people have assumed that when time, situations and people coincide, it's as a result of random circumstances. I doubt such randomness is possible in a universe filled with order, where cause is always behind an effect and even causes have causes. That which is seen as synchronicity (the timely linking of events or items of a similar nature) is considered to be acausal. Synchronistic events are the result of the law of Like attracts Like. For this law to activate it needs to be directed, although such direction can be, but is not necessarily, deliberate. The directors and users of this law are:

- The magicians and miracle workers who work their magic through like objects or images

- The individual person when engaged in strong or definite mental or emotional focus

- The cosmic rulers as described in astrology that direct our destiny through the interaction of similar energies to those embedded in the karmic template in our soul

From the benign to the life threatening, an alignment of events can forge a path that cuts through possible disaster—provided a clear access to each dimension is available via the chakras. Our chakras are powerful, invisible sensors and receivers with potentially unlimited access to the different dimensional levels. If the chakras have become clogged or twisted as a result of fearful, painful and traumatic experiences, our daily journey through life reflects that state. When the chakras are clear, they can ensure a life filled with serendipity.

In order to bring about a desired result, the unconscious mind seeks and finds the resources needed through the chakras. This often includes using the chakra connections between people, which brings into play the 'Like attracts Like' law in a variety of ways. Through the chakra energy centres, the unconscious organises and manipulates the environment and the people in it and, much like the Global Positioning System (GPS) navigation device, can plot the fastest route to a destination or a desired result within moments.

The conscious mind can play a part in creating coincidence. The following experience was doubtless a product of my own determination that I would reconnect once again with my lost friend.

THE TRUTH SEEKER

I had last seen my friend Christine in New Zealand prior to my move to Norfolk Island in 1970. We kept us in touch through letters after she moved to Perth in Western Australia. Unfortunately, when I moved back to New Zealand temporarily before coming to Australia, we lost touch.

In 1972, I arrived in Australia. Although Australia isn't a small country, I determined I would meet up with Christine although statistically the likelihood of my doing so was almost zero. Whenever I thought of her it was with the conviction we would meet again.

In December 1978, I travelled by train from the Central Coast where I lived, to Susie's (my friend from Norfolk Island) place in Sydney. After a day with Susie, I caught the train home. As was usual at that time of the day, there were no seats available. Since I was on a double-decker train, I sat on the stairs and read my book. When the train stopped and some people alighted, I wasted no time in moving into a vacated seat.

The train moved off. As I looked out of the window in order to see where we were, I groaned, 'Oh no!' We were just leaving the Woy Woy station. My station! I couldn't believe it. I *always* knew when I'd arrived at my station. I sat stunned at my lack of sense and proceeded to persecute my stomach with images of the meal I'd have to wait for.

I stepped off the train at Gosford where I ran into a young man I knew and bemoaned my miserable fate as I advised him of my extended trip. With solicitous concern, he guided me to the platform from which I would be able to catch the next train back, and then remained with me to ensure I was safely delivered on to the train when it arrived. While we were talking, a train from Sydney pulled to a stop in front of us and as the passengers alighted, a woman walked up to me.

'Joan?'

'Christine!' It was my lost friend! We quickly exchanged phone numbers as she had to rush to catch a connecting train. Stunned from the encounter, I commented to my companion, 'Now I know why I missed my station.'

Christine had been living about forty-five miles (seventy-two kilometres) from me for around nine months and was planning to leave the area three weeks later. The window of time in which we had to connect wasn't long, considering she travelled by train to and from work each day while I travelled by train only occasionally.

JOAN L BOLER

All aspects of who and what we are as souls, operate through our chakras. Our unconscious minds influenced us to take actions to ensure our reconnection, and in so doing it used the chakra connections formed through our friendship. In this instance, my unconscious blocked my usual need to check what station I was at, ensuring I missed my stop and bringing me into contact with a person who would guide me to a position on the platform that would bring Christine directly into my path.

Destiny ensures what is meant to happen, does happen. In retrospect it is possible to see a sequence of connections that seem to come together to aid, or ensure, a specific result.

Paul and I had gone our separate ways. I was looking for work, and since there was very little on offer on the Central Coast, I headed down to Sydney to register with an employment agency. I was returning home on a train that stopped at Hornsby station halfway through its journey. As the train pulled out of the station, I glanced up to see Paul walking along the aisle towards me. I hadn't seen him for some time and was surprised he was not only on a train, but that of the six to eight carriages on the train he had joined the same carriage I was in. Paul rarely travelled by train. During the next few minutes, he informed me that the previous night, after he finished his work with the band, rather than drive home at the late hour he had stayed at a friend's place. In the early hours of the morning he was awoken by the sounds of a crash. An out of control driver had rammed into his parked car. Driving it home wasn't an option—hence the train trip.

Coincidentally, the friend he had stayed with the previous night had spoken to him of people she knew who were looking for someone reliable and capable to look after their office. A few hours later, after Paul had checked out the details with his friend, he gave me their name and phone number. When I phoned the woman I spoke to was charming, but advised they had already employed someone. However, she continued to talk to me for a while and seemed impressed with my experience and abilities. She concluded our conversation with, 'Give me your phone number, in case the person we have employed doesn't work out.'

Paul, displaying the strong intuitive abilities usually found in those born under his Sun sign Pisces, stated, 'This is your job. You wait and see!' Over a week passed before I received a phone call. The lady with whom I'd spoken advised me the woman who had accepted the position and been due to start work on the Monday hadn't turned up. Within a few days, I had been for an interview and had commenced the job I was to remain in for the next eight years. This reconnection with Paul also resulted in our becoming a couple again.

THE TRUTH SEEKER

In times of need, I usually find help is close by. Perhaps this comes about because I trust my needs will be met. Just prior to the conclusion of one of my trips to visit my son, serendipity intervened. Chris had moved to a new location. His directions were quite clear when he advised me he was now living in the main street of Southport, a densely populated area on the Gold Coast of Queensland. As Southport was familiar to me from previous visits, I didn't deem it necessary to ensure I had a map of the area. The trip from Sydney was a long one, and apparently some of my brain cells were taking a break, so when I arrived in Southport I headed for the Gold Coast Highway thinking 'main road' instead of 'main street'.

As I drove along the highway, I felt something wasn't right. When I sighted a public telephone (this was pre cell phone days), I pulled over. A friendly young man who was just hanging up the phone said, 'You go ahead and use the phone. I need to get more change from the shop.'

It seemed not only my brain wasn't working that day! I attempted to phone Chris for directions, but my phone card, although it still had a balance on it, failed to work. The young man returned with his change. Not sure what my next move should be, I told him of my dilemma and added I had come up from Sydney to visit my son, Chris. 'Oh, you're Chris Boler's mum. I saw him in the supermarket about an hour ago. He said you were coming. If you turn around and take the first right and then the first right again, you will be in Scarborough Street (the main street)—he is at number 200 on the left hand side.' My son, and my son's dog, greeted me enthusiastically five minutes later.

Did my problem solving unconscious anticipate my problem and ensure the meeting between my son and his friend? And what of his friend's need to make a phone call from the public telephone that I needed to use around the same time? Manipulation in this instance seems to have been expedited by the unconscious through chakra connections that provide a direct link between one person and another.

Many people report incidents of running into people they know, or people who know people they know, when they're far from home. There seems to be no reason for such connections, but they happen anyway. In random people connections, it would seem possible each of the persons connecting have been drawn together to the same place at the same time because of their common chakra connection to the same third party.

When I was living on Norfolk Island, I met with some people who had flown over from Whakatane, a small town in New Zealand's North Island. This town neighboured the one where I was born and had lived until I was eleven. I mentioned this to the people I was with, and one of them responded with, 'Do you know Bill F and John F?'

'Yes!' I replied, 'My father and my brother.'

My father and brother hadn't lived in the town for many years and it was unlikely they were the only people these people knew in the relatively close town. Does a 'like attracts like' situation occur, where the unconscious draws people together with common people connections? It is a simple matter for the chakras to intuit this connection. It seems possible the unconscious looks for ways in which to bring awareness, and alerts the conscious mind by throwing up images or thoughts of the person or persons and places both parties have a common knowledge of.

While chakras and personal people connections appear to be the usual way in which coincidental connections are made, the versatile unconscious is not limited to personal connections. Rather, it seems 'like attracts like' can be applied to objects as well.

I was still a young woman and was travelling to work along the motorway when the motor in my little Fiat 500 died and I cruised to a halt. I groaned as images of my being late for work beset me. Then as I looked in the rear vision mirror, I was astonished to see another Fiat 500 roll to a halt behind my car. My Fiat 500 was some years old at that time and there were hardly any of these little cars left on the road. This was bizarre!

Disbelief was still crowding my brain when the young male driver found his way to my car window. After some disparaging comments about his own car and its troubles, he asked what the problem was with my car. It had stopped. That was the extent of my knowledge. Those were the days when males' love affairs with their cars invariably saw their heads under the bonnet of a car while their vocabulary ran almost exclusively to spark plugs, carburettors, valves and engines. Ignorant females could only wonder at the attraction to the grease and the mechanical parts that seemed to be a messy, noisy, evolution of their brother's Meccano sets.

Superior knowledge and ability was flaunted by the young males of the time, or of any time for that matter, and five minutes later the motor was making promising noises. Grateful, I offered my rescuer thanks and a lift to wherever he needed to go to get help. Apparently, he had a friend who lived not far away and proceeded to walk off towards a group of houses.

THE TRUTH SEEKER

The young man's timely intervention negated the need for a tow truck, a mechanic and the resultant costs, and ensured I avoided having to make embarrassing apologies at work and also receive a reduction in my wages.

Two weeks later I had a flat tyre—outside a garage that sold and replaced tyres!

Were the chakras involved in these incidents? I needed help for my car. Help was sought by my solution seeking unconscious using the scanning abilities of my solar plexus chakra in locating a 'like' vehicle with a driver who knew how to fix my car. At the time of this incident, I wasn't aware it was possible to programme the unconscious, so that was an unlikely cause. Since each of us are, through energetic fields, connected to 'like' astrological energies, they doubtless also play a part in all coincidental incidents whether serendipitous or otherwise. In this particular case, the astrological alignments during that two week period contributed towards a positive and quick solution to my vehicle problems on two occasions.

It is probable astrological energies are involved in all serendipitous incidents. In the above situations, the energies worked beneficially to ensure a positive and desirable outcome in each case. This could only happen if the prevailing astrological energies met with harmony in the like energies of my soul.

An aspect of this phenomenon that also needs to be considered is the time factor. The unconscious mind works outside time, so a problem that is to arise in the future can be solved in the present or the past by setting in motion the events that lead to the desired situation or the required solution.

Over the years when I have been prevented from following through with plans, I often discovered later that had they eventuated, an undesirable situation would have been the outcome. For this reason I have learned to trust that changes in plans are in my best interest and, for the most part, remain calm in the face frustrating situations. Trust is the key to letting go of fear. With deep belief or trust that all that happens is in our best interest in the greater scheme of things, fear and its consequences can be eliminated.

In a world where people are learning to take responsibility for their own lives, rather than leaving it up to those who claim authority, the realisation we are intimately involved in all that happens in our lives can give us power over circumstances. Who wouldn't wish to invite serendipity into their life? We can choose to use or abuse the laws that are a fundamental part of our lives—so long as we know about them. The laws relating to the chakras are complex, but these powerful and amazing energy centres need to be understood and respected.

Kundalini

The way we are made is remarkable. When looking at chakras and their associated bodies, we see a magnificent and perfect design. The multiple layers of our psychic and spiritual makeup are sealed with spiritual energy so negative energies can't enter our personal domain. The chakras play a pivotal role in managing our progress as souls through *kundalini* (Sanskrit), the movement of a spiritual force that radiates up through all the chakras, from the base to the crown. Because the force of kundalini activates from the base chakra, it's associated with that chakra.

Kundalini is an amazing process that activates naturally and automatically throughout our lives. As it moves through the chakras, it allows greater access to the powers within—powers that, in part at least, have been developed through our accomplishments. For example, strength of will leads to achievement with the power of the mind, while empathy and caring enhances the perception of the nature of others and provides a source of power for the implementation of the miraculous.

Most people have no conscious awareness of kundalini in action. Many of the indications are subtle and may happen during sleeping hours or over long periods of time. Some people invoke kundalini and prepare for it so there are no, or very few, negative energies in its path. The conscious kundalini experience varies from person to person. Those whose energies are clear may experience ecstasy and/or transcendental states. For most, the subtle workings of kundalini continue throughout their life, gradually increasing chakra function.

Kundalini is not to be taken lightly, nor are there short cuts to achieving true psychic awareness through its premature activation. It can be activated accidentally or deliberately, and can fully open one or more of the chakras before the person is ready. The usually benign ways to bring about kundalini activation include prolonged meditation and exercises during the meditative state. With deliberate activation, preparation is a wise precaution along with the guidance of an experienced person. With or without guidance, if activation happens to a happy well-balanced person, it can prove to be a very positive experience.

THE TRUTH SEEKER

Unfortunately, a positive result is not likely to be the case when kundalini is raised through extreme trauma of which rape, especially in a younger person, is one, while the use of drugs, is another. Puberty is an especially vulnerable time. Whatever the cause, unless the chakras are clear, the results can be distressing to devastating. Each of the chakras can hold within the damage caused through the difficulties and traumas that result from the painful experiences we learn from. For some, kundalini activation results in the clearing of the chakras over time through physical illness or depression. For others, it opens the door to a paranormal world that reflects the fears and negative energies jamming up their system. Mental illness, including schizophrenia and paranoia, can result.

A man of around thirty-five came to me for advice. He was very distressed about attacks of paranoia he had begun experiencing the previous year. He mentioned that a woman claiming 'special powers' said she could stop the attacks—at a cost of $2,000.

'You know,' I said, 'Marijuana can have that effect.'

'I always avoided drugs until last year when I started using marijuana,' was his response.

In another situation I was reading a young woman's palms and noted her mind line revealed the possibility of mental problems. I said to her, 'You should avoid mind altering drugs, for their use can open you to the negative aspects of the psychic world.

'Is that what caused it?' was her response.

Perhaps the most frightening result of the premature opening of the chakras is experienced by the person who harbours strong feelings of guilt, fear, anger, hate or self-loathing. Each of these emotions breaks the Law of Love that governs all in existence. With the opening of some chakras, the lower astral dimensions can be accessed along with the unpleasant entities that inhabit them. Alternatively, the unconscious mind can produce scary hallucinations. Once again, like attracts like occurs in the encountering of unpleasant entities or frightening hallucinations. It's as though life is holding up a mirror saying, **Look. This is what the energy inside you looks like.** Clearing that energy is necessary for recovery to take place.

Through the process of kundalini, each of our chakras gradually opens like a flower coming to full bloom. The more the powers of the chakras become available to us, the more clearly we are able to use them. Most people can make use of the paranormal abilities that lie within to the degree they have already developed them. When we are in a harmonious and balanced state, these energy centres are able to work in cooperation with our environment and bring about the aligning of events so solutions to problems are delivered, almost before they arrive.

This is a like attracts like universe, and never is this clearer than when dealing with other dimensions. Kundalini is a little understood spiritual process that accelerates the development of the nervous system so more advanced abilities are possible. This wonderful process is part of a spiritual system that works towards an awareness that involves love in all its aspects. Such love is the frequency of the higher dimensions and is the passport to them.

More than Physical

It is impossible to grow spiritually and not to also grow in paranormal ability. It doesn't follow that all psychics have developed spiritual awareness and work from a spiritual space. The fact they possess paranormal ability reveals that one or more of their chakras have opened—probably as a result of kundalini activity. Which chakras are open, and how accurately and well they operate, reflects the degree of development of the characteristics related to that chakra.

The witch I mentioned earlier was a powerful psychic. While witchcraft is a spiritual path chosen by many, it was not my chosen path. Even had it been, I wouldn't have accepted this man's offer I join his coven, as the nature of witchcraft in this man's world was a lot about his superiority and power over others. While he was capable of compassion and caring towards those who accepted him unconditionally, he had been tortured and burnt in a previous lifetime because of his then involvement with witchcraft, and that experience coloured his every action in this lifetime. He had at some time in his past developed a very strong mind and therefore had developed his strength of will to a degree that increased his psychic ability. Due to his pain, he had developed compassion that had enhanced his emotional connection to and understanding of others. His charismatic personality revealed another well-developed skill that also played a part in his psychic ability to attract others. In addition, as a witch, along with the drawing upon the psychic energy of those in his coven, he could have called on various non-physical energies and entities, so additional power became available to him.

THE TRUTH SEEKER

In this lifetime, he had become a benefactor to those who followed him, and a judge of those who in his opinion did wrong or rejected him. He used his powers to punish. In a sense he was punishing those who burnt him at the stake. He was probably punishing those very same souls who were involved in his previous death by fire. One punishment he dealt out involved causing a fire through employing psychic ability. His actions mirror the behaviour of his earlier persecutors.

This man told of his grandmother who had been a feared black witch in Europe during his childhood. He confessed he had been a black witch during his earlier years, and he had used others without conscience or concern for their well-being. Then he chose to become a white witch—to be compassionate and help others. A step forward on his spiritual journey—but only a step! A white witch, or any spiritual person, would not judge or punish in the way he was doing.

This man had yet to let go of a deep, deep fear. A fear others had been responsible for instilling in him when they subjected him to a shocking death. In his need to feel safe, he seeks to control others. The anger that bubbles beneath the surface and found its outlet in punishing those he judged deserving reveals he had yet to forgive. Until he does so, this cycle of punish and be punished will continue.

As we evolve and clear away the mental and emotional blocks that clutter our energy centres, we become more and more aware of our power, the spiritual world, and our own spirituality. I use the word 'spiritual' to describe energies of indescribable magnificent power, unlimited unconditional love, infinite intelligence, knowledge, wisdom and vision, and boundless, invigorating creativity.

Healing the Damaged Chakras and Auras

For those who have been damaged through the premature opening of the chakras, there are a number of possible options. For the most part, orthodox medicine does not take into account, or understand, the psychic effect of the individual's own negative energies. By opening to spiritual possibilities and recognising our multidimensional nature, it's possible to cure the emotional and mental damage caused by the premature activation of kundalini.

Personal responsibility for the state of the soul must be taken in order to progress along the path towards health, happiness and enlightenment. To that end, the behaviour that has caused the damage must cease, whether it's the use of psychedelic substances or any other form of self-abuse. Since self-destructive behaviour can be sourced to emotional issues within the person's psyche, these need to be addressed.

In order to change their psychic environment, those who are exposed to schizophrenic type experiences need to eliminate the negative energies within and replace them with non-judgemental self-love. Clearing of the negative enables such people to move forward and raise their energies, so they only psychically encounter beings of the higher dimensions. This is not easy to achieve as their world is full of fearful experiences, and the medical profession can only offer medications that block but do not heal.

I don't think that once the chakras have been opened, it is possible to return them to how they were. Healing through meditation can contribute towards the recovery of those who have opened their chakras prematurely. There are many methods of healing the chakras through regular meditation. The one I usually work with involves visualising and bringing the pure colour of each chakra down through the crown chakra, commencing with the red of the base chakra. First, I allow the colour to extend throughout the body to the extremity of the energy fields, healing all energy related to the colour red. Then I move the energy to the base chakra where it balances that chakra's energies and removes any energy that isn't of a positive nature. I repeat the exercise for each of the chakras, using the appropriate colours.

Since those who have problems with their chakras are also likely to have breached the boundaries of their auric field, it's a good idea to finish each meditation with an aura sealing. This can be achieved by visualising, or requesting of those in spirit, a powerful golden spiritual energy to seal the aura in order to ensure the negative energy of others cannot penetrate its field. This latter exercise can be employed at any time of day or night. A spiritual healer who is aware of and who understands kundalini activity can also help such people by assisting in the clearing of negative energies. Since our health, mentally, emotionally and physically, is reflected in our aura and chakras, a spiritual healer can see where to focus healing energy. For the most part, real healing is achieved through exposing and healing, possibly with the help of hypnotherapy, damaging and destructive emotions and their causes.

It is worth considering that all over the world throughout history mankind has been experimenting with and using psychedelic substances. Since access to the non-physical dimensions can be achieved through drugs, as well as through a life of caring for self and others, transcendental experiences and expanded states of awareness induced through drugs have probably played a significant role in the religions of the world, in religious beliefs, and in the spiritual progress of many.

While drugs have not contributed to my psychic abilities and paranormal experiences in this lifetime, I recall a life as an American Indian shaman some eight hundred years ago when I enhanced my awareness with the aid of substances that were broken down into a powder in a bowl. I lived a very spiritual life and was able to experience a connection to the animals and the land. This type of experience is truly amazing. Somehow, in that life, I was poisoned when the psychedelic substance I usually used, mistakenly or otherwise, included a toxic ingredient. Immediately after ingesting the substance, I knew I had been poisoned. My whole body went into crisis almost immediately and I died.

We are all psychic beings, although some of us are more developed than others. Today there are millions of people worldwide who have experimented with and become involved in taking mind-altering drugs. Many get caught in the web of peer approval and promised highs that, depending upon the type of drug used, can result in an addiction so consuming that all else in life pales into insignificance. The cost to the emotional, mental and physical health can be crippling, while the drug related deaths of many warn of the possible fatal consequences. Financially, drug taking can breed desperation that can lead to criminal activities. In spite of this, there are large numbers of people who have experienced aspects of the psychic and spiritual kingdoms through both limited drug use and habitual drug taking. Since the majority of those who have had such experiences harbour both positive and negative energies within, it is possible for them to have experienced both the positive and the negative during their experience of the inter-dimensional.

While it's easy to focus on the negatives of drug induced experiences because they can cause devastation, there have been positives. Awareness of our supernatural nature, encountering non-physical beings and lifting out of the physical body are just some of the possible experiences. This is no small matter as it can open up the desire within the individual to journey along the spiritual pathway. However, it should be remembered that since psychedelic substances interfere with brain function, the reliability of such experiences is brought into question.

Swiss scientist Albert Hoffman (1906-2008) synthesised and ingested lysergic acid diethylamide (LSD), thereby learning of its psychedelic effects. Seventeen years of research followed, which demonstrated many benefits of its use. The life-changing transcendental experiences that enabled spiritual awakening enhanced the lives and psychic capabilities of numerous individuals. For ten years, LSD was used in psychoanalysis with great success. Unfortunately, misuse in the 1960s led to its use being very much restricted.[123]

The vast amount of knowledge available from this research reveals potential for transformation in those who ingest LSD responsibly. For those needing psychiatric therapy, LSD offers the possibility of healing. The knowledge that LSD is again being researched is encouraging. America, the UK, Germany, Switzerland, Spain, Holland, Israel, Peru and Brazil are among the countries involved in psychedelic research.[124]

I don't recommend the use of psychedelic substances for recreational use, or many of the available substances for any use at all. However, I do believe further investigation will confirm that some substances, such as LSD, may offer opportunities for healing disturbed people. Perhaps the future will see an opportunity for those who experience mental illness to be helped through the use of psychedelic substances in a safe environment supervised by professionals.

There is another method of healing disturbed souls that doesn't require the use of drugs. Psychosynthesis was developed by Italian psychiatrist Roberto Assagioli (1888-1974). His holistic approach to psychoanalysis, which is still being used and developed upon today, encourages personal development through recognition of the spiritual aspect of human nature and of love. He advocated the improved use of will, intuition and creativity in order to bring about a balance and harmony that encompasses all aspects of the person including the spiritual.[125] [126]

Whatever method is used, the key to success is the purging of negative behaviour, attitudes, and energies, and opening to love and its restorative powers. I hope that from the above-mentioned methods of healing, one or two become mainstream so the use of medication that doesn't heal, and that not only limits mental and emotional function, and can have physical side effects, is no longer necessary.

---

[123] 'About Us—Who we are.' *Albert Hoffman Foundation.* www.hofmann.org/about/mission.html, (accessed 12 Dec 2011)
[124] Grof, Stanislav, 'The consciousness revolution', p. 3. *Articles by Stanislav Grof.* www. stanislavgrof. com/articles.htm. (accessed 12 Dec 2011)
[125] Crampton, Martha. 'What is Psychosynthesis?' *Association for the Advancement of Psychosynthesis.* http://aap-psychosynthesis. org/what-is-psychosynthesis. (accessed 23 Apr 2014)
[126] Firman, John & Gila, Ann (2002). "Introduction". *Psychosynthesis—a Psychology of the Spirit,* SUNY Press, 2010, pp. 1–3.

THE TRUTH SEEKER

Spiritual Within

Enlightenment, which is always through paranormal experience and the chakra doorways, heals and opens up exciting possibilities often described as crazy, impossible, or even due to witchcraft, and yet the paranormal experience itself confirms humanity's multidimensional identity. Such experiences change human physiology, while enhancing the soul as they underpin the desire to extend ourselves in the achievement of our goals and for a fuller and happier existence for all on the planet.

For most people, the opening of the chakras is a gradual process linked to our spiritual growth as we incorporate more and more of love and its aspects into our nature. For those who experience premature opening of the chakras, the only true pathway to healing is through developing spiritual love for self and others and letting go of all thoughts and beliefs that invite fear. As we grow in our capacity to love, we can begin to discover and work with our multidimensional bodies and their chakra gateways, and as a result our reality becomes filled with purpose, excitement and creativity. Happiness begins to knock on the door of the soul, and undreamed of possibilities begin to become reality.

We all follow different pathways to our own spirituality and no human being or belief system has the monopoly on mystical knowledge and experience. The spiritual identity of each and every individual on the planet is a reality that demands recognition.

JOAN L BOLER

Chapter 8

Love—the Universal Law

One word frees us of all the weight and pain of life: That word is love.

Sophocles[127]

Love and its Aspects

In any given human experience, something remarkable is happening. Beyond the pain, the horror and the fear, there is a precious essence growing as humanity's baser energies evolve. Over lifetimes the diverse energies within each of us that are in various stages of development come under the astrological influences that ensure development through challenge to the soul. This experiential growth owes much of its potency to male/female interaction.

As a young child, feelings of love for my mother were overwhelming. My love for my father and my siblings was also deep and strong. What I found astounding at the young age of seven or eight was that the huge love I felt for one didn't take anything away from the love I felt for any of the others. This was my first remembered awareness that love was boundless, and the significance of my discovery coloured my view of life from that point on. In my adult years I was surprised by the depth of love I felt, not only for my own children, but for the children of my friends and siblings, and in fact any children. Most unexpected was my reaction to those people who over the years I gave guidance to during psychic readings. The quality and quantity of pure love I felt towards them seemed to reach into forever. But emotional love, no matter how strong, can be vulnerable without the supporting wisdoms and characteristics that have been hewn through life's lessons that have carved their imprint deep in the soul.

Love has depth and breadth and encompasses all that is, for it is not just a one-dimensional feeling of love towards special others. It has a sense of self

---

[127] *Oedipus at Colonus,* line 1616.

and a connection to all those who share, if only for a moment, this life's experiences. Whatever causes us to care, to love ourselves and others also motivates us to grow and develop. Our capacity to love includes respect, honour, truth, strength, power, integrity, loyalty, tenacity, flexibility, discrimination, compassion, wisdom, creativity, courage, discipline and trust. Love removes a range of negative feelings, especially fear, hate and judgement.

For the people who lack love or its supporting attributes, their journey of discovery and learning is still in its infancy. All the well-established religions of the world teach rules for living a spiritual life. They exhort followers to adhere to behaviour that, for the most part, reflects conduct that those who care about others abide by. Although not always understood as aspects of love, that is what all the characteristics are. No matter its intensity, without the strength and wisdom of its supporting facets, love lacks depth and substance and can prove to be unreliable.

The Masters of the past exhorted their follows to live in a manner that would contribute to their spiritual growth.

> *With an open mind, seek and listen to all the highest ideals. Consider the most enlightened thoughts. Then choose your path, person by person, each for oneself.*
> Zarathustra (1500-1000 BCE?) Persian founder of the Zoroastrian Religion.

> *Just as treasures are uncovered from the earth, so virtue appears from good deeds, and wisdom appears from a pure and peaceful mind. To walk safely through the maze of human life, one needs the light of wisdom and the guidance of virtue.*
> Siddhartha Gautama, Supreme Buddha (563-483 BCE) Indian founder of Buddhism.[128]

> John 13:34-35 (NIV). [34]*"A new command I give you: Love one another. As I have loved you, so you must love one another.* [35] *By this all men will know that you are my disciples, if you love one another."* [129]

> Jesus (6-4 BCE—27-30CE) Jewish Rabbi and founder of Christianity.

---

[128] *The Three Building Blocks of Virtue*
[129] Biblestudytools.com. www.biblestudytools.com (accessed 13 Jul 2013)

THE TRUTH SEEKER

Do you know what is better than charity and fasting and prayer? It is keeping peace and good relations between people, as quarrels and bad feelings destroy mankind.
Muhammad (Abu al-Qasim Muhammad Ibn Abd Allah Ibn Abd al-Muttalib Ibn Hashim (570-632CE) Saudi Arabian founder of Islam. [130]

Most of those we meet in life are accomplished in many aspects of the Law of Love, but our presence in the physical reveals that the spiritual laws, as governed by the astrological forces, still have more to teach us.

Spiritual Evolution

Evolution takes humanity from the basic and unrefined to the complex, the creative and the spiritual. That born of base raw material, eventually becomes a being of great beauty and power through interaction with life. As we journey through lifetimes and are challenged physically, mentally and emotionally by astrological forces, growth takes place. Within each individual, energies that align with each zodiac sign are, over time, taken from base to great, from negative to positive.

Aries — 'I AM'
Balancing ego

Negative: Confrontational, self-indulgent, aggressive, impulsive, brutish, irascible, egotistical
Positive: Energetic, courageous, adventurous, self-assured, animated, vibrant, quick-witted

Taurus — 'I HAVE'
Developing inner strength

Negative: Jealous, possessive, greedy, stubborn, mean, indulgent, secretive
Positive: Reliable, loyal, warm-hearted, easy-going, persistent, patient, sensual, steadfast

---

[130] Hadith, Sunan Abi Dawud 4918

Gemini — 'I THINK'
Bringing about mental, emotional and physical harmony

Negative: Superficial, anxious, guilt-ridden, unpredictable, intrusive, calculating, duality
Positive: Enquiring mind, youthful, effervescent, witty, articulate, adaptable, intelligent

Cancer — 'I FEEL'
Working towards emotional stability

Negative: Moody, manipulative, ultra-sensitive, unstable, possessive, excessively emotional
Positive: Considerate, empathic, loving, protective, careful, resourceful, intuitive

Leo — 'I WILL'
Developing inner power

Negative: Arrogant, pretentious, patronizing, intolerant, domineering, meddling, inflexible
Positive: Self-assured, generous, warm-hearted, charismatic, creative, open-minded, faithful

Virgo — 'I ANALYSE'
Discrimination and assimilation through attention to detail

Negative: Perfectionist, conformist, worrier, overly critical, unforgiving
Positive: Conservative, industrious, practical, detailed, analytical, intelligent

Libra — 'I BALANCE'
Developing inner calm and balance through intuition

Negative: Indecisive, procrastinates, passive-aggressive, self-indulgent, martyr for peace
Positive: Diplomatic, cultured, charming, peaceful, quick witted, clever, intuitive

Scorpio — 'I DESIRE'
Directing desire and passion towards that which is of value

THE TRUTH SEEKER

Negative: Jealous, obsessive, vindictive, possessive, manipulator
Positive: Thrilling, compelling, intuitive, passionate, strong-minded, compassionate

Sagittarius — 'I REASON'
Illumination through reason and being open minded

Negative: Irresponsible, insincere, careless, tactless, acts superior, unrealistically optimistic
Positive: Optimistic, happy, good-natured, honest, loves freedom, intellectual, inspired

Capricorn — 'I USE'
Defining responsibility, Order and boundaries

Negative: Tight-fisted, resentful, pessimistic, defeatist, controlling
Positive: Practical, cautious, methodical, ambitious, persevering, mischievous humour

Aquarius — 'I KNOW'
Employing the enquiring mind to uncover truth and express humanitarian consciousness

Negative: Unemotional, detached, headstrong, opinionated, contrary
Positive: Genius, humanitarian, honest, inventive, independent, loyal, curious

Pisces — 'I TRUST'
Developing spiritual awareness and trust rather than blind belief

Negative: Blind belief, escapism, delusional, ungrounded, secretive, indirect, follows
Positive: Intuitive, sensitive, selfless, kind, spiritual, trusting[131] [132]

---

[131] De Pascale, Marc, *Book of Fate,* Thomas Nelson (Australia) Limited, Sydney, 1970/2000 ('I ...' description phrases.)
[132] Parker, Julia and Derek. *K. I. S. S Guide to Astrology*, Dorling Kindersley Pty Limited, Sydney, Australia, 2001..

JOAN L BOLER

Each individual soul needs to develop in all areas. For this reason, our experiences throughout time brings wisdom in many different ways in each person, with layer upon layer of learning creating a well of experience and turning each of us into unique individuals.

The Middle Road

Aristotle (384-322 BCE), a Greek philosopher, believed that in order to live morally it is necessary to find the mean between two opposing possibilities (for example, courage is the mean between cowardice and foolhardiness).[133] Buddhism also teaches of living according to the 'middle road'—living in balance between extremes in behaviour.

In Chapter Four 'Transformation', I discussed how the astrological north and south nodes have an impact on the life of a person to confront and bring about change within. In relationships, it is often the powerful Sun signs that can be attracted to the opposite sign in order to achieve the middle road or balance that the opposite sign offers.

The Piscean person, unless they have strong grounding earth energy in their make-up, is a soul without a rudder who is attracted to the stable, the reliable, the responsible and the unchanging. The Piscean seeks stability on an unconscious level. Responsibilities lie heavily on the shoulders of the Piscean and they frequently are unable or do not wish to deal with them. These delightful dreamers lack boundaries, and as a result possess such a flexibility of attitude that they rarely judge others. They have an abundant capacity for emotional love and a tendency to become emotional junkies. In relationships, the romantic Pisces falls in love with those who appear strong and in control of their lives. They are the believers of the zodiac, and fantasy and illusion are usually a constant in their lives. If they are not living on an emotional high, they are searching for the elusive dream that will take them there. If life becomes too difficult, Pisces will often turn to drugs and alcohol in order to experience the high that can remove them from an otherwise dreary and depressing world. Or if their love life has lost its high due to life's practical demands, they may seek it elsewhere.

A woman in her late thirties placed a photograph in front of me of a man she had met in America. They had become lovers on her recent visit, and were now in frequent telephone contact and planned to get together again soon. As I looked into the face of the man, I could see familiar Pisces features,

---

[133] *The World Eook Encyclopedia.*Ibid. 'A' p. 630

THE TRUTH SEEKER

and as I tuned into him, I could clearly feel the way in which the Pisces energies were influencing his attitudes and behaviour.

'He has a strong Pisces energy.' I stated.

'He *is* a Pisces,' she replied.

I could feel the emotional attachments, responsibilities and commitments around him.

'Oh yes. He is married with a son. But he doesn't love his wife,' the woman advised.

The emotional Piscean tends to equate love with emotion alone without taking into account what it is that can cause emotions to turn on and off. In the face of demanding responsibilities, his emotional love when challenged with the everyday presence of the difficult and mundane, had turned off. True to his nature, this man longed to break free of the demanding, responsibility-laden life he had become enmeshed in. But emotional love can just as easily turn back on again when confronted with emotionally based situations.

The woman then asked me, 'Will he leave his wife for me?'

While she was an outgoing and practical woman with an abundance of earth energy who longed for romance, he was a romantic with feet of clay. Her main astrological energies were earth (practical, reliable, methodical, feet on the ground) and fire, (ego, creative, action passion). She needed and was attracted to the romance, the emotion and the fantasy that her more serious, ordered life lacked. I explained that should this man leave his wife for her (and I did not think it likely for, in spite of his not being 'in love' with his wife, he did love her and the child), there was no permanent romantic future for her where this man was concerned.

Each of these people needed to develop within their own makeup, the energies they were looking to others to supply in order to find balance. The Piscean man needed to embrace responsibility and all that that entailed so he could become competent and gain satisfaction from the role life required from him. Both the women in his life needed to become gentler and kinder to the inner self instead of expecting the need for such nourishment to the soul to be supplied by others.

JOAN L BOLER

The Hook

All energies attract and repel. We are energy.

Life on this planet focuses on the development of our ability to love. For the most part, male/female energies provoke, invite, ensnare, demand and entice in order to ensure interaction on an intimate level. No man remains an island. Even those who would deny their own sensuality must sooner or later accept and honour this aspect of the human experience. Denial and cutting off from our sexuality may, for a time, allow a person to escape into a safe environment where their feelings aren't challenged, but eventually life will ensure they are confronted.

It is by going into, and dealing with, the intense emotions evoked by sexual love that energies such as fear, anger, frustration and jealousy are confronted. Such feelings, that make the individual feel bad, are the result of limited or wrong attitudes, beliefs and feelings. These feelings challenge the soul on a deep level and provide an opportunity to learn the lessons that lead to happiness, fulfilment and enjoyment of life. Those experiences we all instinctively seek and unconsciously know can be. Relationships force growth through happiness and pain, and result in the eventual understanding of unconditional love of self and of others.

Unconditional Love

Many speak of unconditional love—a non-judgemental love that accepts others with all their capabilities, inconsistencies and limitations. While we may talk about it and attempt to apply it, many don't fully understand what unconditional love is. As a psychic reader, I have been exposed to the inner beliefs and motivations of those to whom I have attempted to offer guidance. Time and again, I have encountered the unhappiness that arises out of misconceptions regarding the nature of love.

An intense young woman who came to me for guidance insisted she loved the man in her life unconditionally in spite of his negative behaviour towards her and other people in his life. Her spiritual purpose in life, she had decided, was to 'save' the young man. Her interpretation of unconditional love was to deny all her own wants and needs and to devote herself entirely to fulfilling his every wish. To her mind, what he needed in order to heal the negative and harmful aspects of his nature was her love and devotion. This young lady was not only an enabler; she was also allowing herself to be exposed to emotional abuse through her partner's constant lack of consideration. In spite of my explanations, she was determined in her chosen course of action.

Unconditional love does not discriminate between the worth of one person and another. Love is not unconditional if it only applies to others and not to self, or if it only applies to self and not to others. As no loving support was being given to the young woman's soul, either by her, or by the young man she had chosen to save, her life was difficult and painful. This young lady needed to learn through experience that her own lack of self-esteem motivated her to attempt to rescue another person. Self-love would require that she be treated with love and respect. Her deficient ego had deceived her into believing in her own worth through becoming a martyr and subjugating her own needs to the wishes of another. This way of thinking is unsurprising, for this is the lie that has been propagated by men and the religions dominated by men for millennia.

The demands of the young lady's relationship effectively took her attention away from her own life and needs. Had she taken responsibility for and directed attention towards healing her own unhappy soul, she could have developed self-esteem and overcome her co-dependent state. Eventually, through experiencing on-going abuse and subsequent disillusionment, new insight would be possible. At that time however, she was not ready to accept such concepts. Recognition of the need to value the self is just as important as learning to place value on others.

Romantic Love

Romantic and immature love ideals can blind people to the gift of love that surrounds them.

I was giving a psychic reading to a young lady who was married with two young children. She was unhappy in her marriage as she felt her husband didn't understand her. I sometimes gain insight into a problem by tuning into a past life of the parties concerned, as often couples repeat the same patterns of behaviour. The knowledge they have done it all before, and unless they get it right this time around they could be doomed to do it all again, can have greater impact.

I tuned into a recent past life she had lived with her current husband. As I described the man's physical appearance in that past life, she confirmed the similarity to his appearance in this lifetime. Further confirmation came when I described his personality. As I continued to tune into that past time, I sensed her dissatisfaction and unhappiness, and I could feel his deep love of his wife and his determination to do everything within his power to make her happy. In both lifetimes he had provided her with a home, supported her and their children, and was a devoted husband and father.

'Yes, he does try very hard to make me happy in this lifetime too,' she said. 'But he doesn't understand me!'

This young woman had the romantic notion her husband would, if he were her perfect partner, intuitively understand her every wish without her voicing it. In the previous lifetime, and again in this lifetime, she had judged him deficient in his role as her 'true love'. This belief was based not upon how he gave his everything to make her happy, but upon his lack of ability to read her mind. The poor man was desperate to understand her, but she refused to reveal anything about her needs and instead insisted he should know. Since he'd failed in his efforts, she was considering leaving him in order to find her 'true love'.

The closeness and understanding she was looking for could not come about until she herself understood the dynamics involved and made the necessary changes to her own behaviour. The empathy and understanding that emerge as a result of two people caring and sharing over a period of time are precursors to the intuitive understanding of another person. This was not happening! It was clear her energies were directed towards fulfilment of her own idealist belief, and an intuitive connection with her husband did not, and could not, exist until she learned to empathise with him over his concerns and share with him her own deeper thoughts and feelings.

No one can penetrate, intuitively or otherwise, the invisible but powerful wall of the mind of a person determined not to reveal their inner thoughts and feelings to another. Should this woman move on to another relationship in an attempt to find a love who 'understood' her, as she was considering, she would once again experience the same lack of connection, because the problem lay with her. However, if she put in the effort, in time she might achieve greater emotional connection and understanding between herself and her husband, and then it would be possible for her romantic ideals to become reality.

It is human to view life from our own experience, for that is the only real knowledge we have. The young woman's experience to date had her believing that if she found her true love, he would automatically understand her. She was shocked to discover that was simply not the case. Each of us has developed the many aspects of our character through experience. There is no shame in our lack of wisdom, just a need to be free to experience life and love, and to learn more.

The Judge Within

We didn't arrive in this world with a rule book and we have the right to learn through experience. And even those whose actions have always been 'right' and 'just' are learning, and although innocent of any deliberate wrongdoing, they can face the consequence of 'wrong' or 'erroneous' thinking.

A woman who was concerned for her daughter, came to me for a psychic reading. In order to gain quick insight into the daughter's situation, I used tarot cards that revealed the daughter was very ill and dying. Since I did not know whether the woman was aware her daughter was only a few weeks from death, I questioned her about her daughter's health.

Her daughter had terminal cancer and the woman's concern related to the pain and suffering her daughter was experiencing. I had absolutely no idea how to help the woman. I called upon my guides—those in spirit who aid me at times when I counsel.

'Your daughter's suffering is purifying her soul. It is becoming more and more beautiful through her pain,' I advised her.

In the discussion that followed, the woman became comforted by the knowledge there was a spiritual purpose behind the suffering and it would not be for much longer.

The knowledge that had immediately come to me from my guides revealed more than I had communicated to the woman. As I felt the additional information might cause her distress at that time, I kept it to myself and pondered the knowledge later. Guilt was the reason the woman's soul needed purging through her self-imposed, albeit unconscious, punishment of pain. Guilt, the judgement of self's imperfections and mistakes, is usually accompanied by an over-developed sense of responsibility and/or a need to be perfect. The need to be perfect reflects an ego dependent on the approval of others or the soul's unconscious memory of the remorse that resulted from wrongdoing. I sensed the woman's daughter was a perfectionist. Spiritually, while forgiveness is in harmony with the Law of Love and cleanses, judgement of self and others breaks that law that demands patience, compassion and understanding. We are meant to learn from acts of bad judgement and imperfect capabilities.

Punitive measures, whether applied to the self in the form of guilt, or to others in the form of judgement, invite unspiritual emotions into the soul. Unhealthy thinking and emotions, such as superiority, inferiority, jealousy, bitterness, and judgement, break the spiritual law, while making mistakes does not. This doesn't mean lawbreakers should not be held responsible for their crimes. Integrity aligned with spiritual intent in dealings with serious law breakers demands first of all the protection of the innocent. Rather than a punitive approach, the time they are incarcerated offers the opportunity to heal the damaged soul. Consideration of what has contributed towards the person becoming an aberrant member of society, and looking to removing causes such as negative social conditions, can contribute to a better life for all.

Human life is full of what judgement would call 'imperfect' human beings. Hitler was born on 20 April 1889 under the astrological sign of Aries. His claim for the superiority of the 'Master Aryan Race' exposed the true nature of idealism—an aspect of base Aries energy. His fervent followers were blinded by their egos, which is also related to the sign Aries. Hitler's goal was to bring power and control to the master race, along with the elimination of what he deemed to be imperfect. His superficial approach to life denied him the ability to see the real value to be found in all life.

At fourteen, Amber Barnett, the granddaughter of a very good friend of mine, revealed wisdom beyond her years when she wrote the following:

What is Normal

What is normal? I don't really know. Normal is just a way of alienating and classing people. Normal is just a standard; a standard in which you are or you aren't. If all of us are unique and different, then why are we being discriminated for just that, being different?

If you saw a person in a wheelchair, what would you do? Many of us would turn the other way or pretend we didn't see them, because we can't relate to someone in that situation.

We can't feel safe in ourselves around them. We don't like to feel threatened by the unknown or unusual. My cousin has cerebral palsy and she is so awesome. Sure, her words get muddled and she is in a wheelchair but she is really just like me. The good thing about my cousin is she makes it easy to be around her. Others might be

THE TRUTH SEEKER

uncomfortable with Jess, but because she's pretty it makes it much easier. I used to get really upset when I didn't understand what she was saying. But now as I spend more time with her I know it's OK to get things wrong. My cousin Jess is in a constant fight with her muscles.

Cerebral palsy is brain damage which results in involuntary movements. Jessica's eyes dart from side to side, which doesn't allow her to take in much information at once. She is one of the most wicked people I know. Her laugh is so infectious you can't help but laugh yourself. Her smile lights up the room and I'm so glad she's in my life. Knowing Jess helped me realise that unfortunate things can happen to good people. But luckily for Jess, she has people around her who love, care and support her. Who knows, maybe if Jessica was what society calls normal, she might not be as cool as she is.

How many of us have blonde hair and blue eyes? Well those of us who lived in the 1940s would have been in serious fear for their lives if we didn't fit these criteria. In World War Two, Hitler dictated what was normal and not. Hitler killed six million people including Jews, gypsies, homosexuals and anyone else he considered not to be pure. Hitler herded these people like animals into concentration camps where he would find sick and twisted ways to torture and kill them.

Before World War Two there was a great depression that spread worldwide. There was a shortage of everything and Hitler took this as his chance to rise. World War Two lasted for six years. My heart aches when I hear about the masses of hurt and death that occurred in these years. As for my cousin Jess, she wouldn't have been saved. He also believed that anyone with a mental or physical disability was a plague to society.

No one should be in dictatorship of what is normal and not. Or be in charge of what is accepted. We should all embrace individuality and difference to make our society colourful and unique. As the old saying goes, if everything in this world was the same this world would be so boring. And I believe this to be true.

Would that all people had the wisdom of that fourteen-year-old!

Cassidy, an autistic child, is the daughter of Trish and my nephew John. Trish wrote to me that she was working with parents who had children who were disabled and/or, who had severe learning difficulties.

JOAN L BOLER

I have found an enormous number of my clients lately are complaining about the fact that they have these kids who have huge learning difficulties or are extremely disabled and are basically a drain on the family. One parent of a child in Cassidy's class asked why her child would even have been put on the planet. He was in a wheelchair, had no muscle control whatsoever and was basically in a vegetative state. He then passed away one night when he was seven years old. I watched a programme on TV that explained the idea of these kids being teaching souls, and that they have chosen this life to teach others the lessons they need to learn. Those who die young from leukaemia or other similar situations are here to teach a lot of lessons quickly. And you tend to notice these kids seem fairly enlightened and much less stressed about what is happening to them than their parents and family are.

This got me thinking about how much we have learnt from Cassidy and how I have seen teachers and other people who are basically forced to spend a lot of time with her and others like her, change dramatically in that time and in their perspective of the situation. They develop a deep love and respect for the kids, even though they are quite difficult to be with at times. Now, I don't know a lot about people like her being teaching souls, but I thought it was information that people could really use today. So many of my clients at work tend to feel me out to see if I believe in any sort of after life and then go on to ask about psychics etc. so they are obviously searching for information. And there are so many more diagnoses today of disabilities such as autism which is known for being one of the most difficult behavioural disabilities to manage.

Once people begin to look for the lessons their child can teach them, I've found their whole spirit tends to change from massive negativity and resentment with a feeling of victimisation and the 'why me?' mentality. They seem to move to a greater sense of possibility, self-reflection and enlightenment, and a new-found respect for their child. You've seen me search for the answers and I've seen others in manic states trying to ' fix' their kids, but sometimes it helps to hear somebody tell you that everything is how it should be and that sometimes you need to leave well enough alone.

Whether we realise it or not, such children are a gift as they teach others numerous lessons about the true nature of love. We are individuals. If we follow the rules made by those who crave perfection, we imprison ourselves and limit our growth and our enjoyment of life.

THE TRUTH SEEKER

Religious Laws

Religious laws, while basically about doing what is right and good, vary in their demands. The simplicity of the three commandments of the Zoroastrian religion—*good thoughts, good words and good deeds*—effectively conveys the behaviour deemed necessary for peaceful co-existence.

The commandments of Judaism and Christianity, which detail specific acts to be employed or forbidden, seem to embody the laws of earlier societies that reflect the need to respect the rights of others in order to ensure peaceful co-existence. While some scholars suggest the source of the commandments as Hittite and Mesopotamian, there also seems to be evidence for considering an Egyptian influence.

The 'Egyptian Book of the Dead' which is dated around 1500 BCE[134] reveals a moral code that probably influenced Jewish consciousness as the Jews were enslaved by the Egyptians during the Eighteenth Dynasty (1550–c. 1292 BCE). Spell 125 recited by the dead commenced with 'I have not', rather than 'You shall not', and protested innocence of a long list of perceived unacceptable deeds. Among those deeds are those also found in the Bible in Exodus:[135]

> **Egyptian Book of the Dead—Spell 125** (like protestation to Exodus referenced in brackets)
>
> **Exodus 20:3-17**
>
> *³ You shall have no other gods before me.*
>
> *⁴ You shall not make for yourself an image in the form of anything in heaven above or on the earth beneath or in the waters below. ⁵ You shall not bow down to them or worship them; for I, the LORD your God, am a jealous God, punishing the children for the sin of the parents to the third and fourth generation of those who hate me, ⁶ but showing love to a thousand generations of those who love me and keep my commandments. (A11)*

---

[134] Taylor, John H. (Ed.), *Ancient Egyptian Book of the Dead: Journey through the Afterlife*. British Museum Press, London, 2010.
[135] Hood, Jared C. 'The Decalogue and the Egyptian Book of the Dead.' *Australian Journal of Jewish Studies*, 2009: 53-72.

⁷You shall not misuse the name of the LORD your God, for the LORD will not hold anyone guiltless who misuses his name. (A9, B38, B42)

⁸Remember the Sabbath day by keeping it holy. ⁹Six days you shall labour and do all your work, ¹⁰but the seventh day is a sabbath to the LORD your God. On it you shall not do any work, neither you, nor your son or daughter, nor your male or female servant, nor your animals, nor any foreigner residing in your towns. ¹¹For in six days the LORD made the heavens and the earth, the sea, and all that is in them, but he rested on the seventh day. Therefore the LORD blessed the Sabbath day and made it holy.

¹²Honour your father and your mother, so that you may live long in the land the LORD your God is giving you. (A1, A2, A3, B17)

¹³You shall not murder. (A4, A17, B5, B12, B21)

¹⁴You shall not commit adultery. (B19)

¹⁵You shall not steal. (A20, A22, A24, A25, B2, B4, B6, B8, B10)

¹⁶You shall not give false testimony against your neighbour. (A1, A3, B9, B24)

¹⁷You shall not covet your neighbour's house. You shall not covet your neighbour's wife, or his male or female servant, his ox or donkey, or anything that belongs to your neighbour. (A19, B3, B7)

Over time, the social laws of ancient lands have been integrated into commandments to reflect man's perception of the expectations of their god or gods. Laws are essential in all societies, and the above-mentioned laws define both social rules and the ideologies of a moral people. The commandments do not necessarily reflect spiritual laws.

Spiritually, no person has ownership over another. This means a husband doesn't own his wife, nor does a wife own her husband. Love is the spiritual content of marriage. The freely given love and respect between two committed people binds them spiritually. Without that loving connection, only the legal contract can be broken. Rather than this understanding being conveyed by the commandment, in Exodus 20:17, the legal and social aspect of marriage that sees the female marriage partner as a possession is supported. The commandment appears to have been created by men, for men. At the time the commandments were written, a man's possessions included his house and his wife, who it seems was considered to be of less value than his home!

In the past in Western society, the laws of the land followed religious belief. But today religion is losing its control over those laws that relate to marriage and relationships. The ideal of marriage between a man and a woman, 'Till death do us part' has ceased to be legally supported through divorce taking many years and being based on fault being proven. The commandment, 'You shall not commit adultery,' is no longer a requirement for divorce. Now, after a period of separation, a marriage can be dissolved quickly and easily and with very little social stigma attached to it. In addition, the marriage of same sex couples is gradually becoming accepted.

Unfortunately, over the ages, religious belief has focused on sexuality as a sin if not conducted within the approved state of marriage, or if it in any way offends religious sensibilities. Spiritually this isn't the case. Love and not man-made laws define whether or not the soul is tarnished by the sexual act. Perfect, socially acceptable behaviour may not indicate goodness and spirituality, and socially unacceptable behaviour does not necessarily indicate a soul bereft of love and goodness.

A vibrant woman, in her late thirties with red hair and brightly coloured clothing, sat down in front of me for a psychic reading. After a cheery greeting, I was feeling brighter for the exchange.

As I began to tune in, I became aware her work situation was going to change and I could sense the suburb she would be moving to. I clairvoyantly saw her in charge of a number of women, and was aware of a lot of cheerful communication happening around her work that included an influx of clients. But I didn't actually see what the work was. Then I moved on to her future, relationships and life generally. There was a relationship around her and I psychically saw her moving to England with her partner. I intuited it would happen in two to three years' time. They would become the parents of two children and, if I recall correctly, both were girls. After around five years, they would move to Hong Kong! Their future looked full of promise.

Some people give feedback and this lady enjoyed doing so. 'I am a working girl,' she advised! I wasn't really surprised or shocked. I have programmed my mind not to invade the privacy of a person's personal life when I read for them. This protects both me and the person receiving the reading.

She went on to say there was indeed a possibility she would be given the opportunity to move to another work location and be in charge of a group of girls. Her Asian boyfriend adored her and they anticipated moving to

England, where he had work connections, in around two years' time. In spite of my seeing two children in their future, she advised they had decided to have only one child. They planned to move to Hong Kong where his family lived after another five years.

Spiritually, there was no wrongdoing on the part of this woman in spite of her profession. The warm positive energy this woman gave out, and the way in which she brightened the lives of those around her, revealed her to be a good person.

We are sexual beings. There are those in our society who without the services of people like this lady would never be able to enjoy their own sexuality for a range of reasons which could include physical handicaps, physical unattractiveness, and an inability to relate to people. The happiness people like her can bring to those less fortunate makes the world a better place. Her nurturing nature ensured she would be a good mother. Heart, not what is considered to be perfect behaviour, gives spiritual dimensions to the soul, and for that reason freedom of choice in our activities is essential.

Since spiritual life is about developing the capacity to love, rather than reflecting the perfect and fulfilling ideals, what does this tell us about a spiritual approach to those who are either gay or lesbian? Some people are born with both male and female genitalia, while others are born with differences that affect their sexual orientation. There are even some asexual people who do not experience sexual attraction at all. Whether differences have their basis in the mental, the emotional, or the physical, each individual needs to be respected for the person they are and not be expected to fulfil a role demanded by some members of society. We are not all the same, nor were we meant to be!

British-American neuroscientist Simon LeVay researched brain structure and sexual orientation. His research, and that of others, reveals the probability that for 8-15% of all males, homosexuality is not a choice. It's a condition where the hypothalamus (an organ in the brain that is different in males and females) is different between heterosexuals and homosexuals. [136] [137] These people don't react sexually in the same way as most of their gender and are attracted to their own sex. Many are capable of deep loving feelings and thrive in a loving relationship. Nature does not obey the rules of those who demand perfection. Those who, like Hitler, would destroy what

---

[136] Eden, Dan, 'Homosexuality is not a choice – A review of scientific research on homosexuality' www. viewzone.com/homosexual. html (accessed 16 Jul 2013).

[137] LeVay S (1991), 'A difference in hypothalamic structure between homosexual and heterosexual men.' Science, 253, 1034–1037, http://postcog.ucd.ie/files/sciencearticle.pdf (accessed 18 Jul 2013)

does not meet their idea of perfection are blinded by their 'ideals'. Some, using religion as justification, demand that those who are 'different' deny their feelings, and obey the moral codes of those whose idea of 'rightness' is learned from the ancient religious beliefs of those who lacked the scientific knowledge and understanding available today. In following such rules, those of different sexuality, cannot be true to their self and are denied the right to seek happiness and fulfilment.

The illusion of goodness in demanding obedience to idealistic moral laws dictated by men has been the cause of much suffering over millennia. Only by removing judgement and accepting each human being and their right to be whom and what they are, can one proceed spiritually. Through all experience we learn, and through the learning we come to recognise and overcome deception in all the attractive guises it can take. 'Good' and 'evil' are the emotional judgement of experiential behaviour which is the outcome of our inner seeking.

Freedom's Song

Freedom is a fundamental essence of the gift of love—the control of others, even for their own good, denies a basic ingredient of spiritual love.

The soul sings to the music within as freedom works its way into our lives. Yet the despot is always there. When not in control, they wait in the shadows looking for the vulnerable. Throughout history, the manipulator has used fear and righteousness in their battle for control. Often with genuine intent and with an *end justifies the means* attitude, they may be deceived into believing what they consider to be the good of all supersedes individual rights. Whether politician or priest, head of a conglomerate or a cause, saving the world or saving souls, if it's necessary to take away the power and the freedom of choice of another, the would-be protector is spiritually blind. Only as each individual begins to overcome fear and opens their mind, is it possible to become immune to the manipulations and to discriminate between truth, myths and propaganda.

Spiritually, we have the right to choose how we will live our lives, and to make, and learn from, our own mistakes. Each of us needs to be free in order to be true to ourselves. True to all the thoughts and feelings within that make us human. The freedom to choose those who would be our partners, whether we have a dozen partners or one, whether we marry or have children, whether we attend church on Sundays or choose to enjoy the beauty of the countryside... All choices are ours. We need not be cast into a role and be subject to others because of our gender, our personal choices or our opinions. The right to choose our own pathways in life, to experience the passion of those interests that draw us, and to pursue happiness should not be taken away from us by those who believe they know what is best and who would control.

Although freedom from the controls imposed by those who would subjugate others is a hard fought war that continues to this day, even harder is freeing the self from the entrapment of personal needs and fears. In order to recognise the prisons others would create, it is first of all necessary to open the doors to the prisons within, and to recognise what it is that gives power to those who would rip our choices from our grasp. When we do not demand ownership of others, we do not become owned by others. When we no longer wish to control others, we will not be controlled. As we relinquish our vested interest in the opinions of others, we are no longer limited by the need for their approval and are therefore are free to pursue our dreams. In truth, freedom results from love that does not need to possess or control; that lives in the present, remains detached in the face of the inevitable and is accepting of life's direction towards the destiny that completes our soul.

Humanity can only progress spiritually through the song of freedom. Unless we are first of all true to ourselves, the voice of freedom is elusive and so is our true identity.

Personal Responsibility

Love is the spiritual law and when it directs the course of a person, no other laws are needed. As it works its magic in the lives of those who have found its treasures, it will find and transform weaknesses and bring great wisdom and a boundless capacity to love and honour self and others.

Today, in the West, we are seeing changes in people's behaviour as they throw off rigid demands, rules and judgements of bygone eras. As a result, members of communities are expressing more compassion and less judgement. Socially there is more openness and fewer restrictions with the right to choose to follow a dream, provided it doesn't break the laws of the land. On the surface, this may appear to remove the protection that the apparently moral and social rules offer, but double standards were rampant in the past and public displays of morality often hid corruption, so any protection promised was an illusion unless backed by harsh penalties.

THE TRUTH SEEKER

In learning to take responsibility for the consequences of actions taken, instead of relying on those who claim the right to protect us by imposing moral rules, we move from the 'child' to the 'adult' consciousness; from being dependent upon others to being in control. As the adult begins to emerge, so too does awareness of responsibility—responsibility for self that includes seeking a healthy and happy lifestyle along with a respect for the individual choices of others, and consideration for, and enjoyment of, all life on the planet.

The inner self comprises thoughts, emotions, and physical needs, along with a compulsion to seek love, happiness and fulfilment. This is only possible through being true to one's self and allowing for the discovery, through experience, of what will enable alignment with the spiritual and with happiness. As we mature spiritually and cease allowing others to dictate how we should think, feel emotionally, and behave sexually, the conflicts between mind, emotions and physical needs reflected in frustration, anger, hate, despair, superiority, inferiority, and all base and ugly feelings, lessen. As we experience emotions that bring happiness, joy, delight, and contentment, we become aligned with the spiritual law. While such feelings may be fleeting for some, they hold the key to what causes these much desired states. When inner battles are resolved, and spirit, mind, emotions and the physical senses are aligned, love, with all the bounty it contains and attracts, is revealed.

JOAN L BOLER

THE TRUTH SEEKER

Chapter 9

Revealing the Unconscious

I see life as a creation each of us paints for ourselves. We do create our own reality in order to be aligned with our destiny. The search then becomes a search for self. It is the most important journey we will ever take.

Shirley MacLaine[138]

The Search for Happiness

The search for happiness takes us out into the world chasing experiences we believe will make us happy. Security, power, fame, and indulgence in the sensual, are some of the experiences we pursue in our search. We search and we find. But do we find fulfilment and happiness or disillusionment and discontent? And if we find the latter, after we have followed all of society's rules, why is that?

Plato, (427?-347? BCE), the Greek philosopher, was a student and friend of Socrates (469?-399 BCE). Like Socrates he believed humanity sought happiness, and he attributed the fact many individuals did not find it, to the idea that many did not know what would, in fact, bring happiness. Therefore, man did not seek to do wrong—he simply sought happiness. Since morality and rightness could result in a healthy and happy life, Plato's view was that virtue was to be desired.[139] It's likely Plato was referring to behaviour that reflected respect and caring for self and others. The various facets of love and its application are not easily understood and, for the most part, are learned through experience. As lessons are learned, the individual can move forward to a more successful and happy life—providing learning hasn't left scars.

---

[138] MacLaine, Shirley. '*About Shirley—Introduction*' www.shirleymaclaine.com (accessed 23 May 2012)
[139] *The World Book Encyclopedia,* Ibid. P; Plato - Ethics P504a..

The learning that can take years or lifetimes may leave in its wake, emotional and mental damage that can result in fears and phobias, loss of esteem, serious mental disorders and a wide variety of issues that need to be addressed. Since memories of many of the traumatic experiences are lost in time, and only found through unveiling the unconscious mind, it is there the search is best begun.

Healing the psyche is very much a modern day phenomenon. In developed countries, it is commonplace for people to seek counsel when emotional issues overwhelm them. The unconscious mind, which holds the key to the greater part of our soul's experience, can become destructive. Beneath the conscious awareness of our desires, beliefs and fears, causes are hidden in the depths of a mind that is both complex and powerful. Accessing the unconscious mind can result in change for the better.

Meditation, self-hypnosis and hypnotherapy provide direct access to the unconscious mind and should be treated with respect. Dreams are the unconscious mind's playground, and through dream analysis much can be learned about the psyche and its current challenges and dilemmas. Similarly, divination accesses the unconscious, and knowledge gained from it can be effective in counselling. Each of the above modes of working with the unconscious provides an opportunity to heal chaos found within.

In today's complex society, time for self and self-awareness is minimal as we rush around fulfilling the demands of a busy lifestyle. The cry from within that something is missing or wrong is rarely heard until pain and anguish reaches crisis point. Many who arrive at this point embark upon a journey. Disillusioned by their forays into activities that promised happiness and fulfilment, that reaped them fleeting pleasure at best, they begin the journey within. Such a journey can lead to happiness through exposing and removing the deeper causes of pain.

Healing the Psyche

The healing of mental and emotional pain has come into focus in recent times. While society is still attempting to come to grips with mental illness, it is making inroads into healing the emotional and psychological damage caused by traumas encountered both in this lifetime and in previous lifetimes.

Throughout history, some, like the Greek physician Hippocrates (460-377 BCE) have recognised mental illness can be caused through a physical abnormality in the brain. Christianity, with its widely accepted superstition of devils and demons, has over a long period of time attempted to cure the mentally ill through exorcism. Lack of success usually resulted in the locking up, persecution and sometimes killing of those who suffered. It was not until 1724 that changes began to take place. Cotton Mather, a New England Puritan minister who had been influential in bringing about the Salem Witch Trials, suffered from guilt and put forward the alternative explanation of mental illness being caused by a physical irregularity in the brain rather than possession by demons. In the Christian dominated West, the long held beliefs that devils were the cause of negative, violent and emotionally unstable behaviour began to disintegrate. In 1808 a German physician, Johann Christian Reil, came up with the word 'psychiatry' to describe medical treatment of the soul. [140] [141] A revolution was taking place and it was not long before the causes of aberrant behaviour were being looked for in both the physical and in the fears hidden deep in the unconscious mind. Austrian neurologist, Sigmund Freud (1856-1939), became the 'father of psychoanalysis', and Carl Jung, (1875-1971) a Swiss psychiatrist, became the founder of analytical psychology. Drugs and counselling were soon seen as solutions.

Out of the social sciences of psychiatry and psychology have emerged many forms of analysis and counselling that reveal the deeper causes of pain and unhappiness, and as a result provide opportunity for healing. The genius of Carl Jung, and his enlightened approach to understanding and healing the soul, has given birth to a process of healing through analysis that recognises childhood can make us prisoners of beliefs that ignore, or misunderstand, the essence of the soul. Disillusionment in the form of unhappiness and depression provide an opportunity for the sufferer (through analysis) to reveal the deceptions that resulted in the denial of the inner self.

We are born into this world carrying forward all the accumulated experiences of our previous lives in our unconscious. Some of these experiences have been traumatic and while they will have created growth in the soul, they may also have left us with insecurities and painful blocks. We are introduced to our new external world through birth. Helpless and dependent, we react to an environment we can't interpret accurately. These early days can be traumatic as a result of an unforgiving environment,

---

[140] Calef, Robert (1700). *More Wonders of the Invisible World*. London England: Nath Hillar on London Bridge, pp. 152 & 156, http://salem.lib.virginia.edu/speccol/calef/calef.html (accessed 9 Feb 2014)

[141] 'Psychiatry's 200th birthday', *The British Journal of Psychiatry*, http://bjp.rcpsych.org/content/193/1/1.abstract (accessed 9 Feb 2014)

incompetent parenting, or health issues. Over the next many years, we learn the rules of this external world.

Love and approval in early relationships has an enormous impact upon our lives. It is the way in which love, or lack of it, is experienced that can cause a child to flourish, to lose itself, or to come somewhere in between. Love that nurtures, supports, guides and disciplines when necessary allows for self-acceptance and self-confidence. During these vulnerable years, the mind of the child has not yet developed discrimination, and therefore absorbs the programmes implied and taught as truths. Reward and punishment in its many forms, especially in the form of love and approval given and withdrawn, can be destructive to the child's ego, as such conduct can create a belief that it's only possible to feel worthwhile through pleasing others. This creates conflict between the need to please others and the wish to pursue individual destiny according to inner needs.

Cultural expectations and beliefs of parents, religion, schooling and society form a framework in the unconscious that can block the free flow of spontaneous expression, creativity and spirituality. As the child matures, if its individuality and its emotional and mental outlook have been compromised its future is, at least for a time, determined. That future revolves around the approval, or lack of it, from others. In order to receive love and approval, some succumb to those who have claimed authority, and as a result do not know how to find happiness and fulfilment for themselves. Others claim freedom of choice, and indiscriminately rebel by rejecting authority while still needing and seeking approval from others. Often this translates into seeking the admiration of those who have gained notoriety through antisocial behaviour. For these people, the foundation for relationships is laid down in rebellion and need.

Co-dependence is the outcome of an emotionally unhealthy state. All dysfunctional relationships reveal those who do not feel love and appreciation for themselves. Such individuals become involved in behaviour such as seeking power, blaming others, cutting off from feelings, becoming embittered, being defensive, being critical of others, focusing on gratification, giving behaviour noble identities rather than viewing the deeper motives, and every sort of deviant behaviour to be found in humanity.

The potential for healing is great once the search into the unconscious mind exposes the past experiences that have had an adverse effect. As a result of deliberately changing attitudes and thinking through effort and often hard work, previous programming in the unconscious is gradually eroded and permanent changes result.

THE TRUTH SEEKER

To date, the academic community has not recognised the spiritual identity of each individual and therefore, the need to connect to that spiritual self in order to become fulfilled and happy. For this reason, many move away from counsellors aligned with the establishment and look elsewhere for answers in order to know and heal themselves. Many of those seeking to help others go beyond their traditional training into alternative methods of healing that take into account the greater self in answer to this need.

The Trance State

The trance state, which is induced either through meditation or hypnosis, offers a way to access information the unconscious mind conceals so dealing with the issues that lie within becomes possible. The unconscious mind is both significant and remarkable. Every thought, action and reaction; every emotion, every fear and all we have ever experienced in our current life and during all our existences since the dawn of time can be accessed through our unconscious. Our stored past together with our attitudes, strengths, and wisdoms result s in reactions to every situation we meet in life. Where our reactions are destructive, revealing the unconscious can hold the key to change.

Meditation has been practiced in the East for thousands of years. Through developing their ability to meditate and turning their attention inward Brahman priests, yogis and many other people on their spiritual journey have developed abilities that have enabled psychic, paranormal and mystical experiences. In the West there are now many who find meditation relaxing and beneficial to their physical and mental well-being.

Research into trance states induced by meditation and hypnosis reveals the heart and respiration rate slow down, stress levels are reduced and, whilst to all intents and purposes the body is in a restful state, the brain is alert and experiences alpha and theta brainwave activity. There is very little difference between the trance state achieved in meditation and that experienced in hypnosis. In meditation the individual usually drops into a light trance, either of their own volition or through the guidance of another person. Hypnosis is a procedure whereby a practitioner, using suggestion, guides the subject into a trance state. Unless otherwise instructed by the hypnotist, the subject will find they are totally aware of, and able to recall, everything said. Because of the lightness of the trance, one would not expect the process to produce significant results. In fact, the effects can be startling, informative and healing. Most, if not all of my trance experiences, whether initiated by myself or guided by a therapist, have not caused me to enter into a deep trance state.

Standing sentinel over the unconscious mind is the conscious or thinking mind, which supervises all input received and blocks direct access from outside sources. There is a very good reason why our unconscious mind needs to be protected. Its ultimate power is daunting. Once a programme is set in place, the unconscious ruthlessly enforces it. If a belief is instilled in the unconscious, it will ensure that no matter how much effort is applied to create change with the conscious mind, failure will likely follow. There are two ways to change deep-seated programmes. The first and fastest is the trance state that provides the opportunity to negate and replace unwanted programmes. It is also important to cease any negative attitudes and behaviour patterns that lead to further unwanted programmes. The second method involves a conscious effort to reprogramme by repeated habit forming activity that rejects previous behaviour. This becomes possible when the attitudes that caused the original problem are changed. Since a child's mind doesn't discriminate, beliefs absorbed in childhood become a fundamental part of their unconscious mind and can cause limitation and blindness of thought that can remain throughout their entire life, and sometimes for lifetimes to come.

The conscious mind, with its militant vigilance, becomes counterproductive when one is attempting to access distant memories and positively reprogramme the unconscious. In order to penetrate this barrier, the therapist first of all uses their voice to talk the subject into a relaxed state, which in turn slows down brainwaves and prepares the conscious mind for shutdown—similar to that experienced prior to sleep. As the subject relaxes, the therapist's voice prevents sleep as it absorbs more and more of the subject's attention to the point where control of the conscious mind is released.

Once a trance state is induced, it is possible for the subject to recall past traumatic experiences, and to re-programme their unconscious mind through positive suggestion. Such healing helps the individual to move forward in their life and leave behind the effects of painful experiences. While patterns of belief may be altered rapidly by hypnotic suggestion, changes in behaviour and attitude are also necessary in order to ensure the change is permanent. We programme our unconscious on a daily basis. If we heal the old programme in the unconscious through determined effort or hypnosis, and then go back to negative thought processes and behaviour, the problem will return.

THE TRUTH SEEKER

As a tool for healing emotional and mental handicaps caused by trauma, the trance state, when used by a skilled professional, is, in my opinion, unparalleled.

Hypnotherapy

Personal experience of hypnotherapy has enabled me to discover for myself, the amazing results that can be achieved through its use. But back in the 1990s I wasn't so sure. While in theory I understood hypnotherapy could solve the problems that had followed me throughout my life, I questioned whether it would really work for me. After all, I had tried self-hypnosis without success.

From childhood, I had reacted to performance related activities with nervousness, hands shaking, mental blocks and memory loss. I had always experienced difficulty during examinations, as my mind seemed to freeze and refuse to make sense of what at a later time became a simple exercise. This limited my scholastic achievements, so I often didn't reach my goals. With great determination, I tried over and over again to talk myself out of undesirable reactions. I continued to confront the situations that gave me grief. In my thirties, I became familiar with the concepts of meditation and attempted self-hypnosis. When this failed, I tried self-improvement tapes—all to no avail.

Around 1994 I was once again reaping the sabotaging results of the delinquent programmes in my unconscious. I was invited to participate in a video using myself and another palmist to provide insights into the workings of palmistry. My hands shook so badly that much of the tape couldn't be used. I had run out of patience with myself. I could no longer tolerate a handicap that prevented me from achieving my goals. It was time to try hypnotherapy. I knew any suggestion a therapist might make that did not agree with my own attitudes would automatically cause my conscious mind to reintroduce itself and reject the suggestion. A therapist who caused me to do this would limit the degree of success I could achieve.

Sally and I met through a shared involvement in the psychic world. As a result of our similar attitudes and ideals, we connected quickly and easily, and it wasn't long before we became friends. Along with her 'inner child' counselling skills, Sally, with her BA in welfare studies, and her diploma in clinical hypnotherapy was the right person to work with me.

After Sally had guided me into a trance state, she suggested I return to the time when I first experienced my blocking reactions. Suddenly I recalled myself at five years of age. I was with my father. I had a metal tobacco tin in my hands containing the words my schoolteacher had given to me to learn. My father listened to me read the words. If I found myself unable to recall a word, he censured me. From his viewpoint, he no doubt felt I wasn't trying hard enough and believed showing his disapproval was the best way to encourage me to make more of an effort. This approach didn't work for me. I tried so hard to learn and remember my words. Fear of my father's disapproval robbed me of my ability to access my memory, so no matter how great the effort on my part, I became nervous and inept under his scrutiny. The on-going failures eroded my self-confidence and my self-esteem.

As Sally guided me forward over the years, during the next few sessions I recalled other situations that reinforced the original programme. I recovered memories of the schoolteacher who sent the 'dunces' into the corner. This induced in me a deep fear of the ridicule such punishment would incur.

I recalled the morning I arrived at school to be met by the school caretaker in the hallway where our belongings were kept. In answer to his query, I confirmed I was the one who had left my gumboots at school the previous day. Upon learning my name, he sneered, 'Bill F---s' daughter,' his tone clearly revealing an intense dislike of my father. I was proud of my father. It somehow diminished me to know an adult didn't think well of him.

The caretaker then introduced me to his own form of punishment. First he took a piece of string and threaded one end through the loop at the top/back of one gumboot and tied a knot. He allowed the string to extend for a number of inches and tied the other end of the string to the top of the other gumboot. Then he hung the string around my neck with each of the gumboots dangling down in front of me like a bizarre necklace. He told me I was to wear them like that all day. At eight years of age, I was sensitive to the scorn and rejection of my schoolmates. My teacher apparently saw nothing wrong with the punishment and didn't interfere. The guilt and embarrassment instilled in me during the ensuing school hours compounded my problem.

As we progressed through the years, Sally, after each recall, gave me inner child healing suggestions that I accepted and reinforced. Eventually we came to an end. The result was remarkable! My nervousness disappeared. Getting the shakes was a thing of the past, and my memory losses in times of pressure were no longer a concern. My ability to teach and lecture was now able to emerge along with my being able to handle many situations previously impossible for me.

In retrospect, I realised my earlier attempts with self-hypnosis had failed for two reasons. To instruct oneself during self-hypnosis brings the conscious mind into play thereby ensuring the trance state isn't maintained. Also, at that time I hadn't yet learned to turn off my very busy mind and as a result had been unable to enter a trance state. It would be many years before I learned to meditate properly.

Each of us is programmed at an early age and, until the discriminating mind develops, those in our environment do the programming. Sometimes a child receives positive programming and sometimes not. The power of the trance state as a healing tool is vast, but so is the damage that can be done when that tool is employed by the ignorant and unwise.

Respecting the Unconscious Mind

Do we throw away a valuable tool because it can be dangerous or unreliable if misused, even though it has the potential to enhance the lives of many? Ignorance in practitioners can result in mental and emotional damage to the subject and inaccurate information being produced. Awareness of the workings of the unconscious is extremely important in order to avoid pitfalls.

The unconscious mind does not reflect or consider, and therefore does not use judgement in its implementation of orders to supply specific information. It simply serves and attempts to obey—creatively when necessary. Accuracy is dependent on the practitioner asking clear, precise questions that don't have an answer contained within. There is evidence of people gleaning expected or desired answers from the questions asked by the practitioner.

Evidence of telepathic communication during hypnotherapy has been noted by therapists. In 1982, A Tozzi reported the results of research into telepathy between hypnotherapist and subject. Significantly positive results were noted in sixteen subjects.[142] Connection between the therapist and patient during dreaming is another example of the possibility of telepathic connection. Over thirty years of practice, Israeli psychoanalyst Ofra Eshel was confronted five times with the 'telepathic' dreams of her patients.

---

[142] Tozzi, A. 'Telepatia in ipnosi. Ricerca personale.' *Minerva Medica*, 1982, Vol. 73 (45): 3213-5.

Eshel, who had not previously taken an interest in psi experiences, was surprised and found it necessary to consider the possibility of information transfer between patient and analyst through telepathy. [143]

Since the unconscious mind is telepathic and can receive knowledge from the practitioner's unconscious mind, the practitioner's strongly held beliefs can influence the outcome.

> **When dealing with the unconscious mind, a genuine desire to unearth the truth is a necessary ingredient in discovering the truth.**

Therapists with an axe to grind can impart that axe to the subject, either through unconscious thought transmission or through suggestions contained in their questions. Many experts reject all information obtained through hypnosis. This doesn't negate its huge potential for healing and self-understanding.

Fear hides itself behind the lies we tell ourselves in order to feel safe. Revealing the fear and dealing with it allows for the release of the deceptions that are the beliefs that would limit us. To those who are vigilant, the revelations of the unconscious mind, with its potential for incredible accuracy, can reveal knowledge of great value.

Dream Analysis

The interpretation of dreams has been the province of seers since Biblical times. Today, the interpretation of dreams through dream analysis can reveal what is having a positive or negative impact on our lives.

Dream analysis works differently to hypnotherapy. It reveals rather than locates and removes. It brings understanding of our attitudes and character, and how these have an impact on our present and our future and as a consequence, on our happiness. With this understanding, we are armed with knowledge of the changes necessary to deal with the issues that have an impact on our lives.

Some years ago I was in a car accident. A newly licensed driver travelling from the opposite direction stalled before making a right hand turn. She

---

[143] Eshel, Ofra. ' Where are you, my beloved? On absence, loss, and the enigma of telepathic dreams.' *International Journal of Psychoanalysis*, 2006, 87: 1603-27.

THE TRUTH SEEKER

restarted her vehicle and immediately accelerated into her turn—without re-checking traffic. I was driving along a road I had travelled many times before. After a slight rise in the road, I approached the green traffic lights. Without warning, the girl's car shot across in front of me as I continued through the traffic lights. There was no time for me to stop. The resultant crash threw me hard towards the car windscreen and roof. My seatbelt prevented serious injury but left me with a great deal of bruising. My shin connected with the dashboard and the hurt I sustained took a number of weeks to clear.

I had always been a confident driver, but my inability to avoid or prevent the accident shattered my confidence. During the next two weeks, I recalled two dreams in which I found myself walking on ground that was soggy and had a shallow covering of water. In my dreams I kept sinking into the ground as walked towards my destination. The dreams clearly showed the ground under me was no longer solid! I realised the 'ground' represented my basic belief and trust in my safety. I made up my mind to put the incident behind me and trust in the future. My previous confidence returned and I had no further dreams of this nature.

Dreaming is a process whereby the unconscious releases its concerns and fears, its joys and its sorrows, its failures and its achievements on a stage where symbols hold the key to translating the deeper meaning. Carl Jung revealed incredible insight into the mechanics of dreams. Through his method of interpretation, dream analysis can unravel the inner issues that have an impact on our daily life.

The human race has accumulated symbols that can be interpreted. What we dream is usually not to be understood in a literal sense. Dream analysis recognises the symbolism pertaining to the unconscious of humanity as a whole; that of a particular race or country or of a belief system or family and that of self. Symbolism is both part of the collective or group unconscious and part of the impact of personal experience.

A young lady who had attended my psychic and spiritual development classes only once before arrived for her second night of learning. Upon her arrival she burst out with, 'I had a very weird dream the other night. I dreamed I had a baby and it had *two* sets of eyes.' I explained to her that giving birth represented new beginnings and her having just the previous week commenced the class was a new beginning. I then pointed out the first set of eyes probably represented the sight of the physical eyes, while the second set of eyes pertained to her ability to develop clairvoyant sight. That she had no knowledge or conscious understanding of the symbolism involved didn't prevent her unconscious mind from dreaming in easily recognisable symbols.

Comprehensive understanding of our own behaviour through dream analysis can be enriching. As it provides us with insight into our fears and sometimes-blind behaviour, the wisdoms gained can provide us with the knowledge required to make the changes necessary in order to bring harmony and balance into our lives.

Divination

Divination is the process of discovering the influences surrounding a person, an event, a situation or a locality. Whilst in the past the diviner was seen to have been inspired by God, divining is carried out through accessing knowledge and understanding intuitively. All psychic abilities are developed skills that can be described as spiritual in the same way a great work of art can be considered spiritual. Each of these abilities draws on the unconscious mind that is creative, powerful and can follow the directions of the individual. Intuition is the unconscious impressing the answer sought upon the conscious. In divination, intuition depends upon the interpretation of like images which is made possible because of the Law of Similars. Many are of the opinion that divination through tarot cards and other mediums is based on superstitious belief, and it has become fashionable in this scientific age to reject divination as unscientific.

For as far back as racial memory and history records, divination has been part of most, if not all, of the world's cultures. It is probably the oldest method of discovering what lies beyond conscious awareness. In Biblical times, dreams were used to divine the future of leaders and of nations. While divining the future of a person through their dreams is a skill that survives to the present day, dreams are not the only source for the visual prompts usually used in divination. A wide variety of tools can be utilised for this purpose.

Divination calls upon the sensitive person to intuit from images information that is beyond the reach of our visual and audial faculties. The future we have created through our past and present journeys into the physical world, and those experiences necessary for our spiritual evolvement can be exposed through the use of media that possess or produce like images. When the psychic reader wishes to access the hidden information contained in the energy field that surrounds the individual they are psychically gaining

THE TRUTH SEEKER

information for, that information is revealed through the chosen medium in like symbols.

When divining, the computer-like unconscious mind does not interpret, and therefore vague ideas result in ambiguous answers. Specific instructions and rules are required in order for the unconscious to be able to deliver the *exact* information required of it. Once information is requested, the answer is revealed symbolically through whichever medium the psychic is working with—that may be tarot cards, tea leaves, coffee grains, runes or any other object or objects that have the potential to form shapes such as clouds, or casting lots using a range of objects. It may seem extraordinary, but when directed by the psychic, the tools used reveal, through images that mimic in symbolic form, the information sought. Sometimes, when there are multiple symbols to choose from, the psychic's attention will be intuitively drawn to specific symbols and these symbols will be significant.

What causes the reader to unerringly be attracted to the 'right' symbolic answer? Essential to the process of revelation is the ability of the unconscious mind of the reader to access the soul of the seeker. The result is intuitive insight matched to the symbolic information received. Providing the reader has a way for the unconscious to reveal the information to the conscious mind, the unconscious can be used to access almost any information requested. There are exceptions. Information can be blocked by the subject themselves or by spiritual design. Sometimes information is blocked when the knowledge sought would cause changes that could have a negative impact on a spiritual purpose in the subject's life.

Tools such as runes and tarot cards have been designed in order to make divination easier. With the tarot, divining can be very complex or very simple. I recall a young woman asking me how many children she would have. The card selected to provide an answer was 'The Aeon' which relates to birth, renewal and awakening.[144] As I focused on the card, I was drawn to the three images lower down on the card. To me, they looked like small babies.

'I have three babies, but two seem to have faded out,' I advised her.

'Would that be because I have had two abortions?' was her immediate response.

---

[144] Akron, Hajo Banzhaf, (Translated from German by Christine M Grimm) *The Crowley Tarot.*, U.S. Games Systems, Stamford, p. 113.

The purpose of most forms of divination is to interpret hidden knowledge. Divination can be likened to dream analysis in that it can expose what is actually happening in our world of emotions, desires, fears and attitudes along with the future we have set up for ourselves. It cuts through belief systems and looks beneath the surface illusions and the blocks we have set up to protect ourselves. It is fast and it is effective, and the revelations have the potential to help people to deal with the difficulties creating limitation in their lives.

Tarot

Tarot, which is probably the most commonly used form of divining in the West, is a pictorial language that is used to reveal what has not yet manifested in the physical world. Today's tarot is the product of a mixed history. The meanings and symbols contained within it can represent knowledge from the world of magic, astrology, numerology, alchemy, the kabbalah and its tree of life, the mythology of ancient Egypt, and the traditions of Mediterranean and Celtic cultures.[145]

The tarot deck has seventy-eight cards divided into two sections—the twenty-two trump cards of the major arcana and the fifty-six cards of the minor arcana. Whilst there is uncertainty as to the source of the major arcana, it reveals the archetypes of the human soul along with the events that have a spiritual purpose in a person's life. A majority of these trump cards in a reading indicates higher forces at work, and therefore the person is not fully in control of their fate—whatever the experience, it is unavoidable and, if challenging, necessary for spiritual growth. From the information revealed, it is possible to help a person understand why they are surrounded by the difficulties that confront them.

According to historic records, the minor arcana arrived in Europe around the fourteenth century as a game of entertainment. The cards incorporate the four suits which have come to represent astrological energies—wands express creative, ego or fire energy; cups express emotional or water energy; swords reveal mental or air energy and disks, coins or pentacles represent the prosperity consciousness, the practical, and sensual or earth energy. These cards are used to reveal the mundane, every day, and usually changeable events in our lives.

---

[145] Crowley, A, *The Book of Thoth*, US Games Systems, Stamford, 1995.

Figure 7 - Author conducting a tarot reading using the Keltic Cross layout.

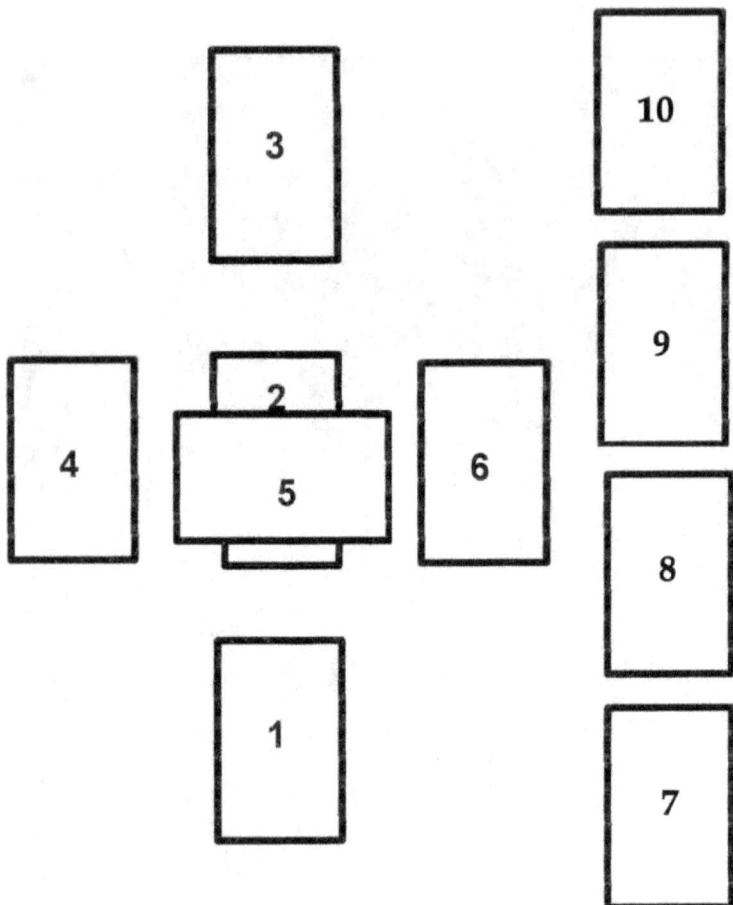

Figure 8 - Keltic Cross layout[146]

Each individual tarot card is complex and can be interpreted in different ways depending on its context. The reader develops a relationship with each card over time, so the appearance of a particular card in a layout immediately indicates to the reader its relevance at that point. The fact that one set of cards may differ from another, or a reader may have a different interpretation of the cards, is unimportant. It is the reader's knowledge and understanding of the card that defines its meaning.

---

[146] Garen, Nancy. Tarot Made Easy. Judy Piarkus (Publishers) Ltd, London 1997. P44-46

THE TRUTH SEEKER

Not only does the reader learn the identity of each card, they can make use of a variety of traditional layouts or develop their own. Since each position in a layout can represent a different aspect or function, more specific information can be obtained. Of the traditional layouts that have been around for some time, the Keltic Cross is both popular and easy to use (Figure 7 page 225 and Figure 8, page 226). The numbers indicate the order in which the cards are laid out.

The function of each card in the Keltic Cross spread, is as follows:

1. Summary of past influences significant to the present.

2. Present state of affairs.

3. Current attitudes, wishes and needs.

4. Issues from the past impacting on the present in order to clear.

5. Shows positive or negative influences that will impact upon the outcome.

6. Near future.

7. How you have responded to the events in the near future.

8. Further developments and new influences.

9. The changes that have taken place within the individual as a result of experiences

10. Outcome.

My personal preference when working with tarot, due to symbolism I can relate to and the complexity and beauty of the cards, is Aleister Crowley's Thoth Deck. English born Crowley (1875-1947), was a clever and educated man who was fascinated with the occult. Throughout his life, he pursued the world of magic, and as a prolific writer left records of both his knowledge and his attitudes. His tarot deck was designed to symbolise the structure of the universe, especially the solar system. It integrates the knowledge of kabbalah, astrology and numerology. The colourful paintings used in each card were the combined efforts of Crowley, who designed them, and London born Lady Frieda Harris (1877-1962), who painted them.

Crowley was reputed, through his involvement in magic and the world of the paranormal, to have been involved in the less spiritual aspects of the non-physical world. As a result, some believe his cards to have a negative energy. Personally, I have never experienced a problem with these cards.

JOAN L BOLER

The energy a person senses from the cards reflects the energy within that person and the beliefs they connect with.

The versatility of the tarot makes it a valuable healing tool. Of all the methods of divination available today, tarot offers a degree of depth with which no other medium can compare. The richness and accuracy of the information gained is limited only by the knowledge and skill of the psychic giving the reading.

Changing the Future

By recognising the cause of the problem, usually found in the individual's attitude or belief, it is possible to aid the person in changing a negative to a positive.

A young woman in her late twenties came to see me. She had a very negative attitude due to her belief she should already have found her partner in life. I checked with the tarot cards and discovered it would be five years before she would meet the man she was to marry. In an effort to change her attitude and in the knowledge the next five years could provide opportunity for personal growth, I pointed out that she was not meant to settle into a permanent relationship at this time, and the next few years would provide her with an opportunity to meet people, have fun and experience life.

Three months later a woman who came to visit me for a reading turned out to be the mother of this young lady. The grateful mother advised me the change in her daughter after the reading had been significant. Her daughter had gone from being unhappy and fearful she was never going to meet her life partner to being happy and outgoing.

In another situation where the person was amplifying their own problem by anticipating the worst possible outcome, I used all my powers of persuasion to shift her attitude. A mature age student of mine consulted me one evening. She arrived looking frazzled and worried. After viewing the layout of the cards, I advised, 'The only problem I see here is a legal issue!'

'That's it!' she replied. 'I have to go to court next Wednesday and I could lose my driving licence!' She related how she had run into the rear end of a vehicle and the driver had been so enraged he had called the police. She had already lost points on her licence, and it was so important to her that she keep her licence that she had retained a barrister to appear in court on her behalf. The card signifying to me this was a legal issue was Adjustment.

THE TRUTH SEEKER

The images on this card include a woman adorned with the ostrich feather of Maat (the Egyptian goddess of justice) and two large scales. Since Adjustment is a trump card, it offered very little hope the court hearing could be avoided.

Such was not the case with the card that followed which was the Failure card. Because I understood the power of the mind, I did not advise her of the placement of this card or what it was saying with regard to the outcome of the case.

'OK. If you are prepared to make the effort and do as I say, you will ensure you will retain your licence.' Upon her confirmation she would do *anything* required to achieve that objective, I continued, 'Each morning when you awaken, and each night before you fall asleep (these are the times when the unconscious mind is most receptive), you will visualise yourself in court, *knowing* all will be fine and receiving a positive verdict. During each day, whenever you think of the court case, you will feel happy and positive about the outcome.'

'Do you believe in angels?' I asked. An affirmative answer had me continue. 'When you go into court on the Wednesday, ask for an angel to be around you to give you support. Next, ask for an angel to be around your barrister so he puts your case across effectively. Then ask for an angel to be around the judge so he sees the case fairly and is sympathetic towards you. And lastly, put your driving licence in the hands of an angel and ask that it be protected.'

As I had effectively worked in this way on previous occasions, I knew I could, if I tuned in on the day, have a positive impact on the situation. At around five o'clock on the Wednesday evening, I headed over to Glebe (a suburb of Sydney) intending to have a meal before preparing for the class at half past seven that this lady attended. I was parking my car when I suddenly recalled Wednesday was the day of the court case. I had completely forgotten and had done absolutely nothing towards helping! As soon as the thought occurred, the knowledge immediately followed it was OK and she was not meant to receive my help. She needed to discover for herself that through focusing her mind and changing her attitude it was possible for her to change the outcome, without any assistance. At twenty past seven she arrived for the evening class looking very serious. Since I already knew the outcome of the court case, I smiled happily at her and she smiled in response. 'How did it go?' I asked.

'It was terrible,' she said, 'I thought I had lost. And then the barrister said to the judge that if I was found guilty of negligent driving, then every driver in

Sydney who had run into the back of another vehicle was also guilty of negligent driving and we would not accept such a verdict and would be back to court to fight it.' She went on to confirm the judge dismissed the case. In spite of her temporary fear in court, she had put in the work and received the desired results. I then advised her of the Failure card to show her she had actually changed the outcome herself.

Ideally, the knowledge we create our own experiences (the good and the bad) should be available to all people, so instead of acting as though the world at large is responsible for their welfare, they look to their own behaviour and attitudes when facing problems. In both of the above situations, the people involved changed what was happening in their future. They had created their present situations and were looking towards unhappy and unpleasant future experiences, but because they changed their attitudes, their future changed for the better.

The Psychic Reader

Psychic readers use their abilities to access, through a variety of means, the unconscious of the person who has come to them for a reading. Like all those who counsel, they draw upon their learning and personal experience in order to inform and aid. Psychic readers are individuals and the advice they impart reflects their personality, bias and attitudes.

Apart from the learning that comes from dealing with life's challenges, most psychic readers have studied one or more subjects that give them insight into both the life purpose of soul of the individual and the current issues the individual is dealing with. Palmistry, numerology, astrology, psychic healing, dream analysis, and counselling are the most common areas of expertise. Many of these people are equipped to aid the individual by revealing ways to heal their soul and improve their life.

Some readers counsel and others tell fortunes. Many people come for a reading expecting to have their fortune told. The main difference between a fortune teller and a good psychic reader is that the fortune teller reveals future happenings as the inevitable future, while the psychic reader can provide advice on the cause of possible future events and how to change the undesirable.

The psychic development classes I attended for a number of years provided me with the opportunity to study the different ways in which people conducted readings. On the evening of the class, we each intuitively read a single tarot card for one other person without knowing whose card we held. On one occasion, a young woman pronounced the person whose card she was reading was depressed. She was reading my card! Perhaps the young woman interpreted my concern regarding the instability of my employment and therefore my financial situation at the time as depression. In my teens and twenties, I had experienced depression and knew what it felt like! Although I was experiencing a time of uncertainty, I was continuing to enjoy my usual round of fun and stimulating activities provided by my varied interests and so stated emphatically I was *not* depressed.

Rather than looking to providing me with a supportive and positive attitude in the face of challenges, her ego demanded she be seen to be *right*, and her forceful reply was, 'Well, you will be!' Such a statement reveals the limited understanding and the harmful attitude of the reader who had no appreciation of the negative effect the power of suggestion could have on a susceptible person. It was not long before my work situation was resolved and in the meantime I continued to enjoy life and refused to allow my uncertain future to cause me grief.

On another night, while attending the same classes, there was one lady who entertained us with her delightfully bawdy sense of humour. This lady was never one to speak quietly, and on one occasion after the class was over and we were talking she advised, 'Joan, you should check your toilet seat. I see you sliding off a toilet seat!' Chuckles emerged from those nearby who overheard.

As no problem with my toilet seat revealed itself, I soon forgot about her prediction. A couple of weeks later during the Christmas to New Year break I took myself off to the Queensland Gold Coast to spend time with my son. On New Year's Eve he said, 'Mum, would you like to come to a party?'

'OK!' I replied and so off we went to join the New Year's Eve revelry. During the evening, I went to visit the 'necessary' where my composure was abruptly shattered when the toilet seat went flying sideways.

Upon my return to the classes the lady who had made the toilet seat prediction said, 'Joan, did you fix your toilet seat?'

Noting a fascinated audience I squirmed. 'Funny you should ask that,' I replied attempting to come up with a way to avoid the inevitable. But with all eyes upon me, the unvarnished truth was all my mind could produce, so I related my embarrassing experience at the party. Raucous laughter followed. This lady was born under the sign of Taurus and was, true to that sign, an earthy person who focused on the physical and sensual.

JOAN L BOLER

Most people given the opportunity to select a psychic reader from a group of readers will unconsciously select one who is, in some ways at least, similar to themselves. When I used to read at psychic expos, I was constantly amazed at the number of people who came to me for a reading who had similar astrological energies to me. Unconsciously at least, people choose someone they feel they can relate to. When no choice is involved, the unconscious can play a part in bringing together the reader and the recipient of the reading for reasons that can range from the mundane to the profound.

Unlike counsellors who have an academic background and training and who depend upon input from the person seeking help, a good psychic does not need verbal input from a person in order to know the cause of their problems. They are not confused by an individual's bias or limited understanding of their situation, and they can provide motivation for change as they can predict the consequences that lie ahead for the person if they do not change.

Perhaps the most important aspect of psychic counselling is the spiritual approach that looks at the bigger picture of the soul's journey.

Psychics and Sensitivity

As sensitives, psychics can be vulnerable to the negative energies of others and avoidance of and protection from intrusive energies is important. Psychics use the unconscious mind to work directly and indirectly with the unconscious minds of others, so they need to have in place boundaries capable of blocking the negative energies of not only those individuals they work with, but also those who might interfere in the reading, mentally or energetically. Protection in the form of white light is the common method used by psychics. But the psychic's own attitudes provide the strongest protection.

Whilst I have rarely been the recipient of negative energy directed towards me while reading, there has been the odd occasion when the person I have been reading for has reacted angrily to what I have had to tell them because it hasn't agreed with what they wanted to hear or with what they had been told by other psychics. The ego is important when dealing with such situations. The ego that requires a total belief in and acceptance of what is revealed by the person being read is vulnerable, as such a reaction reveals the psychic's feeling of wellbeing is dependent upon the opinion of others. Protection is assured when the ego does not have a vested interest in

THE TRUTH SEEKER

approval of the client whose reaction is as a result of their own attitude and is not the responsibility of the reader.

One such case I recall was that of a woman in her late thirties who wanted to know when she would meet the man she was to settle down with and how many children she would have. I intuited from the cards she would not meet the man she was looking for until she reached her mid to late forties, by which time she would no longer be able to conceive children.

I advised her it would still be some time before she was to meet the man she would settle down with.

'What about children,' she demanded. 'Will I have children?'

I knew I was walking into hazardous territory, 'Not unless you are prepared to break your own rules.' Without her saying so, I knew she was determined to have children with a life mate. I also knew unless she was prepared to conceive through a less ideal relationship, she would not have children.

'What do you mean?' She began to throw off sparks of angry energy.

I explained.

She stood up and thrust her hands at me as she stated palm readers had told her she was to have two children. I advised her I had studied palms for many years and had found the lines attributed to revealing the number of children a person could expect to have, were not reliable. (This incident provides an example of palmists who accept the accuracy of what they have read without checking for themselves.) The woman refused to accept what I said.

'What do the palms say?' she insisted. I told her according to what was written in palmistry books, she had two lines on her palms that were supposed to represent children.

'We will leave it at that!' Bristling with anger, she walked away.

I was aware such a situation would not have occurred without a reason, and so I considered why she had come to me rather than to someone who would confirm her beliefs. As with all who trust in a belief, sooner or later a confrontation with reality arrives. Her happiness in the present depended on her knowing her dreams for the future would be fulfilled. Her need to reinforce the predictions of others, and remove the niggling doubts that had begun to emerge due to the time lapse since the last supportive reading, had motivated her to come to me for the expected confirmation about future relationship and children.

Fear and denial walk hand in hand. This lady needed to take responsibility for her own happiness instead of waiting for fate to deliver it to her. Perhaps it was time for her to hear the truth, and although for the present denial took precedence, her personal doubts had been reinforced by the reading. Disillusionment had the potential to motivate her to start taking responsibility for her own happiness. Unfortunately, her abrupt departure deprived me of an opportunity to talk to her about the ways in which she could begin to change the behaviour patterns and thinking that were robbing her of her self-esteem and her happiness.

It is the responsibility of each person to assess information received from those who counsel through psychic readings on its merit. Not all readers are knowledgeable and gifted, and the information gained may not have been accurately interpreted by the recipient, even if correctly reported. Words can be misunderstood. The lady in front of me was denying my statement her husband was a 'visionary'. Through the cards, that clearly portrayed the visionary aspects of his mind, I had tuned directly into his energy and could feel his mind working visually with creative ideas that frequently ventured outside the 'square'. As I sought a way to enable her to relate to what I was saying, I thought to ask her what her husband did for a living. 'He's a film director,' was her reply. I was then in a position to detail the way in which her husband used his visionary mind. While sceptics believe a psychic is 'fishing' when they attempt to obtain confirmation regarding the information they are receiving, accuracy depends upon confirming a communication is both correct *and* understood. Doubtless, there are times when misunderstandings between the reader and the recipient of the reading go unnoticed.

Often during my years of reading for people, I was confronted with those who were deeply depressed and looking to me for help. Mental boundaries, created by the spiritual understanding of the reader, can provide protection from the unhappy energies of others. It is very easy to allow depressed energy to penetrate boundaries, and while empathy is a natural reaction for a caring person, acceptance of the rightness of another's pain as part of their learning and/or healing process enables the reader to remain detached from that pain. This is important, because if the reader takes on the negative energy of the person they are reading for, their potential for healing the other person is very much reduced or lost. A reader who cares has a valuable healing resource and can flood the sufferer with a beautiful, loving, healing energy, while at the same time giving advice to the person as to how they can change their situation and claim their power.

THE TRUTH SEEKER

The spiritual purpose of a reading is to help the person to heal. In order to heal others, energetically and through counselling, the psychic needs to be centred and free from the frustrations of daily life. Meditation is an excellent way to achieve this state. While visualising being surrounded by a white light can be helpful in blocking negative energies, it can be negated by the reader's own reactions. A clear mental attitude that is totally free from judgement towards a person's situation is essential. A strong spiritual energy and spiritual attitudes can provide the reader with impenetrable boundaries.

Interference in Readings

The lack of understanding as to how readers work sometimes results in the failure of the psychic to give accurate information. The reader's trance state is fundamental to accessing information in a reading. When in a trance state, the psychic can be affected, on an unconscious level, by the negative emotions and mental attitudes directed at them by others. Distractions of any sort can pull the psychic out of the trance state. For this reason, when psychic ability is being tested the environment should be free of those with disagreeable or pessimistic attitudes that can have a negative impact on the psychic's ability.

My boundaries have always proven to be strong but they didn't block out the telepathic intrusion of a lady in a hurry. Five minutes before the completion of a reading, my focus was disrupted when I felt a strong energy agitating for me to hurry up and finish. The impact of this was very much like having a heckler constantly interrupt a speech. When the next person arrived for their reading, I asked if she had attempted to rush me. 'Yes,' she said. 'I am in a hurry and I wanted to see you as soon as possible.' She then proudly explained she had kept sending forceful messages to me to hurry up. Her spontaneous excitement as she realised her efforts had been successful, was infectious and we both laughed. I then suggested perhaps she could resist the urge to act in a similar fashion in the future in consideration of the person currently receiving a reading. Since it hadn't been a negative communication, although it was invasive and had pulled me out of my trance, such a situation was unlikely to be repeated and so I didn't attempt to work on setting up boundaries.

It is not only strong mental focus that can have an impact on the psychic's ability when giving a reading. On a number of occasions, people who have come to me for a reading have blocked me from accessing their information. Perhaps in order to test the psychic's abilities they decide not to allow a reader to receive any clues from them, or maybe they fear a secret will be revealed. Without realising it, they create a barrier. For the psychic it is like hitting a brick wall. No one can penetrate another person's energy if that person has blocked his or her self. The mind has the power to set up mental boundaries and each of us has the ability to take total charge of our own boundaries.

While a good psychic reader will probably achieve an average eighty per cent accuracy with regard to future information, and up to one hundred per cent when dealing with issues surrounding the person's life, very little, if any, information can be gained if the unconscious of the person cannot be accessed. Inaccurate readings can be the result of one form or another of interference. Over time, I learned to stop the reading when confronted with blocking. Had I continued, neither the person receiving the reading nor I would have been happy with the result. In order to receive an accurate reading, the person seeking answers through a psychic, needs to be prepared to be open with them.

The Search for Self

At some point in each soul's evolution, the search for happiness becomes the search for self. The search for the truth of who and what we are. That discovery usually results in efforts to heal the unconscious and to eliminate the blocks that limit.

There are many ways of working towards the healing of the psyche. The intent to heal attracts support of the universal energies and brings into our lives enlightening information and experiences that can aid us. Healing frequently demands experiences that require confrontation of the painful and its causes. Although what is attracted may not always be palatable, meeting life head on is an approach filled with potential for change for the better.

For many, the most effective method to uncover the wounds of the past and conquer them is through hypnosis and accessing the unconscious mind to discover and treat their cause. Whatever their area of expertise, those who work towards the healing the psyche draw upon their studies and their personal experience in order to offer knowledge that can aid the person seeking guidance. In the world of healing, it is desirable the practitioner, whether a hypnotherapist, counsellor, psychic reader or spiritual healer, be endowed with caring and insight.

THE TRUTH SEEKER

As spirit beings, we create the reality we experience on our earthly jaunts. During those times we are in tune with our greater selves, we know all we experience is of our own choosing. We know the wisdom of our universe works with us so we fulfil our destiny. We know we are part of all that is, all that has been, and all that will ever be.

JOAN L BOLER

Chapter 10

Extra Dimensional Travellers

If I take the theory as we have it now, literally, I would conclude that extra dimensions really exist. They're part of nature. We don't really know how big they are yet, but we hope to explore that in various ways.

Edward Witten[147]

Our Multi-Dimensional Universe

Throughout the ages, man has dreamed of flying. He has envisioned conquering the skies. With innovative imagination, he has sought ways to defy gravity. Records of designs for wings, and attempts to fly with those wings, reveal the danger some have been prepared to face in order to reach the heavens. Conversely, there have been those who have claimed to fly. They claimed they flew over landscapes, or travelled at apparently impossible speeds to distant destinations. They claimed to leave their physical body and journey, in what appears to be a lighter body, to anywhere of their choosing in the physical world. Some adventurous souls claim to have travelled to distant planets and to other galaxies, while still others claim to have visited other dimensions including the heavenly kingdoms.

According to science, we live in a multi-dimensional universe and if the universe is multidimensional, then so are we. The physical body houses multiple layers, and the consciousness of each individual has the potential ability to move progressively through its lighter bodies until it experiences itself as pure spirit. Throughout lifetimes, we traverse these different dimensions, taking our consciousness with us at death as we enter the worlds of spirit. Some souls find themselves leaving the physical body without the finality of physical death. According to those who travel out-of-body, the experience is a conscious one where the mind is in control and can make decisions and carry them out. These people can provide us with insights into the various aspects of such experiences.

---

[147] Witten, Edward, Theoretical Physicist (Researcher Superstring theory) "Viewpoints on string theory" *Nova*, www.pbs.org/wgbh/nova/elegant/view-witten.html (accessed 11 November 2014)

JOAN L BOLER

The Research

There have been various efforts to research the out-of-body experience psychologically, statistically and experimentally. Scientifically inexplicable data has accumulated over recent years leaving little doubt the evidence supports claims by those who leave their physical body to travel to a variety of destinations.

The question as to whether these experiences are the product of an unstable mind was looked into in 1987 by American professors of psychology, Jerome Tobacyk and T. Mitchell PhD. Their conclusion was that out-of-body experiences were not associated with psychological disorders of any sort.[148]

Surveys by D S Rogo in 1984, into the incidence of out-of-body experiences, cited data from over sixty studies and reports that revealed as many as ten to twenty per cent of the population report at least one experience.[149] Surveys also reveal that an out-of-body experience is a common result of the use of psychedelic substances.[150]

Some research has focused on the stimulation of various areas of the brain that have resulted in out-of-body experience sensations being recorded. In 1958, Canadian neurosurgeon Wilder Graves Penfield, reported such results.[151] Professor Olaf Blanke, MD is Director of the Laboratory of Cognitive Neuroscience, Lausanne, Switzerland. In 2002, he, along with neurological colleagues at the University Hospitals of Geneva and Lausanne, while working with a subject who was being evaluated for epilepsy treatment, applied electrical stimulation to the brain's right angular gyrus (area of the brain linked to complex language function). The subject experienced sensations such as sinking into the bed, falling and seeing her legs and the lower part of her body lying on the bed from above. The brief experiences may have been the beginnings of an out-of-body experience. Further evidence, like leaving the area and travelling distances and seeing what is confirmed at a later time by others, as achieved by experienced out of body travellers, is needed in order to confirm this.

---

[148] Tobacyk, J & Mitchell, T (1987(, 'The out-of-body experience and personality adjustment. ' *Journal of Nervous and Mental Disease* 175: 367-369.

[149] Rogo, D S, (1984) 'Researching the out-of-body experience: The state of the Art. Anabiosis:' *The Journal for Near Death Studies* 4: 21-49.

[150] Luke, David P. 'Psychedelic Substances and Paranormal Phenomena: A review of the Research.' *Journal of Parapsychology*; Spring/Fall 2008, Vol. 72 Issue 1, pp. 86 & 87.

[151] Penfield W, *The Excitable Cortex in Conscious Man*, Liverpool University Press, Liverpool, 1958..

THE TRUTH SEEKER

The following research relating to a person proficient in leaving his physical body provides clearer insight into the experience. Laboratory experiments were carried out in 1973 by American psychologist and parapsychologist Dr Robert Morris (1942-2004), at Duke University and involved Keith (Blue) Harary and his kitten. The kitten was placed in a cage with a grid of twenty-four squares and its agitation was measured by the number of squares it entered and the number of meows. The kitten was markedly calmer when visited by Harary. Fellow researcher, Hartwell, on four separate occasions sensed Harary's presence even though he had no prior knowledge of an intended visit.[152]

There are also documented case histories like that of Mr S R Wilmot. Wilmot and a Mr W J Tait were sharing a cabin on the steamship *City of Limerick* in October 1863. A visit from Wilmot's wife was independently witnessed and commented upon by Tait. Wilmot's sister, who was also travelling on the steamship, likewise confirmed the sighting. Upon his return, his wife advised Wilmot she had been anxious about him and experienced a sense of visiting him over water. She was able to provide a description of the stateroom.[153]

There are those who claim to have had an out-of-body experience whilst apparently in the dream state. Such was the case of Martha Johnson from Plains, Illinois who on 27 January, 1957 reported she had a dream where she travelled to her mother's home almost a thousand miles away in northern Minnesota. She saw her mother, who was bending over something white and doing something with her hands, look up at her. Martha then woke up and noted it was 2:10 am. When Martha received a letter from her mother dated 29 January, it said, *Did you know that you were here for a few seconds? I believe it was Saturday night at 1: 10, January 26th or maybe 27th. It would have been after two at your time... I looked up and there you were by the cupboard just standing smiling at me... I think the dogs saw you too... They got so excited...* A second letter from her mother in February 1957 explained she had been bending over something white because she had been ironing.[154]

In 1935 the famous medium Eileen J Garrett, set up a test using observers Dr Mühl in New York, and Dr Stevenson in Reykjavik, Iceland. She then

---

[152] Broughton, R S, *Parapsychology: The Controversial Science*, Ballantine, New York, 1991. pp. 338-9.
[153] Braude 2003, pp. 262-66—based on Sidgwick, 1891.
[154] Braude, Stephen E, *Immortal Remains: The Evidence for Life After Death*, Rowman & Littlefield, 2003, p. 262.

projected herself from New York to Reykjavik and provided details to verify the experience.[155]

It is possible to see the similarities between the out-of-body experience that Eileen J Garret set up, and the experiences mentioned in Chapter Five 'Our Extraordinary Senses' regarding the use of distant viewing as a spying technique during the Cold War. The difference lies in the method used. Out-of-body experiences require the soul, along with the etheric double of the physical body, lifts out of the physical body, while with distant viewing the mind clairvoyantly accesses the distant site.

Dr John Palmer was a psychologist at the John F Kennedy University in Orinda, California during the mid-1970s when he began to experiment with out-of-body experiences. He worked with a number of subjects at different times with a degree of success. One interesting fact he discovered when he started monitoring brain waves was that those of his subjects who had a genuine out-of-body experience (defined by the subject's ability to describe the target picture accurately) preceded it with over thirty percent theta waves. When a person is thinking, feeling or doing, the brain neurons communicate through electrical pulses creating brainwaves. While beta waves register at 14-30 cycles per second, and accompany intellectual activity, alpha waves occur at 8-12 cycles and appear when we slow down and relax, and delta waves measure ½-3 cycles and occur when deep sleep is taking place. The uncommon theta waves have been found to occur when inducing altered states of consciousness or when intense efforts are made to create mental images.[156]

Out-of-body experiences are fairly common, but are yet to be explained scientifically. There are numerous witness accounts to confirm the soul of a person has travelled to another place. Not only has the individual been seen clairvoyantly by others, the ability to recall details of the circumstances surrounding the out-of-body experience provides convincing evidence of the actuality of the experience. What is happening and how it is happening can't be explained without taking into account the multidimensional nature of our makeup.

---

[155] Garrett, Eileen J, *My Life as a Search for the Meaning of Mediumship*, Oquage, New York, 1939.
[156] Palmer, John. 'ESP and out-of-body experiences: EEG correlates'. (In Research in parapsychology, 1978 Roll, W. G. ed. Metuchen, N. J; *Scarecrow Press,* 1979).

THE TRUTH SEEKER

The Etheric Body

Esoteric knowledge from the East that more recently has infiltrated the West describes an energetic double of the physical body called the etheric or subtle body. This body is similar in appearance to the physical body but lacks its density and is not usually apparent to the human eye. This energetic body that survives the grave is an integral part of each of us and normally exists in harmony with the physical body and penetrates all aspects of it.

We all leave our bodies when we are sleeping, even if all we do is float three to six feet (a metre or two) above our bed. A sign of having done this is the falling sensation and landing with a jolt as we suddenly wake. At such times, our subtle body has been either floating or 'travelling' while we sleep and our body has called it back. This can occur when a noise disturbs us or when nature requires a bathroom visit. Few recall the nocturnal excursions many of us take.

The subtle body is connected to the physical body through a ribbon or cord of energy. It is through the cord's energetic connection to the subtle body that the physical body can recall its travelling counterpart at any time. This cord disintegrates at death, severing our connection to the physical world.

One evening, a young man attending one of my classes, talked of his amazing out-of-body travels to various destinations. The most awesome excursion he indulged in, he enthused, was flying out some distance from the earth and looking back down upon the planet. He complained his one problem was the cord that extended from him and back to earth. He had attempted on a number of occasions to break this cord, and was frustrated by his inability to do so. I explained to him he would need to die in order to achieve that, so no doubt he subsequently ceased his futile efforts.

In the West, there has been an almost total lack of understanding of what is happening when an out-of-body experience occurs. In the past, people have believed in witches who flew at night and despatched evil. The Christian perpetrators of the witch hunts that lasted for many centuries introduced the belief that Satan and his demons formed pacts with witches.[157] Some of those who have naturally, or with the aid of hallucinogenic substances, involuntarily left their physical body were faced with the possibility of a confrontation with Satan or creatures of evil intent. It is time for all such notions to be lain to rest. The more known and understood about whom and

---

[157] Miesel, Sandra. 'Who burned the witches?—A multitude of myths. *Catholic education resource centre.* http://catholiceducation. org/articles/history/world/wh0056.html (accessed 12 Feb 2014)

what we are, the less hold such superstitious, fearful, nonsense will have on people.

Consciousness outside the Physical Body

Although I have frequently experienced falling back into my body, I have not achieved the ability to travel out of body at will. However, I have experienced a variety of spontaneous out-of-body experiences.

At twenty-six, I was the mother of two, very active young children. One afternoon, after I had sent the children to bed for their nap, I took the opportunity to rest as I was feeling somewhat exhausted. My head hit the pillow and I promptly dropped off to sleep. Suddenly, I was startled awake. With a shock, I realised I was floating up near the ceiling, and was four feet (1.2mtrs) above the bed! The 'I' that was floating was an energetic substance while my physical body was on the bed! As I floated in this subtle body, my normal conscious awareness, with its logical mind and emotional responses, accompanied it. Meanwhile my awareness included my physical body lying on the bed, but unlike my subtle body, my physical body did not seem to house my thoughts or my feelings.

Without conscious determination or effort on my part, I began to slowly drift down towards my physical body, and gradually I merged with it. This was totally weird! My left hand was the last part of me to merge. Once again, there was just one 'me'! Shaken, I considered what to do next. *If I moved, I might come apart again!* After around five minutes, I felt stable enough to move without the danger of splitting apart, so I cautiously left my bed.

Disbelief at the impossible conflicted with the knowledge that what I had experienced was real. Over the next few days, I absorbed the experience and its implications. I was not just a physical body. Nor was my survival dependent upon the continued existence of my physical body! This was mind altering! From that time, I knew I was still a complete person without my physical body, and the physical was a part of me I needed in order to operate in the physical world. In fact, I felt as though my corporeal body was like clothing I had put on. The individual that was me had remained intact and operated free of the physical! For the first time in my life I knew without doubt that the ongoing survival of the soul was not only possible, but also probable.

Many years later, during the time when I was reading for people, I conducted two separate readings where the recipients' mothers appeared to be dead. With the first reading, I used tarot cards that indicated the lady's mother was dead. However, she advised me her mother was not dead, but suffered from Alzheimer's disease. Only a few weeks later I read for the second lady. This time I clairvoyantly saw her mother in spirit, and was able to communicate with her. The mother was clear of any confusion, had all her normal mental faculties, and she was happy. Once again, I was advised the mother had Alzheimer's.

The implications of these two readings, along with out-of-body understanding, suggest the possibility that when Alzheimer's reaches a certain stage, the patient's soul, housed in the subtle body, separates from the physical body. I had evidence one of these mothers was, at least part of the time, living an out-of-body existence while only a basic physical consciousness remained operating in the physical world.

The significance of Alzheimer patients being able to experience full conscious awareness, even though for the most part, they have lost the ability to express that awareness through the physical body, is huge. This possibility is confirmed in Chapter Six, 'Mind Powers, Magic and Miracles' by Pim van Lommel[158] who reported brain dead patients claimed that during their coma they were above their bodies and fully conscious and aware of all going on around them. The possibility that those who, for whatever reason, cannot communicate through the physical body are still aware of what is happening around them is a game changer. Medical people attending to their needs, and the loved ones who visit them, have the opportunity to ensure communications comfort and reassure the patient, so what may be to them an isolating and frightening experience becomes a much less traumatic one.

Pronounced Dead

Since there are many who have never had an out-of-body experience of any sort, one wonders what causes some to experience it and others not. For some, the use of psychedelic drugs has resulted in one or more experiences, while for others, like me, they occur spontaneously but rarely. For a few people, out-of-body experiences are commonplace. For my brother, regular out-of-body experiences literarily had a shocking starting point.

---

[158] Van Lommel, Pim. 'Near death experience, consciousness, and the brain a new concept about the continuity of our consciousness based on recent scientific research on Near-death experience in survivors of cardiac arrest.' *The Journal of General Evolution*; Jan 2006 Vol. 62 pp. 134-151.

JOAN L BOLER

When our mother was hospitalised for some months, and then recuperating for a further period of time, my brother, my two sisters and I, went to live on a farm in the Bay of Plenty with friends of the family. School holidays saw the family we were staying with deciding to visit their relatives on a farm in Whaharoa (near Hamilton). Anticipation saw us excitedly clambering into the family car and on our arrival the very large family greeted us. The children were of all ages, and in the ensuing hours we all had great fun playing. When it was time to go, it was decided that my brother John, then aged thirteen, and my sister Yvonne who was nine, would remain for a few more days on the farm.

Yvonne and John played with the other children around the barn. Entertainment at John's expense was introduced by some of the young girls as they grabbed the gumboots he was about to put on, and threw them on to the barn roof. John quickly climbed up to retrieve them. Wasting no time, he ducked under the power lines above the barn, grabbed the gumboots and threw them back down to the ground. Then without conscious thought, he reached up and grabbed hold of the power lines through which 415 volts of electricity were running!

Pandemonium broke loose. Yvonne looked up and saw John hanging from the power lines. The children's yelling and screaming brought their father from the house. He hurriedly fetched a ladder, placed it next to the fuse pole and climbed up to remove the fuse.

In the ensuing confusion of activity that included John being lifted down from the barn roof, some of the older children gathered around Yvonne to distract her. In between their attentions she watched as John was carried unconscious inside to one of the bedrooms. Yvonne's need to go to him to ensure that he was all right was frustrated by the older children as they guided her to another part of the house to play games. In spite of the advice that John was asleep, Yvonne determined she would see for herself he was not injured. But each attempt to slip away was thwarted. After a time, she managed to sneak into the hallway unnoticed. She found John lying on the bed apparently sleeping and injury free.

The local doctor and the Waikato hospital were called. The doctor arrived and pronounced John dead. This devastating news was then relayed to our parents.

The matron from the Waikato hospital arrived at the farm in the ambulance after a trip that would have taken a minimum of forty-five minutes. Today that trip is approximately 35-45 miles (56-72.5km) and is estimated to take around one hour (normal driving) on roads that would not have been up to

THE TRUTH SEEKER

today's standard. The Waikato Hospital in Hamilton had recently acquired a portable iron-lung machine from Australia (the first portable machine of its kind in New Zealand), and it had been installed in the ambulance. The matron, who wished to trial the new machine, placed John inside it.

John has no memory of the next twenty-four hours. As consciousness emerged, John became aware of a being surrounded by a very bright light. He looked down a long tunnel to tiny white figures that were moving. *I'm in heaven and I can see the angels*, John thought. Then he found himself slowly drifting towards them. John's descent down through the tunnel of light continued, and as he drew closer, he realised that he was looking into a room that appeared to have no roof. The five people in the room were doctors and nurses standing around an occupied bed. John was still drifting down and was at a height of about three storeys when he realised the person lying in the bed was himself. At the same time, he could hear a male person calling, 'Wake up John!'

John's descent in his subtle body continued until he reached his physical body, and then, without any intent on his part, he proceeded to merge with it. He entered face first, which meant that once he was in his body, he needed to turn over. As this was happening, he was able to see everything going on around him, even though the eyes in his physical body were closed. As he opened his eyes the doctor said, 'John, can you please open your hands.' John did so.

'Wow. Not a mark!' The doctors then advised him that since they had thought his hands would be burnt, they had attempted to open them in order to treat them but they had been unable to do so. John had had an out-of-body experience even though he didn't understand what had happened.

The fact John survived was remarkable. That he survived without apparent injury was cause for amazement and celebration. But had the experience left its mark?

A Super Hero

John returned to the farm in the Bay of Plenty where everyone greeted him enthusiastically. His homecoming presumed a return to normal and from the viewpoint of those around him, this appeared to be the case, but it was not long before the effects of John's electrocution began to emerge.

JOAN L BOLER

The room John slept in was at the back of the house and was furnished with three single beds. His friend, the fourteen-year-old son of the family we were living with, was in the bed next to him, while the other bed was sometimes occupied by one of the adult sons.

Bedtime arrived. As John lay on his back, in bed in a semi-dozing state and feeling very pleasantly relaxed and light, he glanced sideways to the bed where his friend was sleeping. Inexplicably, instead of finding his friend lying across from him, he was actually lying about two feet (61cm) lower. Shocked, John attempted to sit up, but as he pushed down with his arms he was propelled even higher.

What have I done? John looked around the room, and in spite of the darkness could see everything clearly. Bewildered, John tried to figure out how he could possibly get back down. He moved his arms and tried to turn over—but that moved him away from his bed and above the floor some distance below. A crash to the floor seemed a distinct possibility! A door slammed somewhere and John instantly found himself back on his bed. Heart pounding, John lay still, not daring to move. Then he dozed off.

The next day, as the usually adventurous John pondered his experience, he decided it had been exciting. The more he thought about it, and the possibilities it offered, the more eager he became to repeat the experience. By bedtime, he was impatiently anticipating a reoccurrence of the previous night. Disappointingly, he just fell asleep. But the night after, John once again found he was floating off the bed. This time he was ready. He began to breaststroke through the air. That worked well enough and so he tried rolling over. Then he successfully negotiated the room several times, floating up and down and over his sleeping friend.

At thirteen, John's only source for knowledge of a human flying came from comic books. *I can fly like Superman!* John reached a conclusion. He was a super hero! His head spun with the exciting realisation. For a thirteen-year-old boy, this was the ultimate dream! As he put his head out the window, the old dog that slept at the back door barked. Satisfied for the present with his achievements, John turned around, dropped promptly on to the bed and fell asleep.

The next night, prior to going to bed, John made sure the bedroom's sash window was down far enough in order to enable him to float through it. It was not long before his adventure commenced. John exited the bedroom via the window. The dogs immediately saw him and barked. Fearful of the adults awakening and putting a stop to his escapade, John, as rapidly as he could and using breaststroke, moved up above the tall trees near the

THE TRUTH SEEKER

driveway. The dogs quietened. John's excursion into the night posed no problem with regard to visibility as he could see as well as he did during the daylight—nothing was blurred or shadowed due to the lack of light.

At this point, John had discovered it was not possible to fool the dogs by sneaking up behind them, as they knew he was there and began to bark. Since the dogs were aware of his presence and he had not realised he had left his physical body, he did not know he was invisible to people. John was sure that he was breaking the adults' rules and he wasn't taking any chances of being seen, and so on this, and future occasions he wished to venture out, he waited until his friend was asleep.

Even super-kids have to start somewhere, so John began to work on developing his skills. Each time he escaped the confines of his room at night, through testing his boundaries he came to understand the extent of his new abilities. Using breaststroke became a thing of the past as John discovered he could float or fly whenever he wanted to. The excitement and thrills he experienced flying up, and then swooping down were greater than any he had experienced in his young life. John soon discovered that when he was in the air, he could stop simply by deciding to. At first, he flew around and above the house, taking care not to go too high in case he fell until he realised he was not going to fall and he could safely fly as high as he wanted to.

John delighted in his flights around and through the trees. He noted that the birds that were awake could see him as their eyes followed his progress. The farm animals reacted in much the same way as the birds. As he moved close to the cows, they noted his presence and watched him, but they didn't seem disturbed. The sheep stared but showed no fear. The horses allowed him to get close and, surprisingly, one horse that became agitated and would not let John near during the day remained calm when he came close during his night time excursions.

Perhaps John felt the calm reaction of the horse might indicate a similar reaction from our pet deer that became skittish if we attempted to approach it during the daytime. The deer was in a paddock and tied to a log which had been placed into position with the use of a tractor, as it would have otherwise required number of men to lift it. John decided to move up close to the deer during his night travels. The animal became so terrified that it dragged the log some seven yards (6.4mtrs) in its attempt to escape what it perceived to be a dangerous threat.

The new location of the log didn't go unnoticed. A lively conversation took place at the dinner table the following day when the men discussed the distance the log had moved. A self-conscious, somewhat guilty John listened to the men who were puzzled and amazed that the deer, with its skinny legs, had been able to move the log so far.

After one of his excursions, as John returned through the window of his bedroom, he noticed the light was on and his friend had gone to the bathroom. As he continued his descent into his bed, he was surprised to see his own physical body on the bed. He returned to it and fell asleep.

Realisation dawned on John that he could fly to anywhere in the area. Although initially he remained close to home, after a time he began to expand his territory. The back of the farm where he had previously been taken by the men held a fascination for the curious John. Where did the track go to? He travelled some miles to where the men had worked and then followed the track further into the bush, enjoying his adventure into previously forbidden territory. Then he began to leave the farm and travel all over the countryside. He made visits to neighbours' places, and on one occasion he followed the road, that we usually took in the school bus, some fifteen miles (24km) to the local store.

The length of time John stayed out, initially around two to three hours each night, changed when he realised he was never tired the next day and he began to stay out longer. Usually he returned to the bedroom because he wished to do so, but on one occasion, while on one of his nocturnal excursions, John became aware of a man's voice calling to him from a great distance. He recognised the voice as that of the farmer we were living with. Alarmed, and believing he would be in trouble, he immediately returned to his body. The farmer, who had being trying for some time to wake John, had become extremely anxious due to his lack of response. He couldn't understand why the vigorous shaking he had given John had taken so long to gain a reaction. I recall being in the dining room and hearing the concerned adult voices coming from John's room. Was it possible that during his absence from his body, John's heartbeat slowed to such an extent that it appeared to the farmer John might have died?

We all missed our mother but were never taken to visit her as she was in Auckland and we were in the Bay of Plenty—approximately five hours' drive by car. John headed off one night down the road as he desperately wanted to see Mum. He moved faster and faster so everything around him became a blur. As he flew, he lifted up high above the ground as he headed towards a destination that, although he had no idea where it was, he somehow 'knew' how to find. Then, from up in the sky he sighted a two storey, red brick, square building and began to descend, slowing to a stop as he reached the upstairs balcony. He walked in through the door and although there were people around, no one took any notice of him. He knew where to go as he walked down a corridor with light green painted walls and a green linoleum floor. He went through a cream door into the room where our mother was. John found Mum on a wrought iron bed, propped up on pillows, dozing. He tried to shake her to wake her up. She started to stir and appeared to look at him, so he sat on the bed and talked to her. He told her how we missed her and loved her and how we all wanted to come and visit her. John left the hospital and in the next instant had returned to the farm.

When John next saw Dad, he told him he had visited Mum. Dad didn't believe him as he knew there was no possible way for John to have done so. John insisted he had visited Mum and gave a detailed description of the building and the room Mum was in. Dad agreed his description was correct, but couldn't get his head around how John could possibly know, and so, at least while he was talking to John, he dismissed his story.

Through his night travels, John had discovered some of the interesting aspects of out-of-body travel—that of being able to fly; of travelling at high speeds; of being able to go directly to another person's presence, even though their whereabouts was unknown; of being able to move from one place to another in an instant, and being able to see as clearly as he could in daylight. The limitations of everyday life in the physical world changed significantly when John left his body. Once we left the farm, John tended to travel only at those times he felt lonely. By the time he reached his late twenties, he had ceased this activity.

The Dream State and Multidimensional Travel

While dreaming is the domain of the unconscious mind that plays out scenarios reflecting the inner issues of the dreamer, the dream state also offers a doorway through which it is possible to access other dimensions—sometimes consciously. These dimensions include those inhabited by beings that no longer reside in, or have never resided in, a physical body.

Brain wave patterns while dreaming are similar to those experienced during meditation, and therefore, it is not surprising paranormal experiences like communications from departed loved ones and prophetic revelations can occur while in the dream state. On many occasions in the past, people have advised me that when they have been dreaming, they have connected to and communicated with relatives who have died.

JOAN L BOLER

Normal conscious awareness whilst dreaming is called 'lucid' dreaming. Roma, a long-time friend of mine was, for many years, able to take control of her dream state and dictate the content of her dreams. This capability can enable the dreamer to be the conscious author of their dreams, so anything the imagination can conceive can be experienced. Lucid dreaming is similar to, but not the same as, an out-of-body experience. Both require conscious awareness and determination. However, events created while in the dream state, unlike an out-of-body experience, are a created fantasy.

The symbolism from life experience and the collective unconscious is drawn upon by the unconscious when we dream. Such symbolism is used to process our responses to the events we deal with daily, especially those happenings that are difficult and emotionally charged. Most of the characters in our dreams symbolise an aspect of our own nature. For example, when a person known to have a judgemental and critical nature appears in a dream, that person can represent that same characteristic within the self. The content of the dream can expose the reason why that facet of the self is being examined. Analysis of dreams can reveal out of balance aspects of the self that, if dealt with, can remove problematic issues.

My friend Sally, who has spent many years working in counselling and hypnotherapy and has studied dream analysis, brings conscious awareness into her dreams. Sally is aware when she is dreaming whether a character portrayed in her dreams is in fact an aspect of her own personality. The following experience reveals a dream during which she connected with her dead grandfather.

> *I was in a dreamlike state at a sandy beach with cliffs. I was walking along the beach when my grandfather visited me. That's when the dream feeling changed. Normally in a dream, I can feel myself talking through the characters or relating to the characters and feeling that they are just aspects of me.*
>
> *In this dream, there was a definite sense of my grandfather being present as it was his energy coming through. I felt his warmth radiating through to me—conveying his love for me. He communicated to me that he was fine and that he loved me very much.*
>
> *My grandfather was the most stable male role model in my life. The 'revelation' experience of having a beautiful, caring, responsive male around, even though he was no longer physically present in my life, was really important at that time, and I experienced a sense of him being around still. He probably decided that communicating when I*

was dreaming was the easiest way to connect with me and to reassure me that he was still present in my life.

Sally has also had various paranormal experiences, including the following, where she found herself being taught to use her paranormal abilities during a conscious state while sleeping.

> *There are a group of people who appear to be working with me in the dream/astral state. They get me to experiment and say, 'Try this now.' They told me that I have done these things before and get me to do exercises. They show me how to fly higher up to different levels.*
>
> *There is one Russian woman in particular I work with on the astral. I have had three very strong astral experiences of speaking Russian. I don't know Russian! I recall this woman saying to me, 'You know how to do this,' as she was showing me how to do psychic kinetic type experiments.*
>
> *The experiments appear to be assisting humans in the physical and in raising the level of consciousness. She was speaking to me in Russian and I understood what she was saying. And I was talking back to her in Russian! The first time it happened I thought, 'That was really weird.' Maybe my fluency in this foreign language was related to a previous life when I was a native speaker of Russian. That happened two other times within a period of two or three months. I wish I could retain the language skills when I come back.*

It is not surprising someone who is gifted and eager to advance her skills involving the paranormal, attracts the aid of those in spirit. Strong desires always attract. Since Sally not only works using her skills in hypnotherapy and counselling, but also practices spiritual energy healing, it is probably not unexpected she seeks to develop her healing skills during her sleeping hours. As she is a healer who can work during her sleeping hours, it follows she is drawn into situations where she can destroy that which is negative and causing pain and suffering.

> *Sometimes I get called to help people—some I know, some I don't. For years, I've had these out-of-body experiences of working with people's souls on the astral plane. Sometimes these are individuals, and often groups of people. They are asleep and need assistance and I feel it is important to help them in terms of guiding them towards the light and channelling this particular energy. In one case that was about extreme positive and negative polarity (good versus evil). It was like channelling a lightning bolt through my hands and pushing it back to these people and shifting their consciousness while actually*

feeling a perceptual shift within myself for the benefit of all beings in the world.

I was called to help a woman I knew, although she was a person I didn't really have a close relationship with. I just landed in the place where she was. I could see she was going through a very dark time and could psychically see imminent danger around her in the form of an entity pushing her into a depression.

I had to deflect and cut away the negativity and draw in archangels' help. I drew energy in from the angelic realm and placed the silver energy around the woman.

I later asked this person how she was feeling and what had been happening around her lately. She said that she had been feeling depressed and that she had had situations around her that were volatile and that she had not been feeling well mentally and physically. She had just started to feel normal and like she had become more balanced. She had more energy. I did not tell her of my activities but I had received confirmation.

These experiences reveal that Sally is able to transcend the dream state in order to access and help souls. Sally is conscious of her normal awareness during her healing activities and experiences an expanded state of consciousness that incorporates her spiritual self. She is also aware that she has let go of ego expectation and the analytical mind. This mixture of out-of-body experiences and conscious dreaming that is part of Sally's world provides a fascinating insight into travel into other dimensions. For those who are interested, there are books that describe techniques for developing the ability to astral travel or lucid dream. It is as well to gain knowledge from those who have already done so before venturing on excursions into the unknown.

Expanded States of Consciousness

Expanded states of consciousness can take us into the higher dimensions where we can explore and seek answers. There is a variety of reasons why a person experiences an expanded state of awareness and travels to the higher realms. The desire for answers is one of those reasons.

THE TRUTH SEEKER

Whilst I know I have had a number of experiences that have taken me to the higher dimensions during my sleeping hours, recalling them is another matter. Sometimes I awaken from a beautiful experience that leaves me with exquisite feelings, and then in a moment the memories dissolve and I am left only with enhanced emotional feelings. At other times, I wake with my head filled with crystal clear knowledge not previously understood or perceived, and yet not having memory of how the knowledge was obtained.

In recent years, I have travelled to other realms when in a meditative state, and experienced visitations with beings in spirit. The advantage of this method is that there is not likely to be diminished memory immediately after the experience, which can too often, for me, be the outcome of an encounter entered into through the dream state. The disadvantage is that while in the meditative state and therefore still connected to the physical, the experiences are nowhere near as powerful.

When I was living on Norfolk Island in 1971, my quest for answers at that time was probably the underlying cause of an amazing encounter. I awoke from a sleep state and found myself in what can only be described as another realm. I became aware of feeling totally awed and sitting on my heels before a seated white-robed masculine being with shoulder length hair. I had no doubt this being had once lived in the physical world, as his essence incorporated the nature of man, spiritually evolved. Possibly the clothing he wore represented clothing worn during his last earthly incarnation. Such was the power and love radiating from this being of light, there could be little doubt this was a Master—one of those great souls who through countess lifetimes have evolved beyond the need for earthly experiences.

The environment around us seemed to be a pure white light. As I absorbed the incredibly powerful love and light energy that radiated from this being, he explained to me mysteries of the cosmos. I was able to see visually and understand the knowledge given to me. His instruction included knowledge of the way in which creation was structured and the laws associated with it. Included in the knowledge I recall was the information that the seeming distance between the planets and all that is in the cosmos as we experience and perceive it when we are in the physical body is a creation. This creation when viewed from the greater reality is an illusion, and the distances experienced do not exist in this greater reality. In the one moment, I was able see the distance and see there was no distance. My consciousness had expanded to total genius state where I could understand physics and scientific concepts effortlessly and I felt great excitement and joy in my understanding of the knowledge I received.

My conscious returned to my physical body. Gradually, as my awareness descended to the comparatively dense state normal to me, my clarity of thought lessened. The experience left me feeling beautiful, very much loved, and humbled. The glow of love surrounded me for days afterwards. This was the first time in my life I had actually *felt* love directed at me and experienced its beautiful euphoric effect that dissolved all the concerns and stresses in my life.

My ability to integrate much of the information that had been revealed during the journey to that other realm was limited by my lack of a scientific education, which would have provided a framework through which I could have understood and retained much more of the knowledge imparted. With the exception of the above-mentioned information, the rest of the knowledge I gained, was lost to my conscious mind.

It seems the information gained by me during this experience, is confirmed by quantum mechanics. Dr Nick Herbert, physicist and author of 'Quantum Reality'[159] in a 1998 interview with parapsychologist Dr Jeffrey Mishlove explained that instant quantum connection of everything implies space and distance are illusionary, *That we are all in one place, that there aren't any places.*[160] This knowledge could perhaps better be understood by considering the dynamics of our dreams. In our dreams, we live through experiences that take us through landscapes that are the creation of the unconscious mind. No physical space is required for these created landscapes. Yet in our dreams we experience boundaries such as solid ground and walls, along with the senses of sight, taste and touch, just as we do in the physical world.

We are living in an amazing time scientifically. For it is a time when science is confirming the knowledge gained by mystics both in the past and in the present. As solid and dense as the physical appears to be, it is a creation. A creation that has boundaries that seem totally solid to us, and yet nothing is as solid as it seems. So complex is this creation, it incorporates billions of creatures on this planet alone. Eventually, when the creation has fulfilled its purpose, there will be no further need for the physical, just as when there is no further need for the heavenly realms, they also will cease to exist.

Consciousness and our true spiritual nature, exists always.

---

[159] Herbert, Nick, *Quantum Reality*, Anchor Books, 1985.
[160] Herbert, Nick, 'Consciousness and Quantum Reality: Interview with Dr Jeffrey Mishlove.' *Thinking Aloud: Conversations on the Leading Edge of Knowledge and Discovery,* 1998, http://www.williamjames.com/transcripts/herbert.htm (accessed 28 November 2014)

THE TRUTH SEEKER

Chapter 11

Encountering the Afterlife

The experiences associated with death were seen as visits to important dimensions of reality that deserved to be experienced, studied, and carefully mapped.

Stanislav Grof[161]

Death

At the moment of death, the essence of what we are as an individual leaves the physical body behind and in its non-physical bodies begins a journey into the dimensions beyond the physical. These are the realms of the soul and divine spirit.

Much has been written on life after death. Some of the information is accurate—some is not. The near-death experience is probably the most common source of information on this subject today, but it is not the only source. Many psychics, from a wide range of religious backgrounds, have clairvoyantly observed the process of death and the heavenly residing places of the departed. This has resulted in information on the dimensions beyond the physical that is consistent and reliable. One of these psychics was Rudolf Steiner, (1861-1925). Steiner was an Austrian mystic, philosopher, writer, teacher and lecturer who was not only interested in social reform, he also looked to the links between scientific knowledge and the spiritual. Through clairvoyance he gained knowledge of the afterlife and said, *Life between death and a new birth is as rich and varied as life here between birth and death.*[162]

Providing the practitioner is competent, hypnosis is another method that can be used to access knowledge of what happens to souls between one life and the next. While the knowledge gained in this way cannot provide proof, it

---

[161]Grof, Stanislav, "Alternative Cosmologies and Altered States", *Noetic Sciences Review*, Winter 1994, pp. 21-29.
[162] Steiner, Rudlof, 'Life between Death and Rebirth' Breslau, 5 April 1913
http://wn.rsarchive.org/Lectures/LifeBetween/19130405p01.html (accessed 10 November 2014)

nevertheless allows the individual to assess the many and varied possible experiences.

Invariably, accurate knowledge comes from those whose experiences include part of, if not all of, the death experience either through dying and being brought back to life, or through observing the dying and recently dead through clairvoyance. Ancient religious beliefs regarding the afterlife, in some cases, reveal details of the afterlife that could only have been obtained through personal experience of it or through viewing it clairvoyantly. Today, it is easier to separate truth from myth in this area of religious belief, as all over the world research into the near-death experience has been absorbing researchers for years, and now there is a large resource of information that provides both details of the process and convincing evidence.

The consistency of the death experience, as reported by people from many different races and a diversity of religious beliefs, along with the evidence provided by, and about, such experiences, demands that serious consideration be given by the religious and non-religious alike to this remarkable phenomena.

The Near-Death Experience

When death has apparently taken place, some people find they have lifted out of their physical body. They observe, from an out-of-body perspective, their own body and the actions of the people around them, including those who attempt to revive them. At this point, they are functioning on the dimension known as the astral plane, which is the closest dimension to the physical. Some souls, especially accident victims, have no immediate realisation they are no longer in their body, because they still have conscious awareness of their earthly surroundings. However, when these souls attempt to communicate with those in the physical, they are ignored, and find that they can make little, if any, impression on the physical world. It is this part of the near-death experience that provides us with verifiable evidence. When these people return to their physical body, they are able to give detailed descriptions of what others have been doing during the time they have been 'dead'. Some only experience this aspect of the near-death experience while others go on to experience dimensions beyond the astral plane.

At some point, the person has a sense of drifting through darkness or a tunnel towards a light that may be described as radiant white, white-gold, yellow-gold or gold. Often, loved ones who have died previously guide and support the newly dead person. On occasion, the person has met a relative they believed to be alive only to have it confirmed upon their recovery the person had in fact passed away. Clear conscious awareness that includes all they are as individuals is continuous throughout the near-death experience.

In Chapter Five 'Our Extraordinary Senses', I mentioned my long-time friend Joy who, like me, was reticent about revealing her clairvoyant experiences. In the following story, she tells of when her father died.

On February 23 1988, my father died of congenital heart failure. For the last two weeks of his life, our family had taken turns to be with him in hospital. He had been taken off the saline drip that had been keeping him alive and was very agitated and didn't want any contact or reassurance. He was watching the clock tick and commenting on the time through the midnight hours. Dad had talked once to my sister many years before about the times he had dreamed of flying to all sorts of places without being aware of astral travelling. He was rather sceptical about anything spiritual and what happened to you when you died. Once Mum had gone he had given up on his life; he was aware that his time had come but resisted strongly. While sitting with him I saw my mother standing beside him. She was saying that we had to let him do this his way. About an hour later, after having a cup of tea while sitting on the bed, he died.

Our family went through the formalities, and within an hour of his death, we left the hospital to go back to the house. I was sitting in the back of the car with my eyes closed. I saw a great tunnel of light with Dad walking away from me through it. The tunnel was approximately three metres high and two metres wide and was a brilliant yellow-gold with the light radiating out from his body. Outside of the tunnel were his own family; Mum, his mother and father and his two brothers. They were keeping pace with him in semi-darkness. He was walking holding up his pyjama pants (bought recently by my sister in the size he used to wear, at his insistence, and much too big for him); he looked back over his shoulder with a huge grin and said to me that it was all right—he was OK.

I was left with a warm feeling and relief, knowing he was happy.

The next stage involves being in the presence of the being of light that religious near-death experiencers recognise as an expected deity—for Christians that is Jesus. This being radiates a love that penetrates every part of the soul in its presence, endowing a feeling of pure bliss. With compassion, humour and without judgement, this being usually communicates telepathically and wants to know what the person had done with the gift of life—who they have loved and what knowledge they have gained. The being then supports them as needed as they experience a rapid review of their life.

While some who go through a near-death experience review of their whole life, others experience only a partial review. At some point during the near-death experience, some perceive the beauty of the heavenly realms. While most people's experiences are positive, some aren't. Those who have been depressed, have unsolved anger issues, deep-seated fears, or are totally self-absorbed, callous and cruel, can report a hellish experience. While some of the features of the negative experience are similar to the positive near-death experience, there is nothing pleasant about them, and upon return to life, survivors look to changing their previous negative attitudes and behaviour.

With some people, the experience ends suddenly and they return to their body. Others are informed by a relative or a spiritual deity that it is not their time or they are given a choice as to whether they will return to their earthly existence. In spite of the blissful state they experience, many see a need to return to the living in order to fulfil a heartfelt wish that might involve the nurturing of others, or to go on working towards desired goals and achievements.

Most of those who undergo a near-death experience, report that there is a lack of awareness of time and space. All *knew* the experience was *real* and were convinced that during the experience they were no longer in their physical body. This is confirmed by the fact that while in the out-of-body state, they felt no pain, but once they returned to their physical body they became aware of the pain associated with the physical trauma their body had suffered. In the aftermath, most people had lost their fear of death, and sometimes they saw the need to make changes in their lives. However, most of the changes experienced were involuntary as their perspective of life and its purpose had dramatically changed. Significantly, these effects did not diminish over time.

While there are variations in the way in which individuals experience their near-death journey, essentially it remains the same no matter their cultural background. Because of this, the scientific community acknowledges the near-death experience, but sceptics argue the cause and reality of the experience.

THE TRUTH SEEKER

Consciousness, the Brain and the Near-Death Experience

Evidence of life after death has been growing progressively since the twentieth century. As a result of advances in life-saving medical procedures, patients who have experienced clinical death have been brought back to life. Of those survivors, some have reported a near-death experience.

In the past, because scientists and those in the medical profession had assumed the brain was responsible for mental function, they considered that when the physical died, the mind and consciousness also died. Now the accumulated evidence allows for a new approach that is open to the possibility that the physical body, including the brain, is the servant of consciousness. The near-death experience provides supporting evidence for the continued consciousness of a person after their physical body can no longer support that conscious awareness.

In 2001, Pim van Lommel, a cardiologist at the Rijnstate hospital in the Netherlands, along with a group of doctors, published his findings in 'The Lancet' (the British peer reviewed medical publication). They reported that at the time their patients experienced cardiac arrest, there was no brainstem activity, no blood flow anywhere in the brain, and electroencephalograph (EEG) readings did not reveal any electrical activity. In spite of this, in the cases where patients recalled a near-death experience, they maintained that their mental functions were enhanced. There were patients who were, from an out-of-body perspective, able to report and have confirmed the activities of the attending medical physicians during the time they were considered to be clinically dead. This provided very convincing evidence the near-death experience did not occur prior to clinical death as maintained by Blackmore 1993[163], Appleby 1989[164] and Owens et al., 1990[165]. In evaluating the differences between those who recalled a near-death experience and those who didn't, it seems that reduced short-term memory function due to lengthy cardiopulmonary resuscitation (CPR) or old age was likely to have inhibited the ability to recall.[166]

---

163 Blackmore, S, *Dying to live: Science and the near-death experience,* Grafton (an imp;rint of Harper Collins(, London, 1993.
164 Appleby, L, (1989). Near-death experience: Analogous to other stress induced physiological phenomena. *British Medical Journal* 298:976-977.
165 Owens, J E, Cook, E W & Stevenson, L, (1990), Features of 'near death experience' in relation to whether or not patients were near death. *Lancet* 336:1175-1177.
[166] van Lommel, Pim. 'Near-Death Experience, Consciousness, and the Brain A New Concept about the Continuity of Our Consciousness Based on Recent Scientific Research on Near-Death Experience in Survivors of Cardiac Arrest'. *The Journal of General Evolution*; Jan2006, Vol. 62 Issue 1/2, pp134-151.

There are arguments as to what defines 'clinically dead' and the above information was refuted on the grounds it is possible to have metabolic conditions that mimic death and the brain is still alive for some minutes after the EEG flatlines. Apparently, flatlining occurs when the brain is receiving no oxygen *and* when the brain is dead, and it is impossible to distinguish between the two conditions.[167]

In spite of the above argument as to whether or not the experiencer is, or is not, clinically dead, van Lommel's report in the Lancet is not the only information available. There are reports about other near-death experiencers who have been dead for days. One such was that of the Russian dissident George Rodonaia who was run over twice by a member of the KGB (Committee for State Security), taken to the morgue in Tbilisi where his body was quick frozen. After three days, as a team of doctors proceeded with the autopsy by cutting into Rodonaia's lower torso, he regained consciousness and opened his eyes. This amazing event caused the man to become a celebrity and official records verify all aspects of the case.[168]

Rodonaia reported that during his death experience he was able to see that in an adjoining part of the hospital, his friend's wife had given birth and the baby girl was crying continuously. Rodonaia could see the baby had a broken hip. He spoke to her, telling her to stop crying as no one understood why she was crying. The baby, who was able to see him, stopped crying. After Rodonaia recovered, his first concern was to advise of the baby's broken hip. X-rays of the baby confirmed her hip was indeed broken.[169]

Time is critical when reviving a patient so the focus of the medical team is upon saving the life rather than performing scientific tests, which would take more time than is available to prove clinical death has taken place. Allowing it is possible an individual who while having a near-death experience still retains minimal remnants of life, it is difficult to imagine the brain could be responsible for the very lucid awareness experienced; nor could the confirmed out-of-body experiences that accompany the near-death experience be attributed in any way to possible brain activity.

Since it can no longer be claimed as conclusive (or even probable) that the brain is responsible for consciousness, the question must be asked, 'What is consciousness and where does it come from?' In the last few hundred years only the religious and/or those who listen to the spiritual stirrings within

---

[167] Crislip, Mark, 'Near Death Experiences and the Medical Literature.' *Skeptic;* 2008, Vol. 14 Issue 2, pp. 14-15.
[168] Williams, Kevin, *Some People Were Dead for Several Days,* 'Rev. George Rodonaia's Unusual NDE' www.near-death. com/experiences/evidence10.html. (accessed 11 Jul 2012)
[169] Atwater, P M H, *Beyond the light,* Harper Collins, London, 1995, p. 81.

(like philosophers and those seeking to understand the human psyche) have attempted to answer this question. Today science is attempting to find answers and these answers when found will confirm the continuation of life after the death of the physical body. That knowledge will effect a massive positive change in human consciousness.

Near-Death Experience Research

As a result of the consistency of near-death experience reports, and the life changing effects upon most of the individuals who experienced them, many scientifically minded people have researched this phenomenon—the following are just a few.

Ground breaking research into near-death experiences was done by Raymond Moody Jr. Moody who gained his PhD in philosophy from the University of Virginia in the 1960s and his MD from the Medical College of Georgia in 1976. Over a period in excess of ten years, Moody's research covered around one hundred and fifty cases of people of different cultures, ages, and genders who had had a near-death experience. His findings were published in 1975 in his best-selling book 'Life after Life'.[170] This book was followed by 'Reflections on Life after Life'[171] in 1977. Considered an expert on the near-death experience, Moody, over a thirty-year period, travelled the world lecturing on the many aspects of death and dying. In 1988, Moody received the World Humanitarian Award in Denmark.

In 1977 Moody's 'Life after Life' was read by Kenneth Ring, PhD, Professor of Psychology at Connecticut University, and co-founder of the International Association of Near-Death Studies. Ring determined that a more structured scientific study could further validate Moody's findings and was the first to provide scientific validation for the near-death experience. He found that the near-death experience was common to people of all races—the religious and non-religious alike, and regardless of sex, marital status, or age. He established that drugs, anaesthesia and medication were not responsible for the near-death experience, and that the clear-minded connected experiences were not hallucinations.[172]

---

[170] Moody, Raymond A, Jr M D, *Life after life*, Bantam Books, New York, 1978.
[171] Moody, Raymond A, Jr M D, *Reflections on life after life*, Bantam Books, New York, 1983.
[172] Williams, Kevin, 'Dr Kenneth Ring.' www.near-death.com/experiences/experts04.html (accessed 24 Sep 2005)

Another scientific study was done over a five-year period by Dr Michael Sabom, a cardiologist at the Atlanta VA Medical Center and assistant professor of medicine at Emory University. In 1982 he produced his findings in his book 'Recollections of Death—A Medical Investigation'. Sabom had attended a presentation by Moody and concluded his reports were either fabrications or embellishments. Along with Dr Sarah Kreutziger, he agreed to investigate the phenomenon scientifically with the expectation that he would disprove Moody's findings. This he was unable to do. Rather, he disproved his own arguments along with those put forward by sceptics.

Sabom investigated a number of patients who had suffered cardiac arrest. Although some of these patients claimed they had no prior knowledge of the procedures that followed a cardiac arrest, they recalled their experience from an out-of-body perspective and described the people in the room, their actions, and sometimes their conversations. They were also able to describe accurately the equipment in the room and what actions were taken by the doctors and in what sequence. These events were checked against actual records and in each case found to be accurate.[173]

Could the unconscious mind have produced the knowledge? Through hypnosis it was found that patients who had undergone general anaesthesia were able to recall conversations between doctors and nurses, but no visual impressions could be obtained. In the late 1970s and early 1980s, although exposure to medical procedures through television and films was not so common as it is today, it is reasonable to consider that such knowledge could have been used by the unconscious mind to produce a reasonable facsimile. Sabom sought to test this theory. Twenty-five control cardiac patients, with similar backgrounds to those who claimed to have observed their own CPR, were selected. They were asked to describe what procedures they thought would take place in the case of cardiac arrest. Eighty per cent of the reports revealed at least one major discrepancy.[174]

Sabom also came across people who, after a near-death experience, claimed they began to have out-of-body experiences.[175] This supports my brother John's experiences as reported in Chapter Ten, 'Extra Dimensional Travellers'.

Bruce Greyson, M D, Professor of Psychiatry at the University of Virginia, studied two hundred and seventy two patients of whom twenty-two per cent

---

[173] Sabom Michael B, M. D. Recollections of Death—A Medical Investigation, 1982: New York, Wallaby Books. Sabom, Ch7
[174] Sabom, op. cit. pp. 154 & 113-114.
[175] Sabom, op. cit. Ch. 8.

had had a near-death experience. He found that those who had had the near-death experience were more psychologically balanced than those who had not.[176]

Peter Fenwick, MD, FRC. Psych, is Emeritus Senior Lecturer at the Institute of Psychiatry, Kings College, London. Along with his wife Elizabeth he did a survey of five hundrfed people who had had a near-death experience. He noted that the 'tunnel' experience was usually experienced by people from Western societies, while other societies sometimes experienced a cave or dark river.[177]

An extremely intensive and meticulous study into the near-death experience was undertaken by Dr Phyllis. Atwater. After three near-death experiences in 1977, Atwater became committed to researching the experience and over a fifteen year period she investigated over seven hundred near-death experiences through interviewing the experiencer and those close to them.[178] Atwater's research went into greater depth in certain areas than previous studies, revealing both new knowledge and enhancing knowledge previously gained. The following are some points worthy of note:

Religious beliefs have an impact on the nature of the heavenly or hellish near-death experience. Hell for strong believers in Christianity is likely to include hot hells of fire and brimstone. Such was not encountered by those of other belief systems or those lacking any belief at all as they tended to encounter cold, lifeless and/or ugly landscapes or a void.[179]

The near-death experience resulted in the enhancement all aspects of an individual—their psychic and mental abilities, their talents and their suppressed issues and problems. Changes also included better health generally; a greater sensitivity to chemicals, pharmaceutical prescriptions and drugs; less tolerance for loud noises; a tendency to attract children and animals; a thirst for knowledge; advantageous alignment of events and a variety of other changes.[180] (It is interesting to note that although I have never had a near-death experience, rather I have had spiritual or mystical experiences, I too have experienced the mentioned changes. It would seem these changes take place as a result of any journey into the higher dimensions.)

---

[176] Greyson, B. (2003). Incidence and correlates of near-death experiences on a cardiac care unit. *General Hospital Psychiatry*, 25, 269-276.
[177] Fenwick, Peter. 'Retrospective Study on NDEs.' *The International Association for Near-Death Studies, Inc.* http://iands. org/research/fenwick1.php (accessed 24 Sep 2005)
[178] Atwater, P M H, *Beyond the Light*, Harper Collins, London, 1995, p. .7.
[179] Atwater, op. cit. pp. 22, 43 & 181.
[180] Atwater, op. cit. pp. 132-135 & 139-141.

Some people recalled past lives during the near-death experience (sometimes as different species on another planet).[181]

Like Sabom, most researchers of the near-death experience come across cases of out-of-body experiences that were verified. Some were incidents where patients had reported the out-of-body part of their near-death experience to medical staff who were able to verify the details, while others were verified by family and friends of the person who, during their time out-of-body, observed and later described their activities.

It is likely that never before in the history of humanity, has there been such large numbers of people who have gone through a near-death experience. As a result, there is now an extensive range of information that can provide many insights into an experience that is still a great mystery. This experience not only holds significance for those who go through it, but also for those exposed to knowledge of its process. Belief that it is scientifically impossible for the mind to survive death is increasingly difficult to justify as evidence seems to confirm that the near-death experience is a genuine experience.

The Clairvoyant View

In circumstances where people die and are not able to be revived, the clairvoyant viewing of the person's transition from the physical world to the non-physical realms reveals additional information. To clairvoyants who witness the soul's progress, it becomes apparent that some souls require time to recover from the physical and emotional trauma experienced prior to death. Following death, there is often a period of time when the soul may be unconscious, sleeping, or only vaguely aware. This can be a time of healing. While many may lose consciousness for a short while, those individuals who suffered the effects of anaesthetics, drugs, shock, or a debilitating prolonged illness that drained their energies, need more time. Such was the case when my friend Carol's mother died.

After a number of months of illness that left her, just prior to her death, experiencing difficulty recognising those around her, Carol's mother passed away. Carol requested that I check into her mother's well-being. As I tuned in, I began to see her mother clairvoyantly. I found her lying down and sleeping soundly as Carol's deceased father watched over her. As is my practice in such situations, I sent loving energy to her mother and advised

---

[181] Atwater, op. cit. pp. 115-122.

THE TRUTH SEEKER

Carol to do the same. Such energy raises the vibrations of the recipient and enables them to more effectively deal with the transitional process.

A few days later I again tuned in, and this time her mother was conscious but not fully aware as she was in the process of reconnecting to, and assimilating, all of her energies, some of which had become scattered and weakened during her illness. Once again, I saw Carol's father watching over her mother.

Whenever I thought of it during this time, I continued to send loving energy to her mother. The third time I tuned in was about a week or so later, and around three weeks after her mother had died, I saw her father with his arm around her mother. Her mother, who had lived to the great age of ninety-five, now appeared young and elegantly dressed. Both she and her husband radiated beautiful and happy energy and looked amazing. I have since communicated with both Carol's parents who had wished to relay an important message to her.

From time to time, there have been those who have died and been brought back to life who claimed there was no afterlife, because when they recovered, they retained no memory of the time they were dead. Not only could their ability to recall have been hampered by loss of short-term memory function, but also, as the above story indicates, consciousness does not necessarily immediately follow death. Certainly, lack of the ability to recall a near-death experience, is not proof life does not continue.

After Death Contact

The death process includes a review of the life that the person has lived that can be preceded or followed by a period of time spent around loved ones. Whether dealing with the near-death experience or the actual death of a person, each individual experiences a review of their life. Sensing, seeing and communicating with their departed loved ones during this time is reported frequently by family members and friends. In the following story, the gentleman took the opportunity to communicate with his daughter and with me.

A burst blood vessel in his stomach took the life of a member of my extended family who had been a heavy drinker for many years. At forty-one, he was still a young man. Very much the family man, his wife and three young daughters, the youngest only three weeks old, were at the centre of his life. On the occasions I met him on family outings, I was aware of his being a very sensitive person whose experience of life did not meet his expectations and left him feeling a lack of control.

On the Sunday evening, I received a phone call advising of his death that morning at 11:36. The next afternoon, with a view to checking on him to see how he was, I tuned into him. His energy was weak while his consciousness was only just beginning to emerge. His reaction to being conscious was confusion. He could not understand how he could be conscious and aware. In spite of his Roman Catholic upbringing, he was experiencing considerable difficulty accepting the fact that he was still a conscious being. (His wife later confirmed his lack of belief in an afterlife.) I surrounded him with love and advised him that he needed to go through a process which would result in his soul's energy becoming clear of any negative attitudes and emotions. This was not a judgement, I advised, rather an insight into his life and its purpose.

Apart from sending him love whenever I thought of it, on the Tuesday and Wednesday I again tuned in to him and saw him sitting with his elbow on his knee and his fist supporting his forehead. He was immersed in what he was experiencing and so I surrounded him with love and left him.

On the Thursday, I again tuned in. This time he was fully alert. His energy was beautifully clear and I became aware, for the first time in the ten or so years I had known him, just what a wonderful mind he possessed. Since it is impossible to pass into the higher planes as long as any negative energy remains, I knew from the vital and positive energy that radiated from him that he was ready to move forward. I said to him, 'You can go into the light now.' (I consider that light is the doorway to the spiritual kingdoms in which everything reflects a beautiful spiritual light.) In response, he informed me that he needed to be with his family.

As the events of this week were unfolding, I communicated with his mother who was traumatised over her son's death. The continuing reports of her son's progress fortified her and helped her to deal with his passing. On the Friday, we all attended his funeral. That morning his oldest daughter, who was five at the time, told her nana that Daddy had come to talk with her during the previous night when she was asleep.

The sad day of saying goodbye was over and I fell into bed exhausted. In the early hours of the morning, I awoke to see him standing above and at the end of my bed. Still in the throes of the deep sleep I had been in, my thought was he had come to me for help in order to move on. 'Oh, I am too tired to do anything,' was my reaction and so I said to him, 'Just go into the light!' He disappeared and I fell back into my deep sleep.

THE TRUTH SEEKER

The next day when some of the family gathered for lunch, his mother asked me if I had had any further communication with her son. I suddenly recalled his nocturnal visit and said, 'He woke me up last night!' I then went on to describe the experience. As I gave the incident more thought, I realised he had not appeared in order for me to help him to go through into the higher realms (he was quite capable of doing so whenever he chose to!), but to acknowledge my earlier support and to let me know he was on his way.

The state of mind that induces delta or theta brain waves, and allows those in spirit to connect with us, is experienced when one is meditating, daydreaming, or dreaming. On the occasions I tuned into and supported this gentleman, I induced a meditative state of consciousness. Since I had not believed he needed any further assistance from me, I had not taken myself into that state again, so when he did wish to contact me it was necessary for him to do so at a time when I was receptive. As is the case with most people, his daughter and I were both receptive during our sleeping hours.

An Anomaly

There seems to be an anomaly with regard to time when one clairvoyantly tunes in. With the near-death experience, the time the person is clinically dead is usually a matter of seconds or minutes, and yet their somewhat involved and lengthy experience includes the 'review' of their life and communication with those in the non-physical realms. I find that when I clairvoyantly view the experience of those who have died, from the time of death to the time of moving forward to the heavenly realms can, in physical time, take anything from days to weeks.

A possible explanation might be found in the idea that the near-death experience is incomplete and a greater time is required in order to complete the process. From reports gained through hypnosis into the existence between lives, it appears that the rapid review is followed by a second review that sees more deeply into the lifetime making it reasonable to consider a greater length of time will elapse before the soul moves on to the greater realms. This may be part of the answer, but I do not think the explanation fully covers the time variations.

The main reason for the time difference, I feel, is that when people are outside time, they can actually experience what would normally take much more time if they were in the physical world. All reports of the near-death experience mention the speed of the review, and at the same time remark on its detail and clarity. Since the events that take place during the near-death experience happen in sequence (although it seems possible that apart from the out-of-body aspect of the journey, some of the experiences can happen simultaneously), it is reasonable to assume that although there is no sense of time, when and if, those experiences are viewed in physical sequential time, the dense nature of the physical slows the accessing of events down and perhaps explains why, when viewed clairvoyantly, the duration of the afterlife journey takes some time.

Ascension

At the times I have had reason to access and observe a person's journey into the afterlife, my occasional clairvoyant view of them going through the process means my visions vary in content as I am likely to see them at different stages. The following involves a friend of mine who had for some years aligned himself with pagans. He was drawn to their relationship with nature, as he was adept at tuning into the consciousness of trees and sometimes into the thoughts of animals. His interest in all things supernatural ensured he had extensive knowledge about what to expect when he died.

I did not anticipate Peter's passing, even though I called in to visit him on the Saturday afternoon that was only days before his death. He had not been well and mentioned he had been having trouble with his back. Peter was a hoarder by nature and his place was always full of clutter. Whilst I was visiting, a thought flashed into my mind, *This place will have to be cleaned out.* This of course was a clue something was going to happen to him, but I did not pause to think what it meant. In fact, I continued my conversation with Peter and immediately forgot about the knowledge I had received. A week later, on the Saturday evening, I received a phone call from his friend Tony to say Peter had died (an autopsy later revealed it was his heart). I was shocked. Peter was only fifty-two and a friend of many years. Tony went on to say a few of Peter's friends were going around to the flat on Monday evening to clean it out—I agreed to join them.

On the Sunday morning, the shock that had left me numb receded, and I began to grieve. When I tuned in to see if I could help him, I encountered Peter's frustration, as he was not ready to leave the physical world. The book he had spent years writing was not yet finished and he had not yet accepted it was too late. I advised him to let go and sent him love at that time, and frequently over the next few days.

THE TRUTH SEEKER

Upon waking on the Wednesday morning, I saw Peter in a large vortex of energy that appeared to me to be a deep iridescent blue with energy sparkling everywhere. This awesome vortex went straight up and was around three or four metres wide. There was no background view of any physical manifestation, like sky and clouds, as I was clearly viewing an event that was taking place in another dimension. The sight was stunningly beautiful. Inside the vortex Peter appeared to be ascending, moving up, as though in an elevator, towards the greater spiritual realms. I had absolutely no doubt I need no longer concern myself over his wellbeing.

At around three that afternoon I tuned into him, curious to see where he was. As I moved my consciousness into a trance state, he immediately came into view. He had completed his journey and was exuding happiness as he beamed down at me from the heavenly regions.

The visual content of this experience left me not only awed, but also with questions. What I had seen was Peter ascending into the higher dimensions. Because of my Christian background, I could not help but compare such a happening with the teachings that Jesus ascended into heaven. Whilst it is difficult to know today the degree of accuracy of what was reported two thousand years ago, there was so much similarity between what I saw and the belief Jesus ascended into heaven, it would be remiss of me not to consider the implications. It seems probable all who migrate to the spiritual realms do so through ascension, which is travel to a different energetic and space-time dimension.

It is taught by the Christian hierarchy that the physical body of Jesus did not decompose, but was resurrected and then he rose up into the heavens. Matthew 28 (NIV) *⁵ The angel said to the women, 'Do not be afraid, for I know that you are looking for Jesus, who was crucified. ⁶ He is not here; he has risen, just as he said. Come and see the place where he lay. ⁷ Then go quickly and tell his disciples: He has risen from the dead and is going ahead of you into Galilee. There you will see him. Now I have told you.*[182]

The concern of the writers of the New Testament gospels seems to have been to establish that Jesus was the prophesied saviour, and like the earlier saviours of bygone eras, he was a begotten son of God. Were they influenced by writings of resurrection and myths born of prophecy? Did they go to great lengths to establish Jesus fulfilled all the criteria? Old Testament verses such as the following perhaps contributed to a belief in a redeemer who would rise from the dead. Job 19:25-26 (NIV) *²⁵ I know that my Redeemer lives, and that in the end he will stand upon the earth. ²⁶ And*

---

[182] *Biblestudytools.com* ibid.

after my skin has been destroyed, yet in my flesh I will see God. Psalms 16:10 (NIV) *[10] because you will not abandon me to the grave, nor will you let your Holy One see decay.*[183] If Jesus was to be seen as the redeemer and the Holy One, his physical body could not see decay therefore after death he would 'awake' or 'arise'. The importance of the resurrection of the body of Jesus in Christianity cannot be underestimated, as it is the main basis for the claim for the divinity of Jesus. Paul in 1 Corinthians 15:14 (NIV) said: *And if Christ has not been raised, our preaching is useless and so is your faith.*[184]

It would appear that, if Paul was in fact responsible for this statement (some of Paul's letters are disputed as they are written at a later date[185]), he did not appreciate the importance of the teachings of Jesus about love and its power both in this world and the next, and the real significance of Jesus was in his message and not in his identity.

The death of Jesus, his resurrection, communication with friends and loved ones and subsequent ascension into heaven does not make sense. Whenever looking for the truth it is necessary to look to the evidence—and we have a lot of evidence today regarding the non–physical realms that was not available to the writers of the gospels of the New Testament and the early Church Fathers. When the writings contradict the evidence of what is true, one questions why.

For what purpose would the physical body have been retained? The physical body is used by those walking the earth, and if, as claimed, the physical body of Jesus did rise from the dead he would once again have been a living human being. Since he was no longer 'dead' it would have been necessary for him to either die again in order to ascend into heaven, or to dispose of his physical body in some way, as the refined dimensions are not of the physical, nor can the physical enter into them. So what could have happened to his physical body?

Every cell in the human body includes the nature of every dimension. The essence of the psychic and spiritual kingdoms is already housed within the physical body of each and every human being, and it is that essence that enters the heavenly kingdoms after death. The physical body cannot enter the less substantial realms. In testament to this, those who enter the spiritual kingdoms during the near-death experience maintain they had left their

---

[183] Op. cit.
[184] Op. cit.
[185] The Bible: A history. Episode 6. http://www.channel4.com/programmes/the-bible-a-history (accessed Aug 2014)

physical body. Transformation of the physical body of Jesus into spiritual matter, if that is possible, would have resulted in a second spiritual body. He would not have needed a duplicate.

If the resurrection was a myth and Jesus did *not* retain his physical body, was it possible for him to have been seen after his death by both loved ones and the multitudes as claimed in the gospels? There are numerous reports of the loved ones of a deceased person seeing them not long after their passing, often before they have been advised the person has died, so it is reasonable to consider that any sightings of Jesus were as a result of psychic vision. Is it possible that because Jesus was a very powerful and highly developed soul, as indicated by his miraculous abilities, that his presence could have enhanced the psychic awareness of all those in his presence, enabling even those with very limited psychic ability to be able to see him?

Errors have been made by those who have claimed religious truth in the past. Divine revelation is granted to those who have followed the teachings of the prophets on love and as a result accessed the spiritual realms. Those who record the knowledge of others, and those who set out to decipher the writings of the ancients, no matter how clever and conscientious they may be, cannot assume accuracy or truth unless they themselves have entered the greater kingdoms of spirit.

The early Church Fathers, in their determination to establish a structured belief system, saw fit to ascribe truth to the resurrection of the physical body of Jesus. That knowledge is not supported by spiritual revelation.

Lost Souls

While some spend only a short time on the astral plane before moving into the heavenly kingdoms, there are those who remain on the astral for lengthy periods and sometimes until they are reborn. Some do not move forward because they do not realise they are dead, or they simply do not know there is an alternative. Most of these souls, who have become caught in the peripheral of the world of the living, can be helped, but they may need a push in order to get them to move on. When these souls communicate with psychics, they aren't necessarily wise and spiritual and their communications and advice should be evaluated.

Suicide is usually carried out by tormented souls who look to an end to their suffering. Mental, emotional or physical pain, or a combination of these forms of suffering, can be devastating. Each individual has their own belief about what happens after death, and this perception can have an impact on the decision to terminate their life. Once death has taken place, those who are severely depressed find it extremely difficult to move on to the heavenly kingdoms, especially if their soul lacks the light of self-love and the love of others. Love sent to these people is of great benefit to them. For some who have left their life before they have achieved their goals the realisation they have made a mistake is almost immediate, because not only do they become aware of the pain their premature departure has caused others, they also realise they have failed to achieve their life's purpose. The finer points of right and wrong become blurred in the light of love. There are circumstances where good and loving people choose to bring about an end to their life for a variety of reasons, foremost among them being to end their physical suffering and the alleviation of the burdens their condition places on others. These people can almost immediately find their way to the heavenly kingdoms. It seems that in intolerable situations, it is the choice of the individual as to whether they continue to suffer or take it upon themselves to end the suffering.

After Peter's funeral, his friend Tony commented that his flat needed to be cleared as he sensed a negative energy. I confirmed I would take care of it. Since I did not have the time or opportunity to go to the flat, I did a distance clearing from home. As is usual for me in such circumstances, I mentally transported myself to the flat, called for help from the spiritual realms, and with the energy provided, methodically worked my way through the flat removing negative energy. Suddenly a light appeared, and I saw someone go into it and then I saw Peter reaching out to receive that person. I did not see if it was a man or a woman who went through, but since the soul of the person was in Peter's unit and Peter was there in the light to receive them, it would seem probable it was the lady Peter had lived with some years before, who had terminated her life when she jumped from the eighth floor window. All she had needed was positive energy to help her move on, and the spiritual energy supplied by those in the spiritual realms provided her with that.

The length of time spent in the realm close to the physical will vary considerably. Lost souls—and this includes some who have very little humanity—may remain for long periods. In order to experience the sensations of life, such souls may be capable of impinging upon a vulnerable soul still in the physical. The aura of a family member or a friend that has been damaged or weakened as a result of difficulties experienced mentally, physically, or emotionally can provide an opportunity for confused souls to become attached to those they care about. Very negative souls may try to improve their lot by attaching themselves to those in a negative mental and emotional state like schizophrenics, alcoholics and drug addicts. The stronger the person's feelings, the greater the feeling of 'living' those departed souls experience. In some cases, the 'voices' the schizophrenic hears are not from their unconscious, but can be the voices of passed over murderers and the like.

Intervention, like in the following case can help the souls who are basically good to move on to the heavenly kingdoms.

In the early 1990s, I was a complete novice in dealing with those in spirit who had not passed into the light. I had been taught the process involved, but was not inclined to look for such situations. One day, a young woman came to me complaining that for the past week she had been experiencing an unpleasant energy around her. In answer to my query as to where she had been when she first noticed this energy, she advised me she had been to the grave of a friend who had passed over some years before. In order to help her, I needed to call upon my teacher's instructions.

As I tuned into the woman's energy, I discovered a young male who, according to what I recalled of the instructions I had received, should be advised to go into the light. I did this. The obstinate soul was adamant he was going to stay exactly where he was! For a moment, I was nonplussed. Then I realised all I had to do was ask for help and in the moment I did so, I intuitively knew what to do. I sent out love to completely surround him and again advised him to go into the light where he would receive help. As I watched, he moved towards the beautiful white light that appeared and he was greeted by a person in spirit. Then he was gone.

Before I had an opportunity to speak, the young woman confirmed his departure, 'Whatever you have done it has worked. The energy has gone.' She advised me the gentleman had not been the friend whose grave she had visited. Apparently, her friend had attached himself to her some months before and another psychic had helped her at that time. It was important this woman realised she needed to take responsibility for the fact her aura was torn leaving her vulnerable. I explained about using protection by visualising herself completely surrounded by a spiritual white light and changing the patterns of behaviour destructive to her aura.

It seems probable the woman who was Peter's lady and the young man in the above-mentioned instance, along with others I have aided in this manner, had not actually experienced being drawn to the being of light upon their death. If this was their first experience of the light, the unpleasant energies sensed by both Peter's friend and the young lady who came to me for help is explained, as neither of these people had experienced the purging that takes place during the review of their life.

Judgement

Judgement after death is taught by a number of religions. The near-death experience does not reveal judgement, rather kindness and understanding on the part of the spiritual entities encountered. However, it is indicated by those who have been hypnotised and have accessed the memories of the between-life time that there is a situation experienced that is perceived as a 'judgement'.

The rabbi Jesus seems to have attempted to reverse the result of the judgement teachings with his repeated entreaties that we should not judge. Matthew 7:1-2 9NIV0 *Do not judge, or you too will be judged. ² For in the same way you judge others, you will be judged, and with the measure you use, it will be measured to you.*[186]

If we programme into our unconscious 'judgement', that judgement will apply to us. There is no place for judgement in spiritual love as the attitude of the being of light, as reported by those who have experienced its presence, confirms. The difference between 'judgement' and 'consequence', which is experienced by the soul, is subtle but it is also significant.

What are the consequences encountered by the soul?

Dr Joel L Whitton is a psychiatrist who successfully treated patients through using hypnosis to access previous lives. He found that patients were able to tell of their experiences between lives and so he recorded his findings.[187] It transpired those who believe they have been 'saved' by following the strictures of the religious beliefs of times past, and who in the name of their belief judged and punished others who defied or did not live up to those beliefs, do not meet their expected rewards. Instead of a heavenly welcome, they were met with the pain of those upon whom they inflicted pain.

From Whitton's work, it would appear at least some may experience a judgement by a group of three or four advanced souls. However, these helpful souls in spirit are not there to judge or condemn. Rather, they are there to help the soul review the life from which they have just departed, and to advise how their damaging behaviour broke spiritual laws. Both the reported experiences obtained through hypnosis, and those from near-death experience, indicate there is **NO** judgement unless the person themselves is

---

[186] *Biblestudytools.com* ibid.
[187] Whitton, Joel L Dr, Joe Fisher, *Life betweenLife*, Grafton Books. Glasgow, 1987.

the judge. 'Evil' and 'good' do not have a punishment or reward metered out, rather there is a consequence, that is the outcome of actions and beliefs, that has an impact on what is not only experienced during the time between lives, but also in the next and subsequent lives of the individual. In their next incarnation, if their actions have been of a very violent nature, the beings may advise that in their following life the person will find themselves born into a situation that offers fewer advantages than their previous one. Opportunity to put things right in the next or a future life is also a possibility that may be considered at that time.

All heaven and hell-like experiences are the result of the state of the soul, which is what determines the plane of existence encountered after the review. Those people who have committed grievous crimes and have badly stained souls, cannot progress to a better afterlife environment unless they receive love and/or prayers from those left behind in the physical. Even then, their progress is likely to be limited. Their opportunity for redemption is usually found in a future life in the physical. Since love is the key to the heavenly kingdoms, those incapable of these feelings find their consciousness cannot reach those higher spiritual levels.

Between lives, those who cannot enter the spiritual kingdoms may experience an unhappy time. During the time spent before their next incarnation, some may find themselves on the lowest plane of existence living a hellish experience as a consequence of their own negative state. If they are of an emotional nature, they can find themselves on a level where negative energies are everywhere. In the energetic kingdoms where energy is attracted to like energy, some souls can find their own nasty energy surrounding them and the same energy reflected back at them from like souls. There is no protection, as in the physical world, against the on-going experience of the horrible nightmarish energies that surround them and others. Those who have become totally self-absorbed and who wallow in meanness, cruelty and self-pity, share with like souls the repulsive substance of their being. Fear filled people may attract monsters and demons, and the most unpleasant of entities that could be real or imagined, while those whose emotions have been annihilated, may find themselves in barren, lifeless and ugly surroundings. Only a small percentage of the population visits these dimensions—the doorway into them is lack of love and caring, fear, self-loathing and hate. Only the purging of all such energies can provide a release during the time in the afterlife.

Unfortunately, there are also good souls who experience a hell type experience—those who have deep-seated fears (trust is a fundamental aspect of the law of love), and those who carry guilt (which is self-imposed judgement) because they have not lived up to the standards they demanded of themselves. Although some Christian churches, including the Roman Catholic Church,[188] believe in a purgatory that punishes people for their sins: this is not how it works. Sins are often not sins at all, but the soul crying out for recognition while the peer programming of 'right' and 'wrong' stands in the way of fulfilment and happiness. Errors of judgement are not punishable crimes; they are simply the way by which we as individuals learn what works and what does not work—what is in harmony with the spiritual law and what is not. It is the emotional and mental damage caused by lack of understanding of how the law of love works that can result in a 'hell' experience for otherwise good people. Love sent to these people can help them to let go or purge the negative, including judgement, from their souls. They can then move on to the spiritual dimensions where their soul belongs.

Since any strong negative thought or emotion can result in a hellish experience, it seems incongruous that beliefs that teach fear and guilt are responsible for the energy within the soul that attracts a hell type experience. Also, encountering hellfire, devils and the like is only experienced by those who believe in the teachings of their existence. It is clear that the beliefs of the individual play a large part in the afterlife experience, as the unconscious can create the most feared nightmare or the most beautiful dream. In light of this knowledge, it would appear to be a wise move for Christians and Muslims (the world's two largest religions), whose teachings can include such as everlasting hellfire and brimstone along with horror devilish creatures, to consider revoking such beliefs as they cause often undeserved and unnecessary suffering.

The majority of souls bypass the lower planes where the hell experience is encountered. The letting go of negative energies takes place in an environment that allows for the understanding of the greater purpose of the life experiences, even though some of those experiences may have resulted in harbouring negative emotions. A state of non-judgemental acceptance of such erroneous behaviour is essential in order for the soul to continue its journey into the kingdoms of light.

---

[188] 'Catholic Doctrine—Purgatory.' *New Advent,* www.newadvent.org/cathen/12575a.htm#I (accessed 24 Jul 2012)

God does not judge. People judge. The afterlife represents the meeting of the self. Whether that meeting reveals glorious kingdoms or hells and horrific encounters is entirely dependent on the state of the soul. We are the creators of our own destiny. *They teach that he who hates shall be hated, and that the one who gets angry shall be punished by anger, and that all sin is punished by it and not for it. This is correct.*[189]

The Afterlife Kingdoms and their Occupants

Since we are all individuals, our perception and experience of life will have an impact on how and what we will experience at the time of death and after. Although there are common denominators in the way in which people pass into the afterlife, the experience is as individual as the people themselves and reflects their emotional and mental state, their character, personality and especially their beliefs.

Creation in the dense physical world takes time to manifest, but as pointed out in earlier chapters, each of us individually and collectively are creating what we experience in the world we live in and we are probably also contributing to the physical state of the world in ways that, as yet, we have absolutely no idea of. When we leave the physical, the world of the soul is encountered. The common thought forms of generations exist in this world, and the programmes of current and past lives manifest in our perception. When we see heaven or hell, it is the heaven or hell of common and/or personal belief—a creation of thought.

In the afterlife experience, although most will find themselves in the established manifestation of their expectations, it is possible for each of us to manifest immediately, whatever we consciously, or unconsciously, choose, and that can often be a facsimile of the familiar living environment of the physical. It is also possible to be anywhere in an instant, at any time, for there is no space and there is no time. We create or co-create the imagery encountered. This is the reason that heaven for different cultures reflects the beliefs of those cultures. As the soul develops, it moves forward into dimensions where the creations of the familiar are no longer needed.

---

[189] *Health* (A Monthly Devoted to the Cause and Cure of Disease), December 1905

Each person, as they encounter the being of light, sees what they expect to see—Buddha, Jesus, Mohammad, an angel or in the case of those without religious belief, the type of being or person they subconsciously feel safe with. Sometimes the being is sensed rather than seen. Often people report that while initially they saw 'Jesus' (or another deity), that identity dissolved as they grew more comfortable and they realised they were in the presence of a great loving being of pure light who radiated the most powerful and perfect love. Is the being encountered the actual soul of the person they recognised? There are those who claim, 'No,' while others claim, 'Yes'.

John Hick (1922-2012), was a British, Anglo-analytic philosopher of religion who has had considerable influence through his innovative work that included religious pluralism. As a young law student, Hick had a spiritual experience and as a result changed his direction in life to encompass theology and philosophy.[190] Hick's 'pluralistic hypothesis' suggests the diversity of the world's religions has resulted in 'masks' or 'faces'. When transcendental experiences take place, images of beings and places reflect the beliefs of the people involved. *Underlying* these experiences is the 'real'.[191] That does not mean that when the soul encounters previously passed over family and friends that these connections are not real, for of course they are. It is the locations and the spiritual beings that reflect the expected.

It is the capacity within to love and care deeply that determines the next stage of the soul's experience. Most souls with love in their hearts and clear energy, take a journey into the light and what we perceive as the heavenly regions.

Ancient Beliefs in the Afterlife

It is apparent from ancient scriptures on the afterlife, that for many millennia humanity believed the consciousness, or soul, of the individual survives death. How much of each religion's belief reflected myth and how much was born of, or was based on, truth, it is now able to be considered with some degree of confidence.

---

[190] 'John Hick'. Internet Encyclopaedia of Philosophy. www.iep.utm.edu/hick/ (accessed 24 Aug 2013)
[191] Hick, John, *An interpretation of religion: Human responses to the transcendent,* Macmillan, London, 1989.

THE TRUTH SEEKER

The Australian Aboriginals varied somewhat in their afterlife beliefs with some believing the Land of the Dead was an island, while others believed it was a place in the sky where their people resided until their spirit was reborn.[192]

The ancient Egyptians believed in the survival of the soul or life force (*ka*), which after death, passes through the dangerous underworld with gods, gatekeepers and other strange creatures. The 'Egyptian Book of the Dead' (a handbook on the afterlife) which dates back to around 1500 BCE, provided spells to aid the soul on its journey and convince Osiris (god and chief judge of the underworld) to allow their entry into paradise. In the final judgement before forty-two divine judges, the person is given the opportunity to plead their innocence and then the ceremony of the 'Weighing of the Heart' takes place. The feather of the truth goddess Ma'at, is weighed against the person's heart, and if it is heavier the person's soul is thrown to Ammut (the female demon soul eater) where darkness awaits. Balanced scales ensure Osiris welcomes them to the afterlife, which is a replication of the place where they had lived before they died.[193]

For thousands of years, from the fourth millennium BCE the people of Mesopotamia (Iraq, part of Syria and part of Turkey) believed one half of the universe was the residence of the living while the other was that of the dead. The spirits of the dead found their way to the underworld (a barren unpleasant place) where they were dependent on the living to provide them with food and other comforts. The kings took with them many gifts to bribe the underworld deities in order to gain favours from them. The description of a barren unpleasant place resembles many of the near-death 'hell' type experiences, which may have provided the imagery for the expected afterlife environment.[194]

From this pagan background, the Persian/Indian Zoroastrian (Greek pronunciation) religion was founded by the prophet Zarathustra who, according to modern historians, was born between 1500-1000? BCE.[195] He had a vision when he was about thirty years of age whilst he was performing a pagan purification rite in the river. In this and following visions, he saw *Ahura Mazda* (God) and radiant beings and asked many questions. He was

---

[192] 'Life after death', *The World Book Encyclopaedia* ibid. – A-L Australasia, p.14.

[193] 'The Underworld and the Afterlife in Ancient Egypt.' *Australian museum.* http://australianmuseum.net.au/The-underworld-and-the-afterlife-in-ancient-Egypt (accessed 28 June 2014)

[194] Ringgren, Helmer (tr. Sturdy, John), *Religions of The Ancient Near East*, The Westminster Press, Philadelphia, 1974.

[195] *The History of Zoroastrianism*—Zoroastrianism: A short overview, www.duke.edu/—jds17/zoroast.html (accessed 4 Aug 2012)

possibly the first to teach of one God. He also taught of good and evil, judgement, heaven, hell and everlasting life, future resurrection of the body, and a final judgement.[196]

Is it possible Zarathustra experienced a true revelation? Since at least some of Zarathustra's knowledge is confirmed by current knowledge and understanding, perhaps the question of judgement could possibly be attributed to the original use of a word meaning 'assessment' or similar, or perhaps the information related to consequence of actions was simply interpreted as judgement. I also wonder at the idea of resurrection. Is it possible 'rising from the dead' was later misinterpreted by the followers of Zarathustra? Could the resurrection have related to the non-physical rising of the soul into the heavenly kingdoms as in the 'ascension', or alternatively, could it relate to reincarnation, in that after death we rise again in another body? Of the possibility of a final judgement I suspect that, as with the early Egyptians, for some, the process involved the negotiating of a difficult underworld journey that confronts with frightening images born of fear (for some, like the hell experience), in order that fear may be expunged along with all unhealthy emotions. Finally, this journey culminates in the weighing of the soul or the final judgement.

Afterlife belief in Judaism originally involved *Sheol*—a pit where people went when they died. The religious focus of the Jews was on the way in which each person lived, that he lived righteously and pleased his God so God protected and rewarded him. Communion with God was sought by those whose devotion was great—hence the great respect for the prophets who guided their people as to God's will. This was a religion about life rather than what happened at death. As a result, less consideration was given to life after death. At some time, the concept of the reincarnation of the prophets emerged. In 586 BCE, the Babylonians conquered Jerusalem and the captured Jews were taken to Babylon. In 538 BCE Babylon was conquered by the Persians who brought with them the Zoroastrian religion. This Persian influence introduced into Judaism the concepts of judgement, heaven, hell, everlasting life, future resurrection of the body, and a final judgement.

The near-death experience reveals that souls, whatever their religious or lack of religious belief, can enter the spiritual realms as the key to entry is love and purity of heart, not religious belief or being the recipient of religious rites. Although based on Judaism, Christianity introduced afterlife concepts that deny that the soul with a pure heart can enter God's kingdom

---

[196] God, Zoroaster and immortals' *BBC - Religions – Zoroastrian. Dualism* www.bbc.co.uk/religion/religions/zoroastrian/beliefs/god.shtml (accessed 27 Jul 2012)

THE TRUTH SEEKER

unless first cleansed through baptism. The idea of Adam's original sin being inherited by all humans from birth seems to have been based on Romans 5:12 (NIV) *12 Therefore, just as sin entered the world through one man, and death through sin, and in this way death came to all men, because all sinned.*[197] Christianity's afterlife beliefs include a place called Limbo where pure souls, like babies who die before receiving the sacrament of baptism go as they cannot enter into the presence of God. Limbo can perhaps in some ways, be likened to time spent by many on the astral plane, where residents have either not yet realised they need to progress to the light, or they do not have the ability to do so. There is no evidence to support the idea of original sin as a barrier to the spiritual kingdoms.

Muhammad, the founder of Islam, was born in Mecca around 570 CE. Like the Jews and the early Christians, his people's lineage was Abrahamic. In his early years Mohamad was exposed to, and admired Biblical scriptures. With their common background it is not surprising that Muslim beliefs in the afterlife are similar to those of the Jews and Christians, whose beliefs incorporated the teachings of the Zoroastrian religion.[198] Muslims believe in judgement and resurrection, paradise and hell—admittance to paradise dependent upon their deeds and belief or lack of it in Allah, Mohammad and the Koran.[199]

Siddhārtha Gautama Buddha (563-483 BCE), was the founder of Buddhism. He sought the answers to freedom from pain and experienced enlightenment, at which time, he recalled previous lifetimes. Buddha taught that in order to gain freedom from the painful continuous 'wheel of life', it was necessary to become free of karma (negative feelings, attitudes and delusions). Focus, rather than being on the afterlife (bardo), was to achieve nirvana and the happiness that accompanies such a state. While Buddhism recognises and venerates deities, it is essentially a non-theistic religion. The 'Tibetan Book of the Dead', believed to have been written in the eighth century CE by Padma Sambhava, is a complex and detailed guide to the afterlife and how to, during the afterlife journey, attain buddhahood and therefore liberation from the continuous cycle of lives in the physical.

Since the evidence we now have reveals the actual process, it is possible to see that some of the afterlife beliefs were likely based upon knowledge

---

[197] Biblestudytools.com ibid.
[198] Bard, Mitchell. 'Muhammad.' *Jewish Virtual Library.*
www.jewishvirtuallibrary.org/jsource/biography/Muhammad.html (accessed 23 Jul 2012)
[199] Abdurrahman Mahdi (co-author). *The Journey into the Hereafter; Islam Religion*
www.islamreligion.com/articles/413/ (accessed 23 Jul 2012)

received through a near-death experience, a spiritual experience, or a vision. That the Egyptian and other deities foreign to the Christian-based West represent energetic entities that we may have given another name to is conceivable. As we look to the religions of the Bible and afterlife beings, we encounter angels. Since the planets were originally seen as angels that apparently flew across the skies, the perception of winged creatures emerged. Although this is not a true interpretation of the appearance of the spirit beings we now call angels, this how our unconscious mind sees and recognises them. It also seems possible some religious interpretation and/or embellishment over time, has distorted to a degree, today's knowledge and understanding of the afterlife.

The Near-Death Experience and Religious Belief

What the near-death experience reveals about the afterlife provides us with the opportunity to more accurately understand religious teaching and to discriminate between the truth and what is born of fallible human perception, by both the writers and interpreters of ancient scriptures. As we look at the afterlife teachings of old and apply them to the knowledge of today, we can see that the revelations of the prophets and spiritual teachers of the past usually held the essence of truth. Since spiritual truth cannot change, such a study into the past reveals that at least some of the knowledge available to us today was also available to those who lived in ancient times.

Unfortunately, in the past and even today, judgement and fear play a dominant role in teachings about the afterlife. The right to enter the spiritual kingdoms is universal and not religious. This is revealed in the convincing evidence of the near-death experience that shows race and creed are not measures by which the spiritual kingdoms are accessed. The history of the various religious beliefs and the way in which they have, over time, misled people in a number of ways shows that as long as scriptures and their translations are the main source of spiritual knowledge, destructive, inaccurate and fearful teachings will continue to dominate.

Religion and science are compatible and must be so in order for truth to be established. Where there is conflict, there is inaccuracy in one or both. There are universal laws that govern all, and due to the abundance of verifiable information available today, we live in a time when it is possible, at least to some degree, to correct the errors of religious and scientific knowledge of earlier times. The truth has spiritual power that can only lead to greater understanding for all humanity.

Chapter 12

Human Interaction with Non-Physical Beings

No evil can happen to a good man, either in life or after death.

Socrates[200]

Inter-dimensional Interaction

Two hundred years ago, if someone had said that in a few generations their descendants would be able to see a person on the other side of the world on a screen in their own home and not only see them, but talk to them live as though they had actually joined them, what would have been the response? Doubtless, total disbelief and derision towards the speaker! And yet today we do just that. With the aid of Skype and similar, we can talk to anyone in the world who has access to a computer or smartphone and the worldwide web.

Scientific studies have revealed information that invites consideration of even greater possibilities. As we look to the research that confirms reincarnation, out-of-body and near-death-experiences, we are forced to consider the existence of life beyond the physical and the existence of multiple dimensions. Reports of those who have used hypnosis and psychic ability to penetrate the truths of those dimensions opens humanity up to possibilities once thought to be the realm of science fiction.

If the continued existence of each person after death of the physical is a reality, what sort of interaction with those in other dimensions can be achieved, assuming we, and they, want that interaction? Research into this subject reveals that while the majority of those living in the physical have never had contact with those in spirit, there are many who have. Of those psychics who interact with spirit, some experience occasional spontaneous

---

[200] Socrates in Plato's *Apology* 41c-d, (tr. Bernard Jowett) http://classics.mit.edu/Plato/apology.html (accessed 28 November 2014)

contact—usually with a passed over family member, while regular contact can be experienced by those who are very open psychically, like sensitive children, clairvoyants, and those labelled schizophrenic.

Of those who are aware contacting the departed is possible, some say we should not disturb them. They believe the departed must focus entirely on their spiritual journey in the heavenly kingdoms, and we would only hold them back if we expected or required them to communicate and interact with those of us still living in the denser physical planes. My personal opinion is that while it's true souls should not be held back from passing into the light, once they have done so, contact is likely to be healing and helpful.

Love is the fabric of the universe. It reaches all dimensions including the physical. It seems unlikely that communicating with those in the afterlife would limit or distract them as such an idea does not take into account the true state of those who reside in the heavenly dimensions. Love is never limited or limiting, and any loving thought or action aligns the soul with that of the Creator. There is no time in the afterlife dimensions. After the death of the physical, humans reside in an existence that lacks the boundaries of time and space where it is possible for all experience to happen simultaneously and clearly. Once free of the physical, we are beings of light, and helping those in the physical world is often used as a way to progress spiritually.

Interaction between those of the different realms, especially communication between souls in the physical and those of human nature in spirit can result in much that is helpful. Those human souls now in the afterlife who care about us often provide timely warnings and intervene in happenings in the physical realm. Angelic beings can also play a part in our welfare and can be called on for help in times of need. While it may be easier for the psychic person to be aware of such contact, anyone who believes it is possible, and whose motives are pure, can ask for, and receive, help. Purity of intent excludes any prayer of a negative nature or that ignores another's freedom of choice.

Will regular and easy contact with those in spirit ever be possible in the future? Will man-made communicators provide the means by which contact can take place? The scientific community needs to recognise the possibility of doing so in order for such ventures to be embraced. In the meantime, those who desire contact have a number of ways to achieve this, each of which includes developing the state of mind that occurs in meditation.

THE TRUTH SEEKER

Humankind in the Heavens

For those earthly souls who reside at present in the ethereal realms, there are many possible ways to experience this existence.

After death, those souls lacking in spiritual awareness are for the most part likely to sleep. For the more developed souls, there is a variety of options. Access to the many forms of artistic expression can hold appeal, and the pursuit of knowledge on a wide range of subjects, including the discovery of mystical truths, attracts many. The possibilities are limited only by individual awareness and interest. Connection with previously passed-over souls, and communication with angels and others of those realms, can also be achieved.

Many in spirit choose to spend time around their family and friends in the physical world and aid them during their more difficult life challenges. Those souls who come around us in order to assist in what we are attempting to achieve are usually called 'guides' and in most cases have an established connection to us either in the current, or a previous, lifetime. Spirit guides are not of the angelic hierarchy as angels are on a different evolutionary path to humans. While it is likely all of us have a spirit guide, I am not able to confirm this. What I do know is that it is possible to have more than one, and they can intervene in our lives in order to change circumstances and events in the physical world when they deem it necessary. Masters also play a role in the lives of those who are living in the physical world. Not only do they work with those in the spiritual kingdoms, they will also choose to work with those spiritually advanced souls who have taken on ventures that will bring enlightenment and spiritual growth to the masses.

It seems it is usual for one guide to stay with each of us throughout our lives while others come and go. We can draw guides to us who have knowledge and expertise in our chosen career, hobby or passion. They can aid us while we perform a certain task or are working on developing a particular skill or aspect of our character. Like attracts like, so guides are spiritually aligned with us. During the years I worked as a reader, there were usually around five guides available to help me. Each was proficient in a different area such as spirituality, mental, emotional and physical health, and assisting in communication with the deceased relatives and friends of those seeking guidance.

The physical world holds an interest for those who wish to become involved in a specific area of expertise. Just as on the earth plane we can aid others on their journey through time, so too can those who now reside in the non-physical dimensions be helped by us. They can attend classes and lectures or learn from our actions. Those interested in the arts can learn from the Masters while they work. Life's lessons and experiences are not a one-way street. We all learn from each other whether that learning takes place in the physical or the ethereal realms.

Most departed souls, during their sojourn into the greater kingdoms, spend time planning and preparing for their next venture on the earth plane. As a result of his explorations into the afterlife through the use of hypnosis on his patients, Psychiatrist Dr Joel Whitton discussed the process whereby each person is encouraged by spiritually advanced souls to take on the difficulties presented by another life in the physical. The challenges the individual is likely to encounter will bring about growth within the soul and also provide an opportunity to remove debts to others that may have been incurred during an earlier lifetime. Whitten noted that some souls reported observing their future mother and moving reluctantly into the body of the new baby at birth.[201]

Whitton's information confirmed the much more detailed research completed by psychologist Helen Wambach who also made use of hypnosis in order to access details of the soul's experience before entry to the physical world. Of her 750 subjects from a variety of backgrounds, many were against abortion as they believed it to be murder (some of the participants were practicing Catholics). All agreed the foetus was separate from the soul. When describing their actual birth experience, many complained of the harsh lighting in the room in which they were born.[202]

Those who remain conscious and aware in the non-physical realms continue to grow spiritually through learning in those realms or through interaction with those still in the physical.

Validity of Spirit Contact

While those in spirit can initiate contact, it's also possible for those in the physical to call on and communicate with those in spirit.

Positive interaction between persons in a corporeal body and those in the dimensions beyond the physical depends on the parameters in place when contact is made. Those who choose to make contact with people in spirit

---

[201] Whitton, Joel L & Fisher, Joe, *Life between life,* Grafton Books, Glasgow, 1987.
[202] Wambach, Helen, *Life before life,* Bantam Books, United States & Canada:, 1979, pp. 98-99.

would be wise to first avail themselves of the knowledge of the best way to do so in order to avoid unpleasant consequences. In a cosmos based on evolution, there are many degrees of awareness, and not all who reside in the realms beyond the physical are to be trusted. Especially vulnerable to deception and unpleasant experiences are the novices who access the non-physical dimensions without appropriate guidance and protection.

I have spent time around people who have received messages from those they claimed were their guides. It was clear from the content of some of those communications that the information was not from an illuminated source. Rather, the knowledge imparted reflected the thoughts and beliefs held by the person receiving the information. The danger of self-deception is very real and therefore, when communications and visions are received, questioning and testing is important, as is requesting spiritual guidance and protection. Inner motives play an important role when dealing with the realms beyond the physical. Hidden agendas can be reflected in the results.

Although I have not had personal experience of destructive non-physical beings, I have read of them and spoken with those who claim to have been caught in extremely undesirable and sometimes frightening encounters. Since negative spirits are attracted to negative energy, spiritual cleansing along with spiritual protection is a wise precaution before entering into a situation conducive to contact. This is especially important when dealing with ouija boards, which are not evil in themselves as they are only a tool and can be used efficiently and safely, or irresponsibly with possible unpleasant consequences.

While in some cases communications via an ouija board can represent the unconscious thoughts of the individuals involved, it is also possible for non-physical beings to use this method to make contact. Reports by those frightened by their experiences lead me to consider the possibility that entities can read the human mind and confront the person with images of their greatest fears. When a random entity is invited to communicate, there are no guarantees as to its nature. As a result, those indulging in this pastime with a group of friends may encounter a negative spirit that can set out to scare, or even to connect to the aura of an individual. This is not an activity for the naive.

The nature of negative spirits is an area of knowledge that invites a lot of conjecture and since I can't call on personal experience in this area, I have to depend on the reported experiences of others. In Chapter Eleven, 'Encountering the Afterlife' I discussed the 'pluralistic hypothesis' put forward by British philosopher John Hick[203]. He maintained the beliefs of the viewer resulted in 'masks' or 'faces' being overlaid on spiritual beings and the imagery encountered in other dimensions. In consideration of this, it seems probable we also interpret the appearance of conscious evil entities. Those in the living, and those who have died, report the sighting of evil creatures, including the Devil. Since only those who believe in the Devil, see the Devil (that was originally the creation of superstitious, fear-filled, religious believers), it can be assumed such a creature does not exist. Rather, it is either an image overlaid on a negative non-physical creature or being, or it's a creature manufactured by the unconscious mind of the person who encounters it. Such a creation would need to use the negative energy the individual carries within themselves in order to have substance. Perhaps both of these possibilities can occur.

If evil entities are involved in any form of malevolent, non-physical encounter, consideration should be given to contaminated elementals (conscious creatures that lack a physical body and play a role in a variety of energetic processes related to the physical world). Another possibility could be debased, departed human souls whose consciousness has not passed into the higher kingdoms after death and who take delight in locating and then intimidating and scaring victims. Since they no longer have a physical body, they can adapt their appearance to be terrifying. An individual's personal beliefs could also result in the overlay of an image.

When I attended my brother's wedding at Lake Taupo in New Zealand, my family all stayed together in a holiday rental property. Each time I walked into the house, I became angry and agitated. As soon as I left, I returned to being my usual happy self. I discussed this with different family members who also admitted to experiencing the bad energy. Although I realised that at some time in the past a very angry and frustrated person had lived in that house, at the time this experience occurred I hadn't become skilled in dealing with such situations, and so I did not perform a spiritual cleansing of the house which is what I would do today. Whether the soul responsible for the energy was still there or not, his negative energy certainly was.

> **Belief and deception walk the same pathway.**

If care is taken when entering into communication with non-physical beings, the possibility of amazing and rewarding experiences is real and is certainly worth the effort put into the preparation for such a venture. In order to avoid

---

[203] 'John Hick'. *Internet Encyclopaedia of Philosophy*. www.iep.utm.edu/hick/ (accessed 24 Aug 2013)

deception, a fundamental aspect of preparation is the removal of *all* fear-filled beliefs.

Intervention

Is there evidence to support the possibility that those in spirit intervene in our lives without our express request? Is it unrealistic to consider the possibility there are perhaps many times when they assist us?

That those who take on the role of guides can intervene in our life in order to protect I discovered one night when attending a psychic development class. The exercise that night was to contact the spirit guide of another person in the class. The young man who was tuning in to me stated, 'Joan, your car was off the road recently.' I hadn't mentioned that fact to anyone in the class, but I confirmed it had. 'Your guides are saying they took it off the road otherwise you would have been in an accident!'

I had not been impressed when I'd suffered the inconvenience of travelling to work on public transport for three days while mechanics attended to the needs of my car. The realisation I had been saved from what might have been a serious accident (I doubt there would have been intervention for a minor accident) caused me to abandon my previous disgruntled attitude and be grateful.

Just because on most occasions there is no way to confirm those in spirit have contributed to a positive outcome where help is given, does not mean it does not frequently happen.

Those in spirit probably employed Paul and me as rescuers when we decided to take a walk one afternoon. Paul and I frequently went on walks during the years we were a couple. Sometimes we would drive somewhere and then walk. At other times, like the time this incident happened, we would walk out my door and head for the local back streets. On this particular day, we deviated from our usual path after around fifteen minutes and turned left instead of right.

Five minutes later, we once again turned left as we encountered a previously avoided rather busy road. We continued for some minutes when at an intersection our attention was drawn further down the side street to a tiny screaming child of around three years of age. As she emerged from a property, she headed across the road as fast as her little legs could carry her.

JOAN L BOLER

As I moved down the street towards her, the screaming, panicked child ran full pelt in our direction.

As I reached out for the child and picked her up, I said, 'It's alright Kristy, I'll take you home to Mummy.' I cuddled her to me and continued to reassure her.

A shocked, 'You know her?' came from Paul.

Indeed, her mother was a friend of mine. We took a short walk to the next side street where we saw her mother frantically walking up and down and calling out for her daughter. The child had somehow found her way out through the back fence of their property and into the property backing theirs. She had then become lost and frightened.

While there was a constant flow of traffic on the road, we were the only pedestrians. One minute earlier or later and we would have missed the child who in her panic would likely have continued across the busy road. This was the only time we'd taken this route on our walks. We were in the right place at the right time. *Who was looking out for the child?'*

Sometimes intervention from spirit is revealed by telepathic knowledge. I was on my way home from my place of work near North Sydney and was driving north along the Pacific Highway towards a blind corner when the thought dropped into my mind there could be someone on a bicycle around the bend. I slowed down as I rounded the corner and in front of me was an elderly gentleman *walking* his bike across the first of six lanes of traffic—in peak hour! I slammed on the brakes and came to an abrupt halt a short distance from the man.

Now I was the one in danger, as my car couldn't be seen by any cars approaching the bend I had just negotiated. To my relief a truck, with its greater height and visibility, came to a halt behind me removing the threat from the rear. Meanwhile, the old gentleman with the bike was still standing in my lane and graciously waving for me to swing past him into the middle lane. Cars were hurtling around the corner at probably more than the seventy kilometre (43.5 miles) an hour speed limit, so I wasn't about to take my life in my hands and follow his direction.

As I looked for a safe solution, I noted the traffic lights and pedestrian crossing around twenty-two yards (twenty metres) ahead. However, I had no opportunity to direct the gentleman towards that possibility as the truck driver, who had more guts than sense, got out of his vehicle and walked man and bike across the road, ending a situation that could easily have resulted in a nasty accident. In this case, not only did I receive a warning which specifically included knowledge of a bicycle, but also I was saved from an almost certain rear-ender due to the timely arrival of the truck.

On many occasions I have thought, *Someone up there is looking after me.* Just as people in the physical world care about us and help us when we are in need, so too can those who no longer live in the physical.

Communication with Passed-Over Human Beings

For the most part, contact with those in spirit is a positive experience. Communications from loved ones can create healing and provide information that can aid and ease the concern of those in the physical realm.

Like most people, I was not born with the ability to communicate with the departed. I developed the skill over a period of time, first through attending classes and then through practicing the skill during readings. For me, much of the communication came in the form of 'ideas' or 'knowing' that dropped into my mind. These were usually accompanied by visuals that could be symbolic or reveal actual people and places and expose events and situations from their past or about their future. My teacher always insisted on gaining verification when communicating with the loved ones of a person before moving forward with the reading. For this reason, I made a practice of describing the person I was seeing clairvoyantly in detail, since I rarely received names and vague descriptions are open to question. Such a description could be, 'I see a dark haired man of around forty years of age. He is of solid build, has blue eyes, rimless glasses, fair skin and a strong nose and jaw.' I include any characteristic that individualises the person and continue to describe the clothes they wear, which can indicate the time period during which they lived, and sometimes I provide details of where they had lived and how they had died. As I speak, I continue to see further aspects of the person's life and personality that I also communicate. Only when I receive recognition do I continue.

Communicating with the departed reflects individual skills and capabilities and there is no end to the process of learning. Up until the following incident, which occurred not long after I began reading outside the class environment, I hadn't realised I was not able to tell if the images I received related to a person who was living or dead.

The man sitting in front of me listened as I described the image of the woman I was being shown. I described her physically, her personality, and details of the kitchen she enjoyed working in. He said he knew who she was. I then described a man. Again, the gentleman confirmed recognition. When I attempted to relay the message I thought was from the woman, who I had assumed was dead, I was unable to make sense of it.

'I don't understand,' said the man. 'Why do you say my wife is giving you a message for her brother? My wife is still alive. It is her brother who is dead!' In the class environment, on every occasion I had received clairvoyant communication from beyond the grave, I had first seen the person bringing the message. Obviously, this was not always going to be the case. Once I realised my mistake, the message for the man's wife from her deceased brother made sense and I was able to impart it with clarity.

Armed with my new understanding, I was cautious when reading for a woman a short time later. As I tuned in, I received an image of a middle aged man. I described the man and where he lived. She recognised him as her ex-husband. I asked her if he was still living. She answered in the affirmative. I then described a younger man that she recognised as their son. Again, I checked and found he was still alive. The next knowledge I received from the spirit world was that there was conflict between father and son. The woman confirmed this was so and advised that her son did not see or communicate with his father. I had become aware that within a few months the young man's father was going to die, so I impressed on the woman that she needed to advise her son it was very important for him to make peace with his father in the near future.

I had yet to discover who the message was coming from. When I asked, the image of an older woman came into focus. The woman immediately recognised her as an older relative who had died recently.

Communication with those in the dimensions that are not of the physical are not the same as communicating through language in the physical, and therefore the exact translation of information imparted is often difficult—sometimes impossible. But the effort involved is usually worth it. Since it is the person in spirit who is in control of the reading, it is usually their agenda that takes precedence. Because of this, unexpected and valuable information can be relayed through readings.

When I'm reading, I call for assistance from my own guides and those of the person I am reading for. There have been many occasions when I would not have been able to help people without the assistance of those in the spirit world.

THE TRUTH SEEKER

I wasn't surprised when a young woman in her thirties asked whether or not she would have children as it's a common question younger ladies ask. Those in spirit usually show me a vision of the children likely to be born to the person in the future. I was therefore very surprised when I clairvoyantly saw the woman actually giving birth in hospital. I remarked to the woman how strange that was, but as she made no comment I continued with the reading. At its conclusion, the lady advised me she was currently undergoing tests in order to discover if she could have children. I realised that had I been shown a scene that included a child or children, she would not have known whether they were the result of a natural birth or adoption.

Time and again I have been given confirmation as to the validity of the information gained from those in spirit. In many cases, the knowledge obtained aids in removing or reducing stress and worry in the person's life. At other times, it can lift emotional pain or change the outlook of a person. In today's complex world, such invaluable help cannot come from sources in the physical that are not privy to such knowledge.

Angelic Assistance

Angels are thought to be the messengers of God, or the gods, who can be called on when their assistance is needed. Individual situations require individual solutions, and angels seem to fulfil celestial roles and are less likely to be found giving advice. Their help seems to be more suited to situations that involve the use of spiritual energy.

A young woman who had come to me for guidance on a number of occasions wished to know whether she would be successful in her bid to purchase a unit. A quick layout of the cards revealed likely success. Three months later, she came to see me again. She had moved into the unit, but was concerned about the 'energies' she could feel. I tuned into her unit and came across the soul of a fairly tall man probably in his late fifties to early sixties who had once lived there. I sent him love and spoke to him saying, 'Look at the light. Go into the light.' Instantly he was gone. A vision of an idyllic scene of a beautiful land followed and confirmed he had gone to a place of great beauty in the heavenly kingdoms. I advised the woman that a man had passed over into the light and that he would no longer bother her, but that if there was still a problem she should feel free to call me.

A day or so later she called me to say that she could still feel an energy in her home that concerned her.

JOAN L BOLER

On the Thursday night after work, I met the young woman at her unit. After she advised me the negative energy was near the table, she left the room. As I approached the table, a solid wall of depression hit me. I became aware that the energy belonged to a very lonely and unhappy European woman who had died in the room.

I directed loving energy towards her and said, 'Go into the light,' to which I telepathically received the response, 'Nobody loves me.' I find it difficult to describe just how heavy and dense her energy was. I can only liken it to the description given to the black hole in space that scientists speak about where matter compresses and becomes incredibly dense.

As I needed advice on how to overcome such an oppressive energy, I asked my spirit guides, 'What can I say to this lady that will make her feel happier so she can move forward into the light?'

'Talk to her about her son,' was the reply. As I did this, she cheered up a little and showed me images of her son as a little boy outside the building on a tricycle. Once again, I surrounded her with love and suggested that she go into the light. Her energy reverted to the heavy negativity, and again she said, 'Nobody loves me!'

It was the end of a long day and I was tired. I needed help. *Please guides, angels, send loving energy through me so that she can go into the light.* An incredible blast of beautiful energy poured in through my crown chakra and then out through my other chakras towards the woman who immediately moved forward to a more peaceful place. As I viewed her new environment, I could see a barrier preventing her from moving forward to the heaven world where most people go. I knew that she had gone as far as she was able at that point in time.

I had spent around twenty-five minutes working with the woman and I suddenly thought, 'What if there are more problem energies in the place?' And so I called upon the angels to stay and please ensure the whole place was cleared. I then called the woman back into the room. 'It wasn't the man,' I said. 'It was a woman.'

'Oh, I know,' she replied. 'The man was over by the TV. He's gone now.' As I turned to leave, I was stunned at the sight of a human sized angel in the corner of the room. The woman had no further problems.

It has been my experience that it is usual for guides to initiate actions to aid us without being asked, while angels seem to only provide help when requested to do so. Having said that, no doubt there are exceptions to this such as their being directed by a higher being or following through on a pre-determined objective.

Spiritual Help for the Sick

Knowledge of spiritual healing harks back to the time of Jesus or even earlier. Today there are many forms of spiritual healing, and for those who work with the universal forces and the inhabitants of the higher spiritual kingdoms, anything is possible. The most common form of healing that I have been involved in is that which contributes to the healing of the soul through bringing awareness and understanding. On each occasion I am confronted with a person who needs healing physically, mentally or emotionally, I look to guidance for the appropriate action to take.

Death leaves grieving loved ones in its wake. For the grief-stricken person whose pain is like an open wound, healing can begin through receiving the knowledge their departed loved ones are happy. A young mother came to me for a reading. Emotional pain radiated from her in great waves. Three months earlier her three-year-old daughter had died. As an empathic psychic, I am flooded with the physical, mental, and emotional feelings of the person I tune into, so encountering such raw pain is difficult to deal with. As I asked those in spirit to show me the child, a scene opened up before me and I was in the presence of the little girl who was being cuddled by a human sized angel. I spoke to the child and asked her if she was able to visit her mother. In the next moment, the child had left the angel's arms and revealed to me how she frequently looked in on her mother. The child was bubbling with happiness as she began to skip around in her secure surroundings. As I transmitted this knowledge to her mother, I could feel her pain ease. Her grieving was not yet done, but the intense, raw pain I had felt on her arrival was gone.

In many instances when dealing with the healing of sickness and disease, healing the physical is not appropriate. For those whose negative behaviour and attitudes are the cause of the illness, it is necessary to first of all overcome the original cause, otherwise, in spite of healing energy being effective, the symptoms are likely to return. Also sometimes the illness is serving a purpose so it is not always appropriate for the sufferer to receive healing at that time. As each situation is different, it follows that the action taken regarding each healing may also be different.

On a number of occasions when I have attempted the physical healing of a person, there has been no healing energy available to me. At such times, I pray to those in the spiritual realms for an alternative way to provide appropriate aid for the suffering individual.

'My mother in England is ill. Can you please send her healing,' came from the frantic woman on the other end of the telephone.

'I'll see what I can do.' As I replaced the receiver, I intuitively knew the daughter needed healing and so I made the request. Since distance is no problem, when the energy poured through me I redirected it. For some ten minutes the energy flowed through me and then it just faded away. Then I asked those in spirit about the mother, but no energy was forthcoming. I understood it was her mother's time to go, so I requested that she receive calming balancing energy to bring her peace during her last few weeks.

When my brother-in-law became ill with cancer, I attempted to send him healing. I don't know whether I was too tired at the time or if he wasn't meant to receive healing. Whatever the cause, no energy was forthcoming. Since that did not work, I asked for three angels to look after him as he underwent surgery to remove his cancerous growth. I also asked for an angel to look after my sister Yvonne who I knew would be going through a very worrying and stressful time.

A day or two after the operation had taken place I was talking on the phone to Yvonne who lives in New Zealand. After chatting for around twenty minutes, she hesitantly told me of seeing three angelic beings floating beside her husband's bed and looking down at him whilst he was resting before his operation. Yvonne advised that these beings were about the same size as a human with pale flesh coloured skin and feathered wings. The free flowing robes they were wearing were made up of numerous teardrop patterns approximately two inches (five centimetres) in length and coloured pale silver, gold and white. Golden blond hair framed their beautiful androgynous faces.

Then Yvonne became aware of three human spirits, who were dressed in black, moving towards the bed, and she viewed them with trepidation. The first, a short woman wearing a veil, approached to within a yard (metre) of the bed. The other two, one of whom was very tall, were also approaching and were at that moment about three yards (three metres) from the bed. Fearful these spirits were harbingers of death, Yvonne told them to go.

The spirits moved back and faded away. At the same time, the angels also started to fade so that Yvonne, not wishing to lose their wondrous comforting presence said, 'No! Not you! You stay please.' One continued to fade from view while she could still clearly see the other two. For about a minute Yvonne continued to be aware of the presence of these angels and then she smiled at them and said, 'Thank you.' She felt them acknowledge her thanks and although they then faded from her view completely, she remained aware of their presence. Yvonne was left feeling a lot calmer and more positive about the outcome of the operation. Her husband subsequently recovered.

To call upon those in spirit to help in times of sickness is helpful to both those making the request and those who receive the benefit of it. Though the effects of healing energies are not always visible, genuine requests for help are always answered in the way that is right for the person, though not necessarily in the way requested. Sometimes the results are minor and may come in the form of acceptance, while at other times the outcome is astounding. At all times they are appropriate.

Archangels

Through the records of the religions of old, we are informed of amazing powerful beings of light that are variously described as gods and archangels. Myths surrounding such creatures permeate the world religions. Just as in ancient times, interaction between humans and great spiritual beings is reported today. What are these beings that are so much greater than the angels more commonly seen by the psychic?

I was visiting my son on the Gold Coast, and one evening while we were out having dinner, my son received a call on his mobile phone. He handed me the phone so I could speak to my distressed old school friend Bernice who was calling from New Zealand. She had gone to some lengths to find and contact me. After flying to Sydney for an operation her friend had died unexpectedly as a result of complications, and Bernice wanted to check how her friend was.

It was probably a week or two after the woman's death that I was able to follow through on the request. In order to achieve this, it was necessary for me to transport my consciousness to another realm. I didn't need to know in advance which realm, as all that was necessary was for me to stipulate who I needed to check up on and immediately I was there.

What I saw was incredible.

I had never met her friend, but somehow I immediately recognised her as she wandered around with other people. There were no boundaries anywhere. No ground or floor, no walls or perspective of distance, just light and people drifting around. What blew my mind was the massive archangel, the size of a tall building a number of stories high, overseeing the occupants of the area of light. Since I had found the answer I sought, I withdrew from the location that I felt was a place that some of the recently passed-over visited until they found their bearings. I was thus able to report back to Bernice that she need have no worries about the welfare of her friend.

Questions regarding the nature of the awesome creature I had witnessed invaded my mind. Given that the appearance of the creature was a reflection or image and not necessarily the way someone of another religious background would have seen it, I had to consider that in some cultures a being of such greatness and power would have been described as a god.

The soul at its highest is found like God, but an angel gives a closer idea of Him. That is all an angel is: an idea of God.[204]

Meister Eckhart

Expanding the Consciousness

Personal knowledge is the most effective way of learning the truth. Those who seriously put the effort in have from earliest times found, or been given, the help and direction to reach their desired goal, be that personal spiritual power, the ability to communicate with the dead and angels, or the ability to expand the consciousness and the heart and to personally access the heavenly kingdoms.

According to different studies on the heavenly kingdoms, there are different levels or dimensions—just as we ourselves are made up of different levels. This agrees with my own experience and observations on the occasions I have witnessed and entered into those wondrous realms.

Meditation can lead to altered states of consciousness and is a proven pathway for those who wish to expand their consciousness in order to meet with those of the non-physical dimensions. However, mediation alone does not guarantee entry to the higher dimensions. The higher levels are reached through spiritual intervention or personal spiritual awareness. As I look back

---

[204] Oliphant Old, Hughes (tr.) 'The German Mystics', Sermon 9, *The Reading and Preaching of the Scriptures in the Worship of the Christian Church*: Vol. 3, William B Eerdmans Publishing, Grand Rapids, Michigan, 1999, Ch. 9 p. 449.

upon my own spiritual awakening that included my being transported into the heavenly realms and brought into the presence of great beings, there is always a common cause. Access to the kingdom of heaven or the God within is achieved through the heart that is filled with unconditional love and purity of intent. Love is the doorway that enables the expansion of awareness to include our greater self, which results in alignment with the Creator and access to the spiritual kingdoms. Luke 17:20-21 (NIV) *[20]Once, having been asked by the Pharisees when the kingdom of God would come, Jesus replied, 'The kingdom of God does not come with your careful observation, [21]nor will people say, 'Here it is,' or 'There it is,' because the kingdom of God is within you.'*[205]

Forays into the spiritual kingdoms that reveal their inhabitants and their surroundings are as amazing as they are rewarding. Beyond beautiful places, exquisite sounds and radiant love is the experience of the wondrous realms of spirit. For those with love in their hearts who experience physical death, and those who are able to move their consciousness to the non-physical dimensions, it is possible to enter such places of absolute harmony and bliss.

---

[205] *Biblestudytools.com* ibid. (accessed 12 Oct 2013)

JOAN L BOLER

Chapter 13

The Invisible Creatures of Earth

Millions of spiritual creatures walk the earth unseen, both when we wake and when we sleep.

John Milton[206]

Our World and its Creatures

In our multi-dimensional world, as we acknowledge the likelihood of the human consciousness being indestructible and accept the possibility of angelic beings, are there other areas of the dimensions beyond the physical that deserve attention?

Planet Earth is teeming with life. The almost limitless variety of life forms has long fascinated and stimulated man's curiosity, and in today's information age, we are aware of many creatures' habits and habitats. Until recent times, we have been unaware of the existence of such miniscule life forms as the germs and bacteria that have had an impact on humanity for as long as there has been human life. Today, it is possible to magnify these miniscule creatures to thousands of times their natural size, proving they exist. This has contributed towards the development of protection against, and cures for, some of the diseases their invasion causes in humans and animals. If it has taken mankind this long to discover these minute life forms, is it possible there are other creatures of Earth yet to be recognised?

We live in a time when research has revealed that our universe is multidimensional. This knowledge along with evidence of mind travel, clairvoyant and telepathic abilities that transcend space and time, evidence that supports out-of-body experiences, and the survival of the non-physical aspect of our identity after the death of the physical begs the question:

> If, in this multidimensional universe in which we reside, consciousness does not depend upon a physical body for its existence, why then would there not be as many entities without physical bodies as there are with?

---

[206] Milton, John 'Paradise Lost' Line 614

JOAN L BOLER

Since the seventeenth century, scientific attitudes have treated tales told by those endowed with clairvoyant sight as fantasy. Prior to that time, most of the population believed in a whole range of spirit beings, including 'the little people', which are also described as elementals or nature spirits. Scientific rejection has resulted in the relegation of all tales of these little creatures to the world of fantasy, with the result that many consider the 'sighted' to be 'not of sound mind'. Awareness of this has ensured that most of the sighted, being of sound mind, keep their knowledge to themselves.

Like most people, for many years I had thought that the little people would, if they existed, have a physical body, and as I had never seen one I thought that they must be the delightful imaginings of creative story-tellers. My years as a physic reader caused me to question my ideas when an individual confided in me their ability to see the little beings. When they spoke of their encounters, their pleasure in their ability to see such creatures shone through their eyes as they shared their experiences without fear of ridicule.

Since I am not a believer and require evidence and facts before I reach conclusions, *if* I reach conclusions, I began to seek out more knowledge of these little beings through information that was revealed by the sighted. I found much that I dismissed, but here and there were reports that rang true.

Researching Information on Elementals

In view of the prevailing attitude towards the existence of elementals, and the difficulties encountered by those brave enough to report and record their knowledge and experience, serious research into this area of knowledge is extremely limited and difficult to check. Investigations into the world of faerie can be carried out via clairvoyant sight or through of out-of-body travel. Both approaches provide information that deserves consideration, even though some of the conclusions drawn about these small beings by those who possess the necessary skills vary on some aspects of the elementals and their lives.

It is claimed by the sighted that dwarves, gnomes, elves, pixies, brownies, imps, faeries, sylphs, undines, salamanders and a wide range of creatures that do not have physical bodies inhabit our world. It seems to be generally accepted that these little creatures are the conscious spirits of the elements of earth, air, fire and water. Most reports maintain that these creatures are small with a human type form. Their bodies are not physical, so it is possible for them, should they wish to do so, to temporarily change their appearance, or to have their appearance changed through environmental influences that they absorb. In an existence that does not have to deal with the limitations of the physical body, such creatures can teleport to wherever they wish in an instant—just as can be accomplished by those who leave their physical body. Their destination can be a desired location, or they can immediately transport themselves into the presence of the person or being that telepathically connects to them.

Animals and other physical life forms have a different type of consciousness to each other and to humans. So too, do these creatures. Their life experiences seem to lack the heavy responsibilities that can be faced by humans, and their lives appear to be simple and for the most part full of enjoyment and fun. It is reported that some of these small beings can be mischievous and problematic to humans who create difficulties for them. In our multi-dimensional world, these creatures exist in a dimension that is very close to and interacts with the physical world.

Findhorn is a village by the sea in Scotland. In 1962 a few extraordinary people came together to develop a remarkable centre for humans who worked with nature spirits. Such was their success in this endeavour that in the barren sandy soil huge plants, including forty-pound cabbages, flourished, attracting the attention of horticultural experts who were at a loss to explain the profusion of herbs, flowers and vegetables.[207] Among those who lived or spent time at the centre over the next few years were people gifted with clairvoyant sight who were able to communicate with the nature spirits and the angelic beings in the area. Through this communication, greater insight was gained into the needs of those non-physical creatures and that of the local plant life. The nature spirits took the opportunity to warn that the callous and overall destructive behaviour of humans towards the planet, and all that inhabit it, could lead to the annihilation of an infinite number of life forms, including humans themselves.

In considering the nature of these beings, their human collaborators, in this case, Ogilvie Crombie, Dorothy McLean and David Spangler[208] were of the opinion that the elementals related to the plant kingdom take delight in and responsibility for the nurturing of plant life. They also thought that these, for the most part happy playful creatures are beings of light that when their consciousness becomes more individualised take on an etheric form that mimics the human body to a degree. The Findhorn people speculated that the elementals' appearance reflects the thought forms produced by humans,

---

[207] 'Beginnings' *Findhorn foundation history*; www.findhorn.org/aboutus/vision/history/#.UPZTU (accessed 16 Jan 2013)
[208] Crombie R Ogilvie, *Meeting Fairies—My remarkable encounters with nature spirits*; Allen & Unwin, Crows Nest, Australia, 2009, pp. 85-87, 160-162, 174 & 194-195.

as their imaginations created images of the creatures of myth, fantasy and creative faerie stories of times past. But their opinion on these points is not the only possible explanation.

Alternative ideas are put forward by English born out-of-body traveller Geoffrey Hodson[209] (1886-1983), who for sixty years lectured around the world for the Theosophical Society. It was his opinion that their radiating 'light' shape lends itself to the human type form and that they alternate between their light form and their more human-like etheric bodies. That they are great mimics is revealed in their manner of dress, which he notes is copied from humans from a variety of historical periods. Hodson relates one instance where he observed a brownie that had noted, and apparently liked, the boots he was wearing. The eight-inch high (20 cm) creature proceeded to mentally produce like boots on its own feet.

Hodson claims that that all plant life, in each of its different stages of development, produces a subtle call (like a sound) that attracts the type of help required from the specific nature spirits equipped to answer that call. While some attend to the atmosphere around the seed, others will ensure that the matter vibrates at the appropriate speed, while still others shape the etheric mould of the plant.

According to Ogilvie Crombie, it is possible for elementals to become contaminated by the evil emotions of those humans who have become immersed in fear and hate. Some nature spirits have, over the centuries, taken on more scary appearances, like goblins. Their original natural appearance may have been quite different from the unpleasant forms they now have. As absorbers and carriers of evil human emotions, these once innocent creatures express these unpleasant energies in ways that provoke fear in those humans who can see them. The polluted creatures need healing so they can return to their original form and nature.[210]

Research into this fascinating subject by reading books written by those who claim to interact with elementals can be a rewarding and illuminating experience. Before dismissing the possible existence of elementals, consideration needs to be given to the fact that science recognises we live in a multi-dimensional universe, and that therefore it is not inconceivable that there are differing types of conscious beings residing in other dimensions.

---

[209] Hodson, Geoffrey, *The Kingdom of the Gods*, The Theosophical Publishing House, Madras, India, 1952, pp. 35, & 99-107.
[210] Crombie R Ogilvie, ibid. pp. 160-163.

THE TRUTH SEEKER

Memories of another Lifetime

Whilst my current lifetime lacks contact with any of these small non-physical beings, recently through hypnosis I re-lived moments of an unusual lifetime around twelve hundred years ago. The living memories I experienced had a powerful impact on me and removed my doubts as to the existence of the little people.

As I began to re-experience that lifetime as a female, I found myself as a toddler playing in the garden in the back yard of the family home. Our cottage was in the woods in Europe. I happily played with my companions who were little creatures dressed in brown. At around twenty inches (fifty centimetres) tall with acorn-cup shaped fitted brown caps on their heads, fair skin, and round childlike faces, they were full of mischief and fun. Over the years, these little woodland creatures giggled and laughed, teased and played with me in the garden and in the woods. As I walked through the trees, I could hear their giggles and knew they were teasing me, hiding from me, daring me to find them.

The brief memories I retrieved from that lifetime included that of two little men-like creatures who were making their way along the edge of the forest that bordered the family property. These very thin little beings had long sharp noses, were dressed in brown with brown hats and were about nine inches (twenty-three centimetres) tall—their serious business-like demeanour discouraged communication.

This carefree existence lasted until I was around twelve or thirteen years of age. Then one day the local serfs seized me while I was walking through the woods some distance from my home. They tied my wrists and raised my arms above my head and then attached a rope to what must have been a tree branch, so even though my feet were still on the ground, I couldn't escape. Not that I attempted to—I had no idea what they wanted of me. The men were dressed in light brown clothes made of coarsely woven material. The tops they wore had hoods that came down to a cape like garment without sleeves, instead having slits for the arms to come through. They were all dressed the same.

While I was secured to the tree, I could see women wearing dull-coloured clothing who stood a distance away. All were serious as they stood waiting and watching. Suddenly one of the men in front of me swung a tool that looked like a pickaxe down towards me, striking me with great force in the chest and stomach. The wound was fatal. Doubtless, these people believed me to be a witch, and to their superstitious minds witches were responsible for death and disease, crop failures and all the disasters that befell their community. I sometimes wonder if the shock of that experience has created a mental block that has prevented me from seeing the little people in subsequent lifetimes.

Jane's Faerie Queen

In March 2005, during a visit to my spiritual healer, Jane, she related to me the amazing events of a weekend she had spent in the Blue Mountains just out of Sydney.

The sequence of events she related was so incredible and different to any she had previously experienced, that she was constantly questioning and doubting. That first day on the mountains produced encounters of a strange nature that were later confirmed by a person living on the property. The second day was both incredible and overwhelming and yet she 'knew' the experience was real.

This is her story.

> *I went away for the weekend in the Blue Mountains. The first day I went walking with a friend around the property. As I was walking, I felt the presence of a 'being' but I couldn't see anyone. It was a very strong sense that someone was walking next to me, but visually no one was standing at my side. My friend was talking away, oblivious of our new companion. When I asked my friend if he was aware of this feeling of a presence, he said that he wasn't, so I naturally doubted this sensation and myself. As I continued to walk, the feeling became stronger until I stopped and tuned into this presence. I began to get an image of this presence in my mind (a third eye sight). It was a very thin and wiry Aboriginal man who was trying to talk to me. I did think that I was rather mad and doubted that this could be real. I listened to what he was trying to say and I could 'hear' information coming into my mind about the history of the land. I continued to walk and listened.*
>
> *As the day progressed, my friend went off and I spent the afternoon with this apparent (I still thought apparent) spirit man. He stood beside a tree and told me to go down to an outcrop of land on the escarpment. He pointed out a rock and told me that it didn't belong there, that it wasn't of this land. I went down to the rock that he*

THE TRUTH SEEKER

directed me to. Unlike the other grey rocks around, this rock was a light brown. I sat down on it and I felt dizzy and nauseous. It felt like it was in another dimension. Weird! It didn't feel like it belonged to the earth. He wasn't happy with it being there.

He showed me really interesting things about rock formations and introduced me to a brother of his—a more serious type. I also got to see other places and learn more of the history of the area.

I came back from the walk early and sat at the kitchen table in the community house. I sat with my back to the staircase that led up to a loft. There was a small chair and a telephone table under this staircase. A man was sitting there as if waiting for a phone call. As there were a few people wandering about the place, I didn't really notice him enough to engage in a conversation. On the table was a book about the history of this particular property. I started to flick through the book and I saw a chapter on the Aboriginal spirit man that fitted the description of the aboriginal spirit I had seen exactly. Then I became aware of the man sitting behind me on the stairs so I introduced myself to this fellow and I found out that he had written the book!!! I asked him for more information and he validated the description of the spirit man—the personality, the little moustache and the body movements. He had lived on or around this property for a while and had met this Aboriginal spirit man a few years before. He had talked and walked with him quite a bit and the spirit man encouraged him to write about the history of the area.

He validated the whole thing. I was so excited!

I find it interesting that Jane, immediately upon her return from her walk, found a book on the table written by a man who had also seen and recorded his interaction with the same Aboriginal spirit man. And directly following this amazing discovery, she was able to discuss and compare her experiences with those of the author. This validation seems to have prepared her for an even greater experience the following day.

The next day we went down to the cave and my friend went off on a different path and I knew I had to go into the alcove. It was like a little enclosure but it wasn't a cave because it was on flat ground with sandy base and not too many ferns. It felt still in there. I felt a pull to my right and all of a sudden, I fell to my knees as a wash of reverence came right through my body. I cried. The feeling of love was so intense that I felt I had to be on my knees in honour of the feeling that was coming through my body. I lifted my head up and I opened my eyes and there in front of me was not just a faerie, but a faerie queen. I don't know how I knew that, but I knew it was. She was standing off the ground. She was quite large, around seventy-five centimetres or two and a half foot in height with a nicely shaped, though broad figure. She was translucent. You could actually see behind her. She was light with form. Her skin was very light and her hair was fair with a double bun and she was wearing a little coronet. Her fine white dress covered her feet. Her wings were translucent and were moving so fast I couldn't really see them.

She hovered in front of me and I said to her, 'You are so beautiful.'

To which she said, 'So are you.'

I replied, 'No, no, you are so beautiful.'

She said straight back, 'So are you.'

I cried.

This faerie was before me radiating such love and respect—it was incredibly moving and this feeling of connection has remained with me. The whole thing felt like a lifetime but it probably lasted thirty to sixty seconds. I was left with a feeling of peace, love and tremendous respect.

Jane's experience with the faerie queen was amazing, and as she related it, I could sense the awe she felt recalling the event. Her experience contains the timeless element common to experiences that encroach on the non-physical realms. A very important aspect of Jane's experience with the faerie is the love she felt radiating from it. Love is such a beautiful and powerful energy that when it flows through your whole being, it leaves you filled with awe and a deep knowledge of its spiritual nature and reality. I recall my amazing experience with the Master who revealed to me how the cosmos worked, and I can appreciate Jane's automatic response of falling to her knees as the beautiful, magnificent energy of such powerful and spiritual beings compels reverence.

The Faerie Narrative

At the end of April 2005 when I went to visit family on the Gold Coast, Jane's story was uppermost in my mind and I related her experience at a family gathering. Among the family members present, was Trish, who was

THE TRUTH SEEKER

fascinated by the idea that faeries could be real. On my next visit to the Gold Coast in July, Trish reported the following:

> *In April 2005, Joan and I were having a conversation in which the subject of faeries came up. Joan spoke about a healer she had been seeing and how she had described to Joan her sighting of a faerie. I was surprised that faeries really existed and asked for more details. This particular faerie had been seen in a hollowed out area of rock and I distinctly remember Joan saying that the wings were barely visible due to the fact that they were moving at such a vigorous speed that you could just see the vibration in the air around the small figure. This stuck in my mind because I had met a young girl at my daughter's day care centre who swore faeries were protecting her and insisted upon having her Tinkerbell toy with her at all times, especially sleep time.*
>
> *In June 2005, I was working back in a Year 6 primary school classroom of my ex-students for a day. During this time the students were invited to write a narrative on any subject that interested them. Upon completion, each student brought me their story in turn for me to proofread and edit cooperatively with them.*
>
> *A young boy Mark[211] who was twelve years of age sat beside my desk leaned over and asked me to read his story. This boy suffered a learning difficulty that made writing extraordinarily hard for him. I noticed that he'd written a substantial amount in comparison to his usual story length. He always wrote about war and horror emphasising and celebrating the violence of it. His father was in the army and Mark admired the position his father was in and intended to join the army when he was old enough. In fact, many children at this school had parents who were in the armed forces as the base was located only a short distance from the school.*
>
> *When I began reading, I was surprised to see that a boy whose stories always centred on fantasies of war and violence was this time about faeries and angels. Granted, there was an element of the story that still drifted back to his normal war related fantasies. However, this time it was really about the faeries. Never had I seen this before in his work. All his past stories had been about reliving war and the historical aspects of war. This seemed to be a really imaginative piece for him.*

---

[211] The names of all the children in this chapter have been changed to protect their identity.

JOAN L BOLER

Flashes of my conversation with Joan came back to me when I was faced with this story about angels and faeries. I was intrigued and decided at this point to delve deeper and see if Mark had written the story from a mythical viewpoint or if it had some deeper meaning.

I asked him if he had ever seen a faerie. I was quite surprised to hear his response, 'Yeah!' as if to imply that I was abnormal having never seen one. My interest prompted me to delve deeper. I asked him if the faeries had wings. He told me that they didn't have wings.

At that moment, another boy (eleven years of age) who was standing behind him waiting patiently for his story to be read responded, 'Yes they do!'

Mark replied, 'No they don't.'

The other boy then informed us, 'They do have wings but they move so fast that you have to look really carefully to see them.'

When I asked if he'd if seen the faeries too, he didn't hesitate in telling me about the fact that he had indeed seen faeries but I was unable to delve too deeply into it as the boys didn't seem overly keen on other class members hearing the conversation. I was able to gain information on their incredibly fast wing movement from the second boy who debated with Mark about whether they had wings at all. Both boys agreed that these faeries were particularly pretty. The boys also commented that the faeries were relatively small but didn't give an indication of just how small they were.

Interestingly, the girls in line were expressing their disbelief with heads shaking and eyes rolling as girls so often do. I found it intriguing that both boys were the two true individuals in the class. They both struggled in certain aspects of their learning and really stood out from the crowd in a number of ways. Both children are extremely warm-spirited. Mark would cry if he could sense either I, or any child in the class was upset. If someone cried, so did Mark— he was so tuned into the emotions of others. He would laugh about the fact that he couldn't help it.

What would the chances be of not just one, but two children in a class of thirty-one admitting to seeing faeries? That both these boys were extremely sensitive children supports the validity of their statements as it is the sensitive child who is likely to see such beings. The reference in this story to the faerie wings moving too fast to be seen complements Jane's observations. It is interesting to note that only a few weeks had elapsed between my relating Jane's original experience, and Trish's class situation. And it was only a few weeks later that Zac came into Jane's life and as a result into mine.

An Extraordinary Child

The story of Zac, a very special open and gifted child who is both sensitive and intelligent, needs to be told in detail. There is no way of proving, or even providing evidence for his ability to see the little people, but among his wide range of psychic abilities and experiences, evidence for the genuine nature of his paranormal abilities, can be found. Also I believe it is important to reveal the impact that some of those experiences have had on him. This child, like many other 'sighted' children, has to deal with a world where a vast number of people have little or no tolerance for those who actually see into the dimensions beyond the physical where the departed, angels, and delightful little creatures can be found.

Zac is born under the sign of Gemini, and his features have the refined almost ethereal look that is consistent with the appearance of many born under this sign. Zac not only sees the various inhabitants of other realms, but is also one of those gifted clairvoyants whose abilities enable him to see auras around people and their chakra energy centres.

Zac's story begins around ten years before he was born. His mum Judy[212], and dad Phil[213] have a friend who is clairvoyant. On her first visit to this lady, his then future mother was told, 'There is a spirit around you who says he is going to be your son.' In fact, she suggested that was already pregnant. Judy was not impressed. She and Phil had been married for a number of years already and had absolutely no intention of having children! And as it turned out, she was not pregnant. A year went by and Judy again visited the clairvoyant who repeated the message from the spirit who claimed to be her future son, 'Tell her I'm still here. I'm not going away. Tell her I'm still here!'

Unimpressed, Judy's comment was, 'Yeah... Yeah... Yeah...'

Over the next few years at around twelve monthly intervals, the same scenario took place and Judy just laughed. But frustration that the clairvoyant was unable to obtain any other information resulted in the

---

[212] Name changed.
[213] Name changed.

clairvoyant explaining that because Zac's spirit was all over her, she found it very difficult to get past him to delve into anything else in her life. The clairvoyant complained that Judy was the most difficult person that she had ever read, because whenever she opened up a connection, she just experienced this energy of her being pregnant with Zac. On one occasion, the clairvoyant told her, 'This is a very special child. I don't know what he will be, or what he will do, but he will be amazing! And he keeps saying, "Tell her I'm still here. Tell her I'm not going away."'

Around two years before Zac was born the clairvoyant said, 'He not only says to me, *Tell her I'm still here*,' but he's got someone by the hand, and is saying, "Ask her if she wants to meet my brother."'

After sixteen years of marriage without children, Zac's parents finally had a change of heart. Zac at last had the opportunity he had been looking for! His parents (who had expected conception to take place sometime during the next few months) did not expect immediate results. But they had not counted on Zac! Zac was conceived on that very first night. Phil, who had fallen asleep, woke up around fifteen minutes later. The room was bright with a light so white and blinding that he had to shield his eyes. 'Why did you turn the lights on?' he asked Judy as he jumped out of bed and flipped the light switch. As the light didn't go out he continued to flip the light switch. To his dismay, the light stayed.

Judy, who had been lying awake in the dark, said, 'What are you doing with the lights?'

He replied, 'I'm trying to turn them off, but no matter what I do…' Suddenly he 'knew' what the light was—it was their newly conceived son and then he said, 'I know what it is—he's here!' His sense of knowing was absolute.

When Judy called to advise the clairvoyant she was pregnant, the clairvoyant replied with a heart-felt, 'Thank God!' She then went on to say that most souls move on when they can't come through the channel they have chosen, but that Zac never wavered and there was never any possibility of him going elsewhere. Zac was born in 1996. Three years later, his brother was born.

THE TRUTH SEEKER

Zac's Helpful Spirit Relatives

Zac's world involved experiences that were funny, entertaining, helpful, bothersome, upsetting, scary and even terrifying. His parents had been exposed to knowledge of the paranormal and weren't strangers to psychic experiences, so when his abilities began to emerge, his mum and dad were supportive of him. Zac, at around four years of age, began to make comments to his mum like, 'There's a spirit in this room.' She encouraged him to talk about what he was experiencing. Then, for a while he didn't say anything, and his parents thought he had lost his clairvoyant capabilities. However, when he was around six or seven, evidence of his psychic abilities re-emerged.

Zac's close relatives from beyond the grave interacted with him. His deceased paternal grandfather was surprised by Zac's capabilities and commented in the colourful language he used while still in the living, *I didn't know you could 'effing' do this!* Embarrassed, Zac related to his parents what his grandfather had said. Fortunately, that gentleman has toned his language down in the regular visits he now has with Zac. His aunty, who died in January 2005, has kept a close eye on him and can be both humorous and helpful. Zac explains one such situation, 'One day when I was at school I couldn't answer this question. It was very hard and I couldn't work it out. I worked it out a little bit, but I couldn't get the answer. But then my aunt told me the answer, and then I saw why it was that answer.'

In March 2005 when Zac was eight, the family decided it was time to find their dream home. They located a beautiful duplex that suited them perfectly and set their hearts on purchasing it. The property was being sold at auction and Judy and Phil were one of a number of interested parties. An attack of nerves had Judy decide not to attend the auction. Zac noted that his dad and brother were not the only family members attending. His deceased aunt and a deceased male relation by marriage were both there. The financially minded gentleman who had been friends with Zac's parents had loved real estate and auctions and had always enjoyed discussing what houses had sold in the area.

The bidding commenced at around eleven in the morning. After it had been under way for a while, one lady emerged as the only real threat to their ownership. The bidding continued to rise taking them closer and closer to their financial limit. Each family member, both living and dead, was feeling the pressure, and as fear that they would lose to the other bidder became a real possibility, the two deceased relatives suddenly disappeared.

The family lived a block away. Judy suddenly stood in response to an overpowering compulsion to get to the auction. *I just have to go there now,* was the thought that took hold of her as she ran to where the property was being auctioned. Both the deceased relatives returned to the auction and advised Zac they had gone to get his mum. As she arrived at the auction, she found her husband ready to pull out because bidding had gone beyond what he wanted to pay. But she felt strongly that this was *their* house and she wasn't ready to let go of the dream! Judy took up the bidding. As Zac watched the proceedings, the deceased male relative stood in front of the other bidder and roared in her face. She stopped bidding. The family had their new home!

There was a number of passed-over friends and relatives of the family who kept a regular check on the family and Zac's activities. On one occasion, Zac was practicing a difficult piece of music on the piano, and just couldn't get it right. Then, after a lot of effort, he finally played it perfectly! He felt a presence behind him and turned, and there were all the spirits clapping him!

The family appreciated the help and attention they received from their loved ones in spirit, and in the early part of 2006 Judy decided to light candles on a regular basis for the spirits so they could all gather and share the love and appreciation the family felt for them. Unfortunately, these positive aspects of co-operation between the living and the departed were not the only type of spirit experiences Zac had to live with.

Frightening and Unpleasant Aspects of the 'Sight'

Troubled souls who have died and not found their way into the spiritual kingdoms may see but not be able to communicate with those on the physical plane—except when a person is like Zac and gifted with the 'sight'. Troubled spirits are not the only unsettling aspects of being psychic. In an energetic world, negative energies can be seen by the psychic and more disturbing, they can infiltrate the sensitive's psyche. Zac had become a withdrawn and anxious child, but his parents, unaware of the stress he was under, had assumed he was just shy and reserved.

On her birthday, Zac's maternal great grandmother appeared to him. This lady, a difficult person during her lifetime who had suffered from Alzheimer's disease during her later years, was intent on terrorising the child. Her frozen stare in Zac's face was really frightening to the young boy. She began to appear in his classroom and maliciously influence the other children to be spiteful and mean to him. Zac's life was wretched, and when

THE TRUTH SEEKER

he turned to his parents they were supportive but at a loss to know what to do! There is no instruction manual for the problems Zac was facing. But they had to do something!

Zac's parents favoured natural therapies whenever possible. During his short lifetime, the only medication Zac had taken was one prescription of antibiotics and Nurofen. When he had a health problem he was usually treated with homeopathic and natural medicines. His mother decided that she had to come up with answers! Without knowing why she did so, she made an appointment for him with a lady who practiced kinesiology, who, it turned out had special abilities that enabled her to deal with Zac's problem. After his second visit to this lady, he jumped down off the table and to his mum's surprise and delight, she discovered over the next few days that the child she had thought was shy and reserved—wasn't. Suddenly he was more relaxed, outspoken, outgoing and happy.

But only a week or so later he came screaming down the stairs saying, 'There are all these people in my bedroom. Tell them to go away!' When there are no boundaries to stop them, lost, past over souls who seek to communicate with those in the physical world can invade the lives of these special people to such an extent, that a bedroom can become like Grand Central Station.

So it was back to the kinesiologist who once again effectively dealt with the problem. Now whenever Zac begins to feel the stress of his world, he asks his mum to take him back to the kinesiologist.

Zac began to see chakras and auras. He describes the energy centres known as chakras as usually being about two inches (five centimetres) in diameter with each having its own colour that can sometimes change. Although the auras of positive, emotionally stable people have lights, and he can sometimes feel what he describes as *a really nice energy* coming from them, sometimes the energy he sees hanging around people is negative, especially when they are experiencing stress or other problems. Such energy looks like black blobs.

Zac not only sees negative energies in people's auras, he can also see the negative energies in the environment. People who harbour emotions like fear, anger, unhappiness and discontent pollute their surroundings with these disagreeable energies. Such unpleasantness needs to be cleared away, or it can cause the sensitive individual to become depressed if it impinges on their energy field. In order that Zac be assisted in dealing with these energies, the kinesiologist suggested that his mum take Zac to see Jane (the spiritual healer who saw the faerie queen). Jane advised Zac that when he encountered negative energy, he could mentally imagine faeries, angels, or dolphins in areas where the negative energy was. By producing positive thoughts, and therefore positive energy, it is possible to disperse negative energies.

Jane also told him to call her telepathically if he was scared. He meant to do so one night but instead of linking with Jane, he connected to his kinesiologist. He was embarrassed and said, 'Oops, I called the wrong person.'

The kinesiologist replied, 'It's okay darling, I'm here.' This lady confirmed at a later date she had indeed experienced this telepathic connection.

Learning to survive in his multi-dimensional environment is difficult for Zac, as he doesn't know when another strange or frightening experience will invade his world. One such incident happened in 2005 when he lay down for a rest during the day. He seemed to fall asleep into a dream, but instead felt himself rising. He could clearly see, in spite of his eyes being closed, that he was moving up off the bed towards the ceiling fan. He became frightened as he thought the fan was sucking him up and he was powerless to stop it. Terror and panic took over as he came to within two feet (sixty centimetres) of the fan! Abruptly, he dropped back down on to the bed. Propelled by fear, he jumped off the bed and ran from his room.

Once he had calmed down and taken the time to reflect on what had happened, he realised that although during the experience he had thought it was his physical body that had risen from the bed, it had in fact been his spirit. This incident reminded him of another time when he was younger when he came out of his room and found himself flying down the stairs.

Not being able to share his wondrous and strange abilities with close friends leaves Zac feeling isolated and different. On one occasion, Zac decided to reveal his ability to a friend at school. He told his friend that he had seen a ghost and his friend said, 'Yeah, right!' His disbelief resulted in Zac not bothering to pursue his claims or to attempt to disclose such information to any other of his friends.

It is a very sad fact that most children like Zac receive no support whatsoever and are left to fight their way through a sometimes toxic maze of entities and energies. With help from his parents, and people like Jane and the kinesiologist, Zac's life has become less difficult, but in spite of this he still has to deal with situations most adults would find extremely daunting. Fortunately, some experiences involve creatures that are helpful and delightful.

THE TRUTH SEEKER

Angels and Angel Cards

Zac sees, talks to and receives help from angels. These beings wear light clothing, have wings and are usually around the size of a woman. However, sometimes he sees them as pure, beautiful light energy without form.

Once, on a flight from Mexico to Los Angeles with his dad, mum and brother, as their plane's altitude dropped on approach to the airport, they ran into a violent electrical storm. The plane shuddered and bucketed around in the wind and the rain while lightning slashed the sky. Zac's noticed his mum had become very agitated and he was concerned. Suddenly, through the window of the plane, he saw a light come out of the clouds, and then from that light, angels emerged and surrounded the plane. Zac told his mother the angels were there and said, 'Look out there. They're all lined up!'

'Fine,' his mother said, and calmed down.

In spite of a rough landing, the plane and its passengers were unharmed. His mother's statement when they were safely on land was, 'I am not getting on a plane without you again. You're coming with me because you've got the safety factor!'

Zac trusts angels, as he knows that they are beautiful loving beings and so at Jane's suggestion, Judy bought him some angel cards. When she gave the cards to Zac, he didn't feel comfortable with them and said, 'These cards aren't new. Someone has used them. They belong to someone else.' So Judy took them back to the shop. There was a different lady in the shop to the one who had previously served her and, although his mother really didn't want to have to explain, she said, 'Look I'm really sorry—I bought these for my son,' she held the cards out to the woman and continued, 'I have a gifted son and he says that these cards actually belong to someone else.'

The woman looked at her in open-mouthed astonishment. Then gathering her wits together she replied, 'I've been looking for those cards all morning. The person who sold them to you, sold you my cards!'

Dwarves, Faeries and Elves

Not only does Zac see angels and the spirits of those who have passed over, at any time when he ventures outdoors, he may come across diminutive creatures such as dwarves, faeries or elves.

JOAN L BOLER

Not long after the family moved into their new home, Zac, on his way to play in the back yard, stepped out the back door on to the patio area. To his astonishment, he viewed a startled dwarf who was standing some ten feet (three metres) from him on the patio. The dwarf was about eighteen inches (forty-six centimetres) in height. He wore a tall, red hat that was about fifteen inches (thirty-eight centimetres) high. He carried a pitchfork in his human-like hands that was almost as tall as he was—hat included. The dwarf had fair skin, ears much the same as those of humans, black eyebrows and wide, round black eyes. No sign of hair could be seen around his hat. His chest-length beard had a white outline and was grey in the middle. The dwarf was wearing a blue, long-sleeved, buttoned shirt with a jacket over the top and long red pants.

As they stared intently at each other, neither made an effort to speak and Zac got the impression the dwarf was not a communicative creature. Then in the blink of an eye, the dwarf was gone, apparently transporting to a place where the human child could not see him.

Often when Zac is in his back yard, or other places around nature, he sees faeries. These fascinating little creatures have wings and travel in groups of four or five. They are about six inches (fifteen centimetres) in height and are surrounded by a luminous bright light, the colours of which may be red, gold, bright yellow or white. They have light-coloured skin, light or dark-coloured hair and are constantly moving. They do not stop for conversation. They just say, 'Hello!' and Zac says, 'Hello!' back.

The elves Zac sees usually spend their time in bushes and trees and have skin that is a light green in colour—similar to the colour of celery. They are around ten inches (twenty-five centimetres) tall and wear long green curved hats that are almost as tall as they are. Their heads around their hats reveal no hair or ears. Their wide eyes have black eyeballs that are more oval than round and are surrounded by white. Their hands only have three fingers and a thumb, and no fingernails. Their long sleeved dark green jackets have brown buttons with a collar and narrow cuffs that are light green. They wear either short or long pants, and wear soft shoes that are green and curled at the toes.

Zac's interaction with the little people was minimal until he met a special little elf.

THE TRUTH SEEKER

The Travelling Elf

In August 2005, Zac was visiting Melbourne with his family. It was a cold night—around seven or eight degrees Celsius, and after having had dinner at a restaurant, they were walking back along Chapel Street to their apartment. Zac passed a small hedge-like bush in a pot with a number of elves crawling around inside it.

When Zac told his mum she said, 'Let's go back!' And so they turned and walked back forgetting Zac's dad who continued on his way. Once he realised his family were heading back the other way, his dad wanted to know what they were doing.

His mum said, 'There's a bunch of elves down there.'

His dad replied, 'Oh, okay.'

The fascinated family returned to the spot where the elves were, relying on Zac to give them details of what he was seeing.

When they left to return to their hotel, one little elf jumped out and followed Zac and his family the three blocks back to where they were staying. Then the little fellow asked Zac if he could come home with him! Zac asked his mum and dad, who agreed. And so the little green elf, who revealed his name to be Jasper, travelled back to Sydney on the plane with them, sitting himself quite happily on the back of Zac's seat. But once they landed in Sydney, the little fellow disappeared.

A few weeks later when the family went on an overseas trip, Jasper joined them on the plane. Their first stop was Bangkok. During their stay, whilst at their hotel, Zac's six-year-old brother Thomas slipped over and received a nasty cut to his head. It was necessary to take him to the hospital where he received three staples. Thomas was hysterical and this made the situation very stressful for the whole family. A few days later, the family went to the markets where Zac purchased a crystal ball with his allowance. He then waved it over Thomas's head, at the same time telling his mum, 'I'm just picking out the bad energy. I'm healing it.'

Whilst they were in Bangkok, they visited the Emerald Buddha. Although not large, at around eighteen inches (forty-five centimetres) tall, the Emerald Buddha is very special. It's made from one piece of jade and is considered one of the most sacred objects in Thailand. Zac could see Thai angels (they looked like Thai people) around the Buddha. The angels realised he could see them and said to him, 'You are a very lucky boy. You have a very good life!'

Jasper popped in and out of the plane as they continued on to England. They settled into their hotel about a block from Euston Station. Jasper found accommodation to his own liking in the park across the street, in a huge tree with lots of foliage.

While they were in London the family went out on excursions. One of their outings was to the Tower of London (a fortress with walls that surround a number of buildings within), which is patrolled by the Beefeaters. One of the buildings is a church. Inside the church Zac repeatedly commented to his parents, 'There's lots of heads floating around here!' Then the guide walked into the church and began to explain that people had been beheaded and were buried under the church. He informed them that prior to the discovery of six hundred bodies buried under the floorboards a few hundred years ago, no one had been aware that they were there.

The family visited Trafalgar Square as his parents had read a book that said that Nelson was a deva (Buddhist name for a divine being or a god) and Trafalgar Square was a sacred place. The book in question, 'The Boy Who Saw True', was a collection of diary entries commencing 1 January 1885 by a child who, much like Zac, saw people in spirit, angels, auras, elves and faeries.

The following text is from that book and records the writer's experiences on 24 January 1887.

> *That nice pupil (in spirit) of E. B's turned up this morning for a bit at our eleven o'clock repast, and told us a few things. He asserted that some souls who were far enough on, and didn't want to have to come back to earth again could become devas or sort of gods or what we imagine are angels. He argued that each country has its deva, and sort of looked after things, but in a way it would be hard for us to understand. He avowed that Lord Nelson, who won the battle of Trafalgar and said 'Kiss me, Hardy,' was now a deva, and if I ever went to London, I would see him on top of the Nelson monument in Trafalgar Square.*[214]

On 7 August 1887, the young boy went to Trafalgar Square. His report of that experience is as follows:

---

[214] Anonymous, *The Boy Who Saw True*, The C. W. Company Limited, 2004, p.157.

THE TRUTH SEEKER

We saw the Nelson Monument in the middle of Trafalgar Square. That spirit was quite right, there is a big being up there with lovely colours. I did so want to stop and look at him properly, but if I'd asked to Cousin Agnes and Cousin Jimmy, let alone Mildred, (his older sister) *would only have thought me dotty.*[215]

While they were in Trafalgar square, Judy's curiosity had her ask Zac, 'Can you see anything here?'

He replied, 'Yes, there are five angels who are flying around the statue constantly, and they don't leave.' The speed that the angels were moving at was similar to that of a brisk walk.

'Can you ask them what they are doing there?' was Judy's next question.

Zac replied, 'I just spoke to another angel who said, *You cannot interrupt those angels because they have a very important job to do."*

In 1887, the child in the book saw 'a big being with lovely colours' whilst in 2005 Zac saw *five angels*. An increase in the number of beings around the monument appears to have taken place. Why was this? Could the being seen by the child in 1887 have been a very powerful spirit that required five angels to replace it, or is it possible that the spiritual work these beings are undertaking now requires greater effort?

That Jasper didn't go on the outings was revealed one night when I was asking Zac for details about the England section of the trip. Jasper had joined us and advised Zac that he didn't do so because he found such excursions boring! Instead, Jasper slept in the tree most of the time and Zac would see him there as the family went on their outings. Jasper did not come back on the plane to Australia with them, but a few days after the family returned home, he turned up in their garden where he now spends a considerable amount of his time.

Jasper pops in and out of Zac's life at will and is as happy inside the house as outside. He teases and plays, and on one occasion brought five of his family who cavorted in the corner of the living room.

The mischievous elf joins the family frequently and brings fun and laughter into Zac's unusual and challenging life. On family outings, this cheeky elf's antics bring delighted amusement as he pops up on Dad's shoulder—or

---

[215] Op. cit. p.186.

anywhere else that takes his fancy. On one occasion, Jasper amused Zac by on sitting on my shoulder and on another occasion, he sat on my head, bringing delighted giggles from Zac.

Zac's gift of the sight and his willingness to share his experiences provides an opportunity for critical examination of his story. If scepticism is put aside, and the evidence examined with an open mind, perhaps it is possible to learn from his sometimes turbulent, sometimes delightful, but never boring life.

Real or Not

As the various aspects of the sightings and dealings with the little people and those beings of other realms are examined, is it possible to glean evidence for their validity?

Jane's and Trish's students' reports that faerie wings move so fast they can't be seen are supportive of each other. In an attempt to identify what the faeries Zac saw looked like, I went to some lengths to find about twenty pictures of faeries to show to him. He found only one that actually bore any resemblance to the little faeries he had encountered, and the one he selected had clear, see-through wings.

Questions arise about the faerie sizes. Is it possible that for beings without a physical body, their size is in some way energy related? Just as the archangels are of a greater size than the angels more commonly seen, so too was the faerie queen that Jane saw of a much greater size than the faeries seen by Zac.

It is interesting to note that Jane's description of the faerie queen did not fit what one would expect, and rather than disproving her experience, it tends to add weight to her story as it is unlikely that she could have been drawing on previously seen illustrations of faeries. It is perhaps unfortunate that storytellers, believing faerie tales to be fantasy, have created their own rendition as to the appearance of the little people. When I showed Zac a few pictures of dwarves, he rejected all of them. Also, the detailed descriptions Zac gives of elves, faeries and dwarves frequently differ from those in works of fiction. It would be difficult to make the argument that exposure to fictional stories and illustrations were the basis for images created by an overly-imaginative mind. Like most children, Zac watched 'The Lord of the Rings' movies. Unlike most children, he was unimpressed that the elves

THE TRUTH SEEKER

were the size of humans. He was indignant that, 'They (the adults who had made the movie), didn't know that elves were not that big!'

As I interviewed Zac, I was looking for evidence of imagination playing a part in his accounts of his experiences. When I probed for further information and details, he frequently answered that he didn't know. He couldn't enlighten me on such details as, 'Do you know where the dwarves live?' 'What do they need pitchforks for?' and, 'Are there female dwarves?' Nor was Zac able to tell me if there were female elves. All elves looked the same to him, but in spite of this he always recognised Jasper, although he had no idea how he did so. A child with a resourceful imagination would most likely have produced creative answers to some, if not all, of these questions.

The angel card incident, the heads seen by Zac in the Tower of London, and his telepathic communication with the kinesiologist provide supporting evidence of his psychic ability. The house-buying situation with Zac's explanation for his mother's compulsive need to get to the auction, and the Nelson monument incidents cannot be easily dismissed.

Further evidence for the reality of Zac's experiences can be found in the fear and emotional reactions he had to some of his more upsetting and frightening experiences. It is extremely unlikely that he faked such reactions. Why would a well-behaved child pretend a fear that distressed his parents and had them frantically searching for answers, and why, when those answers were found, did he become a happier child? The answer seems clear. Zac was experiencing exactly what he said he was experiencing. Of course, an argument could be raised that Zac was hallucinating, but the validation of some of his experiences, tends to negate hallucination as an explanation.

Many children lose the sight after they reach puberty. Why is this? Zac claimed he didn't see any of the little creatures when his mind was focused elsewhere such as when he played sport. Perhaps some of these children lose their ability because they learn to focus their minds. This could possibly occur without any intention on the child's part, as their lives become more focused on the demands of the physical world. Alternatively, deliberate effort by some children to prevent their sometimes traumatic psychic experiences that can result in punishment and ridicule has led to their shutting down their abilities by intentionally refocussing their mind as soon as their psychic abilities activate. It seems an indictment on society that such children are driven to cope in this way.

I found myself wondering about whether it was Zac's thinking of him that brought the little elf into his presence. It seems likely that a telepathic connection had formed between them, so when Zac thought of the little elf, it transported to his presence, and when Zac became absorbed in what was going on in his environment, Jasper became bored and took himself off to find more interesting company.

The mysteries surrounding our world are many. At present, detailed knowledge of those around our planet who are not anchored in a physical body is only possible for those who have the sight. The rest of humanity cannot categorically say that they exist. Nor can they say that they don't! For this reason, it seems both arrogant and thoughtless to treat reports of the little creatures described in this chapter with superior disdain. This becomes especially so in light of the fact that such an attitude has not only denied us access to many more like revelations, but has also been responsible for pain and suffering experienced by the sighted.

In time, as we become more in tune with who and what we are, more and more of us may be able to see and enjoy such delights as the enchanting creatures described in this chapter. Science is continually inventing new ways of obtaining knowledge pertaining to our world. Magnification has revealed the microscopic physical world, and it is now possible to *see* the heat signature of the physical body through the invention of infra-red goggles. Perhaps it is possible that in the future science will invent special glasses or a special type of camera that will be able to sense and allow us to see the finer spiritual energy and reveal these creatures. In the meantime, an open mind would encourage more of the sighted to provide us with knowledge of the intriguing creatures that their gift of sight allows them to witness.

THE TRUTH SEEKER

Chapter 14

Religion, Belief, Spirituality and Truth

Spirituality is not about emotional security, it is about finding truth.

Tom Butler-Bowdon[216]

Religion

In order to understand his world and define his place in it, man has long sought to find answers and explanations—to identify the nature of all that is. Religion and spiritual beliefs have dominated societies in all countries of the world. In earlier times, for many peoples, religion combined the revelations of the prophets and the study of the skies and the planets along with interpretation of nature's opposing forces of violence and nurturing. In a world that lacked the scientific knowledge available today, producing answers to life's mysteries created the illusion that some measure of control had been gained.

We live in a world where nature is a force to be recognised and respected for its ability to challenge and destroy. In this age of communication we are witness to the lives of people devastated by great floods that destroy their community; fires that rage through bush land, destroying homes and taking lives; molten lava from volcanic eruptions that leaves grotesque remnants of devastation in its wake; tornadoes that rip through towns exploding buildings, and earthquakes that bring down great buildings and turn towns into rubble and burial grounds. In spite of the devastation, today we recognise that such happenings are not the result of the fury of the gods, but are the forces of nature in action. This was not always the case.

Religion in its infancy expressed beliefs that nature's violence was brought about by jealous and angry gods that needed to be appeased through promises of faithfulness and sacrificial offerings. The punishment dealt out by the gods was believed to be due to a lack of faith. Since no physical

---

[216] Butler-Bowdon, Tom, *50 Success Classics: Winning Wisdom for Work and Life*, Nicholas Brealey Publishing, London, 2010.

cause could be seen for the sometimes devastating effects of disease, mental illness and a whole range of undesirable experiences, the idea of negative spirits was introduced to explain the effects of these invisible creatures that brought ill.

Throughout time, and in the different nations, prophets like the Jewish Rabbi Jesus, have emerged, and their enlightened communications have resulted in spiritual wisdoms. These wisdoms have been integrated into belief systems that contain legends and myths, many of which have survived to the present time. As a result, today as in the past we see a wide diversity of ideas and beliefs about the existence and nature of God, or the gods.

Through belief in a greater consciousness, individuals and communities have been able to express their racial, cultural and spiritual goals. Through these shared goals, they have achieved success in many of their endeavours and produced people of great spirituality who have variously shown courage, compassion and wisdom.

However, religious belief has also resulted in the horrendous. Some of the greatest crimes against humanity have been committed by the religious in the name of their god or gods. History tells of human sacrifices in the old religions that have been superseded in relatively recent times by the torture and killing, of men, women and children who were the victims of religious belief. A history of holy wars continues to this day.

How could this happen? Was, and is, 'belief' a major factor in the disintegration of goodness in otherwise decent people? Is belief without truth blind and does it stand in the way of spiritual progress?

Belief seen as truth separates one religion from another and one person from another. There are thousands of such 'truths' with variations between not only each religion, but also between each sect and denomination within each religion, all claiming their own truth is the only truth.

For millennia, believers have trusted in the authenticity of Biblical writings. Is it time to allow truth into the religion and let go of uncompromising dogmatic belief?

Truth in Religion

We live in a time of unveiling. The search for truth in religion takes into account, first and foremost, the evidence for spiritual knowledge currently

THE TRUTH SEEKER

available—like that gained from research into the paranormal, reincarnation, out-of-body and near death experiences—along with the mystical experiences of those who have penetrated and travelled to the greater dimensions and experienced expansion of awareness. Through the eyes of archaeology and the discovery of long lost ancient writings and modern translations of many ancient texts, we look to the gods and myths of old and their beginnings to find truths that have been hidden or lost for long periods of time. There is much evidence from the pre-Christian era, to support the migration of religious ideologies, myths and legends from one race of people to another.

Through listening to others, insight into inner motives, along with unexpected gems of knowledge, can to be found. On different occasions, I have had the opportunity to discern the underlying reason behind the beliefs held by many different people. I began to understand why some people would follow one belief system, while others followed another. I noted that some simply followed the lead of others. However, over time I came to recognise that those who were enthusiastic believers of a particular religious outlook were drawn to beliefs that aligned with their own personality and makeup as individuals. For example, those who believed in an angry and punitive God seemed to find an outlet for the fear and/or the anger (suppressed or otherwise) that lay within. Obedience, usually seen to be an admirable and spiritual trait, had at its source fear, and frequently reflected a damaged ego.

What I learned from believers often led to my reassessing my own ideas, although I never questioned the knowledge that was anchored in personal transcendental experience. The following opportunity to expand my knowledge literally landed on my doorstep.

One morning back in 1973, I was down on my knees scrubbing the kitchen floor. Encouragement came in the form of loud, upbeat pop music. Immediately I completed my chore, I went for my reward—a cup of tea. As I turned on the electric jug, the knowledge suddenly came into my mind that *the Jehovah Witnesses are here to see me.* An automatic response had me heading into the dining room and making my way towards the lounge room in order to reach the front door. I stopped. How ridiculous was that? Why would I think that Jehovah Witnesses were here? As I moved to return to the kitchen, I glanced towards the lounge room windows through which I could see the two people standing on my front porch. I quickly turned down the din coming from the radio and answered the door. It was indeed two Jehovah Witnesses—a man and his wife.

These two lovely people discussed with me then, and on many future occasions, aspects of their beliefs, and over the years I learned much from and about them. They informed me of an error in Biblical translation that related to the word 'camel'. (That same information is found further on in this chapter.) Their beliefs did not influence me to change my own opinions, rather they motivated me research more of the Bible. I enjoyed our discussions and was conscious of the importance of keeping our communications to the most significant aspects of religion—the teachings on goodness and love. To bring in many of my views would have immediately alienated them and that would have meant a lost opportunity. No one can change the beliefs of another, only they can do that, so I did not venture down that road!

All knowledge that refutes long held religious views attacks the very basis of religious belief. Each time a specific belief is revealed to be false questions inevitably arise as to the validity of other beliefs. And this is as it should be. The very acceptance of belief, which is often seen to be a spiritual attribute, carries within its boundaries, limitations and controls that can restrict, break and distort the essence of the soul.

The Gods of the Ancient World

As we travel back in time to the religions of old, we find gods and goddesses that the human mind conceived as it studied its worldly environment, the sky and the planets. The people of ancient Egypt, Mesopotamia, Greece, and Rome all adored gods that reflected their understanding of their world. As astronomy/astrology developed throughout the lands, they saw the sun, moon and planets as gods or goddesses, while the sky, as the domain of the gods, was known as the heavens. As ideas spread from one nation to another, each modifying the concepts to reflect their own identity, consistent themes can be seen throughout the different nations as the gods and myths of one culture were adopted by another.[217]

Extensive archaeological digs throughout the world are contributing an amazing array of knowledge about our distant past, including the religious ideologies and beliefs of many ancient cultures. In 1799, the Rosetta Stone that provided a key to translating Egyptian hieroglyphs was discovered, enabling access to historical information that reaches back over seven thousand years. Insight into the spiritual beliefs of the Egyptians, and the

---

[217] Schoener, Dr. Gustav-Adolf (Tr. Denson, Shane), *Astrology: Between Religion and the Empirical* www.esoteric.msu.edu/VolumeIV/astrology.htm (accessed 14 Oct 2014)

influence that those beliefs have had on world religions even to this day, can now be studied. From as early as 2500 BCE, the beginnings of astrology are evident in Egyptian records, and by 2100 BCE Sumerian records revealed more defined concepts. Over time, the influences of the growing knowledge reached Greece and Rome. At that time, there was no separation between the study of the planetary positions and the constellations, their seasonal influence and the spiritual impact upon the lives of the people. Such knowledge encompassed astronomy, astrology and religion.[218]

The ancient gods of Egypt were a colourful lot. Atum (man wearing a double crown) was the first and the creator god. Amun (often symbolised as a ram or a man with a ram's head or alternately as a man with a hat of ostrich feathers) was king of the gods. Anubis (the man with the jackal head or the jackal) was the god of death. Aten (the Sun and a version of the Sun god Ra) was considered to be king of the gods during the reign of Akhenaten. Horus (man with hawk's head), was the protector of the pharaoh. This was a culture rich in gods, each of which was allotted a role in protecting, aiding and overseeing the wealth and wellbeing of the Egyptians during life, and for some of the gods, after death.[219] Neith was one of the oldest virgin mother goddesses. Isis, the goddess of protection (woman with throne as headdress or cow's horns with Sun disc), was mother to Horus and wife to Osiris.

The ancient Sumerian-Babylonian gods reflected the planet's identities—Shamas gave light and life like the Sun and Sin inherited the likeness to the Moon, the God Marduk took on the nature of Jupiter while Nabu was likened to Mercury.[1] Ishtar, the mother and love goddess, is the likeness to Venus and the equivalent of the Egyptian goddess Isis.

The ancient Greeks also had many gods: among them were twelve main gods that ruled over different aspects of the world and of life. Apollo was the God of music and prophecy and one of the most important gods. It is possible to see a link between the twelve main gods and the signs of the zodiac in astrology. Ares has dominion over war while the astrological sign of Aries is ruled by Mars—the martial planet. Poseidon's domain was the sea, which corresponds with the water sign Pisces. Hermes was the winged messenger god that corresponds to the sign Gemini and its ruling planet Mercury.[220] As with the Greek gods and the gods of other cultures of the

---

[218] Op. cit. pp. 32-33 (accessed 1 Nov 2012)
219 'The gods and goddesses of ancient Egypt.' *Gods and Goddesses—Ancient Egypt.* http://www.ancientegypt.co.uk/gods/home. html (accessed 19 Oct 2012)
[220] Hemmingway, Colette & Sean, 'Greek Gods and Religious Practices.' *Heilbrunn timeline of art history.* The Metropolitan Museum of Art. www.metmuseum.org/toah/hd/grlg/hd_grlg.htm (accessed 19 Oct 2012)

ancient world, the identities of Roman planetary gods aligned with archetypes found in astrology.

As we look to the beginnings of Judaism, it is possible to trace a belief in the gods of the heavens or the skies. The early Israelites claimed their god to be YHWH (Jehovah or Yahweh). This god was perceived to be a god who would look after them and who was superior to the gods of other nations and as a result would enable them to destroy, or be protected from, their enemies. At this point in time YHWH was not considered to be the only god as is evidenced in Exodus 20 (NIV) *²'I am the LORD your God, who brought you out of Egypt, out of the land of slavery.³' You shall have no other gods before me.*[221]

In 925 BCE, the House of David was annihilated by King Shishak of Egypt. The Israelites supposed that their angry, jealous god had punished them for being seduced into adoring other gods. In spite of this, archaeological evidence confirms that the early Jews continued to adore other gods, especially the fertility goddess Asherah (Babylonian identity for the planet Venus[222]). Inscriptions have been found that refer to 'Yahweh and his Asherah'. In the following Old Testament verse, it seems likely that the 'Queen of Heaven' (a sky goddess) was Astarte who was originally called Asherah. Jeremiah 44:17 (NIV) *¹⁷ We will certainly do everything we said we would: We will burn incense to the Queen of Heaven and will pour out drink offerings to her just as we and our fathers, our kings and our officials did in the towns of Judah and in the streets of Jerusalem.*[223]

In recent times, archaeological digs have produced thousands of figurines of Asherah and other gods from the period before 586 BCE when the Temple of Jerusalem was destroyed by the Babylonians and the captured Jews taken to Babylon. No figurines have been found that postdate this period.[224] [225] At least part of the reason for this could have been as a reaction to the destruction of their temple, which was seen as Yahweh's punishment of his faithless people. It is also likely that the influence of the Persian Zoroastrian religion played a part.

It was during their time in Babylon that the Jews were exposed to the Zoroastrian religion. The Persians invaded Babylon in 539 BCE, and their

---

[221] *Biblestudytools.com* ibid. (accessed 11 Oct 2012)
[222] Schoener, Dr. Gustav-Adolf ibid. p.33. (accessed 14 Oct 2014)
[223] *Biblestudytools.com* ibid. (accessed 11 Oct 2012)
[224] Dever, William G, *Did God Have a Wife?* (Eerdmans, ISBN Wm. B. Eerdmans Publishing Co., Grand Lakes, Michigan, 2008.
[225] Glassman, Gary, Wrote, produced & directed documentary *The Bible's Buried Secrets*, SBS ONE, 12&19 Sept 2010.

THE TRUTH SEEKER

one god Ahura Mazda was forced upon the Babylonians. The Persians freed the Jews from slavery, and from that time on the nature of the Jewish god bore a remarkable resemblance to the god of the Zoroastrian religion. Ahura Mazda was the creator and seen to be omniscient, omnipotent, omnipresent, beyond the concept of human understanding, unchanging, the creator of life and the author of all that was good and joyful.[226] Judaism's Yahweh became the Creator, and took on characteristics attributed to Ahura Mazda. Perhaps it was at this point in time when, in recognition that there was only one God, it became necessary that the planets instead of being known as gods became known as angels.

Many of the spiritual understandings of the religions of those earlier times (including Judaism) can be shown to be anchored in beliefs that grew out of astrology.

Myths and Legends of Old

As we look back to the myths and legends of ancient times that had an impact on humanity's attitudes towards spiritual understanding, today's ability to reveal misunderstandings and inaccuracies enables a clearer picture of the truth.

In 1839 British archaeologist Austen Layard found the oldest heroic literary epic in existence when he discovered the Sumerian Royal Library of Ashurbanipal that included 'The Epic of Gilgamesh'.[227] It was not until 1872 that the tablets, written in cuneiform (wedge shaped) script, were translated by George Smith.[228] Incomplete writings of this story date back to 2000 BCE, and more complete versions to 1646–1626 BCE. The story refers to King Gilgamesh who appears in the list of Sumerian kings as the fifth ruler of the first dynasty of Uruk (Iraq) between 2750 and 2500 BCE. This indicates that the story probably dates back to that time.[229]

There are many major points in common between the Gilgamesh Epic and the Biblical flood story of Noah and the ark. Authorship of Genesis was

---

[226] 'Zoroastrian beliefs about God.' *BBC— Religion and ethics.*
www.bbc.co.uk/religion/religions/zoroastrian.shtml (accessed 18 Oct 2012)
[227] 'Library of Ashurbanipal.' The British Museum
http://www.britishmuseum.org/research/research_projects/all_current_projects/ashurbanipal_library_phase_1.aspx (accessed 24 Jan 2015).
[228] Cuneiform. www.ancient.eu.com/cuneiform/ (accessed 6 Jun 2013)
[229] See 'The epic of Gilgamesh' Academy for Ancient Texts
www.ancienttexts.org/library/mesopotamian/ (accessed 1 Dec 2013)

traditionally attributed to Moses who led the Israelites out of Egypt after the building of the Egyptian cities of Pithom and Rameses. Exodus 1:11 (NIV) *[11]So they put slave masters over them to oppress them with forced labour, and they built Pithom and Rameses as store cities for Pharaoh.*[230] These cities were built for Ramesses II who lived around 1279-1213 BCE.[231] The exodus took place after this time. Modern scholars are of the opinion that the Genesis flood story was written in the fifth and sixth centuries BCE.[232] [233] Contemporary scholars generally accept that the Gilgamesh epic was a source for the Genesis story.[234] G A Rendsburg (whose study and research included that of Biblical literature, the history of ancient Israel, and the relationship between ancient Egypt and ancient Israel) offers a detailed summary of reasons as to why he believes Genesis 6-9 is one complete story *paralleling perfectly the Babylonian flood story tradition recorded in Gilgamešh Tablet XI, point by point, and in the same order.*[235] Gilgamesh is a literary classic of the ancient world; pertinent cuneiform documents have been discovered in a range of places including Anatolia, Megiddo (Armageddon) and Ugarit.

While the development of astrology and astronomy contributed to belief in many gods and goddesses, within the religious beliefs of the ancients in Egypt, Europe, Asia, Africa and America was a common belief in both the virgin mother goddess and the human–divine saviour. One of the earliest recognised gods was the Earth-mother goddess (Isis, Gaia, Maia, Ceres Rhea or Cybele and Demeter) as the immortal virgin—the mystical source of all life on the planet.

In his writings 'Pagan and Christian Creeds: Their Origin and Meaning' Edward Carpenter (1844-1929), pioneering mystic socialist, philosopher and poet and advocate for sexual freedom, wrote the following description of the

---

[230] Biblestudytools.com (accessed 11 Oct 2013)
[231] 'Ancient Egypt, Ramesses II. http://euler.slu.edu/~bart/egyptianhtml/kings%20and%20Queens/Ramses-II.html (accessed 7 Jun 2013)
[232] Van Seters, John (1998) "The Pentateuch" In Steven L. McKenzie, Matt Patrick Graham. *The Hebrew Bible today: an introduction to critical issues.* John Knox Press, Westminster, p.5.
[233] Sarna, Nahum M, *Understanding Genesis,* Jewish Theological Seminary of America, New York, 1966.
[234] Davies, G.I (1998). "Introduction to the Pentateuch". In John Barton. *Oxford Bible Commentary.* Oxford University Press, Oxford, p.37.
[235] G. A. Rendsburg, "The Biblical Flood Story in the Light of the Gilgameš Flood Account", in Joseph Azize and Noel Weeks (eds), Gilgameš and the World of Assyria: Proceedings of the Conference held at Mandelbaum House, The University of Sydney, 21-23 July 2004 (Leuven; Paris; Dudley, MA: Peeters, 2007), 115-125: 115. (Rendsburg acknowledges that similar arguments had earlier been put forward by Gordon Wenham, "The Coherence of the Flood Narrative," Vetus Testamentum 28:3 (1978) 336–348.)

relationships that involved both a virgin-mother-goddess and the saviour child.[236]

Anyhow, and as a matter of fact, the world-wide dissemination of the legend is most remarkable. Zeus, Father of the gods, visited Semele, it will be remembered, in the form of a thunderstorm; and she gave birth to the great saviour and deliverer Dionysus. Zeus, again, impregnated Danae in a shower of gold; and the child was Perseus, who slew the Gorgons (the powers of darkness) and saved Andromeda (the human soul). Devaki, the radiant Virgin of the Hindu mythology, became the wife of the god Vishnu and bore Krishna, the beloved hero and prototype of Christ. With regard to Buddha St. Jerome says 'It is handed down among the Gymnosophists of India that Buddha, the founder of their system, was brought forth by a Virgin from her side.' The Egyptian Isis, with the child Horus, on her knee, was honored centuries before the Christian era, and worshiped under the names of 'Our Lady,' 'Queen of Heaven,' 'Star of the Sea,' 'Mother of God,' and so forth. Before her, Neith, the Virgin of the World, whose figure bends from the sky over the earthly plains and the children of men, was acclaimed as mother of the great god Osiris. The saviour Mithra, too, was born of a Virgin, as we have had occasion to notice before; and on the Mithras monuments the mother suckling her child is a not uncommon figure...

The old Teutonic goddess Hertha (the Earth) was a Virgin, but was impregnated by the heavenly Spirit (the Sky); and her image with a child in her arms was to be seen in the sacred groves of Germany. The Scandinavian Frigga, in much the same way, being caught in the embraces of Odin, the All-father, conceived and bore a son, the blessed Balder, healer and saviour of mankind. Quetzalcoatl, the (crucified) saviour of the Aztecs, was the son of Chimalman, the Virgin Queen of Heaven. Even the Chinese had a mother-goddess and virgin with child in her arms; and the ancient Etruscans the same... where it is said 'an ambassador was sent from heaven on an embassy to a Virgin of Tulan, called Chimalman. . . announcing that it was the will of the God that she should conceive a son; and having delivered her the message he rose and left the house; and as soon as he had left it she conceived a son, without connection with man, who was called Quetzalcoat, who they say is the god of air. 'Further, it is explained that Quetzalcoatl sacrificed himself, drawing forth his own

---

[236] Carpenter, Edward, *Pagan and Christian creeds: Their origin and meaning*, Ch. 10. Project Gutenberg www.gutenberg.org

blood with thorns; and that the word Quetzalcoatlotopitzin means 'our well-beloved son.'

It is from a backdrop of astrology, ancient legends and myths that Christianity was born.

The New Testament Scriptures

Two thousand years ago, Christianity, a sect that followed the teachings of the Jewish Rabbi Jesus, emerged. Today, due to the information now available, we are able to ascertain the reliability and the significance of the scriptures and the people of those times.

Biblical writings have been, and are, considered by many to have been inspired by God. Therefore, for those who believe this, if it is written in the Bible, it is true. The following verses explain, in part, the reasoning behind such a belief. 2 Peter 1:20-21 (NIV) *[20]Above all, you must understand that no prophecy of Scripture came about by the prophet's own interpretation of things .[21]For prophecy never had its origin in the human will, but prophets, though human, spoke from God as they were carried along by the Holy Spirit.*[237] Had the writers of scripture accurately recorded only the words of true prophets, then this could be applied to the Bible, providing no changes were later made to the original writings. But much written in the New Testament is not about the words of the Prophet Jesus, rather, many of the scriptures appear to have been written by those who had heard eyewitness accounts, or who at a later time had gathered together as much information as they could from different sources.

The following statement which provides possible support for claims made by many as to the truth of all that is written in the Bible is open to interpretation. 2nd Timothy 3:16-17 (NIV) *[16]All Scripture is God-breathed and is useful for teaching, rebuking, correcting and training in righteousness, [17]so that the man of God may be thoroughly equipped for every good work.*[238]

Is it possible that Timothy was saying that all spiritual writings are inspired just as today great compositions that move and create change in millions of people's lives are inspired? The significant question is—supposing Timothy was stating that God actually spoke through the writers of the Bible and

---

[237] *Biblestudytools.com* ibid. (accessed 20 Oct 2012)
[238] *Biblestudytools.com* ibid. (accessed 11 Oct 2012)

therefore these writers could not err, how is it possible to know that Timothy was making a statement that was true? And indeed, to which scriptures was he referring? Was it all scripture, the Old Testament, or one, or all, of the gospels, letters and epistles that eventually were included in the New Testament? And what of the scriptures that weren't included in the New Testament like the Gospel of Thomas? If he believed all Biblical scripture was the word of God, does that make it true? Why would his opinion define the religious approach of all of Christendom, especially as it was Timothy and not the prophet Jesus, who made this claim?

The assumption that all scripture is accurate must also suppose that the translation of scripture be without error. If not, how could two to three thousand year old writings be relied on? Research challenges the belief that all Biblical scripture is the word of God.

The gospels of the New Testament are thought by scholars, to have been written a number of decades after the death of Jesus and over a period of time by different authors. This would indicate that at least some of the authors were not eyewitnesses. Although there is no evidence to support the claim, the gospels are ascribed to Matthew, Mark, Luke and John. It could be argued that general acceptance in the early days confirms that they were indeed, if not the writers themselves, the source for the information contained in each of the gospels. It seems likely that the records of the ministry of Jesus were, prior to and following his death, communicated orally or in a collection of writings that included myths and legends that were brought together at a later date.

The Synoptic Gospels (Matthew, Mark and Luke), are believed to have come from the same source and their similarities are difficult to dismiss. From this, we can conclude that they can't be used to confirm or validate each other. In the gospel of John (which was written in Greek) there are a number of statements that claim that Jesus was divine. These claims reported by the writer's need to be viewed in conjunction with what is known, and thought to be likely, about the authorship of the Gospel of John. It is considered by scholars that the writings of John were pieced together over time, and while some believe that John was the original source, most don't, rather they attribute the text to the 'Johannine Community' that traced its traditions to John. Many authors are thought to have been involved in the writing of the Gospel of John which reached its final form around 90-100 CE. In the Gospel of John, some of the events that are recorded are out of sequence, which lends support to the idea that data from different sources was combined.[239] [240] This gospel seems to be the least reliable source for finding valid information on the life and teachings of Jesus.[241]

In a land where a number of different cultures intermingled, although Hebrew and Greek were spoken Aramaic was the main language and is considered by scholars to have been spoken by Jesus.[242] [243]

There are differing opinions as to the original language used by the writers of the Gospels, especially as they were written over a period of time. It is generally thought that the writers (however many there were) were, in the main, Jewish and therefore spoke Aramaic. Since the words of Jesus were also most likely spoken in Aramaic, their translation to any other language would have been necessary—whether that translation was from the written or spoken word. There are basic differences in the writing of Aramaic and Hebrew to the writing of Greek. Aramaic and Hebrew words are written without vowels from right to left and require understanding of the concepts discussed, especially since a single word can have several meanings. For example, the Aramaic word 'rookha' can mean 'holy ghost', 'spirit', 'wind', 'life', 'rheumatism', 'in spirits prophecy' or 'soul'.[244]

Greek is written from left to right and each word has a distinct meaning. All languages have idioms that can result in wrongful interpretation. The literal translation of the Gospels into Greek, at least in some cases, does not take into account the differing ways of thinking and of expressing ideas that do not easily, if at all, translate to another language.

George M Lamsa, (1892-1975) a native Assyrian, grew up in a Christian culture that had remained isolated from the Western world until the beginning of the twentieth century. The Aramaic (Syriac) language of his people had survived almost unchanged from the time of Jesus and included many of the ancient sayings and expressions. Lamsa became a distinguished scholar, lecturer and author. His area of expertise was the Bible, which he transcribed directly from Aramaic to English in his work 'Holy Bible: From

---

[239] Harris, Stephen L, *Understanding the Bible,* Mayfield, Palo Alto, 1985, p. 355.
[240] 'Gospel According to John'. *Encyclopaedia Brittanica* www.britannica.com/EBchecked/topic/304610/Gospel-According-to-John (accessed 12 May 2014)
[241] Harris, Stephen L ibid. pp. 302-10 & 367-432.
[242] Barr, James. 'Which language did Jesus speak', *Bulletin of the John Rylands University Library of Manchester,* 1970; 53(1) pp. 9-29
[243] Porter, Stanley E. *Handbook to exegesis of the New Testament,* Brill Academic, Leiden, the Netherlands, 1997, pp. 110-112. See also Hamp, Douglas, *Discovering the language of Jesus,* Create Space, 2005 pp. 3-4
[244] Lamsa, George M. *Idioms of the Bible explained,* Harper Collins, New York, 1985, p. 105.

the Ancient Eastern Text'.[245] The Christian Church of the East received early copies of the New Testament written in Aramaic that had no need of translation.[246]

Lamsa's translations from Aramaic reveal mistranslations such as the following:

> Mark 10:25 (NIV) *It is easier for a camel to go through the eye of a needle than for a rich man to enter the kingdom of God.* [247]

In Aramaic, the written words for 'rope' and 'camel' are almost identical, except that the word 'rope' has a very slightly taller stroke.[248] Suddenly, not only does the verse makes sense with the correct translation, but also we receive confirmation that the original New Testament writings were in Aramaic and that this error occurred when the written word 'rope' was translated into Greek.

The influence of the New Testament of the Bible on the writings in the Quran can be seen in the following:

> Quran 7:37-38 *Heaven's gates shall not be opened to them, nor shall they enter paradise until the camel passeth through the eye of a needle.*[249]

The Bible contains the wise instruction: Thessalonians 5:21 (NIV) *[21]But test them all; hold on to what is good.[22] Avoid every kind of evil.*[250] There is much to admire and emulate in both the Old New Testaments, and within the pages of the Bible can be found an abundance of that which is spiritual and has the potential to enlighten, inspire and bring comfort and peace. But the writers of the Bible were many, and they were human beings with differing opinions, attitudes and capabilities. Some wrote of spiritual ideologies handed down over time and some reported, to the best of their ability, the myths and legends of old. Their personal beliefs and attitudes were likely contained in those writings. The original scriptures were rewritten time and again over the centuries by scholars of varying cultural

---

[245] Noohra Foundation, *Biography of Dr George M Lamsa*. www.noohra.com/Index.pl?glamsabio (accessed 21 May 2013)
[246] Younan, Paul D. *History of the peshitta* www.peshitta.org/ (accessed 3 Jun 2013)
[247] *Biblestudytools.com* ibid. (accessed 30 Oct 2012)
[248] Lamsa, George M. *The holy bible: from the ancient eastern text*, Harper San Francisco – a Div. Harper Collins, (originally published A. J. Holman Co. 1933) p. XVI.
[249] Rodwell J M (tr.) *The Koran*, London Orion Publishing Group Ltd., 2005, p.98.
[250] *Biblestudytools.com* ibid. (accessed 30 Oct 2012)

backgrounds and differing linguistic abilities, religious beliefs and knowledge.

Geza Vermes (1924-2013) was a Hungarian born Jew who converted to Catholicism at six years of age and was later ordained a priest only to leave the priesthood in 1957. Vermes was a professor of Roman and Jewish history who sought to convey a truer picture of Jesus. He maintained that Jesus was a Jewish preacher—a fact seemingly overlooked by both Christians and Jews. Vermes was the first scholar to translate the 'Dead Sea Scrolls' and was considered a foremost authority. His work showed that Biblical texts were not necessarily strict reproductions of earlier writings, but were rewritten to reflect thinking of the time.[251]

Theologian, writer and lecturer in Biblical studies Dr Paula Gooder in the documentary 'The Bible: A History' discusses with historian Tom Holland a problem with regard to some of Paul's letters in the New Testament. Scholars dispute up to six of the thirteen of Paul's letters. Some of the writings postdate Paul, and it is thought that these letters were probably rewritten by later members of the Pauline Christian community whose thinking disagreed with that of Paul, especially his attitude of equality regarding gender. Only seven of the letters are not disputed.[252]

For many Christians, the Bible is considered fact and becomes the rod by which all else is measured. The Bible has many inconsistencies, and those who claim authority produce creative arguments to explain away discrepancies. In the case of the 'camel' passing through the 'eye of the needle', an explanation, that is not supported by fact, dates back to the fifteenth century and perhaps even as far back as the ninth century. It was suggested that the walled city of Jerusalem had a number of gates, one of which was very narrow and known as 'The Needle'. It was surmised that in order for a camel to pass through this gate, it would have had to have its load removed.[253]

From a perspective that takes a more complete look at the life and times of Jesus, it is possible to begin to separate truth from myth.

---

[251] 'The Dead Sea Scrolls and Jesus: the life work of Geza Vermes.' *The Spirit of things*. www.abc.net.au/radionational/programs/spiritofthings/the-dead-sea-scrolls-and-jesus3a-the-life-work-of-geza-vermes/4729428

[252] *The Bible: A history*. Episode 6 www.channel4.com/programmes/the-bible-a-history (accessed Aug 2014)

[253] Morris, Leon, The Gospel according to Matthew, Wm. B. Eerdmans Publishing Co, Grand Rapids, Michigan, 1992, p.493.

THE TRUTH SEEKER

Who Was Jesus?

Christianity began when the Prophet Jesus commenced his ministry, the foundation of which was his new covenant of love. The religion that emerged as a result of the birth, life and death of Jesus has had an immeasurable effect on the lives of billions of people. While it is clear that *some* of what is written about Jesus, like the virgin birth and the resurrection, indicates a belief in that Jesus was *the only begotten son of God*, much of what is written about the life and teachings of Jesus does not support these stories.

In their zest to produce a religion of greatness, the men of those early years fashioned a religion that merged ancient legends such as those related to resurrection, myths of a divine family, and the fulfilment, through the birth of Jesus, of prophecies of a great leader being born to the House of David.

In the Old Testament there are prophecies, like the following, regarding a future king and saviour. Jeremiah 23:5-6 (NIV) *⁵'The days are coming,' declares the LORD, 'when I will raise up for David a righteous Branch, a King who will reign wisely and do what is just and right in the land . In his days Judah will be saved and Israel will live in safety. This is the name by which he will be called: The LORD Our Righteous Saviour.'*[254]

It will be noted that Jesus did not fulfil this prophecy as he never ruled the land, Israel did not become safe, and his birth did not lead to his reigning on David's throne, or over his kingdom. In spite of the lack of prophecy fulfilment, in an apparent attempt to link Jesus to the early prophecies the New Testament, in Matthew I, records the genealogy of Jesus. Verses 1-16 trace his ancestry from Abraham to David, and then from David through to Joseph, clearly claiming that Jesus was descended from David through his father Joseph's line. Matthew 1: 15-16 (NIV) *¹ Elihud the father of Eleazar, Eleazar the father of Matthan, Matthan the father of Jacob, and Jacob the father of Joseph, the husband of Mary, of whom was born Jesus, who is called Christ.*[255] This record reveals Jesus to be the son of Joseph.

Matthew continues to relate the story of the virgin birth, which immediately invalidates the claim that Jesus was born of the House of David through Joseph and that he fulfilled the earlier prophecy. It seems naive to suggest that if Matthew wrote the entire gospel ascribed to him, he would have written two different stories regarding the parentage of Jesus, each contradicting the other. Scholars agree that the gospels of Matthew, Mark

---

[254] *Biblestudytools.com*. ibid. (accessed 30 Oct 2012)
[255] *Biblestudytools.com* op. Cit.

and Luke came from a single source. This being the case, why is it that Mark, unlike Matthew and Luke, does not discuss the birth of Jesus or his genealogy? Since Mark's gospel deals with the ministry and miraculous achievements of Jesus, it seems reasonable to consider the possibility that his gospel did not include the records linking Jesus to David and the virgin birth, because they were added at a later date to the Matthew and Luke versions.

So, was Jesus acknowledged as the child of the Virgin Mary and therefore the begotten son of God during his lifetime, or did such a story emerge only after his death? As we take a closer look into the identity of Jesus through the gospels of Matthew, Mark and Luke, we find that the words of Jesus, as recorded, reveal who and what he was. Also revealed is his relationship to and with his family.

As an adult, Jesus clearly had a normal family relationship with his mother, brothers and sisters, even though they apparently did not appreciate, or recognise, his authority as a spiritually advanced man.

> *Mark 6:1-4 (NIV)* *¹Jesus left there and went to his hometown, accompanied by his disciples. ²When the Sabbath came, he began to teach in the synagogue, and many who heard him were amazed. 'Where did this man get these things?' they asked. 'What's this wisdom that has been given him? What are these remarkable miracles he is performing? ³Isn't this the carpenter? Isn't this Mary's son and the brother of James, Joseph, Judas and Simon? Aren't his sisters here with us?' And they took offence at him.*
> **⁴ Jesus said to them, 'A prophet is not without honour except in his own town, among his relatives and in his own home.'** [256]

Jesus recognised that the very fact that he came from a local, typical family that included brothers and sisters created a stumbling block to the recognition of his worth—as a prophet, not as the begotten son of God. Jesus did not dispute his relationship to his siblings, rather he acknowledged them when stating that his family did not hold him in the esteem his disciples did. The Catholic Church maintains that the word 'brethren' or 'brother' (translation of the Greek word 'adelphos') also referred to cousins at that time. Can their claim likewise be applied to the translations from the early Christian Church of the East which has been translated directly from the original Aramaic to English in which the words 'brothers' and 'sisters' are also used?[257]

---

[256] *Biblestudytools.com* ibid (accessed 11 Nov 2012)
[257] Lamsa, George M. *The Holy Bible: From the Ancient Eastern Text,* ibid. Mark 6:3

The following verses in each of the gospels of Matthew, Mark and Luke, stand out as Jesus himself confirms the correctness of who Simon Peter thinks he is.

> Matthew 16:15-16 (NIV) *"[15] 'But what about you?' he asked. 'Who do you say I am?' [16] Simon Peter answered, 'You are the Christ, the Son of the living God.'"* [258]
> Mark 8:29 (NIV) *"[29] 'But what about you?' he asked. 'Who do you say I am?' Peter answered, 'You are the Christ.'"* [259]
> Luke 9:20 (NIV) *"[20] 'But what about you?' he asked. 'Who do you say I am?' Peter answered, 'The Christ of God.'"* [260]

The expression the 'Christ' or 'Messiah', meant the anointed or chosen one, (a term applied to kings, prophets and priests). [261] [262]

Only in the Matthew version is there mention of the *Son of the living God*.

It was not uncommon for the people of early times to assign to kings and chosen ones the title 'Son of God'. The records reveal that title was used in Rome where Julius Caesar (100-44 BCE) was described by his adopted son Emperor Augustus as the 'Son of God'.[263] Also called 'sons of god' were leaders in China since 1000 BCE[264]; Japan[265]; the ancient Near East; Mesopotamia and ancient Egypt,[266] where from the fourth dynasty, the pharaoh was known as the 'Son of Re' (the Sun god and creator); ancient Iran; Anatolia/Asia Minor; the Levant (modern Syria, Lebanon, Israel, Palestine and Jordon), prophets were given the title 'Son of God'; Cyprus and the Arabian Peninsula.[267] [268]

---

[258] *Biblestudytools.com* ibid. (accessed 2 Nov 2012)
[259] Op. cit.
[260] Op. cit.
[261] *Our Rabbi Jesus.* http://ourrabbijesus.com/articles/what-does-the-word-christ-actually-mean/ (accessed 10 Jun 2013)
[262] "Origin of the name of Jesus Christ' 'Christ.' *New Advent* www.newadvent.org/cathen/08374x.htm (accessed 10 Jun 2013)
[263] Rhee, Helen, Early Christian Literature, Routledge Early Church Monographs, 2005, pp. 159–161.
[264] Russell, Bertrand, *The Problem of China*, http://www.gutenberg.org/ebooks/13940 (accessed 1 December 2014)
[265] Boscaro, Adriana, Gatti, Franco & Raveri, Massimo (eds.) *Rethinking Japan: Social Sciences, Ideology and Thought II*. Japan Library Limited, 2003, p. 300.
[266] Collins, Adela Yarbro &, John Joseph, *King and Messiah as Son of God: Divine, Human, and Angelic Messianic Figures in Biblical and Related Literature*. Wm. B. Eerdmans Publishing, Grand Rapids, Michigan, 2008.
[267] 'Re', *Encyclopaedia Britannica*.www.britannica.com/EBchecked/topic/492674/Re (accessed 7 Jun 2013) and 'Son of God' http://en.wikipedia.org/wiki/Son_of_God (accessed 5 Oct 2014)

The Old Testament refers to 'sons of God (elohim). Sometimes 'elohim' is translated as 'God' and sometimes as 'angels'. From the following verse, it can be seen that in the early days of Judaism, as in other religious belief systems of the time, it was believed that the gods or angels (the planets)[269] had children with human women. Genesis 6:1-4 *When men began to increase in number on the earth and daughters were born to them, ² the sons of God saw that the daughters of men were beautiful, and they married any of them they chose.³ Then the LORD said, 'My Spirit will not contend with man forever, for he is mortal; his days will be a hundred and twenty years.' ⁴ The Nephilim* (offspring of gods and human females) *were on the earth in those days--and also afterward--when the sons of God went to the daughters of men and had children by them. They were the heroes of old, men of renown.*[270] Taking these verses into account, it would seem that Jesus could not be a 'son of God' as a planet was believed to be a son of God. The offspring of a god through human women were known as 'nephilim' and were the heroes of old.

According to the Catholic Encyclopaedia, when used in the Old Testament, the term refers to *persons having any special relationship with God. Angels, just and pious men, the descendants of Seth* (the third son of Adam and Eve), *were called 'sons of God'*. However, when the term is applied to Jesus in the New Testament, it confirms his divinity.[271]

It would seem that the meaning applicable in this case, is that Jesus was a 'just and pious man' or a man 'having a special relationship with God'. That the term 'Son of God' meant that God took the place of his physical father can't be supported.

Jesus had already stated that he was a prophet (Mark 6:4), and he confirmed the accuracy of Simon Peter's statement with the words in Matthew 16 (NIV) *¹⁷Jesus replied, 'Blessed are you, Simon son of Jonah, for this was not revealed to you by man, but by my Father in heaven'* [272] Simon Peter identified Jesus as having a special relationship with God and also, because he was a prophet, as having been anointed by God. Jesus confirmed that his answer as correct.

---

[268] Roukema, Riemer, *Jesus, Gnosis and Dogma*. T&T Clark International, 2010.
[269] Altmann, Alexander. 'Astrology.' *Jewish Virtual Library* www.jewishvirtuallibrary.org/jsource/judaica/ejud_0002_0002_0_01531.html (accessed 10 Jun 2013)
[270] *Biblestudytools.com* ibid. (accessed 11 Nov 2012)
[271] 'Son of God', *New Advent* www.newadvent.org/cathen/14142b.htm (accessed 28 Jul 2013)
[272] *Biblestudytools.com* Ibid. (accessed 12 Dec 2012)

THE TRUTH SEEKER

Jesus often referred to God as his father. It is obvious that he saw God as the spiritual father of not only himself, but also of each and every human being. Matthew 6:9 (NIV) *[9]'This, then, is how you should pray: 'Our Father in heaven, hallowed be your name, [10]your kingdom come, your will be done on earth as it is in heaven...'*[273]

It seems clear that the story of the Immaculate Conception (that identified Jesus as the begotten son of God and therefore divine) was not known at this time either to Simon Peter or to Jesus. The disciples of Jesus gave a number of different ideas about who Jesus was, none of which included his being the begotten son of God and being born of a virgin. Matthew 16 (NIV) *[14]They replied, 'Some say John the Baptist; others say Elijah; and still others, Jeremiah or one of the prophets.'*[274]

In considering Biblical statements as to how the apostles and his disciples viewed Jesus, there are many where he was addressed as 'Rabbi' (teacher), such as Matthew 26:25, 26:49 and Mark 9:5, 10:51, 11:21 and 14:45. It is clear that Jesus was seen as a spiritual teacher, but how else did others see him while he was alive? Those who sought his death, called him 'King of the Jews' and crowned him with thorns were referring to the prophecies relating to a descendant of David. Where did the virgin story come from? It's clear that Jesus himself, the apostles and his disciples thought he was a chosen one of God and one of the prophets.

The virgin birth stories could only have been introduced by those who believed the myth that the gods (planets) impregnated human women. Their beliefs were based on the statements in Genesis and the earlier legends of the virgin births of the older religions.

We are all made up of ***all*** the materials of creation—if the Creator is omnipresent, it is impossible for it to be otherwise. In Chapter Seven 'Our Multidimensional Identity', I discussed the presence of chakras and the layers of non-physical bodies that each individual is made up of. As separate conscious beings, we descend from the non-physical realms, so our spiritual self, as an aspect of the Creator, becomes clothed in the physical at birth. It is not necessary for God to impregnate a woman in order for His essence to manifest. Manifestation of the Creator takes place through the individual consciousness aligning with that of the Creator whose essence is love. We are an idea of God expressed in the physical, and as such we are spiritually all children of the Creator.

---

[273] Op.cit.
[274] Op. cit.

The Jews, prior to their enslavement by the Babylonians, saw Jehovah as their own personal God while they were His chosen people. At a time when it was believed Earth was the centre of the universe, and no understanding of multiple universes existed, explanations for the unknown were introduced and often accepted as fact. Since most of humanity at that time did not have knowledge of, or understand, the inner spiritual makeup of human beings, inconsistent, unlikely, and impossible ideas were included in the beliefs of the people. As the records of most of the ancient religions worldwide reveal, lack of scientific and spiritual understanding resulted in beliefs that allowed for men to be impregnated by the God or the gods.

The evidence points to the probability that Jesus was a very spiritually advanced man, and while his ability to perform miracles may have seemed to support a claim of divinity, Jesus himself, in the following, discusses how like him each and every human being can perform miracles.

> Mark 11: (NIV) *[12]The next day as they were leaving Bethany, Jesus was hungry. [13]Seeing in the distance a fig tree in leaf, he went to find out if it had any fruit. When he reached it, he found nothing but leaves, because it was not the season for figs. [14]Then he said to the tree, 'May no one ever eat fruit from you again.' And his disciples heard him say it........ [19]When evening came, Jesus and his disciples went out of the city. [20]In the morning, as they went along, they saw the fig tree withered from the roots. [21]Peter remembered and said to Jesus, 'Rabbi, look! The fig tree you cursed has withered!' [22]'Have faith in God,' Jesus answered. [23]'Truly I tell you, if anyone says to this mountain, 'Go, throw yourself into the sea,' and does not doubt in their heart but believes that what they say will happen, it will be done for them. [24]Therefore I tell you, whatever you ask for in prayer, believe that you have received it, and it will be yours.'* [275]

Jesus appears to display the very human response of anger towards the tree that did not bear fruit that could have satisfied his hunger. I noted in Chapter Six, 'Mind Powers Magic and Miracles', that I had found that anger was a powerful force in bringing about the manifestation of what I commanded and even what I wished. I am of the opinion that it is the depth of caring involved that makes anger such a potent force.

---

[275] *Biblestudytools.com* ibid. (accessed 9 Mar 2013)

THE TRUTH SEEKER

In another example of the humanity of Jesus, Luke says 17:26-27 (NIV) *²⁶'Just as it was in the days of Noah, so also will it be in the days of the Son of Man. ² People were eating, drinking, marrying and being given in marriage up to the day Noah entered the ark. Then the flood came and destroyed them all.'* ²⁷⁶ It would seem that either Jesus was incorrectly reported, or like all Jews at that time, he accepted the Jewish story of Noah and the ark and was not aware that the original story was about a Sumerian. Lack of knowledge does not reduce the value of the life and teachings of Jesus, except for those who would only acknowledge him and follow his teachings if he had been the begotten son of God.

I do not *know* that both parents of Jesus were human, but no person can claim to *know* that Jesus was the begotten son of God! In fact, I do not *know* whether all that is written on the life and teachings of Jesus actually related to him or to another. Perhaps the 'teacher of righteousness', referred to in the Qumran Dead Sea Scrolls Damascus Document, which according to scholars dates from around 100 BCE, was a source for some of the events or teachings included in the New Testament. In a similar scenario to that experienced by Jesus, the Teacher of Righteousness was one anointed by God, or a messiah, who came up against the 'wicked priest' who persecuted him.[277] [278] What I do know is that someone lived, probably around two thousand years ago, who left a treasure of wise spiritual knowledge that can help others to become a prophet and Master. If most of the documentation in the synoptic gospels relating to the *teachings* of Jesus are accurate, then not only all the spiritual evidence, but also much of the gospel evidence says he was indeed a human person, albeit an advanced one.

Lack of understanding has led to the loss of the real treasure contained in the teachings of the self-proclaimed prophet Jesus. In the claim that 'Jesus was the only begotten son of God',[279] Christianity distracted from the knowledge that Jesus was teaching the way, to those who would listen, to become a prophet like him. Islam also, in its teaching that Mohammad was the last prophet, reveals that Islam does not yet recognise the truth of our individual spirituality and the potential for each and every one of us to become a prophet and Master.

---

[276] Op. cit.
[277] Black, Matthew, *The Dead Sea Scrolls and Christian Doctrine: The Ethel M. Wood Lecture delivered before the University of London on 8 February 1966*, The Athlone Press, London, 1966, p. 24.
www.biblicalstudiesorg.uk/pdf/emwl/scrolls_black.pdf (accessed 4 Jun 2014)
[278] Frederick Fyvie Bruce 'Teacher of righteousness.' *Jewish Virtual Library*
www.jewishvirtuallibrary.org/jsource/judaica/ejud_0002_0019_0_19666.html (accessed 4 Jun 2014)
[279] John 3:16 *Biblestudytools.com*. ibid. (accessed 11 Oct 2011)

JOAN L BOLER

Following in the Footsteps of Jesus

In order to follow in the footsteps of Jesus, it is necessary to understand that along with new revelations of the spiritual, his teachings were about a ***new*** covenant of love that superseded the laws laid down by the forefathers of the Jews. John 13:34-35 (NIV) *³⁴'A new command I give you: Love one another. As I have loved you, so you must love one another. ³⁵ By this everyone will know that you are my disciples, if you love one another.'*[280]

In a time when Judaism looked to the skies as the heavens and the home of God, the planets were seen as angels rather than the gods other nations named them and the forecast saviour would bring peace in the land of David, Jesus revealed a spiritual truth: Luke 17:20-21 (NIV) *²⁰Once, having been asked by the Pharisees when the kingdom of God would come, Jesus replied, 'The kingdom of God does not come with your careful observation, ²¹nor will people say, 'Here it is,' or 'There it is,' because the kingdom of God is within you.'*[281] This statement not only revoked the idea that the kingdom of God was to be found in the skies above, but also reveals Jesus was a mystic. As a mystic he experienced the world of spirit within which incorporates the essence and power of love.

The following statement by Jesus negates all the fear-filled teachings of a God that was the product of human concepts; a jealous, angry, judgemental God that rejected simply because a person belongs to the wrong race or the wrong religion and thought differently. Matthew 7:7-12 (NIV) *⁷Ask and it will be given to you; seek and you will find; knock and the door will be opened to you. ⁸For everyone who asks receives; he who seeks finds; and to him who knocks, the door will be opened. ⁹Which of you, if his son asks for bread, will give him a stone? ¹⁰ Or if he asks for a fish, will give him a snake? ¹¹If you, then, though you are evil, (If therefore, you who err*[282]*) know how to give good gifts to your children, how much more will your Father in heaven give good gifts to those who ask him! ¹²So in everything, do to others what you would have them do to you, for this sums up the Law and the Prophets.'*[283]

As we look to the ministry of Jesus, it is possible to see that his focus was upon teaching about spiritual love and caring. This love conflicted with Judaism's many laws, rules and punishments. His teachings were about a

---

[280] *Biblestudytools.com* ibid. (accessed 21 Mar Oct 2013)
[281] *Biblestudytools.com* ibid. (accessed 20 Oct 2014)
[282] Lamsa, George, *Translation of the Peshitta* 'Matthew' www.studylight.org/bible/glt/matthew/ (accessed 13 Oct 2014)
[283] *Biblestudytools.com* ibid.

love that forgives and does not judge self or others or punishes the breaker of moral laws; that sees all people as equal and does not discriminate because of race, gender or different thinking and is non-violent. Jesus, on a number of occasions, attempted to point out where spiritual values lie. Mark 3:1-5 (NIV) *¹Another time he went into the synagogue, and a man with a shrivelled hand was there. ²Some of them were looking for a reason to accuse Jesus, so they watched him closely to see if he would heal him on the Sabbath. ³Jesus said to the man with the shrivelled hand, "Stand up in front of everyone.' ⁴Then Jesus asked them, 'Which is lawful on the Sabbath: to do good or to do evil, to save life or to kill?' But they remained silent. ⁵He looked around at them in anger and, deeply distressed at their stubborn hearts, said to the man, 'Stretch out your hand.' He stretched it out, and his hand was completely restored.*[284]

Unfortunately, idiosyncrasies of the Aramaic language that were neither understood nor translated to reflect their true meaning have resulted in considerable confusion. The following texts became the basis for the sacrament of Holy Communion. The Catholic Church teaches that Holy Communion is *necessary* for salvation, and that without it the individual would be unlikely to be able to resist the temptations of serious sin.[285]

The real meaning of the texts involved throws a totally different light on what the Rabbi Jesus was communicating at the time. Jesus used concepts of eating (absorbing, or taking into oneself) to get the message across that the application of his new covenant of love would bring spiritual life, while the teachings of their forefathers did not. John 6:48-51 (NIV) *⁴⁸'I am the bread of life. ⁴⁹Your forefathers ate the manna in the desert, yet they died. ⁵⁰But here is the bread that comes down from heaven, which a man may eat and not die. ⁵¹I am the living bread that came down from heaven. If anyone eats of this bread, he will live forever. This bread is my flesh, which I will give for the life of the world.'*[286] The bread from heaven is the spiritual love that flowed through Jesus. The ministry of Jesus and his teachings informed *those who had ears to hear*[287] of the love which would enable everlasting life, awareness of the non-physical kingdoms and the spiritual power within.

In a similar vein, Jesus says in John 6:53 (NIV) *⁵³Jesus said to them, 'I tell you the truth, unless you eat the flesh of the Son of Man and drink his blood, you have no life in you.'* This Aramaic expression (its use supports

---

[284] Op. cit.
[285] 'Holy Communion' *New Advent.* www.newadvent.org/cathen/07402a.htm (accessed 18 July 2014)
[286] *Biblestudytools.com* ibid. (accessed 20 Nov 2012)
[287] Matthew 11:15. *Biblestudytools.com* ibid.

the claim that Jesus spoke Aramaic) was commonly used and understood in the time of Jesus. *Eat and drink* translates to *take on* or *receive into yourself,* much as we might say, *take it on board. My body and my blood*, translates to *what I say and what I do.* 'Or *follow my teachings and live as I live.*[288] *No life in you* relates to spiritual life that emerges with the practice of the kind of love that Jesus taught. It is this spirituality that opens the doors to the spiritual kingdoms for all mankind no matter race or creed, or in which age a person has lived or will live.

As a result of confronting the then corrupt religious establishment, Jesus suffered and died. The scriptures reveal that on many occasions, the priests were confounded by their inability to discredit Jesus who was undermining their power, and so they sought his death. Mark 3:6 (NIV) *⁶Then the Pharisees went out and began to plot with the Herodians how they might kill Jesus.*[289] 'Mark 12:12 (NIV) *¹²Then they looked for a way to arrest him because they knew he had spoken the parable against them. But they were afraid of the crowd; so they left him and went away.*[290] Mark 14:1 (NIV) *¹Now the Passover and the Feast of Unleavened Bread were only two days away, and the chief priests and the teachers of the law were looking for some sly way to arrest Jesus and kill him.*[291]

Spiritual love heals, removes anguish and provides the strength to fight for and even to suffer as Jesus did in order to expose the spiritual truth—that love itself, and not a person or a belief, is the redeemer.

> **Those following in the footsteps of Jesus, live by the 'Law of Love' and fight against religious ignorance and corruption in order to enable that which is of a spiritual nature, to flourish both within the individual soul, and in the community in which they live.**

Authority

After he became Emperor in 312 CE, Constantine declared Christianity to be the religion of the Western Roman Empire (Anatolia, Syria, Egypt and Greece). The religion of the Empire had, up until that time, relied on the

---

[288] Lamsa, George M. *My neighbour Jesus in the light of his own language people and time,* Harper & Brothers, USA, 1932, p.84.
[289] *Biblestudytools.com* ibid. (accessed 1 Oct 2014)
[290] *Biblestudytools.com* ibid.
[291] *Biblestudytools.com* ibid.

protection of numerous gods and goddesses. Thirteen years later, mainly due to disagreements within Christianity relating to the specific way in which the divinity of Jesus was to be viewed, Constantine ordered that the church hierarchy define Christian belief.

In 325CE, Constantine called for the first Council of Nicaea in what is known today as Turkey. Over a period of two months and twelve days, Emperor Constantine, along with three hundred and eighteen bishops, most of whom were Greek, attended. Why was there not a greater representation of bishops from the other lands at this momentous meeting, especially from those nations that spoke Arabic? Most of the Greek bishops were, no doubt, attempting to discern the truth using the Gospels as their guide. However, with their roots buried in their own ancient religion and a language quite different to that used by Jesus and his contemporaries, did they understand that the references in the Bible to the 'son/s of God' did not confirm that God impregnated the mother of Jesus as those who spoke the Aramaic language would have?

The far-reaching effects of the bias in the Christian leaders present at that time, plus the decisions made during the Council of Constantinople in 381CE, resulted in the Nicene Creed which outlined what was to be, the new Christian dogma. The Nicene Creed demanded belief in Jesus as the only begotten son of God, who was born of the Virgin Mary and who, after he was crucified, rose from the dead and ascended into heaven where he sits at the right hand of God and will come again to judge the living and the dead.[292]

The early Church Fathers transferred Roman tradition of popery from the old religion to the new[293][294] and became the dictator of belief and the moral conscience of the people. In the application of this power, they assumed, and later claimed, infallibility. In justification, they turned to the Bible and the words of Matthew. In Matthew only, the verses relating to Jesus being the Christ continue to include the following statement: Matthew 16:18-19 (NIV) *[18]And I tell you that you are Peter, and on this rock I will build my church, and the gates of Hades will not overcome it. [19]I will give you the keys of the kingdom of heaven; whatever you bind on earth will be bound in*

---

[292] 'The Nicene Creed.' *New Advent*. www.newadvent.org/cathen/11049a.htm (accessed 24 Oct 2006)
[293] Rüpke ,Jörg, 'Communicating with the Gods,' *A Companion to Roman Religion*, Blackwell, 2010, p.226.
[294] North, John A, '*The Constitution of the Roman Republic,*' *A Companion to Roman Religion*, Blackwell, 2010, p.226.
p.268.

heaven, and whatever you loose on earth will be loosed in heaven.' [295] Was this statement a true validation of authority—that Simon Peter was the first pope and leader of the church of the Jewish rabbi, Jesus? Since Jesus himself was seen to be the *only begotten son of God*, and thought to have had the right to speak on God's behalf, it was assumed that his designated successor inherited the right to introduce laws, determine beliefs, and be God's voice on earth. As we look more closely at what Jesus is reported to have said, it would seem probable that the verses involved have been misunderstood.

- **Matthew 16 (NIV)** [17]***Jesus replied, 'Blessed are you, Simon son of Jonah, for this was not revealed to you by man, but by my Father in heaven.*** [18]***And I tell you that you are Peter, and on this rock I will build my church...'*** Jesus tells Simon that he is blessed for having received a spiritual revelation from God, and is doubtless referring to Simon's spirituality when he uses the words 'Peter' and 'rock', (both words mean 'foundation'). All Jesus taught had its foundation in the spiritual. In fact, if Simon had achieved a state of spiritual awareness, as Jesus seems to imply, then he personally, like Jesus, had developed, at least to a degree, the spiritual awareness of a prophet. There can be little doubt that it is this spirituality to which Jesus was referring when he used the word 'rock'. Confirmation of this can be found in Matthew 7:21-27 (NIV) [21] *'Not everyone who says to me, 'Lord, Lord,' will enter the kingdom of heaven, but only he who does the will of my Father who is in heaven...* [24] *'Therefore everyone who hears these words of mine and puts them into practice is like a wise man who built his house on the rock.* [25]*The rain came down, the streams rose, and the winds blew and beat against that house; yet it did not fall, because it had its foundation on the rock.'* [296] It seems that Jesus desired to have his church based, not upon Simon himself, but upon his teachings of spiritual love that result in spiritual awareness and access to the spiritual kingdoms. Mastery is not something that can be handed on to another person. Rather, it is earned through a spiritual way of life.

- ***'And the gates of Hades will not overcome it.'*** The word 'Hades' is a translation from 'sheol' which simply means 'place of the dead'. It would seem that Jesus was saying that his church, which was of the 'kingdom within' and the world of spirit, would not die and go to the 'place of the dead' like the physical body, because death has no power over that which is of the spiritual. However, the Church, in

---

[295]*Biblestudytools.com* ibid. (accessed 21 Sept 2012)
[296] *Biblestudytools.com* ibid. (accessed 30 Sept 2012)

consideration of other New Testament verses, sees 'Hades' or 'Hell' as a place of punishment where the damned go after they die.[297] Matthew 25:41 (NIV) [41]*'Then he will say to those on his left, 'Depart from me, you who are cursed, into the eternal* (ongoing[298]) *fire* (mental suffering, torment) *prepared for* (created for[299]) *the devil and his angels*[300] (Evil forces; opposition, the corrupt person)*'*.[301] Matthew 25:46 (NIV) [46]*'Then they will go away to eternal* (ongoing) *punishment, but the righteous to eternal* (ongoing) *life.'*[302] John 5:28 (NIV) [28]*'Do not be amazed at this, for a time is coming when all who are in their graves will hear his voice.'*[303] The Apocalypse of St John the Apostle: Revelation 20:14-15 (NIV) [14]*Then death and Hades were thrown into the lake of fire. The lake of fire is the second death.* [15]*If anyone's name was not found written in the book of life, he was thrown into the lake of fire.*[304] Revelation 21:8 (NIV) [8]*But the cowardly, the unbelieving, the vile, the murderers, the sexually immoral, those who practice magic arts, the idolaters and all liars-- their place will be in the fiery lake of burning sulfur. This is the second death.*[305] The symbolic (mental torment and suffering) or mythical use of the images of fire and brimstone (sulphur) in the afterlife is shown to be false in Chapter Eleven, 'Encountering the Afterlife'.

- *'I will give you the keys of the kingdom of heaven.'* While the keys to the kingdom of heaven include non-judgemental love, goodness and the resultant spiritual awareness, it is possible that Jesus was at this point also referring to the way in which to induce a transcendental state of consciousness that enables access to the spiritual kingdoms.

- *'Whatever you bind on earth will be bound in heaven, and whatever you loose on earth will be loosed in heaven.'* The spiritual laws have always been there—they never change and cannot be added to or taken away from. The physical world is subject to the laws of the

---

[297] 'Hell—Name and place of hell'. *Catholic Encyclopedia* www.newadvent.org/cathen/07207a.htm (accessed 7 Aug 2013)
[298] This word, although very similar in meaning, is more accurate than the word 'eternal', as while suffering may be ongoing, it is not part of that which is spiritual and therefore eternal.
[299] This I have changed as it is not possible that God created torment of any sort. In his ignorance, man does this.
[300] Biblestudytools.com ibid. (accessed 30 Sept 2012)
[301] Lamsa, George M. *Idioms of the Bible explained* ibid. pp. 50-59.
[302] *Biblestudytools.com* ibid.
[303] Op. cit.
[304] Op. cit.
[305] Op. cit.

spiritual kingdoms. Following the spiritual laws gives access to spiritual power, which in turn, gives power over the physical world—*not* the other way around. The process of earthly actions being registered in the spiritual realms explains the law of karma. The results of the positive and negative actions and the decisions that each human being makes while on the earth plane are registered on the non-physical levels and attract consequences in the current incarnation and, unless purged, are carried forward to the next incarnation.

History records the consequence of the decisions made at this time and in the centuries that followed by the Christian Church.

The Reign of the Church

In order to discover the truth, we must first experience that which is untrue. The long rule of Christianity has provided many with the opportunity to learn through the consequence of their beliefs and actions that which is and isn't spiritual, that which brings happiness and that which destroys it. Today, the results of that learning can be seen in the emergence in the West of the more compassionate and open-minded attitudes of the masses.

During the first three centuries before the rule of the Church, Christianity saw its followers choosing to live spiritual lives based on the teachings of Jesus that placed the focus on love, forgiveness and non-violence. Christianity had moved forward from the earlier teachings of the Old Testament to be a more compassionate religion that did not agree with or adhere to some of the old laws, especially those that related to violence and forced religious belief. One such change involved the excommunication of dissidents rather than the earlier approach of Judaism that prescribed torture and death.

In 308 CE Lactantius, a Christian supporter, wrote 'Divine Institutes' in which he stated: Divine Institutes V:20 *'Religion being a matter of the will, it cannot be forced on anyone; in this matter it is better to employ words than blows... It is true that it must be protected, but by dying for it, not by killing others; by long-suffering, not by violence; by faith, not by crime. If you attempt to defend religion with bloodshed and torture, what you do is not defence, but desecration and insult. For nothing is so intrinsically a matter of free will as religion.*[306]

When, with the apparent saving grace of Constantine, Christianity became accepted as the Church of the Western Roman Empire, it totally changed the dynamics of the religion. The masses, instead of choosing to become Christians because they recognised the goodness in the teachings of Jesus, were compelled to follow the new religion. In order to enforce obedience to the Church, the clergy looked to the Old Testament and its ideas of compulsory belief and harsh penalties. Emperors succeeding Constantine decided that they were responsible for enforcing Christian doctrine.[307] In 407 CE, a law was introduced declaring heretics (those who thought differently), to be criminals who could be punished through exile, confiscation of property or death.[308] [309]

In their fervour, and often through violent means, the Christian Church brought under its authority many kingdoms, and managed, from its early days until the sixteenth century, after which time its power gradually became more diluted, to hold power over many countries and ensure that in each country its representatives were the authority on what behaviour and thinking was, and wasn't, acceptable. In recognition of the Old Testament writings, kings and queens were decreed by the Church to be the chosen of God. Strict adherence to a multitude of rules and beliefs was demanded, even though beliefs and rules changed over the centuries. What was right in one century could be considered wrong in another. The right to gain knowledge from sources other than those approved by the Church was denied. Science was only accepted as long as it did not interfere with the Catholic teachings that were deemed to reflect the word of God and therefore God's truth and perfect knowledge.

Those who seek power are attracted to opportunities that afford them power. The Church, as a major political power over many centuries, attracted not only those who wished to serve God, but also those who were hungry for power. The ministry of the Popes embraced political power and used violence and force, both of which were anathema to Jesus, as a method to increase their power and/or to bring more souls to God. The breaking of spiritual laws in the Church's approach to its ministry heralded the

---

306 'Inquisition.' New Advent, www.newadvent.org/cathen/08026a.htm & www.newadvent.org/cathen/08736a.htm (accessed 13 Oct 2011)
[307] Op. cit. (accessed 17 Jun 2013)
[308] 'First council of Nicaea,' 'Inquisition' 'The Nicene Creed.' *New advent.* www.newadvent.org/cathen/11049a.htm (accessed 24 Oct 2006).
[309] Kieckhefer, Richard, "Papacy", in Strayer, Joseph Reese, *Dictionary of the Middle Ages 9*, Charles Scribner's Sons, 1989.

corruption that, to a lesser and greater degree, has dogged its reign to this day.

Some of those who reigned as popes did not adhere to ecclesiastic law when they took office and are now identified as anti-popes. Some, if not all of these anti-popes, and also some of the clergy in the times during their reign, are known to have lived decadent and corrupt lives and were involved in numerous crimes including murder. [310][311][312]

Acknowledged by the Church as anti-popes were: Hippolytus, third century; Novatian, 251; Felix II, 355-365; Ursicinus, 366-367; Eulalius, 418-419; Laurentius, 498-501; Constantine II, 767; Philip, eighth century; Anastasius, 855; Leo VIII, 956-963; Boniface VII, 974; John XVI, tenth century; Gregory, 1012; Sylvester III, 1044; Benedict X, 1058; Honorius II, 1061-72; Guibert or Clement III, 1080-1100; Theodoric, 1100; Aleric, 1102; Maginulf, 1105; Burdin (Gregory VIII), 1118; Anacletus II, 1130-38; Victor IV, 1159-64; Pascal III, 1164-68; Calixtus III, 1168-77; Innocent III, 1178-80; Nicholas V, 1328-30; Robert of Geneva (Clement VII), 20 September 1378 to 16 September 1394 and Amadeus of Savoy (Felix V), November 1439 to April 1449. [313]

However, corruption was not only to be found in the anti-popes and their followers. Dr Joseph Martin McCabe (1867-1955) was born in England, became a priest in 1890 and left in 1896 after becoming disillusioned with the Church both as a Christian institution, and as a source of spiritual truth. He wrote that, *Centuries of trafficking in ecclesiastical appointments, deceit, scandals, immorality, aggression, frauds, murder and cruelty, and the true disposition of the popes is knowingly falsely presented by the Church today.*[314] This does not mean that the Church as a whole was corrupt, rather, that over periods of time, some of those in positions of power were corrupt.

Early Christians recognised the spiritual wisdom to be found in the teachings of Jesus. Much of this was lost when the religion was taken over by the Empire. In those times, 'right' was about following the rules—a teacher/child consciousness that accepted the correctness of those in power making rules for society to follow in all areas of their life including religion.

In order to ensure the rules were followed, penalties were introduced. Although the Church Fathers employed measures that they, and most

---

[310] *Catholic Encyclopaedia*, i, p. 31 and vi, pp. 793-4; xii, pp. 700-03, passim.
[311] Bishop Frotheringham, *The Cradle of Christ*, 1877.
[312] *Catholic Encyclopaedia*, Pecci ed., ii, pp. 289, 294, passim; also vi, pp. 791-95.
[313] 'Antipope', *New Advent*, www.newadvent.org/cathen/01582a.htm. (accessed 1 Aug 2013)
[314] McCabe, Dr Joseph, *A History of the Popes*, C. A. Watts & Co, London, 1939.

people, accepted as their right, they were breaking the spiritual law in demanding belief and enforcing that demand. As we look to the history of the Church, it is possible to see that in spite of the genuine desire by many of the Church Fathers to do what is right, the false ideas that were integrated into their beliefs and forced on the people contained the seeds of evil that blinded the clergy and the faithful and in many cases led to their spiritual downfall. Since no experience is a waste, getting caught in the backlash provided hard lessons that eliminate errors of thinking.

A Religion Built on Fear

Fear has been at the heart of Roman Christianity. Imprisoned by fear, the faithful were bound to react in ways that expressed that fear, for that which we hold within will sooner or later be let loose. Fear is a powerful motivator, and all it takes is for something or someone to light the fuse and a consciousness of violence will be released.

Fear underlined the Church's ministry in the following ways:

1) The punitive policies of the Church promised persecution, torture, imprisonment or death as punishment for disobedience to their teachings.

2) The fearful belief in an everlasting fiery hell in the afterlife was vigorously promoted by the Church.

3) Over time, fear of the devil evolved into horrendous teachings, the like of which rivals one's worst nightmares.

As we look to the source of the belief in demons and devils, it is possible to see that inaccurate translations of some of the verses in the New Testament led to the adoption of many false beliefs, especially those related to hell and demons. In the time of Jesus, demons or devils described insanity, and Satan was another word for 'evil' or 'bad'. Matthew 8:31 *The demons begged Jesus,* translates to, *The insane men begged Jesus.* Luke 8:2 *Seven devils* translates to, *Seven bad habits or inclinations.* Luke 10:18 *I saw Satan fall* translates to, *I saw evil destroyed.* [315] The Church's horrendous teachings of the devil and its ability to tempt and to take over and control the soul resulted in mass paranoia. Suppression and control by violence were seen as valid ways in which to destroy the devil and the people who were deemed to be under its control.

---

[315] Lamsa, George M. *Idioms of the Bible explained* ibid. pp. 50-59.

The Church hierarchy, after Constantine, saw themselves as divinely appointed. Religious belief was seen to be a gift of God that removed the individual's right to an opinion. In order to suppress heresy, ecclesiastic laws and penalties were introduced and became imperial law in 407 CE. Over the centuries, laws that included the death penalty for certain kinds of heresy were applied. In the thirteenth century, such tyranny had evolved into the Inquisition.[316]

By the thirteenth century, Catharism, a heretical Christian religion, had become a serious threat to the Catholic Church in Europe, so tougher measures were seen to be necessary. The Pope set up a tribunal to which he appointed permanent judges as inquisitors. In 1252, torture was authorised by Innocent IV and became a valid way in which to obtain confessions.[317] Since, in many cases, only a confession would stop the torture and the pain, victims sooner or later admitted to whatever sin they were accused of. Punishment for the guilty included confiscation of all their worldly goods, imprisonment (sometimes for life), serving as galley slaves on ships, or death. Men, women and children judged as evil, were burnt at the stake, drowned, garrotted or beheaded. In addition to the Cathars, also considered deserving of such fates were the converted Jews who, under the threat of death, became baptised as Christians and then continued their own religious rites and ceremonies in secret. The Inquisition did not completely come to an end until early in the twentieth century.[318]

As fear spread its poison, horrendous teachings of the devil included the belief that it was possible for humans to have sexual intercourse with demons and pacts with the devil. Such ideas were not only held by the uneducated, but also by those who were held in high esteem like Saint Thomas Aquinas (1225-1274 CE) and Saint Bonaventure (1221-1274 CE).[319] Witch-hunts by the fearful in many countries sought out those who had knowledge and abilities that might give them unnatural power over their contemporaries. Fear, superstition and wrong belief over many centuries entrapped those who would do what is right to doing that which is evil.

Rather than being recognised as the outcome of breaking the spiritual law through wrong behaviour and erroneous thinking, suffering became valid punishment for those who transgressed. Conversely, those who were obedient to the Church and its rules suffered because they followed those

---

[316] 'Inquisition—New Advent ibid. (accessed 24 Oct 2006)
[317] 'Inquisition—II The Suppression of Heresy by the Institution known as the Inquisition.' *New Advent*. www.newadvent.org/cathen/08026a.htm (accessed 24 Oct 2006)
[318] Drewery, Laurett and Alcock, Michael. (shown on SBS 2009) *Secret files of the inquisition*. Inquisition Production Inc. MMVI: Sydney Aust.
[319] 'Witchcraft.' *New Advent*. www.newadvent.org/cathen/15674a.htm (accessed 25 Apr 2014)

rules. Such suffering, they were promised, would reap them rewards in heaven. Thus, the truth became concealed that the Creator does not deal out suffering; the individual invites it when breaking spiritual laws. To inflict suffering in the belief that it affords the opportunity to purge sins or demons, and to teach acceptance of suffering as a way to earn rewards in the afterlife, reveals a misunderstanding of the life and teachings of Jesus. However, such teachings reduced the likelihood of rebellion against the harsh manmade laws and systems that frequently resulted in misery and privation for the masses.

The Church's fearful teachings resulted in the use of violent, punitive measures to eradicate sin and evil. Jesus did not teach fear: rather he taught love and trust in God. Neither was violence the way of Jesus. Luke 6:29 (NIV) *²⁹If someone strikes you on one cheek, turn to him the other also. If someone takes your cloak, do not stop him from taking your tunic.*[320] When punishment was the given treatment for those who had sinned, Jesus said, John 8:7 (NIV) *⁷When they kept on questioning him, he straightened up and said to them, 'If any one of you is without sin, let him be the first to throw a stone at her.'*[321] Jesus had attempted to show these people that we all err and therefore we should not judge others.

> **Fear, the most powerful, negative, manipulator of human behaviour, is the underlying cause of all evil actions.**

Perfection and Idealism in the Church

The Zoroastrian religion taught that God was the author of all that was good and joyful.[322] Jesus also taught kindness, compassion, non-judgement and caring. These emotions invite, and establish, beautiful, loving, joyful and happy feelings in the soul. When love is within it is expressed in moral and honourable behaviour by all who harbour such emotions and attitudes. As we cast our eyes back over the years, it is possible to view and understand what contributed to the destruction of loving spiritual energies in the souls of the faithful over the centuries of Christian rule.

---

[320] *Biblestudytools.com* ibid. (accessed 30 Aug 2013)
[321] Op. cit.
[322] 'Zoroastrian beliefs about God.' BBC— Religion and ethics.
www.bbc.co.uk/religion/religions/zoroastrian.shtml (accessed 18 Oct 2012)

JOAN L BOLER

There are limitations to every person's knowledge, and those who wish to promote good do the best they can with the knowledge and understanding that they have. Decisions regarding the truth of the life of Jesus and his teachings have over many centuries, for the most part, been made in good faith by the Roman Catholic Church, and although the Reformation began the breakaway from the Church that eventually resulted in many separate Christian denominations, for the most part the belief systems set up by the Catholic hierarchy were retained by the rebel Christian religions.

The Roman Church, during its early days, promoted models of perfection in every walk of life. By adopting the ancient myths found in the gospels, Christianity became focused on the superhuman aspect of a man who performed miracles and whose mother came to represent idyllic purity.

From time immemorial, humanity has acknowledged its limitations when faced with the often destructive forces of nature. They sought to find a super being with amazing powers that could protect or save them. Over millennia, myths and legends grew and spread across the lands. In spite of Jesus claiming that wielding great power was possible for those who followed his teachings, this truth was ignored. In the aftermath of the life and death of Jesus, there were those who sought to record, as accurately as possible, what they knew of his life. Some saw him as the prophet he claimed to be—a man sent by God. Others decided he must have been the forecast saviour. This was confirmed for many by the miraculous powers he had displayed. After the death of Jesus, as time went by virgin birth myths were overlaid on the original records and it wasn't long before the more popular god-man identity emerged and took precedence.

Since Jesus was to be accepted as a god-man, then his mother also had to be seen as a model of perfect womanhood. It is probably not surprising that Mary, as the claimed virgin mother of Jesus, who never knew man, came to be a person revered for her chaste life. The Roman religion, prior to the acceptance of Christianity, had a reverent attitude towards virginity. The goddess Artemis was the goddess of chastity[323] while the highly regarded Vestal Virgins were Priestesses of the goddess Vesta. The Vestal Virgins were chosen when they were six to ten years of age and were expected to remain virgins for their thirty years of service.[324]

---

[323] Cartwright, Mark, 'Artemis – Definition' *Ancient History Encyclopaedia* www.ancient.eu.com/artemis/ (accessed 19 Apr 2014)
[324] Mark, Joshua J, 'Vestal Virgin— Definition' *Ancient History Encyclopaedia.* www.ancient.eu.com/Vestal_Virgin/ (accessed 19 Apr 2014)

Mary, the mother of Jesus, inherited goddess-like status based upon the claim that she, as a virgin, gave birth to Jesus (the son of God). In addition, according to Catholic teachings, throughout the remainder of her life Mary remained a virgin. This belief resulted in the need to deny that Jesus had brothers and sisters, and to insist that Mary's marriage to Joseph was never consummated in spite of the following statement. Matthew 1:24-25 (NIV) *²⁴When Joseph woke up, he did what the angel of the Lord had commanded him and took Mary home as his wife. ²⁵But he had no union with her until she gave birth to a son. And he gave him the name Jesus.*[325] And in another version of the same verse, Matthew 1:24-25 (English Standard Version) *²⁴When Joseph woke from sleep, he did as the angel of the Lord commanded him: he took his wife, ²⁵but knew her not until she had given birth to a son. And he called his name Jesus.*[326]

Both versions clearly state that Joseph consummated their marriage after the birth of Jesus.

The purity of the Virgin Mary was glorified and came to represent the highest spiritual state. As a result, the purity desired by Christianity was not the purity of mind unsullied by judgement or guilt, or the heart free from fear and filled with love and joy. Rather, purity became a superficial ideal that denied all that was not perfect and imprisoned its followers in a world of denial that was destructive to kindness, compassion and the joy of life. Over the centuries, procreation became a base act for many. Abstinence and denial of the flesh were seen as a pathway to the spiritual and many chose, or were forced into, a life of abstinence as a member of the clergy.

Many attempted to follow the perfection that was promoted—to their detriment. Their version of the spiritual encouraged physical abstinence, and in fact, sexual feelings were deemed to be unspiritual and the devil's tool by many. Of those who were committed to living pure lives, denial of their natural physical needs could result in frustration and lack of fulfilment. Such inner feelings were often released through judgement, jealousy, bitterness and intolerance towards the behaviour of others. By following demands for perfect righteous behaviour, which included acts of charity, good Christians doing their duty for promised recompense in the afterlife, failed to experience the immediate emotional rewards of a caring heart.

Over recent centuries, puritanical attitudes towards sex in both Catholic and Protestant churches culminated in the sexual corruption of many simply because they saw their natural physical needs as evil. Doubtless, some who

---

[325] *Biblestudytools.com* ibid. (accessed 21 Jun 2013)
[326] Op. cit.

believed that they were evil and beyond help experienced a grotesque twisting of the soul that led them to expunge their conscience and travel down corrupt pathways. When base nature won out, responsibility for the potent feelings that emerged was often delegated to demons, devils, witches and all manner of entities. Guilt, denial and blaming the devil in themselves and others for the 'base' desires of their physical nature turned the sexual act into an act that was solely physical.

Wrong belief removed the wholesomeness and beauty from what has the potential to be, at the least, a joyful experience. More importantly, rather than standing in the way of spiritual advancement, when the loving act between two people combines the physical, mental, emotional and spiritual, the spirituality of the people involved is enhanced.

Unfortunately wrong values impacted upon the behaviour of many 'righteous' Christians as they judged others as 'fallen' or 'heathen', and took it as their right to punish, victimise and destroy the lives of those found wanting. From early times, most religions promoted the myth of the superiority of men who were charged with the responsibility of the lesser female. In Christianity, the creation myth of the temptress Eve supported the idea that females were seducers. As a result, men were able to blame women for their own shortcomings.

For millennia, in many cultures the almost total removal of the rights of females has cast them in roles that enslaved. While little is said in the New Testament as to the attitude of Jesus towards women, he always treated them with respect and listened to what they had to say. In those times, men did not usually discuss ideas with women as they considered them inferior. This was not the attitude of Jesus. John 4:27 (NIV) *²Just then his disciples returned and were surprised to find him talking with a woman. But no one asked, 'What do you want?' or 'Why are you talking with her?'*[327] He was happy to impart spiritual knowledge to those women who wished to learn. Luke 10:38-42 (NIV) *³As Jesus and his disciples were on their way, he came to a village where a woman named Martha opened her home to him. ³⁹she had a sister called Mary, who sat at the Lord's feet listening to what he said. ⁴⁰But Martha was distracted by all the preparations that had to be made. She came to him and asked, 'Lord, don't you care that my sister has left me to do the work by myself? Tell her to help me!' ⁴ 'Martha, Martha,' the Lord answered, 'you are worried and upset about many things, ⁴²but few*

---

[327] *Biblestudytools.com* ibid. (accessed 11 Jul 2013)

THE TRUTH SEEKER

things are needed—or indeed only one. Mary has chosen what is better, and it will not be taken away from her.[328]

The callousness and judgement, seen as normal by 'righteous' Christians, was still commonplace in my parent's time. When I was around ten years of age, I was taken to visit a lady in hospital who would have been in her early forties at the time. She died three or four years later. When I became an adult, her story was told to me.

This fine young woman of the Catholic faith was raped by her friend's fiancé at the place she resided. In her distress, she knocked on the doors of three of her neighbours. Each door was shut in her face. Callous as this behaviour sounds, it is understandable. From the early days of Roman Christianity, it was necessary to suppress and deny feelings of compassion and empathy in favour of judgement as guided by the Church. Her neighbours were likely afraid for themselves and their family as, just by being associated with someone who was now a fallen woman and had *asked for it*; they themselves could face being ostracised by the 'good' people of the community. As was to be expected in that time, the man suffered no consequences.

The young woman was ruined and therefore not a person to be seen with or associated with. She could never expect to marry, as she no longer met the ideal of being 'pure'. The trauma and her social disgrace had an impact on her mental state and she was admitted to a mental institution, which in those days were prisons and places of horror that often included violent shock treatments (electroconvulsive therapy). What she suffered during her time there can only be guessed at. At some time, it was decided by the medical experts that a frontal lobotomy would help her. This operation left her paralysed and she spent the rest of her life in a hospital bed.

In my own generation, young women I knew were advised by priests who believed in the sanctity of marriage above all else that they should remain in a marriage where the husband drank excessive amounts of alcohol and was verbally and physically abusive towards them and/or their children. The prevailing attitude at that time, which doubtless dated back through the centuries where women were considered to be inferior and the property of men, was that if they were abused by their husbands, it was because they deserved it. Therefore, the women, and not the men, were judged as the guilty party.

---

[328] *Biblestudytools.com* ibid.

In Australia, well-meaning Christians wished to 'save' children from those they judged to be heathens. Up until the 1960s, they were responsible for the removal an estimated 100,000 Aboriginal and Torres Strait Island children from their parents. These children are now referred to as 'The Stolen Generation'.[329] The attitudes of those times also resulted in taking of children from 'genetically poor' families and from unmarried mothers and placing them in institutional care.[330] Many of these institutions have since been found to have been places of physical and sexual abuse. I imagine that other Christian countries have a similar history as a result of ideas that had their foundation in Christian idealism.

Most of the Popes of Rome were pious men who sought only to fulfil the will of God as they saw it. The evil that was exposed as a consequence of the application of their teachings enabled great spiritual advancement. Many people in their previous lifetimes have lived through situations that were painful and yet illuminating as a result of following the rules of Christianity. As we look to the remarkable changes that have now taken place within religious communities, that in the main, today work towards a supportive and caring community, it is possible to see the good that has come out of the suffering. We, over many lifetimes, awaken slowly to what spirituality truly is. As we travel together through time, we follow many roads, each of which offers learning, especially those that take us along a road filled with difficulties and hardship.

If in the past we lived under Christian rule, we choose that experience in order to grow in spiritual awareness.

Karmic Consequences

It seems likely that during our past lives, many of us have lived through times of unjust, fearful and cruel religious practices. The insecurities, fears and guilt that we harbour today may encompass past lives steeped in being the recipient, or the perpetrator, of persecution, torture and death. It would have been almost impossible for any of us, during such times, to have avoided the influences of religion. Heretics and infidels have experienced the horrendous at the hands of the pious. Today we are the product of our past lives.

---

329 'Stolen generations fact sheet.' *Reconciliation Action Network.*
http://reconciliaction.org.au/nsw/education-kit/stolen-generations/ (accessed 10 Jul 2013)
330 'Senate Committees'. *Parliament of Australia* Ch. 2:10
www.aph.gov.au/Parliamentary_Business/Committees/Senate_Committees (accessed 10 Jul 2013)

THE TRUTH SEEKER

For many years, I suffered from neck problems and on one occasion when I visited my spiritual healer friend, Jane, I asked her to check my neck as it was bothering me more than usual. As I lay down, she placed her hands around the back of my neck and acknowledged the pain and discomfort I was experiencing. She then commented that she felt that my neck had been bent when I came through the birth canal and suggested that I had carried it forward from a previous life. She advised that she would look to it after she had worked on grounding my energy.

Rather than wait for her to finish, I decided I would attempt to recall the relevant lifetime and the original reason for the damage that caused my neck to bend forward. I had preconceived ideas about what I was likely to discover and fully expected to be confronted with a decapitation, hanging or some similarly gruesome experience. But I had asked about a life that related to my neck being bent forward, and as precision is the domain of the unconscious mind, that is what I got.

As I relaxed into a trance state, the first image that I saw was a woman in black with a black veil over her head. At first, I thought that I was looking at myself as a Muslim woman. But as the scene became clearer, I realised that the woman was a nun and she was kneeling down with her head bowed as she cleaned the stone floor of a church.

In line with the Christian teachings of the time, she saw herself as a worthless sinner. I could feel her extreme unhappiness, lack of self-esteem and overwhelming desire to be a 'good' person. This nun was a subservient, earlier me, who saw her only value in serving in whatever mundane capacity was required of her. So ingrained was the belief in her lack of worth, that she avoided all contact with others by lowering her head so eye contact did not occur. In this way, she isolated herself, convinced she had nothing to offer.

As Jane completed the grounding healing work on me, she returned her attention to my neck. I did not mention to her the past life recall I had just experienced. After allowing healing energy to pour over the affected area, and then ensuring that I was in a relaxed state, Jane guided me into a meditation and said, 'You will go through a doorway into a spacious area. The Karma Lords are there. You will now revoke all vows of poverty, chastity, and obedience.' In stunned silence, I hastened to mentally revoke the nun's vows. My studies had made me aware that such vows could have an impact on the soul of a person for many lifetimes. I was more than happy to purge the limiting programmes from my soul.

JOAN L BOLER

My devastated ego in that earlier time took many lifetimes to recover, but my state of mind in that time could not be attributed to the teachings of the Catholic Church alone, for I knew that each of us create and attract that which we experience. As the lifetime prior to my being a nun could likely offer insight into the cause of my total lack of self-worth, it was there that I looked.

It was the time of the Crusades. My growing years, as a male member of a fairly important family, exposed me to talk of God's holy war. To be one of God's warriors, fighting to take control of the Holy Lands from the infidels fired my young and idealistic imagination. At around sixteen or seventeen years of age, I headed off on a quest that seemed to my young mind to be of the greatest importance. Head held high, and very proud of myself and my lofty intentions, I left my home and made my way on my handsome white horse towards the Holy Lands.

Like most young men from a family of significance, my fighting skills had been honed, so I was not a novice in combat. My ideal of testing my skills in battle consisted of equal and fair fighting. But that was not all that I experienced. What I was also confronted with was the shocking and unholy slaughter of those who were considered infidels. With superior weaponry, and from their elevated position on their horses, the almost invincible crusaders invaded towns and villages and massacred defenceless men, women and children in the name of God. This was not something I could live with or remain part of.

Devastation, horror and guilt followed me throughout the remainder of my life. I became a priest and attempted to bring about a change in the attitude of the Church's hierarchy, but even though I took my pleas to the highest levels, they fell on deaf ears as I was met with fear or corruption at every turn. The guilt that plagued my soul carried forward into my next life. The deep shame I felt ensured I was receptive to the Church's teachings regarding the worthlessness of mortals who were considered sinners by nature.

It is not difficult to find in the world today, those who justify 'holy' wars and religious persecution. What lies within the hearts of those who leave pain and devastation in their wake in the name of their God? The motivation behind such is fear, which results in anger, hatred, and the desire for control. Mankind does not need religion in order to kill and destroy, but with religion, violent behaviour can be justified.

Each individual who works towards the elimination of that within, that brings about the manifestation in our lives of the appalling contributes towards the world becoming a better place for all to be. As spiritual awareness increases, the prejudice, hatred and lack of respect for others that has been woven into religious belief can be recognised and purged.

Spiritual Victory

Who are the victims that suffer in the unholy execution of the unethical demands of religious belief? The fear and the programming that cause good people to behave in ways that are both cruel and unspiritual soil the soul of both the recipient of abuse and the one who issues the command demanded by their belief. In spite of this, there is potential in adverse experiences for spiritual growth.

My conflict with the unspiritual attitudes of the powerful Catholic Church appeared again during what was probably the fifteenth century in Europe. My brief recollections of that lifetime focused on my rebellious attitude towards the dominant Christian control. As a well-bred woman in my twenties, my spiritual outlook conflicted totally with that of the Church, and, incensed by the wrongness of the forced strictures, the cruel punishments and the subterfuge necessary for survival, I felt compelled to speak out in spite of the danger of doing so. I was taken to a public area where I was ordered to place my head on a wooden block. Decapitation followed.

In the early sixteenth century, I was a well-educated young man of good birth. I lived in a city enjoying a pleasant lifestyle and was a recognised and respected young man about town. I freely expressed my opinions on the politics of the day, along with my ideas about religion—especially regarding the Catholic Church and what I perceived to be the double standards of the city's current bishop. The bishop was a heavy-set man who wore a cyclamen coloured biretta (a square cap, four cornered with tassel on the top) and the same coloured cassock. (Curiosity about the Bishop's attire led me to the library to check. I had thought the biretta and cassock to be a relatively recent mode of dress for bishops. However, research revealed that such ceremonial dress was around from the fifteen hundreds on.)

Due to the esteem I was held in by those around me, I did not expect the repercussions that my outspokenness might have brought a less known and less respected individual. But one day, when I was aged around thirty, I was passing through a country town where I was unknown to the locals. As I made my way across the town square around which shops displayed their wares, the only person I noted was a man on a horse-drawn cart bringing his goods to sell at the local shops.

JOAN L BOLER

Suddenly, I was grabbed from behind and my hands were tied behind my back. The two men who had apprehended me escorted me to a stone building that belonged to the Church. I was placed in a private cell which was to become my home over the next ten years. To the front of this cell were bars, while on the right, too high for me to see out of, was a small barred window, and on the floor was a straw pallet. The bishop who had given the orders for my capture and subsequent incarceration ensured that my disappearance remained a mystery to those who would have rescued me. The only time I was removed from the cell was to receive the lash. It would seem that the bishop wished to change my thinking and, to his way of thinking, save my soul. I refused to recant my views or show repentance for them, as my intuitive understanding of the falseness of idealism in religious belief had been carved into my soul lifetimes before when I had, in my naivety, joined the Crusades. Finally, ten years after being taken, my soul left my weakened and tormented body as it collapsed like a piece of flotsam, lying half on and half off the straw pallet that had been my bed.

Another lifetime once again picked up the religious theme and ensured that the experiences of the previous lifetimes were to become the basis for spiritual growth. This life was in Europe in the latter half of the nineteenth century. I was a young girl who at around six years of age was placed in the hands of nuns. My well-dressed mother seemed to have little interest in my welfare, and after a while her visits ceased. I had no knowledge or memory of a father. I imagine I could have been illegitimate. By the time I reached my teens and began to think for myself, I came into conflict with the strictures, boundaries and beliefs that surrounded me.

I wanted to be free to live my life as I wished, but I was expected to become a nun. When I rebelled they saw fit to have me exorcised and literally dragged me before the priest who performed the ritual cleansing. It seemed I had no say in my future, and my rebellion at my lack of freedom of choice resulted in my spirit eventually being broken. In spite of this, I knew that the nuns, who I loved and who had been my family for most of my childhood, cared deeply for me. Over the next ten years, and mainly because of their loving concern, I surrendered, and by the time I was twenty-eight I had become a nun. This was not a lengthy lifetime. At around forty, I died of an illness that caused me to have difficulty breathing and left me with the feeling I was suffocating—very much aligning with the emotional suffocation I experienced throughout that lifetime as a result of my lack of freedom of choice.

The remarkable aspect of this lifetime was that sometime during the process I went through, I developed humility. This was not the sometimes-promoted 'humility' that comes from the total annihilation of self-esteem, the like of which I had experienced when living as a nun many lifetimes earlier. Rather, I experienced a humility that assesses but does not judge right or wrong, good or bad, and that bows to the greater power of love in spite of the perhaps misguided motives of those seeking to control.

It was not until my current lifetime that the sequence of events that commenced with my experiences at the Crusades and resulted in loss of life or freedom in a number of lifetimes, that I finally removed the judgement from my soul and allowed myself to be free to experience and live my life without the heavy guilt of the past. As a consequence, I now find it easy to forgive the shortcomings and errors of judgement of myself and of others.

The horrors and difficulties of lifetimes of confronting religious fanaticism, has, step-by-step, changed my soul and brought me wisdom regarding that which is truly spiritual. Through learning the dangers and wrongness of beliefs that demand killing people of another race and creed in the name of God, recognising the judgement within that was directed towards the Church hierarchy that dissolved into humility led to the love and forgiveness of myself for own actions. In spite of all the suffering, the barriers to happiness within my soul have been, for the most part, removed. This new and fragile awareness needs refining and reinforcing until it infiltrates all aspects of my being.

Belief

Does religious belief encourage spiritual growth or retard it? This is not a simple question for it is clear that religious belief can result in both great and admirable actions and conversely in actions that are unimaginably cruel.

Hinduism has been around for about five thousand years and teaches a way of living rather than requirements of belief. Buddhism began in the fifth century BCE in India and also doesn't demand adherence to a belief. This allows for the possibility that as new knowledge comes to light, both scientifically and spiritually, there is no conflict, just new awareness. This does not mean that communities do not develop their own beliefs, simply that the religions do not demand them. Both these religions teach reincarnation. Consideration of a process of spiritual evolution through many lifetimes is denied to most of the followers of the major 'belief' religions.

JOAN L BOLER

With over two billion members worldwide, Christianity is the world's largest religion followed by Islam with over one and a half billion.[331] As multidimensional beings, we travel the long road from the base to the spiritual, gaining an ever-increasing ability to penetrate and align with the higher spiritual dimensions both during life and after death. The greater design reveals that no one person can develop spiritual awareness in just one lifetime, because each of us learns through individual experience and therefore great periods of time are necessary.

The 'belief' religions that insist that we live only one earthly life favour the idea that those 'chosen' and/or faithful to a 'belief' will be 'saved'. Those who wish to be among the chosen or saved look to knowledge that can provide them with guarantees. Three major religions search for, and find, many of their beliefs in the Bible. Even though the followers of the belief religions may be in agreement with each other and their trust in what has been written in earlier times, they cannot promise spiritual truth in God's name. Gandhi reiterates to those ready to listen, the truth about belief. *An error does not become truth by reason of multiplied propagation, nor does truth become error because nobody sees it.*[332] Life itself, as designed by the Creator, provides evidence as to what is and isn't true.

Each belief places a condition on the truth and therefore creates a wall inside the mind that rejects all that contradicts it. Each wall of belief builds a prison for the believer, hiding truth and denying freedom of thought and action. Belief is the panacea for those who place their welfare in the hands of others. Its price is limitation, loss of freedom and spiritual blindness. Spirituality does not depend on the Old or the New Testaments of the Bible, rather it is found through love. Until one is ready to question the very essence of belief, to discard the *knowing* of belief and replace it with possibilities, maybes and maybe nots, and in fact the unknown, spiritual truths sought will be hidden.

In an age when, in many countries religious belief is a choice and not a requirement of survival, each individual is responsible for the beliefs they allow to be part of their world. However, those who are indoctrinated as children, or forced to accept and live by the moral rules and beliefs of others, suffer the consequences as though they themselves were personally responsible for their creation. No incorrect or negative religious belief could survive without the silent will of its followers.

---

[331] 'Worldwide Adherents of All Religions.' *Encyclopaedia Britannica*. www.britannica.com (accessed 25 Nov 2014)
[332] Young India 1924-1926 (1927), p. 1285.

THE TRUTH SEEKER

While I, or anyone else for that matter, could provide arguments that contradict what is written in this chapter by simply quoting a conflicting verse from the Bible, such arguments cannot, on their own provide proof for any point of view. The Bible records the myths, legends and beliefs of the Jewish people from around 1200 BCE to the first century CE. It cannot be proven that the claimed authors for the scriptures, are the true source, nor can it be shown that the information it contains has been accurately transcribed and reported. The truth of historic events needs to be proven through physical evidence while statements made on the nature of spiritual love require confirmation by those who are aligned with it, and statements made regarding the spiritual kingdoms can only be defined by those who have been there. If one truly searches for the truth rather than confirmation of what they believe, or would like to believe, truth will find them.

> **Belief and superstition walk hand in hand. While the religious person who is righteous, follows what they believe is the law, the spiritual person follows the heart, and therein lays the reason that righteousness can lead to callous behaviour and the unspeakable, while when love and trust are the rulers within, justice and compassion follow.**

Religion – The Future

All religions are based on an, often ancient, accumulation of knowledge put forward and recorded by members of a race or group of people who seek the spiritual. While there is much of true spirituality to be found within the belief religions, there is also that which is neither truth nor spiritual. As the masses become more educated, better informed and more aware, the future of belief religions is brought into question. Can they adapt quickly enough or will they disintegrate? Could Christianity lead the way in removing the blindfolds and releasing the faithful from the bondage that belief has placed on them inhibiting true spirituality?

Today in most religions, the teachings promote goodness and spiritual growth, and many blossom under the umbrella their religion provides as its adherents work together in co-operation and kindness. As we move away from the stifling controls of the past, we move towards a society of much healthier emotions, and therefore with a much greater potential for happiness and fulfilment. As people experience the opportunity to explore and enjoy life, they become kinder and more tolerant. Today, more than ever during the past two thousand years, people in many countries are living in ways that reflect the teachings of Jesus.

In a time when truth is opening the eyes of the masses, it would be a great loss to humanity if all the wisdoms of ancient times were cast aside. The sharing and appreciation of the beautiful loving teachings to be found in the Bible bring nourishment to the soul. The very deep reverence with which most of the religious follow their various rituals, and the demands their religions make on them, reveals a deep love for that of the spirit. So strong and deep can religious faith be, that history is overflowing with those who have through their own choice given their lives for their beliefs.

In a world of diversity of souls, there are great souls that stand out as an example to us all. It is not only in the past that such souls existed. They have been around throughout time, and are very much present today.

In recent times, we can look to Mohandas Karamchand Gandhi (1869–1948), better known as Mahatma (Great Soul) Gandhi. Gandhi was a political and spiritual leader. He worked to change the religious class-consciousness of India at the time, to remove the demeaning attitude towards the untouchables and to increase the rights of women. In his efforts to free India from English rule, he endorsed civil disobedience rather than violent action.

Mother Teresa (1910–1997) was a nun in the Roman Catholic Church and another indomitable spirit of our times. Her capacity to love was boundless, and in her deep concern for the welfare of the poorest of the poor, she founded missionaries all over India and later in one hundred and twenty-three countries. She worked with Catholics and non-Catholics alike, and looked to the welfare of the sick including those with AIDS and leprosy. For the dying, she offered the comfort of the religious rites and needs of their own faith. In 1979, in recognition of her far-reaching and selfless efforts, she was awarded the Nobel Peace Prize.

Neither of these people was perfect and both had their critics, but undeniably they were spiritual giants who had a positive impact on the lives of millions of people.

Among the great souls alive today, who can deny the spirituality of His Holiness, Tenzin Gyatso, the fourteenth Dalai Lama who was awarded the Nobel Peace Prize in 1989? Constantly looking for ways in which to bring about peace in our time, he meets with people of all religions and their leaders, and expresses kindness and love with every word while his beautiful spiritual energy shines through. This wise, gentle, and delightful

THE TRUTH SEEKER

soul leaves in his wake simple teachings that align with those of the great teachers of the past. Among his wisdoms is, *There is no need for temples, no need for complicated philosophies. My brain and my heart are my temples; my philosophy is kindness.*[333]

Walking among us are spiritual heroes who quietly go about their lives for the most part neither seeking nor receiving recognition. Spiritually evolved souls are everywhere, expressing a love that includes compassion and kindness.

That which is spiritual is universal and the rightful inheritance of all souls. As we move forward into a new era of information relating to our own identity and our place in the universe, this greater understanding and knowledge can begin to build a bridge between the differing religions and therefore between nations.

Spiritually, there are no barriers between man and man except those man creates through the manmade boundaries of beliefs, be they religious or otherwise. By opening the heart and mind to those of different faiths and spiritual beliefs in both the East and the West, by becoming familiar with the basic shared truths and considering the different 'masks' and 'faces' of the spiritual beings of other religions, one can add richness and depth to spiritual awareness. Through tolerance, sharing, and respect, we all can learn from each other. In order to have peace in our time, or in the future, the religions of the world need to lose not their spiritual identity, but their manmade beliefs.

My explorations into my past lives over a long periods of time have enabled me retain in-depth knowledge of some lives and random glimpses into others. I have seen myself both as male and female, and living lives that seem to cover every race on the planet. I have experienced a life as an Egyptian boy child, seen myself as a large African male, lived as a young boy in India and been the Arab leader of a nomad people. I have recalled a variety of Asian lives and known America from a lifetime as an Indian, I have regained memories of a Greek lifetime along with lives lived in England and Europe. Needless to say, I have experienced many and varied religions.

Through living and experiencing many ways of worship, and the many beliefs of the differing religions of the world, I developed through their disciplines and gained insight through the various approaches to spirituality.

---

[333] Pibum, Sidney, *The Dalai Lama: Policy of Kindness*, Snow Lion Publications, New York, 1990, p. 52.

JOAN L BOLER

Much of my character and strength, compassion and love of humanity, and my spiritual awareness, has developed through experiencing the sometimes erroneous teachings, as well as the spiritual disciplines, of the various religions.

Religions are manmade harbours for the people, and have the potential to provide an environment of community interaction and support and be a source of spiritual knowledge for those who seek it. Within each religion are those spiritual individuals who have the opportunity and ability to work within their religion to purify its ideals so only the spiritual remains. To that end, it is hoped each religion can rid its identity of the beliefs born of fear and the misguided superficial idealism introduced by earlier religious hierarchies. In the relinquishing of all belief, truth can be discovered.

No matter which religion, if any, is followed the majority of humanity seeks the truth. An elusive part of us is looking for answers. Our search for truth began way back in time, and we continue that search through many lifetimes, gradually discarding what we find to be false. We have lifetimes in which to continue our search, and although we may pause for a while, caught in an apparent safety net of blind belief, the deeper purpose of our search will continue until life enables us to confront that which is not truth and takes us closer to the great happiness and amazing realities that are to be encountered through what is our true identity.

It is, I like to think, time to teach the way for each and every person wishing to do so, to become a prophet and Master, to have power over the physical, and to spread the potent power of love and truth into all the regions and religions of the world. While great courage is needed in order to let go of belief and its underlying fears, if there is love within, there is courage. For those who seek the pinnacles, who would leave the 'safe' behind, the journey promises the amazing, the awesome, the fulfilling and the truth. *No bird soars too high if he soars with his own wings.* [334]

---

[334] William Blake, Proverbs of Hell, line 15.

Chapter 15

Mysticism

Great indeed is the sublimity of the Creative, to which all beings owe their beginning and which permeates all heaven.

Lao Tzu[335]

Mystical Heritage

Profound knowledge of the spiritual nature of the cosmos has throughout the ages been bequeathed to humanity through a stream of mystics who continue to emerge to this day. The inter-dimensional travellers, both in the past and in the present, of the old religions and the new have journeyed, through expanded states of awareness into the dimensions beyond the physical. These are the prophets and adepts of the ancient and modern worlds. The knowledge reported in the past, at least in those parts of the world in which the information has been recorded, is for the most part the same information that is being revealed by those in our own time. The ancient Sanskrit writings that describe the earth as having many planes of existence and the Hebrew Kabbalah that explains creation are just two of many ancient sources that are being confirmed by modern mystics.

In the kingdoms beyond the physical, beings of light of varying degrees of complexity and intensity, exist and evolve through the multifaceted, invisible dimensions of the cosmos. From the denser beings that border the physical, to those in the higher dimensions where the purest forms of consciousness are expressing the spiritual—all are part of the divine creation and the divine plan. The permanent residents of those kingdoms that are described by their witnesses as gods, devas, angels, or elementals, also share these realms with those humans who are, at present, no longer living in the physical. There is a considerable difference between not only each being,

---

[335] Wilhelm, Helmut (ed.), Lao Tzu, *The I Ching or Book of Changes,* Princeton University Press, New York, 2011, Book III p. 370.

but in the accumulated experience that has combined to make them what they are.

In this day and age, mysticism and the experiences of the mystics are studied by a range of academics, many of whom recognise the consistencies and probable validity of such experiences. Although this area of study holds many mysteries that are yet to be unravelled, and some answers must be left to the future, that does not mean there is not an abundance of knowledge already available to the seeker. The consistency of the knowledge imparted, much of which aligns with my own experiences even though expressed in different ways, provides considerable evidence that most of the information is, when not decorated with belief, valid.

Secrets of the Cosmos

As we look to the mystics of our time, their writings bring clarity to ancient texts and truths that have in the world of Christendom been hidden for millennia with only a privileged few gaining access to the sacred knowledge, in many cases, through breaching the boundaries of the physical world, with or without the help of esoteric teachings like those found in the Kabbalah. The knowledge imparted by such mystics frequently goes beyond my own experiences, and yet links into and compliments what I know to be true. Their teachings enable me to form a more complete picture of the way in which the cosmos works.

There are many, especially in recent times, who have written of what they have learned of the higher dimensions and the source of life. One such person, Geoffrey Hodson, has left very detailed records of his experiences in the non-physical kingdoms.

Geoffrey Hodson (1886-1983) philosopher, teacher, yogi, mystic, clairvoyant and prolific writer was a British subject who spent time serving with distinction in the British army during the First World War, at which time he witnessed the misery caused by war. A spiritual and humanitarian man, Hodson wished to advance his own awareness and raise the consciousness of humankind. His journey led him to the Theosophical Society and the yogi practices of the East that in turn led to his illumination and learning through the teacher archangels and the Masters. His ministry included becoming a priest in the Liberal Catholic Church, travelling the world three times giving of his knowledge and writing over four hundred articles and over sixty books and booklets.[336] His clairvoyant abilities were tested by scientists, three of whom attested to his extra-sensory abilities.[337]

In his book 'The Kingdom of the Gods', Hodson records how his knowledge and experience of the non-physical dimensions commenced with a series of mystical experiences where he interacted with a god-like angelic being that revealed advanced knowledge and understanding to him. He was exposed to knowledge of a cosmos filled with a myriad of conscious life forms and beings which are continuously created through the emanations from the Infinite, Divine Will of the Logos or God that is the Source, the Divine Law and Creator of the manifest universes and is all that is. Hodson explains that in order to manifest, the God consciousness, through reflection, enables a positive-negative second state in which lies the male-female potential, which in turn allows a third state—the process of propelling all the ideas and archetypes from this three-in-one state through seven rays from which intelligent shining sub-rays are emitted. This, according to Hodson, is the process of creation, which is repeated throughout the universes, galaxies and solar systems, and their physical and non-physical worlds. Eventually the process of creation is reversed and all return to the source.

Hodson tells of a complex and diverse hierarchy of the conscious beings belonging to our solar system. These include solar archangels and planetary archangels that oversee the hierarchies of omnipresent or all-pervading (by whatever name they are called) gods, angelic hosts, shining ones or devas that have a human-like form. Each of the god-like beings has a purpose that usually involves the process of the evolution of conscious life on the planet. A variety of angelic bodies oversees differing facets of the lives of humans, the spiritual aspects of which are presided over by an archangel. There are archangels to oversee the established countries, while the administration of the karmic law falls to the Angels of Karma. Archangels and angelic hosts, along with the Masters, play a part in overseeing all the religions on the planet, and in each building that is dedicated to the god or gods, angels are to be found. There are gods of the mountains, gods of the oceans and gods of the land, which may encompass a myriad of conscious entities, including elementals. Since physical objects such as rocks have a non-physical conscious counterpart, they too are included. There is nothing on our planet devoid of a conscious existence. And all the kingdoms are presided over by angelic/god beings.

---

[336] Keidan, Bill; 'Geoffrey Hodson—Introduction.' www.geoffreyhodson.com (accessed 13 Mar 2013)
[337] 'Clairvoyant-Investigations—Science'.www.geoffreyhodson.com (accessed 14 March 2013)

The degree to which these great beings are involved in the life of humans is extensive, and just as nature spirits are intimately involved in the growth of all types of plant life (Chapter Thirteen 'The Invisible Creatures of the Earth'), so too are angels involved in the formation and growth of the human embryo and its physical, emotional, mental and etheric bodies. From conception to birth, they play a role in the construction and formation of the future housing for the individual soul's entry once again into the physical world. In each human born, the macrocosmic is reflected in the microcosmic.[338]

Jesus taught, *Be perfect, therefore, as your heavenly Father is perfect.* Matthew 5:48-48 (NIV).[339] In confirmation of this, Hodson, who was a Christian throughout his life, stated that human beings are progressing towards perfection through lifetimes on earth, and although Christians are taught that the only perfect human being was Jesus, there are others who are also Masters. Hodson himself communed with and learned from the Masters, and throughout history and in the different cultures, there have been those who like Jesus had divine visitations—for example, the Persian prophet Zarathustra and Siddhartha Gautama the Supreme Buddha—along with the many men and women who have displayed superhuman powers and reached, or almost reached, perfection.[340] For the serious seeker, Hodson's work is worth researching.

The mystic's goal is to become an adept or Master. Access to the cosmic mysteries through expanded states of consciousness is real, and the knowledge gained is irrefutable, but this does not automatically mean that the mystic knows all the answers and is therefore infallible. Since we live in an extremely complex universe, there is a variety of ways in which information is perceived and the degrees of perception and awareness employed or reachable at any given time can vary considerably. All humans have opinions, including those who are mystics. Just as in science there is so much that is supposition based on available knowledge, in a universe so vast and complex, the mystics can draw their own conclusions and have their own ideas about what they have learned and experienced.

---

[338] Hodson, Geoffrey, *The Kingdom of the Gods*; ibid.
[339] *Biblestudytools.com* ibid. (accessed 14 Mar 2013)
[340] *The inner government;* www.geoffreyhodson.com (accessed 14 Mar 2013)

Kabbalah and Creation

It would seem that information on creation has been around for a long time. Believed to precede the Jewish Kabbalah, the claimed sacred geometry of the 'Flower of Life' (which is made up of circles that represent the source and the stages of creation), have been found in both Assyria from around 645 BCE, and Egypt no earlier than 535 BCE.[341] The symbols that make up the Flower of Life have found their way into Pagan, Hermetic, Wiccan, Christian and Jewish religions and represent common concepts of creation.[342]

The Jewish Kabbalah (to receive) is based mainly on the 'Zohar' and has a history that is thought to date back to the early days of Judaism. The Kabbalah contains Jewish understanding of the esoteric, mystical knowledge that seeks to explain the mysteries of the divine, the creation process, the spiritual purpose of creation, and the methods by which that purpose can be achieved by those on a spiritual pathway. The knowledge revealed in the Kabbalah is in line with the teachings of the mystics, including Hodson, and incorporates the understanding of astrology.

The Kabbalah's 'Tree of Life' describes creation. The following are the ten aspects of the Tree of Life that reveal the creation and the metaphysical workings of the universe.

1) Kether: The Crown — Is all and In all. 'I am that I am' Infinite, intelligence, power, light, creator—**(God is existence, not a being).**
2) Chockmar: Wisdom (force) — Reflects divine qualities of the Crown creating division. Cosmic maleness.
3) Binah: Intuition/understanding (form) — Primordial wisdom; the womb of life; cosmic femaleness.

These first three branches form the trinity that is the basis of all creation.

Knowledge — (branch without number, sound or colour) Change from force to form.

4) Chesed: Mercy/abundance/greatness — Formation of matter; will to live; expansion and abundance.

---

[341] Furlong, David. *The Osirion and the Flower of Life* – Article by Malcolm Stewart
[342] 'Flower of Life.' *Wikipedia*, http://en.wikipedia.org/wiki/Flower_of_Life (accessed 17 Jun 2014)

5) Geburah: Strength/severity/justice — Governing principle; awareness of right and wrong; counteracts evil.
6) Tiphareth: Glory/beauty — Love that connects the spiritual to the physical.
7) Netzach: Victory/firmness — Intuition; unconscious awareness and feelings; desire. Artistic and imaginative.
8) Hod: Majesty/glory in splendour — Intelligence; discrimination and rationality. Scientific and intellectual.
9) Yesod: The Foundation — Purifies intelligence; brings about unity.
10) Malkuth: Sovereignty/the kingdom — Manifestation completed as it brings about the merging of spirit, soul, mind and body.

The Tree of Life describes the process of life creating, through Itself, the many. Each of the branches of the tree, with the exception of the first, is associated with planetary influences and interlinks with the knowledge in astrology. While the Kabbalah represents the evolution of spiritual understanding in Judaism, from the twelfth century onwards, its wisdoms attracted followers of Christianity and Islam.[343][344][345][346]

It would seem that in order to create and experience the many possible aspects of what can be, the Source of All that Is, began a process of creation that included ideas of beings whose consciousness was separate from, and yet still connected to, the original source. The human was just one of many of the self-aware conscious beings that come into existence to inhabit a cosmos of universes, galaxies and worlds.

On this planet at least, most human beings have lost awareness that each and every person is a part of 'All That Is' with the result that we are always seeking to become reconnected to the source and to achieve the ability to express, through the individual soul, the spiritual being that we are. To that end, each of us can find our own pathway through love, creativity and learning, and in so doing, express all that we are and can be, both as a soul and as spirit, and to see the many faces of God in those around us. At first, we descend from the divine and then we, as ideas, ascend back to the divine through many lifetimes.

---

[343] Rich, Tracey R. '*Kabbalah and Jewish Mysticism.*' www.jewfaq.org/kabbalah.htm (accessed 5 Oct 2013)

[344] Afilalo, Rabbi Raphael. '*Authentic Kabbalah—The history of Kabbalah*' www.kabbalah5.com/history_of_the_Kabbalah.htm (accessed 5 Oct 2013)

[345] Williams-Heller, Ann. *Kabbalah – Your path to freedom*, Theosophical Publishing House Illinois USA, 1990.

[346] 'Kabbalah', *Jewish Virtual Library*. www.jewishvirtuallibrary.org/jsource/Judaism/kabbalah.html (accessed 5 Oct 2013)

THE TRUTH SEEKER

Defining the Mystical Experience

Studies into mysticism reveal that many people, no matter their race or creed, lay claim to having had spiritual experiences. The Stanford Encyclopedia of Philosophy reports that in defining the mystical experience, religious visions, out-of-body experiences, telepathy, precognition and clairvoyance are not included in research by philosophers into mystical experiences. While interpretations of the experience can be confused by both the experiencer and the philosopher examining the experience, when 'explaining away' is taken out of the equation, it is possible to recognise and consider consistent similarities. One of those similarities is the realisation by mystics that the purpose of transcendental experience is to help bring about human transformation.[347]

There are a number of different approaches taken by philosophers when defining the mystical experience. For example, Walter Terence Stace (1886-1967) worked at Princeton University as a professor of philosophy from 1932 to 1955. Stace[348] separates mystical experiences into two basic types—'extrovert' and 'introvert'—that are to be found *in all cultures, religions, periods, and social conditions*. Another approach is put forward by Zaehne, who sees an additional overall experience. A gifted linguist, Robert Charles Zaehner (1913–1974) was a British academic who specialised in Eastern religions and wrote books on mysticism. According to Zaehner,[349] there are basically three ways of experiencing mystical consciousness:

1) That experience where consciousness is extended outside the self to experience a oneness with nature. (This is the type of experience I encountered in my previous life as an American Indian shaman. Also, in this lifetime, when I sought to change the weather, I once again became one with the energies of nature and then took a conscious, active role in redirecting the storm.)

2) An experience that reveals undistinguishable unity with all that transcends space and time.

---

[347] 'Mysticism'. *Stanford Encyclopaedia of Philosophy*. http://plato.stanford.edu/entries/mysticism/ (accessed 23 Aug 2012)
[348] Stace, Walter T, 1961, *Mysticism and Philosophy*, Macmillan. London, 1960. The Teachings of the Mystics, New York and Scarborough: *New American Library*.
[349] Zaehner, R C , *Mysticism, sacred and profane*, Oxford University Press, New York, 1961.

3) An experience of a God-like being where awareness of self is retained. (Both of the following spiritual experiences are of this type.)

Of the many ways in which a spiritual experience can happen, there are some that allow access to the higher realms and its truths, some that involve visits from the residents of the higher realms and still others that transport one to the higher realms in the ethereal body, while the most profound experiences leave behind both the physical and the etheric bodies.

In the following experience, I remained totally in my body while Spirit enveloped me.

Paul came into my life not long after my then fourteen-year-old son, had been taken to live in another state by his father. In spite of promises that my son could visit during the school holidays, over the next two years I had very limited telephone contact with him and did not see him at all. I was devastated. Paul's gentle and loving nature, along with his incredible sense of humour, brought a ray of sunshine in my life. One night Paul called in for a visit. Seemingly out of the blue, he advised me that he thought we needed a break from each other and that perhaps we should go out with other people.

I hadn't seen it coming. The emotional blow hit my stomach and felled my soul.

Silently I screamed, 'GOD HELP ME!'

Immediately a powerful loving being's energy surrounded me and merged with my soul. The love that poured into me brought about a feeling of great happiness and bliss. 'Would you like a cup of tea?' I asked Paul. And for the next hour or so, we laughed and chatted happily. I was aware of the beautiful loving being for a period of three days as its potent love penetrated, surrounded, strengthened and nurtured me.

Was it God the Supreme Being who came to my aid, or was my call answered by the god that governs and is omnipresent in this world? The answer to this question is not important. I only had to call and my prayer was immediately answered. I suspect that all gods, by whatever name and from whichever religion, are an aspect of and fulfil the will of the Supreme Creator.

THE TRUTH SEEKER

As I look back on that incredible experience and the exquisite perfection of its love, I wondered about Jesus and his comments about his relationship with God, (assuming his remarks were accurately reported and translated). In John 10:30 (NIV) Jesus said, *I and the Father are one*.[350] Did Jesus constantly feel the presence of God in his life through the love that penetrated his soul and therefore knew that what he taught was in alignment with God's purpose? Or did he simply mean that a loving attitude caused his spiritual thinking to become aligned with that of the Creator?

In the following experience, which was the most awesome in my life to date, I travelled to a very high spiritual dimension leaving behind my physical *and* etheric bodies.

After a year's separation from my husband, I had returned to my marriage. My desire to do what was best for my family superseded my own needs and wishes, and I fell back on my earlier religious and social programming that included such ideas as *children are better off with both parents.*

It was only a matter of months before I realised my mistake. Instead of the improved situation I had anticipated, the still self-absorbed man, who was again drinking heavily, was now experiencing alcoholic blackouts. These blackouts resulted in behaviour that lacked any indication of the thinking mind and often revealed a lack of ability to relate to or recognise the physical objects in his environment. On one occasion, he twisted the laundry tub tap spout and managed to rip it off—the torn metal revealing the considerable strength and determination involved.

Although in returning to my marriage I believed I had acted in what I had thought was the *right and responsible* way, my outlook was wrong and I was about to be enlightened. On this particular night, I was weighed down with concerns for my family.

Suddenly I woke to find myself in an expanded state of awareness that was still 'me' but included awareness of my spiritual self. I was no longer in, or had any sense of my physical body or even that of my etheric body. I was pure spirit energy! I was light! I was love so great and powerful that the beauty and endlessness of it defies description. I was power and nothing was beyond my power to create. I had unlimited intelligence and wisdom and was in communion with a great loving being whose absolute love

---

[350]Biblestudytools.com Ibid. (accessed 23 Aug 2012)

surrounded and permeated all I was. No physical experience comes close to the blissful state I was in.

Three questions emerged from my soul—no conscious thought authored them. The thought that expressed the first question revealed my deep concern and feeling of responsibility for the immature man in my life. The moment the question formed, I knew I needed no answer; I instantly recalled I had known the answer before I entered this lifetime. I knew that spiritually I was not responsible for him, and that the welfare of his soul was under the care of the greater spiritual forces.

The second question focused on the emotional pain that had invaded my life off and on (mostly on) over many years. The answer took me another three years to digest and accept, as the implications of the knowledge imparted were foreign to my way of thinking at that time.

The pain was not important. What was important was that through the pain, I was learning and growing, becoming wiser, learning to appreciate myself, learning boundaries, and where to place my trust and where my responsibilities really lay. This lesson, I later learned, was indicated in my astrological chart, which revealed I had a Pisces South Node (unconditional and romantic love that lacks judgement and boundaries) and the lesson of my Virgo North Node (discrimination through looking deeper to the motives of self and others).

The third question I can no longer recall.

There was no way to gauge time whilst I was in this state. Gradually my awareness returned to my physical mantle, and I left the realm of weightlessness, perfect harmony and happiness.

In the aftermath, I was amazed I had never before realised how uncomfortable and heavy the human body is. My mind found it difficult to believe the experience I had had—and yet there was no question it was real. During the next three days, nothing could diminish my heightened awareness of the love that continued to surround me. Of course, the love is always there, but the more I became caught up in day-to-day living, the less I was able to sense its presence.

I cannot give my awesome experience to others—I can only relate it and say that this experience changed my soul at its deepest levels. Fear, that most limiting energy, no longer had reason to reside in the corners of my soul.

THE TRUTH SEEKER

In spite of the understanding gained from the experience, I did not immediately leave the marriage. At that time, my husband had managed to run up thousands of dollars in debt, and I felt conscience bound to help him clear that debt before leaving. As time went on, it became obvious that no matter what I did, I was never going to stop the rash business and spending habits that continued to take us deeper into debt.

Over the three years following my experience, I digested the knowledge I had gained and began to realise that instead of being in a position to help my husband through being a loving, supporting and caring person, I was an enabler in that the responsibilities he neglected, I took on. Additionally, I began to question whether I was contributing to his feelings of inferiority that led to behaviour where he was constantly attempting to build his own self-confidence—at the expense of mine.

I began to reverse the programming of the past and threw away roles that had been drummed into me since childhood. I was not less intelligent, less capable or less worthy because I was female. My needs should not be always sacrificed to the wishes and needs of others. I was not sinful in the eyes of God. From that time on, I ceased to see myself as unimportant and insignificant. I now knew myself to be a beautiful and incredible being and recognised the need to expect I be treated with consideration and respect by myself as well as by others. I recognised my responsibility lay not in putting others' needs ahead of my own, but in looking to my own well-being and happiness, and that included seeing to the well-being of those dependent on me. As my outlook aligned itself with what I had learned, I became free to follow my dreams, to express the truth of who and what I was through my intelligence, creativity, knowledge, sensitivity and capacity to love.

The experience raised many questions within me, but I was at a loss as to how to go about finding answers. Fortunately, although at that time I was a novice in attracting through the mind, a few days after this experience, I was walking down George Street in Sydney when I passed the Angus and Robertson book shop and saw a book on display called 'The Highest State of Consciousness'.[351] The book consisted of a collection of articles that researched and looked into the spiritual experience from differing perspectives. This amazing book provided me with not only the answers that I sought, but also brought me a vast resource of valuable information.

---

[351] White, John (ed.), *The Highest State of Consciousness*, Anchor Books, New York, 1972.

Through reading that book, I came to realise that many people had had similar and different experiences to mine, and that considerable research had been done in this area.

Like the iceberg that reveals only a small aspect of its true dimensions while most of its majesty is hidden, normal human awareness is dwarfed by the extent and power of its spiritual identity within.

All That Is

What is God and what is Its relationship to humankind?

As a child, I was taught about God the Father in the heavens who looked down upon me and judged all I said and did. As a young adult, my ideas evolved and I perceived God to be a mysterious and supreme being way beyond my realm of knowledge and experience, a being I imagined must possess an infinite capacity for love. This understanding was confirmed by my spiritual experiences.

There is a common idea presented by mystics that all that is, is God, and that God can express Itself through each and every sentient being, everywhere and at all times. In order to understand this possibility it is necessary to accept that there are layers to our consciousness, just as there are layers to our body that incorporate all the dimensions. In consideration of the various states of consciousness I have experienced, while each has been amazing, it seems to me that the possibility of a greater expansion of consciousness on my part could enable awareness that incorporates All That Is. Logic says that if the Creator God is everywhere and in all that is, and science says everything is connected, then separation is a created illusion. If that is so, each conscious being is also God albeit experiencing for the moment a separate consciousness.

That consciousness, as it evolves and begins to express that which is of a spiritual nature, is expressing that which is God. This seems to be the meaning of the following statement by Jesus. Luke 18:19 **(NIV)** [19]*'Why do you call me good?' Jesus answered. 'No one is good except God alone.'*[352]

The following quotes appear to reflect the awareness gained from the second experience described by Zaehner, which I have not personally

---

[352] *Biblestudytools.com* ibid. (accessed 11 Jul 2013)

THE TRUTH SEEKER

experienced—that of being one with everything. Over time and even until today, there have been mystics who have claimed to be one with God in a variety of ways.

> *He who experiences the unity of life sees his own Self in all beings, and all beings in his own Self, and looks on everything with an impartial eye; he who sees Me in everything and everything in Me, him shall I never forsake, nor shall he lose Me.*[353] ~ *from the Bhagavad Gita—discussion between Pandava prince Arjuna and the god-king Krishna. (written fifth to second century BCE).*[354][355]

> [21]*That all of them may be one, Father, just as you are in me and I am in you. May they also be in us so that the world may believe that you have sent me. John 17:21 (NIV)*[356] ~ *Jesus (1ˢᵗ century CE) — Jewish Preacher and founder of Christianity.*

> *I am Not, but the Universe is my Self.*[357] ~ *Shih-t'ou (700-790 CE) — Japanese Zen Master.*

> *I am God.*[358] ~ *al-Husayn al-Hallaj (858-922 CE) — Islamic Sufi Mystic*

> *The eye by which I see God is the same eye by which God sees me.*[359] ~ *Meister Eckhart (1260-1327) — German Theologian, Mystic and Philosopher.*

> *To know God and to live is the same thing. God is Life.*[360] ~ *Leo Tolstoy (1828 –1910) —Russian writer.*

> *Now I am nimble, now I fly, now I see myself under myself, now a god dances within me.*[361] ~ *Friedrich Nietzsche (1844-1900) — 'Thus Spake Zarathustra'*

---

[353] *Bhagavad Gita* tr. Shri Purohit Swami.
[354] Fowler, Jeaneane D, *The Bhagavad Gita: A Text and Commentary for Students*, Sussex Academy Press, Eastbourne, 2012, p. 2.
[355] Upadhyaya, Kashi Nath, Early Buddhism and the Bhagavadgītā, Motilal Banarsidass Publ. 1998, p. 16.
[356] Biblestudytools.com ibid. (accessed 11 Jul 2013)
[357] Wei Wu Wei, *Open Secret*, Hong Kong University Press, Hong Kong, 1965.
[358] *The Mathnawi of Jalálu'ddín Rúmí*, Vol. 4, part 7, edited by Reynold Alleyne Nicholson (1940) p.248.
[359] Meister Eckhart, Sermon no.12, *Werke*, ed. Niklaus Largier, Deutscher Klassiker Verlag, Frankfurt am Main, 2008, vol 1, p.148.
[360] Tolstoy, Leo, *A Confession*, Digireads 2010, p.34.

JOAN L BOLER

The only Real Existence is that of the One and only God, who is the Self in every (finite) self.[362] ~ *Meher Baba (1894–1969CE), born Merwan Sheriar Irani — Indian Mystic and Spiritual Master*

Truth is that Divine Force that dwells in every individual's heart. It is the all-pervading, eternal Reality, uniting all individuals, and finally, linking all of existence in one divine awareness. That Divine Force is called God.[363] ~ *Swami Rama (1925-1996) —Yogi Master, Himalayas*

You don't look out there for God, something in the sky, you look in you.[364] ~ *Alan Watts (1915-1973) — Master's degree in theology and a Doctorate of Divinity and interpreter of Zen Buddhism*

---

[361] Nietzsche, Friedrich, *Thus Spake Zarathustra*, translated by Thomas Common, 1891, http://philosophy.eserver.org/nietzsche-zarathustra.txt (accessed 17 November 2014).
[362] Baba, Meher, *Meher Baba's Universal Message*, Meher Spiritual Center, South Carolina, 1971.
[363] Swami Rama, *The Essence of Spiritual Life*, Lotus Press, Urraranchal, India, 2004.
[364] Watts, Alan, *Self and Other: A lecture*, http://terebess.hu/english/watts2.html#self (accessed 17 November 2014).

Chapter 16

Our Intelligent and Spiritual Universe

There are only two mistakes one can make along the road to truth; not going all the way, and not starting.

Anonymous

Our Intelligent Universe

We live in an intelligent universe. How could it be otherwise?

If one aspect of life stands out as significant in its ability to bridge the gap between the scientific and the spiritual, it is consciousness. Profound answers begin to emerge when we realise that it is not the physical creature that produces consciousness, it is consciousness that produces the physical creature. All we view changes and begins to fit as consideration is given to this fact.

As the knowledge recorded in this book deals with each aspect of life experience, the weight of overall evidence demands a new look at all we thought we knew. An open mind, ruthless self-honesty and confronting fear and its crutches are basic requirements in the undertaking of what for many will be a giant leap. With the strength that comes from demanding, expecting, and facing the truth, it is possible to deal with the formidable, the unbelievable and the fantastic.

As we open to new possibilities, we find that spirituality is not about the ideologies that traditional religious teaching would have many of the world's people believe. By now it is perhaps time to consign all beliefs that turned spirituality into a demanding, limiting, unexciting, and often painful way of life, to the place where such ideas belong—in the archives. That does not mean the spiritual path is always easy. It is not. But for the seeker looking for joy, happiness, and fulfilment, it is the only pathway!

As travellers in time, and also outside time, we grow spiritually through experience—mainly in the physical world. We discover the truth through disillusionment. The illusion is constantly changing while love remains—deepening and growing until we realise the truth. We are spiritual beings and we repeatedly come down from the spirit realms in order to experience and know ourselves, and to fulfil our own destiny and that of planet Earth.

Creation is about us. It is about every creature and consciousness in a cosmos filled with universes. And it is about the Absolute Creator. All are interwoven in a great cosmic plan with billions of possibilities and the underlying spiritual force of love that encompasses it all.

Astrological Ages

Religions have reflected our search for, our connection to, and our understanding of, the greater forces of the universe. The universe in turn has the prime objective of ensuring the spiritual evolution of all life forms. Although the influences of all the signs of the zodiac have an impact in varying degrees on behaviour and thinking, it is the ruler of each age, that lasts around 2,160 years, that has the greatest overall impact on humanity as a whole. As we scan the behaviour of the human race over millennia, it is possible to see a design in the very gradual spiritual evolution through the experiences of humanity.

In order to progress along our spiritual road, at allotted times, the astrological energies or entities challenge specific weaknesses in humanity. Most astrologers believe we are emerging from the astrological Age of Pisces while some believe we are still in it. Around 2,000 years ago, give or take, the commencement of rule of the sign of Pisces heralded a time when that aspect in each of us that deals with the Piscean energies, was to be confronted. The nature of Pisces is emotional and feels safest when connected to, and working in harmony with the community, and to this end, will tend to trust to the beliefs of the masses that prevail at any given time. Non-confrontational by nature, the Piscean nature will hide that which may not meet the approval of, and cause conflict with, others. The romantic *seeing the world through rose coloured glasses* Piscean nature loves fantasy and myths that allow escape from the mundane. The lessons around the Piscean myths that have been explored through Christianity during the reign of Pisces, have brought realisation to many individuals the dangers of being caught up in illusions.

Trust in the spiritual is the prime objective of the forces that rule Pisces—without that trust, fear is let loose. Fear blocks us from the spiritual and cripples the soul. Although the causes of limitation in our lives may appear

THE TRUTH SEEKER

to be many, each has its source in fear. Fear of being hurt; fear of being rejected; fear of losing a loved one; fear of lack; fear of being harmed; fear of failure; fear of the unknown; fear of the future—there is an endless list of what we find to fear. Fear creates a wall between our conscious awareness and our spiritual self and undermines love of self. It leaves us feeling powerless and dependent upon others. It denies self-worth and looks for emotional security in spiritual guarantees. It exposes the child within who is dependent on the parent or establishment. In order to let go of fear, there *must* be trust or at the very least, a peaceful acceptance of the possible dangers and losses that life can bring.

The astrological sign of Pisces is about learning *what* to trust. Each of us has been following our own journey of discovery under the rule of Pisces during the past two thousand years—a journey that has allowed us through many lifetimes to experience disillusionment through exposure to the consequences of beliefs born not only mythical stories, but also of fear. Pisces teaches that total trust is possible through knowing and trusting in the spiritual and yielding to a greater purpose. The personal revelation of our spiritual identity, which can come through a near death experience or through an expanded state of consciousness, is an amazing gift and is experienced by a soul when the time is right. Such a journey within usually occurs when a soul's conscious awareness is reaching into the spiritual. Once personal experience reveals our true spiritual identity, a journey that holds wondrous possibilities begins and doorways that were previously hidden allow for personal journeys into the realm of spirit.

In order to break free of belief's prisons and move into the Piscean positive aspects of unconditional emotional love, it is necessary to activate Aquarian energy. With the coming, or arrival of, the provocative Age of Aquarius, its truth seeking energy is released, and the veil that hid and protected that which was false, is lifted, revealing truth.

The Age of Aquarius is the age of the mind—of science, truth and the power of the mind emerging. Aquarius also heralds the humanitarian age where differences between peoples are not only respected, but also enjoyed and appreciated. The force that is Aquarius invites genius as it penetrates the unconscious of humanity and demands we use our minds and seek *truth* through a scientific and open-minded approach. What has gone on behind closed doors in religion, government or commerce is no longer safe. Shameful secrets long hidden are now fodder for the media, and governments run for cover as their sometimes amoral behaviour in war zones and invasive strategies for gaining information on friend and foe alike, are exposed. Christian establishments are reeling from the belated confessions of the abused children of an earlier generation. And documentaries such as the 'Secret Files of the Inquisition',[365] based on actual records released by the Vatican in 1998, have revealed the true horror of the attitudes and behaviour of a Church caught up in the erroneous, fear-filled, superficial interpretation of the spiritual. The dishonest dealings of financial institutions and multinational businesses are also under scrutiny. The emerging consciousness of the Aquarian Age will demand transparency and accountability.

Although Piscean consciousness still holds many in its thrall and locked into the belief systems of past ages, a new wave is sweeping the earth and its peoples. Education is opening minds and science is reaching into the world of the paranormal. World communication and trade connects the far corners of the earth and narrows the gap between peoples of all races and creeds. Further change is inevitable as the Aquarian energy infiltrates our lives.

The Open Mind

The first step towards finding truth is to at all times, even in the face of the seemingly impossible, retain an open mind. An open-minded approach is based on questioning everything and not dismissing the improbable or seemingly impossible without thoroughly researching the evidence. And even then, when evidence is inconclusive, retaining an open mind. Whereas the Piscean Age represented the common attitude, that was expressed as —*I believe*, or, *I don't believe*, the Aquarian age will find more and more people taking personal responsibility for their opinions and independently investigating and saying—*I know*, or, *I don't know*. English philosopher Francis Bacon (1561–1626) once said, *If a man will begin with certainties, he shall end in doubts; but if he will be content to begin with doubts, he shall end in certainties.*[366]

While education has removed many of the religious superstitions that over great periods of time have captured the masses, many today accept, information, especially that of a scientific nature, provided by the established authorities in societies without due consideration. Perhaps this tendency commences with schooling where the teaching of information that could be supposition is imparted as though it was known fact to be learned and accepted. A child receives a constant stream of information, which becomes the framework from which life and the world at large is viewed

---

[365] Drewery, Laurett and Alcock, Michael. (shown on SBS 2009) *Secret files of the inquisition*. Inquisition Production Inc. MMVI:. Sydney, Australia.
[366] Bacon, Francis, *The Advancement of Learning*, 1605, Book I, v, 8.

THE TRUTH SEEKER

and acted on. The pattern in childhood of learned acceptance of apparently authorised facts, becomes a programme in the unconscious, so not only can absolute trust in a recognised authority result, but also, the tools required to investigate and evaluate independently are not developed. The true educator, rather than teaching *what* to think, facilitates the individual to use their own mind to explore, understand, and assess all available knowledge on any given question. In more recent times, this approach has begun to infiltrate the more enlightened education systems and has the potential to change the consciousness of humanity on a deep level.

The search for truth invites a healthy scepticism, demands a degree of self-honesty that is able to recognise and expose personal vested interest and an acceptance that answers do not have to be conclusive. There is much that cannot be proven. This fact does not invalidate a truth. The following story tests to the maximum the willingness to allow that even the most incredible and unbelievable, that lacks an atom of proof, can possibly be true. In a cosmos full of surprises, the following experience has to stand out as one of my most confounding.

Back in the 1990s, a friend who was traumatised over the very recent death of her son came to visit me. It seemed that a psychic reading could offer her some helpful understanding. As I tuned in, I became aware of a being with very strong energy around her, attempting to gain my attention. I immediately knew that I was sensing an alien. I also knew that the being was a male and I could feel a mental type of love radiating out from him. I was dumbfounded as I felt the energy of the personality and character of the alien. I had become adept at recognising the nature of a wide range of human energies, but the energies I encountered then were so foreign that I had absolutely no frame of reference for them.

Once he had gained my attention, the alien showed me an image of a city on his home planet. The land was a light brownish earthy colour. The beautifully sculptured and smoothly finished buildings were made of the same earthy substance and were designed with a lot of curves that were very pleasing to the eye. I did not see any trees or plant life in that vision. Unfortunately, in my trance state, it never occurred to me to attempt to discover what this alien looked like.

As I related his message, along with what I had seen, to my friend, she advised that she had been aware that she had an alien guide.

JOAN L BOLER

Had anyone communicated to me a story such as the one I have just imparted, I would probably have reacted with a healthy dose of scepticism, and of course many who read this may do just that, and if they avail themselves of further information available on the subject, that is so much better than *believing* my story is true or false! But *I* knew that what I had experienced was real. I cannot explain how this alien could be a guide, but I had no option but to accept I had encountered an alien. Since the alien guide was relating to me from the non-physical dimensions, I was left with more questions than answers, foremost amongst them was, *Are all or most of the numerous reports of alien encounters, actually happening on a non-physical level, and are UFOs (unidentified flying objects), if they **are** alien space ships, inter-dimensional, intergalactic, or both?*

In order to have any hope of assessing the possible validity of such an experience, research into what is reported on the subject, is perhaps the first step. While there are a lot of apparently hysterical reports on aliens, there have also been serious researchers. John E Mack, M. D. (1929-2004) was born in New York and was Professor of Psychiatry at Harvard Medical School. For his biography on T E Lawrence, he won the Pulitzer Prize in biography.[367] Mack worked with over one hundred alien abductees and compiled some very impressive and interesting information. In his book 'Abductions—Human Encounters with Aliens',[368] Mack recorded the stories of abductees who had, in his opinion, experienced a transcendental, but real abduction. Through the use of hypnosis, he was able to access the memories of the on-board ship experiences that revealed a relationship between the aliens and the abductees, in that the human abductees were alien souls and were originally from the same planet as the aliens. Of note is that these people were consistently warned by the aliens regarding the destructive and dangerous way we are abusing our planet—ways that can not only lead to its destruction, but also cause problems for our neighbouring planets and galaxies.

In the early 1990s I viewed a documentary called 'UFO Miracle of the Unknown,'[369] (can be viewed on YouTube) when it was shown on television. This film about aliens and their spacecraft showed interviews with people who claimed to have had personal experience of aliens. While many of the millions of sightings of UFOs by people all over the world can be explained by physical phenomena, some cannot. Reports of sightings by responsible and reputable people, including military officials, astronauts,

---

367 *Biography of John E Mack, M D.* http://johnemackinstitute.org/biography-of-john-e-mack-m-d/ (accessed 16 Oct 2013)
368 Mack, John E. *Abduction—Human encounters with aliens,* Pocket Books, London, 2007.
[369] *UFO miracle of the unknown'.* Documentary written and directed by Yin Gazade, and produced by Royal Atlantic Film & Manfred Kage and co-produced by Coriolys Film.

pilots, scientists and police, lend validity to the reality of an alien presence around the globe, as do the many films of flying objects that not only travel at speeds as yet impossible for earth-made aircraft, but also move with a manoeuvrability that defies belief.

Interestingly, a week after my viewing of the documentary, a man who was attending the same psychic development classes as me discussed his shock upon watching that same documentary. He recognised the design of the spaceship from a number of what he had previously thought had been dreams of being taken aboard a spacecraft. The description of the way in which the spacecraft was powered, and the interior design, fitted his 'dream' memory exactly. The dreams had commenced during his childhood and had recurred from time to time over the years.

In the words of Mark Twain, *Truth is stranger than fiction, but it is because fiction is obliged to stick to possibilities, truth isn't.*[370] There is much that we encounter through what others have claimed to have witnessed that is easy to dismiss. But to do so, does not honour or respect 'truth', rather it protects the 'safe' boundaries we have drawn for ourselves that sooner or later, in the face of truth, must be destroyed.

Quantum Mechanics and Consciousness

Quantum mechanics has challenged the great minds of our time to the extent that American theoretical physicist Richard Feynman (1918–1988), who in 1999 was voted by one hundred and thirty of the world's leading physicists to be one of the ten greatest physicists of all time,[371] said, *Anyone who claims to understand quantum mechanics is either lying or crazy.*[372] In spite of the discoveries that to a great extent are still steeped in mystery, physicists today are looking at consciousness in new ways because of their exposure to the world of quantum physics.

I do not have a clear understanding of quantum mechanics, but I do know from personal experience of the existence of dimensions beyond the physical world, of the 'no time', 'no space' reality; of the potential super

---

[370] Mark Twain, *Following the Equator* (1897), ch. 15.
[371] 'Physics World poll names. Richard Feynman one of 10 greatest physicists of all time.' *Caltech.* http://www.caltech.edu/article/12019 (accessed 13 Nov 2013)
[372] Yirka, Bob. *Phys. Org.* 'Survey shows physicists can't agree on fundamental questions about quantum mechanics.'
http://phys.org/news/2013-01-survey-physicists-fundamental-quantum-mechanics.html (accessed 13 Nov 2013)

powers we can access; of non-physical conscious beings; of the continuation of individual consciousness, and many of the aspects of the supernatural that are described in this book. The ongoing evidence and proof that has come my way regarding the extraordinary realities that are part of our greater existence have confirmed for me time and again the validity of my experiences. That many have similar experiences to my own supports my claims. Just because it is not possible to scientifically prove much of the paranormal, does not mean that its existence should not be seriously considered, especially now that quantum mechanics has changed our view of the world and gives possible explanations for that which is neither seen nor measured by the physical eye.

Many scientific minds today are looking into the way in which consciousness and intelligence works. Stuart Hameroff, MD is recognised for his theories on consciousness. Hameroff has from 1975 onwards worked at the University of Arizona where he became firstly professor, and then emeritus professor of anaesthesiology and psychology. He also became Associate Director for the Centre for Consciousness Studies. His scientific publications on consciousness and quantum space-time are compatible with reincarnation and other psychic and spiritual experiences.[373] It is time to move beyond the traditional approach that maintains the brain is the source of our conscious awareness and mental ability, and look for answers that explain the inexplicable.

Creation

As soon as recognition is given to the possibility of consciousness not only *not* being dependent upon the physical body, but also being potentially indestructible and therefore capable of surviving death and returning to life through reincarnation, a whole new perspective regarding the how and why life on this planet, will need to be sought.

Today, science depends upon experimentation and examination of the results. Although at present, science recognises that the cosmos is multidimensional, it only has the tools to investigate from the outside! But what if investigations were only considered complete if, and when, they were studied through the conscious mind entering the non-physical dimensions?

---

[373] Hameroff, Stuart, *Media – Quantum consciousness*. 'The brain's connection to funda-mental reality: The little book of bleeps.' www.quantumconsciousness.org (accessed 22 Jul 2013)

THE TRUTH SEEKER

The twentieth century, thanks to Einstein, saw great leaps in the understanding of light. But how does light feel and does it produce sound? On one of my visits to the higher dimensions, I had an amazingly beautiful experience when I found myself in a dimension of pure, beautiful energies. I could see an angel to my left that seemed to be there for me for the duration of my excursion. A golden light penetrated and illuminated all before me. Then as I moved forward, I merged with energies that were of luminescent white with iridescent fine sparkling colours running through it. I felt and heard that energy. The pristine energy reminded me of a crystal, but there was nothing hard about the energy that was so pure it defies description, and no sound on earth can compare to the beautiful harmonics the energy was producing. The closest sounds to these harmonics I have heard come from Tibetan bell bowls, but the sounds I listened to while in the non-physical realms, transcended those and were even more beautiful and ethereal.

As science today researches and finds answers, what does it have to say about creation? One of the most recognised and undeniably brilliant cosmologist and theoretical physicists on the planet today put forward his theory in the documentary 'Stephen Hawking's Grand Design'.[374] Hawking's thoughts are accepted as probable by many, both in the scientific and non-scientific worlds.

Hawking discusses the fact that in our everyday experiences everything that happens has a cause and therefore it follows that man would assume a cause for the Big Bang and the creation of the universe. Hawking theorises that since science has shown that protons can pop in and out of existence without energy causing them to do so, and since there was no causal energy before the Big Bang, it is not necessary to have a god in order for the universe to have formed, especially as the Big Bang produced equal amounts of positive and negative energy so everything adds up to zero. Time is a factor also considered relevant. Before the Big Bang there was no time and therefore, according to Hawking, there was no possibility of a creator existing.

Hawking's theory is based on the assumption that consciousness in itself requires time in order to be, and therefore since prior to the Big Bang there was no 'time' or 'space', no creator could exist. The reports of those who have out-of-body experiences, near-death experiences, spiritual experiences and recovered memories of the time between lives, all confirm that when in the non-physical dimensions, time and space as we understand them cease to

---

[374] Hawking, Stephen. *Stephen Hawking's Grand Design*; Produced by Darlow Smithson Productions Ltd for Discovery Channel. MMXI Discovery Communications, LLC.

exist. And yet, conscious awareness is continuous, and eventually that awareness returns to the physical and the laws that govern it.

In the physical world, energy is required as a cause, but what of the non-physical? For those who have entered the higher realms of the non-physical, the experience is very much about what 'is'. Mediation, when the mind is stilled, can move our conscious mind into a state where there is no time or space. This is an existence where ideas are intuited, or *known* in their completeness; where consciousness is; awareness is; knowledge is; understanding is; exquisite loving feeling is, and will is, but conversely, unlimited power also is. How can that be?

For millennia, holy men and women, especially from the East, have been providing information, as observed from the inner experience, of the Creator; the structure of the universe; its creatures and their purpose. Today scientific mystics are contributing their knowledge to the world at large.

Czechoslovakian born Itshak Bentof (1923-1979) moved to Israel where he spent time in the Science Corps of the Israeli Defence Forces. Later he moved to the United States where he became sought after as an inventor of industrial and medical products. His scientific interests led him into researching consciousness. His endeavours took him into the mystical dimensions through ever-expanding states of consciousness. The extent to which he was able to expand his mind, and the intelligence he was able to gain, provides insights and answers that are both daunting and amazing. Bentof conceived of the holographic model of the universe that gains wide acceptance today. He said, *I am attempting to build a model of the universe that will satisfy the need for a comprehensive picture of 'what our existence is all about'.*[375] The workings of this model are described in his book, 'Stalking the Wild Pendulum'.[376] [377]

Apart from understanding the workings of the holographic universe from knowledge gained from his out-of-body travels through the cosmos, Bentof, like many others before him, gained knowledge of gods, devas, angels and other beings that he maintained were all evolving. Bentof was able to compare his experiences and the knowledge gained with others, and found consistency and agreement. His scientific approach revealed a greater interest in how the universe worked rather than the incredible beings that he

---

[375] Bentov, Itzhak, *Stalking the Wild Pendulum: On the Mechanics of Consciousness,* Destiny Books, Destiny Books, p. 2.
[376] Op. cit.
[377] Bentov, Itzhak with Mirtala, *A Cosmic Book: On the Mechanics of Creation,* Destiny Books, Vermont, USA, 1988.

encountered. He describes a *modest continuous bang universe,*[378] with back to back black and white holes. At the point where the Creator is found, there is no time. According to Bentof, the old universe is absorbed into the black hole and re-emerges from the white hole. He describes a continuous process in all life that involves movement in and out of time—a pattern is found in the macrocosm and microcosm. Reincarnation is an example of this.

In his explanation of the absolute and creation, that contradicts the assumptions of Hawking, Bentof explains that pure consciousness, that encompasses all potential manifestation, is operating at unimaginably high speeds so that the frequency of the wave is flat, which means that It is not only creating, It is also totally at rest.[379] This would explain why the no time, no space state allows for total stillness and receptive awareness and, at the same time, the power of the creative forces.

Appropriately, Stan Grof who wrote 'Beyond the Brain' says, *Western science is approaching a paradigm shift of unprecedented proportions, one that will change our concepts of reality and of human nature, bridge the gap between ancient wisdom and modern science, and reconcile the differences between Eastern spirituality and Western pragmatism.*[380]

As we look with new eyes at creation itself and the emergence of the physical, perhaps it is easier to recognise that consciousness has always played a part in all that is. It is time for scientists and physicists to investigate consciousness and work with those who have achieved the ability to penetrate the multiple dimensions through expansion of the mind.

Creation and Evolution

The contents of this book discuss knowledge that goes beyond the physical and extends into realms that until recently were rejected by the world's scientists and often misunderstood by religious believers. As we look to the views put forward by creationists and evolutionists, we are left with unproven and unsubstantiated ideas. Dr Wernher von Braun (1912-1977), a German rocket scientist and NASA director of the American space program, said, *It is in scientific honesty that I endorse the presentation of alternative theories for the origin of the universe, life and man in the science*

---

[378] Op. cit. p.14.
[379] OP. cit. pp. 17-18
[380] Grof, Stanislav, www. stanislavgrof.com/ (accessed 4 Nov 2013)

classroom. It would be an error to overlook the possibility that the universe was planned rather than happening by chance. [381]

The theory of Charles Darwin (1809-1882), of evolution by natural selection that suggests that small changes, could over millions of years, become great changes. The question is, what directs those changes? The complex designs of all living organisms required intelligent input in order to exist. DNA is a programme. Who or what designed or wrote the programmes essential to every creature in our world? As every creature and all plant life is viewed, the incredible complexity and amazing versatility encountered is bewildering. Each creature's integrated design compliments its needs and its environment in every way. The designs, similar in basic areas to those of other of nature's creations, are nonetheless unique and perfect.

Scientists look to the building blocks of a life that are to be found in DNA (deoxyribonucleic acid) which is responsible for turning genes on and off and hence the possibility of turning on dramatically different genetic possibilities. DNA mutates as environmental forces (ultra violet light, nuclear radiation, and some chemicals) have an impact on it, or when cells copy DNA incorrectly prior to cell division. Research reveals that there seems to be evidence that, rather than reacting to circumstances and building defence mechanisms against a threat, survival is random and dependent upon those already possessing inbuilt resistance. Perhaps it is both.

Consciousness, it's independence of the physical and it's ability to impact on the physical, as discussed in previous chapters, can provide answers that fit. Reports of elementals playing a part in the process of the life of plants, and angels' involvement during the gestation period of the human embryo could explain the turning on and off fail-safes for different attributes, in members of the same species. Consider also the possibility that minor improvements over time are caused by the individual mind that can, as in the case of neuroplasticity, actually cause physical changes to take place. Could determination by the individual, as in *I will do that* cause the unconscious to set in motion the creation of the necessary changes.

Without incorporating the impact of consciousness and its ability to impact upon the physical, the existence of a creature such as a bird cannot be explained. Every part of the bird is designed for flight. How did a bird develop an inbuilt guidance system, lightweight bone structure, wings and claws and clothe itself in perfectly designed feathers that allow it to capture and glide upon the air currents? How were all these attributes and more co-

---

[381] von Braun, Wernher, from a letter to the California State board of Education 14 September 1972.

ordinated and designed before the bird even knew there were air currents to glide upon?

Creationists, many of whom believe the world and all its creatures were created by God in six days, cite the Bible as proof. Whether the 'days' cited in the Bible are considered to be actual 'world days' or 'ages', creation is supported by the evidence, but perhaps reality is considerably different to that believed by religious creationists.

With another look at the macrocosmic and the microcosmic, the possibility that the ability to create is the potential of all spiritual beings including ourselves needs to be considered. The 'ideas' (gods, devas, angels) designed by the Absolute Creator God is in agreement with what mystics have said. It would seem possible that the actual process of creation could involve beings in spirit that were themselves creations. Assumptions cannot be made without evidence as to the identity of the consciousness or multiple consciousnesses that were, and perhaps still are, involved directly in the creation of life on the planet. When one begins to accept the possibility that the physical world and its inhabitants are multidimensional with a greater consciousness in the invisible realms than usually expressed through the physical creature, we can begin to see creation in a new way.

As we look to the spiritual evolution of human beings, we can see that as the soul evolves, more and more of that which is of the spiritual is expressed through the physical. What appears to be random selection is possibly the impression of the soul on the physical with guidance from realms beyond the physical. As we keep in mind the claims we are all connected, all creation is an expression of the Creator, and at least some of the creations are also creative, it is possible to appreciate the comment by John Wheeler (1911–2008) who was an American theoretical physicist, *We are tiny patches of the universe looking at itself and building itself.*[382]

The Truth Within

Eventually there is nowhere to go, but to the truth. At present, we stand on the brink of a revolution of the mind. A revolution that will enable us to bring the power of our minds into service. The search into the unconscious

---

[382] From an interview with John Wheeler by Tim Folger, "Does the Universe Exist if We're Not looking?", *Discover*, Vol.3, no.6, June 2004, p. 44.

is the search for self. It can transport each of us through the physical into the metaphysical. And through that journey, we can become the conscious authors of our destiny.

We are, first and foremost, spirit beings. As spirit beings we descend down into the dense physical matter of this world we call Earth. Energetically, Earth is home to a myriad of energies, some wild and some magnificent, all described in astrology. It seems possible that we, as spirit beings, have taken on the transformation of energies from the basic to the beautiful. Through many lifetimes, we continue our task of refining the materials that we work with. Initially, the energy we enter into is so dense that all knowledge and memory of our true identity is lost. Yet it is not possible to remain that way. The further we bring the spiritual into the physical world, the greater the impact we have on the spiritual evolution of the world. Each and every soul who recognises and expresses the spiritual enhances and improves the lives of others.

The greatest soul in the physical that I have come into personal physical contact with I have never spoken to, I have never met and I have no idea of his name. But when my soul connected to this anonymous person, he was able to lift it to great heights that left me both enriched and awed. In 1991, I decided to attend the Mind, Body, Spirit Festival in Sydney for the first time with a friend from the bushwalking group. There was a great deal to fascinate me as I wandered around with my friend, enjoying investigating the products of the various stalls. Abruptly my attention was drawn to a small Buddhist monk who was with two other monks, each of whom was dressed in the orange robes that identified them. This small monk was around three yards (2.7mtrs) away from me, his attention focused on a display at the stall adjacent to the one in front of which we were standing.

I had no conscious awareness of a reason for my interest, but as my attention focused on him I began to feel the most amazing loving energy radiating out from him. Contact with his energy raised my own energy to a level where I experienced bliss. Over the next hour or so, I wandered around feeling so wonderful, so happy and so peaceful, it was as if the energies of the heavenly kingdoms surrounded me, and in fact that was exactly what had happened; this man was expressing his god-self or spiritual self.

Whether we are conscious of it or not, we are all influenced, in varying degrees, by those around us. Some enhance by their presence while others drain. Positive loving people uplift others in their environment. As each of us develops spiritually, we not only show others by example, how to live and enjoy a better life, but also the spiritual energy we expel in the natural course of our lives enhances the lives of all those in its proximity. We are

THE TRUTH SEEKER

like a sea of energy, connected to yet separate from each and every being on the planet.

All that we are becoming through life's processes can only be glimpsed. The following incident provides insight into the future possibilities for human beings to become what today we would regard as super-beings.

Before Paul and I became a couple, I attended dances at the club where he was a musician in the dance band. One night, I was talking to a woman behind the bar when I noticed Paul was on his break and sitting across the room with the rest of the band. To my astonishment, I suddenly found myself filled with power as I experienced an expanded state of awareness. A powerful band of energy extended out from somewhere below my stomach area to connect to Paul. I later discovered that the source of this energy was the sacral chakra. The fact that the bar was in front of me and Paul was on the other side of the bar did not seem to in any way limit the power or capability of this chakra.

This vortex of energy accessed, and enabled me to feel energetically, Paul's nature. The explosion of energy revealed a love of life and humanity along with an innocence and purity to be found only in those who do not judge or become imprisoned by society's rules. *How could so much energy fit inside one person?* I wondered in absolute amazement. At the same time, I sensed a mind that was crystal clear, and I knew without a doubt that this man did not take drugs or in any way abuse or limit his mental capabilities.

In my mind's eye, which I now know as the third eye chakra, I was seeing above Paul, another image of him—smaller in size and upright whereas Paul himself was sitting down. By this time in my life, due to previous out-of-body experiences, I was familiar with the concept of an astral or etheric body and realised what I was seeing was Paul's non-physical counterpart. Since it is possible for the non-physical layers of the body to float out of the physical body when in a trance-like state (which no doubt in Paul's case could be accounted for by his total immersion in his music), I assumed that this was what I was viewing.

It was not my intention to invade Paul's privacy in any way. The experience happened without conscious intent on my part. There was no sense of distraction as I continued the conversation I was having with the lady who was serving me a drink. As I left the bar, my amazing experience came to an end. But at that time, as stunned and awed as I was, I had no idea what had happened. It was not until I came across information on the energy centres called chakras that the answers began to come.

JOAN L BOLER

In reviewing this experience, it is possible to see that it revealed a capability to, in the same moment, give full attention to a conversation and yet to also, with total clarity, receive non-physical information both visually and intuitively, and to make observations about the information received through the chakras. This ability to deal with different situations at the same time is reported to be an aspect of the afterlife by those who experience a near-death or inter-dimensional experience.

Is it possible that as we expand our consciousness more and more into spiritual awareness and understanding, we will be able to operate as spiritual beings, with all the power that entails, through the human physical form, so that at all times we can maintain clairvoyant and psychic awareness and bring into our everyday lives the power of the mind and its miraculous abilities without having to induce a trance state? Conscious psychic awareness through the chakras, which is normally only achievable when in a trance state, is obviously possible. It is not unrealistic to consider that what I experienced for a matter of a minute or two could become a continuous experience. I imagine that such could be achieved when all the chakras are totally clear and in tune.

As we begin to awaken from our long sleep and open to the potential within and without, we look to a future with the promise of mysteries that are ours to unfold and discover, to experience and enjoy. We are life seeking to discover ourselves, to fulfil our destiny, to become all that we are capable of becoming—magnificent, creative, loving, happy, powerful beings. For the seeker of truth, the world becomes an intriguing and exciting place to be. As the internal truths are revealed and understood, our power, oneness and rightness in the world, brings peace, joy, fulfilment and happiness.

THE TRUTH SEEKER

JOAN L BOLER

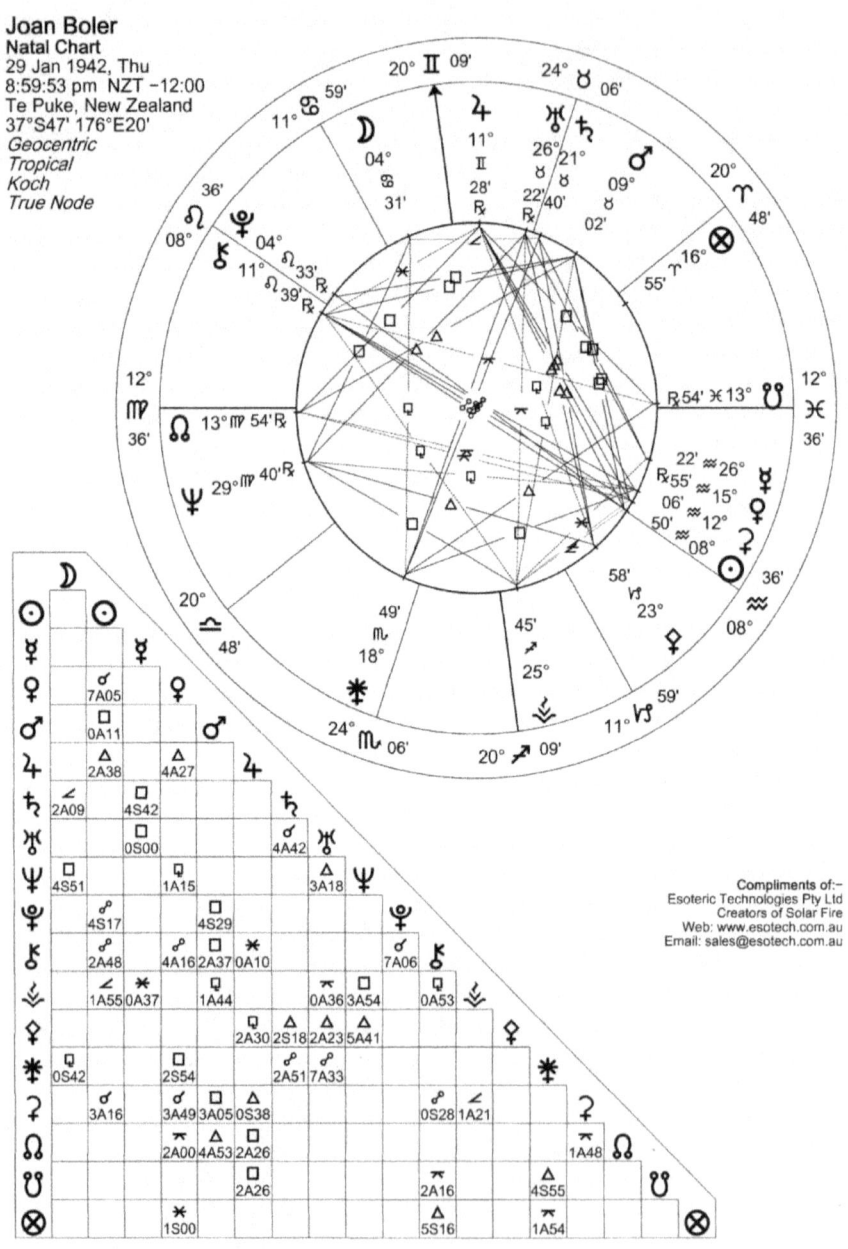

Figure 9 - Geocentric Natal Chart

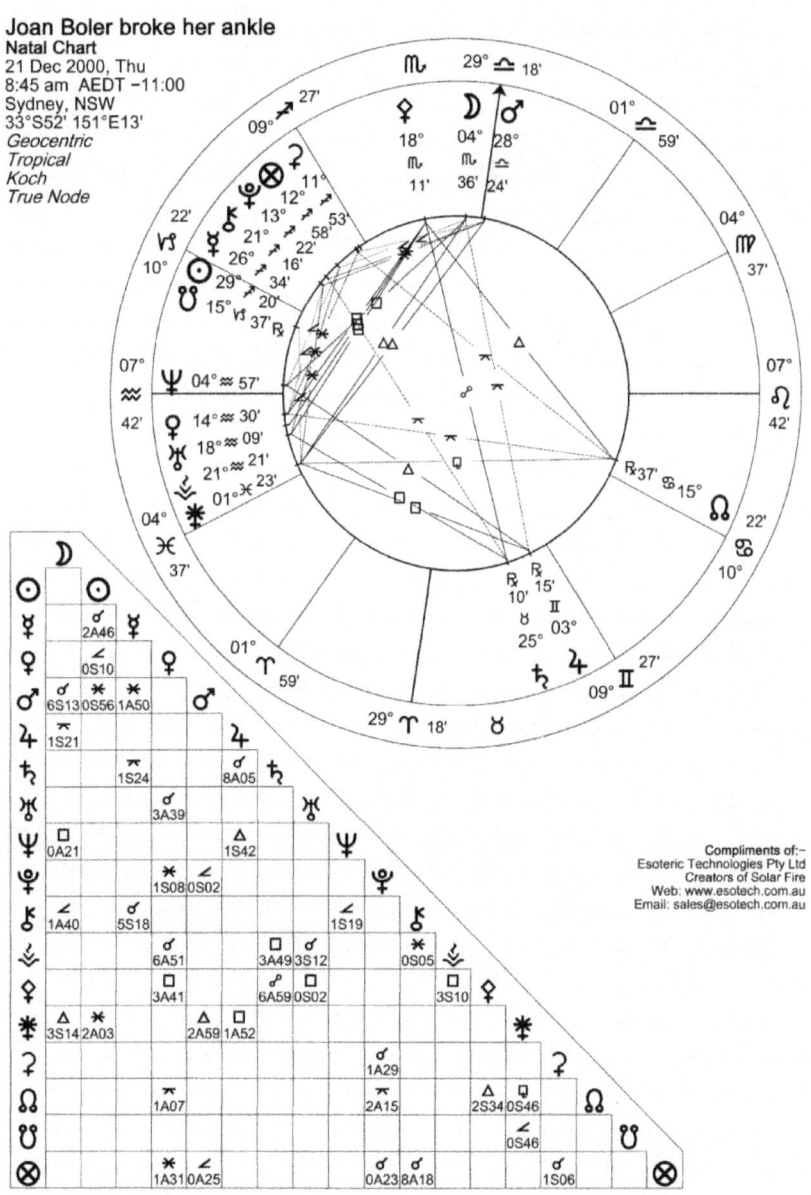

Figure 10 - Geocentric Event Chart

JOAN L BOLER

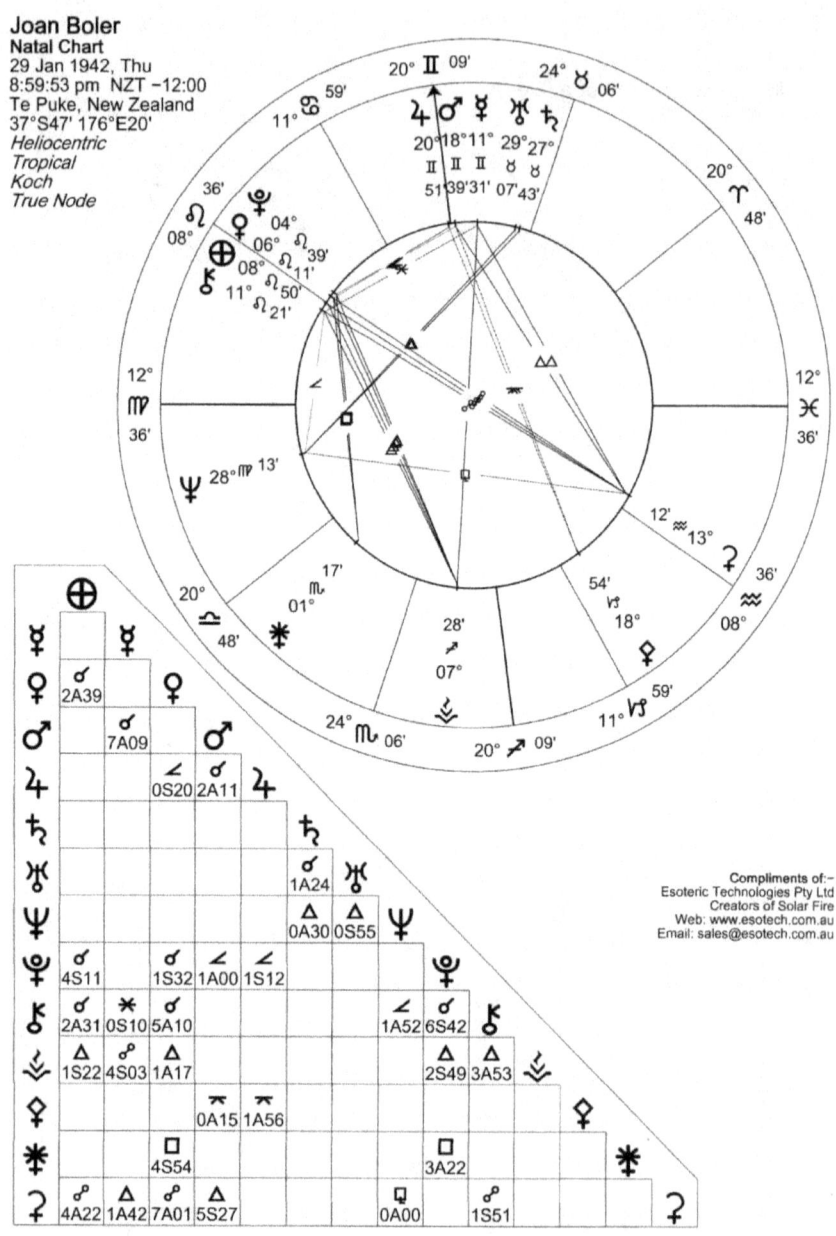

Figure 11 - Heliocentric Natal Chart

THE TRUTH SEEKER

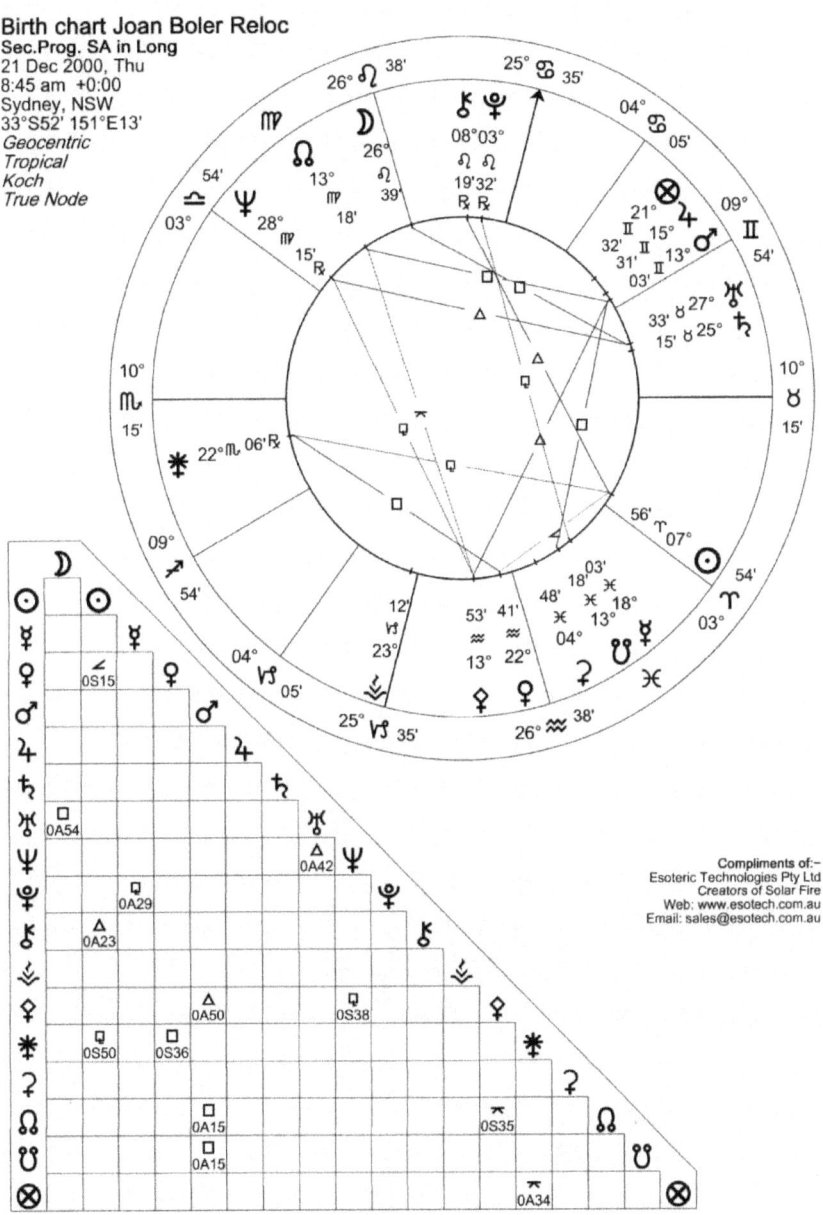

Figure 12 - Geocentric Second Progress Chart

www.ingramcontent.com/pod-product-compliance
Lightning Source LLC
Chambersburg PA
CBHW061925220426
43662CB00012B/1808